Somebody Should Do Something

The MIT Press's publishing mission benefits from the generosity of our donors, including Eric Klose.

Somebody Should Do Something

How Anyone Can Help Create Social Change

Michael Brownstein, Alex Madva, and Daniel Kelly

The MIT Press
Cambridge, Massachusetts
London, England

The MIT Press
Massachusetts Institute of Technology
77 Massachusetts Avenue, Cambridge, MA 02139
mitpress.mit.edu

The MIT Press would like to thank the anonymous peer reviewers who provided comments on drafts of this book. The generous work of academic experts is essential for establishing the authority and quality of our publications. We acknowledge with gratitude the contributions of these otherwise uncredited readers.

This book was set in ITC Stone Serif Std and ITC Stone Sans Std by New Best-set Typesetters Ltd. Printed and bound in the United States of America.

Library of Congress Cataloging-in-Publication Data is available.

ISBN: 978-0-262-04978-8

10 9 8 7 6 5 4 3 2 1

EU Authorised Representative: Easy Access System Europe, Mustamäe tee 50, 10621 Tallinn, Estonia | Email: gpsr.requests@easproject.com

Contents

Note to the Reader

An appendix that goes into more depth on some of the central concepts of this book is available online at www.somebody-book.com. For the sake of readability, there are no numbered notes in the main text, but readers can find further discussion of our sources in the notes section.

Introduction

By the 1920s, US car companies had a problem. More and more people were driving, but more and more people were getting killed in accidents too. Compared to a decade earlier, there were three to four times more traffic fatalities. In cities, about three-quarters of these deaths were pedestrians. A conflict was brewing about who belonged in the streets—cars or people.

One response was to try to restrict how fast cars could go. Over 10 percent of Cincinnati residents (42,000 in all) signed a petition in 1923 supporting a law to force automobile makers to install "governors" in the engines of cars that would prevent them from going over 25 mph. Unsurprisingly, the car companies resisted. Evidently, so did people who liked to speed. The industry-backed no-vote campaign squashed the proposal before it could become law.

Despite their success in Cincinnati, car companies realized that if the country was going to be redesigned for cars, they had to respond to the widespread perception that cars endangered pedestrians. Local victories weren't enough. They needed to change the conversation.

What followed was a public relations blitz to convince Americans that cars don't kill people, people do. John Hertz, who founded Chicago's Yellow Cab Company and Hertz Drive-Ur-Self—which went on to become the car rental company Hertz—in 1926 declared, "We are living in a motor age . . . and we must have not only motor age education, but a motor age sense of responsibility. . . . The streets are for vehicle traffic, the sidewalks for pedestrians."

The Chicago Motor Club searched for an expression to both describe and criticize irresponsible pedestrians. The term they coined is still with us: *jaywalkers*. It was an effective insult. A *jay* was a country bumpkin, someone clueless about city life. Hertz, revealing something about his own political sensibilities, declared, "We fear the 'jay walker' worse than the anarchist."

Of course, reckless drivers also bore some of the responsibility for accidents. In 1922 the American Automobile Association offered $25 to whoever could suggest the best new epithet for an irresponsible driver. The winner, we are delighted to report, was *flivverboob*.

According to historian Peter Norton, the car companies' strategy was to deflect responsibility from themselves to individuals. They understood that the country's skyrocketing traffic deaths could threaten the rise of the motor age, and they wanted to get out in front of the problem before social movements and lawmakers solved it for them.

This basic script has played out again and again since the 1920s. "Guns don't kill people, people do," the National Rifle Association (NRA) infamously claims. Smokers are "intelligent enough to make their own decisions," Anne Browder of the Tobacco Institute said in 1985. If individuals are responsible for traffic deaths, handgun murders, and lung cancer, then car, gun, and tobacco companies can keep making money. You might lower your personal chances of getting into an accident by avoiding jaywalking or flivverboobing, but the motor age will plow ahead, undisturbed.

Fast-forward to the twenty-first century and ask yourself, What can I do to help solve any of the big problems cars create, from traffic deaths to climate change?

One option would be to focus on *personal choices*. You could sell your car and buy a bike instead. You could try to convince your friends and family to quit driving and take the bus. You might hope that, like the individual drops of water that fill up a bucket, these small changes will add up to big ones.

We feel this, and do things like these in our own lives. But we also worry that we're buying into a century's worth of propaganda. Isn't this exactly what the car companies wanted, each of us taking on the responsibility of dealing with the problem they created? Sneaky PR aside, your personal choices can feel pretty inconsequential. Giving up your car isn't going to move the needle on the national traffic fatality rate. And how many people can you, personally, persuade to give up their own vehicles? The US is an awfully big bucket to fill drop by drop. And that's just the US.

So you could consider an alternative: pass better laws. Rather than fret about your personal choices, *change the system*. You could advocate for "congestion pricing" that makes it expensive for people to drive into cities. Or get your city to invest in bicycle infrastructure, public transportation, or European-style car-free zones in city centers. These are all ways of changing the systems that shape the choices individuals make.

But while focusing on your personal choices can feel insignificant—or like succumbing to corporate propaganda—trying to change the system can feel overwhelming, a gargantuan undertaking with long odds of success. You probably know how to ride a bike, but what about implementing congestion pricing or ending car culture?

A Better Picture

The philosopher and novelist Iris Murdoch once remarked, with characteristic elegance, that "man is the creature that makes pictures of himself and then comes to resemble the picture." We've come to resemble the picture painted by Hertz, the NRA, and Big Tobacco, inheriting a view of ourselves and social change that is compelling, entrenched—and wrong. It seems to offer a stark choice: if you want to make change, you can focus on yourself, or you can focus on the system. You can quit driving, or you can try to end car culture. That's a terrible choice, since the first seems ineffective and the second beyond our reach.

The three of us spent a long time feeling stuck about what we could do about the biggest problems we collectively face, problems like climate change, racism, and yes, car culture. It seemed to us that we were being forced to choose between personal choices or systems and social structures.

This book is about getting unstuck. Our personal choices *do* matter, just not the way we usually think.

Part of why it's hard to see this is that would-be changemakers are constantly told they have to choose: change people or change systems. "You can't save the climate by going vegan," a *USA Today* op-ed proclaimed in June 2019. "Corporate polluters must be held accountable." This widely circulated essay argued that focusing on individual actions like what to eat and how to travel "distract from the systemic changes that are needed to avert this crisis."

From our perspective, the authors are right that the climate crisis is only going to be solved with systemic change. They're also right to be suspicious of putting the responsibility for change at the feet of individual consumers.

But the authors' overall message falls short: They make what we shouldn't do much clearer than what we should. "Don't change lightbulbs," they say, "change [the] energy system." The first part of this message seems straight-forward. Stop stressing over individual actions like how to light homes and stock fridges. Got it. But what to do instead? What can any of us do to hold corporate polluters accountable and overhaul energy infrastructure? The philosopher Robin Zheng put the crucial unasked question this way: "what is my role in changing the system?"

Lurking in the background of USA Today's op-ed—and behind the domi-nant cultural conversation about social change—is the portrayal of people as isolated from each other, with limited reach, able to adjust a few things here and there in their own personal lives but not much else. It highlights divisions rather than connections, boundaries rather than pathways of influ-ence. It underlines opposition: real-deal change is taking down the car com-panies or fossil fuel industry rather than making changes in your own life.

We need a better picture, one that highlights how personal choices are connected to systems and structural change. We need a picture that fore-grounds our most powerful personal choice: to work together with others. As the writer Bill McKibben put it about climate change, "the most impor-tant thing an individual can do is be somewhat less of an individual, joined together with others in movements large enough to make those changes on [a] more fundamental level."

We need images and models and stories that help us see what kinds of personal choices merely make us feel good but are basically ineffectual, and what kinds actually have the potential to create transformative social change. This book assembles these images and models and tells many of these stories. It offers them in service of getting unstuck.

Structural Change and Individual Change

The most pressing social problems are incredibly complex. Take climate change. There's no one fundamental solution because climate change is an "everything problem." It results from how billions of people commute and travel, grow food, make clothes and medicine, ship things around the world, get rid of trash, build homes and roads and cities, and keep them-selves warm in the winter and cool in the summer. Each of these factors contributes to climate change, and they're all interconnected.

Climate change encompasses laws, institutions, political economies, cultures, and all the interconnections between them. Call these *social structures*. Seriously addressing the problem requires *structural change*.

Everyone doesn't contribute equally, of course. An average American refrigerator uses more electricity in a year than the average person does in Kenya, Nigeria, or Tanzania. The US and the European Union have produced about half of all historic greenhouse gases, but their people, especially the wealthy, are likely to be shielded from the worst of its effects. (No one will be completely shielded, though.) These facts have led many people to realize that climate change—in addition to requiring a massive overhaul of energy systems, food systems, and so much else—is also a matter of justice. Responding to it fairly will require redistributing global wealth and power.

No one thinks solving these sprawling everything problems will be easy. But pure uncut pessimism can be paralyzing, and isn't justified anyway. In the US, at the time we're writing this book, per capita carbon pollution emissions are below where they were in 1913. The clean energy economy is growing furiously. As we'll see, there are all kinds of ways in which people can contribute to making progress on these everything problems.

Still, coming to grips with the structural nature of a planet-sized problem like climate change makes it incredibly difficult to know what to do about it. This can be demoralizing. The three of us grew up in the era of "reduce, reuse, recycle," a slogan that made things seem simple. If everyone cared enough and did their part, we could solve the problem. One of us—Michael—even had a recycling-themed bar mitzvah, replete with giant balloons that looked like the Earth. (Sorry, sea turtles.)

Thirteen-year-old Michael was naïve, but having tangible things to do is an appealing alternative to "change the whole system." How does one go about changing social structures anyway? Where to even start? The three of us know how to recycle—though even that can be a source of confusion and marital friction—but we don't know how to decarbonize the power grid, let alone redistribute global wealth and power.

It's all too easy to be daunted into inaction. Between 1985 and 2022, Greenland lost one trillion tons of ice—that's 30 million tons melted *every hour*. But the angst-inducing size of the problem is no excuse for accepting the status quo, sticking our heads in the sand while vacationing in Fiji. If we don't stop pumping carbon pollution into the air, Fiji won't be there anymore. It will be underwater, along with Bangkok, Ho Chi Minh City,

Jakarta, Manila, New Orleans, Shanghai, the West Netherlands, and a whole bunch of other places.

The burdens of climate change fall disproportionately on the world's communities of color. And racism is itself another complex, structural, everything problem. Understanding how to combat it also requires unlearning myths many of us were taught as kids, which, like the corporate picture of climate change, focuses attention on individual bad guys and good guys. Whatever the problem, its causes and solutions have faces and names. The fairytale about racism is that it came from villains who hated Black people and was fought by heroes like Frederick Douglass, Abraham Lincoln, Rosa Parks, and Martin Luther King Jr. who vanquished them. The general lesson we learned as kids is that evils like racism are caused by racists, just like pollution is caused by litterbugs.

The reality is that racial injustice is embedded in a dense thicket of interconnected social systems. Racial segregation, for example, wasn't just started and perpetuated by individually racist homeowners or race-baiting politicians. And it didn't end after civil rights activists like Parks and King marched and dreamed. Segregation is an essential throughline of American history, running from the founding fathers through slaveholders and outspoken segregationists to New Dealers and mortgage bankers, all the way up to the present and the nice white parents who just want their kids to go to the "best" schools.

Just as it's naïve to think that we can recycle our way out of climate change, it's similarly naïve to think that systemic racism will be overcome when each of us becomes a little less prejudiced. Treating everyone fairly and kindly is an excellent thing to do, but that alone won't undo the racial wealth gap or eliminate medical apartheid.

So what are you supposed do? Bias and prejudice are relatively easy to recognize, even if they are hard to completely avoid. But how do you challenge systemic racism? Can you do it without quitting your job and becoming a full-time revolutionary?

People Who Change Systems That Change People

For the purposes of this book, we're not going to try to convince you that climate change and racism are bad, or explore the essence of what makes them so. We'll just assume they're bad and assume you agree. We're not going to make specific policy recommendations either. We're not wonks. We're three philosophers frustrated by the wrong lessons we were taught about these systemic problems. We've spent a long time thinking about what a better picture, and a better set of tools for thinking about social change, would look like.

In the chapters that follow, we'll meet union organizers, reproductive rights activists, city planners, and a whole bunch of ordinary, busy, imperfect people who have found ways to connect their personal choices to systemic change. One thing that unites these people is that they see systems and institutions as mutable, and see themselves as *part of* those systems and institutions, not separate from them. This is the central idea we'll explore, mapping out its implications across a whole swath of contexts. The people we'll profile have found ways to take advantage of human beings' unavoidable, radical interdependence. That we're so deeply interconnected is an idea found across contemporary social science.

Our focus will be on climate change and racism, two areas where the old picture—individual choices outmatched by systemic forces—retains a strong grip. There's another reason too: race and climate change are intimately related. As Fijians and people of color the world over have been telling anyone who'll listen, the effects of pumping billions of tons of carbon pollution into the atmosphere are devastating their communities *now*. Still, our main point of departure will be how these issues arise in the US, the context we three are best poised to study. Where we can, though, we'll venture a more global perspective.

The book has three parts. The first diagnoses the problem of "either/or" thinking about social change that stems from the seemingly forced choice between making better personal choices and changing the system. The second offers a different way to think about social change, anchored in a more accurate picture of human nature. The third explores ways of putting this picture into practice.

From learning to pay attention to systemic causes of injustice to building social movements, we need a "both/and" approach. We need to make personal choices that help change systems and to build systems that help people make better choices.

I The Problem of Either/Or Thinking About Social Change

1 You Do You: The Misdirected Individualist History of Climate Activism

People Start Pollution . . . So People Can Stop It?

If you've watched any TV show or movie made between 1930 and 1990 that features a Native American character, chances are you've seen the actor known as Iron Eyes Cody. He starred in movies alongside Roy Rogers and John Wayne and in TV shows like *The Cisco Kid*, where he played Chief Sky Eagle. His career was illustrious. Cody appeared in over 200 films and 100 TV shows. He was a close friend of Walt Disney. He has a Hollywood star. He chants in the background of Joni Mitchell's 1998 song "Lakota."

As you might have guessed from his name, Iron Eyes Cody didn't just play Native American characters onscreen. He lived the role. Off camera, he was usually seen wearing the same beaded moccasins and fringed leather he wore on camera. He appeared in documentaries discussing Native American sign language. He was reputedly very generous to Native American charities. Often, he spoke about his Cherokee father and Cree mother.

Maybe this wholeheartedness contributed to the success of Iron Eyes Cody's most famous role. He played the "Crying Indian" in what is usually regarded as the most successful public service announcement (PSA) of all time. Launched on Earth Day in 1971 by a group called Keep America Beautiful, the PSA opens with Cody paddling his canoe down a pristine river in full buckskin. Ominous drums beat in the background.

But the river turns out to be not so pristine. First you see a single piece of floating trash. Then, as if you've flashed through the Industrial Revolution on a geologic timetable, Cody is surrounded by litter, heavy industry, and a crowded highway. Just after Cody pulls his canoe onto a trash-strewn shore, a driver speeds by and tosses what looks like a week's worth of garbage at his feet. Cody remains silent. A stern-sounding narrator reads the famous words, as Cody slowly turns to face the camera, a tear sliding down his cheek: "Some people have a deep abiding respect for the natural beauty that was once this country. And some people don't. People start pollution . . . and people can stop it."

The PSA was immediately celebrated. It won multiple awards and is widely cited as instrumental in reducing roadside litter. Even when tested today, the decades-old ad is rated highly, and audiences endorse its message.

Timing might have been one factor driving the ad's success. In 1971, collective acknowledgment of the genocide that Native Americans suffered at the hands of European Americans was growing. The ad evokes a sense of guilt for those horrors and then yokes one guilt to another: culpability for polluting the planet. But the ad doesn't just leave viewers to stew in shame. It also empowers them. People start pollution, but *people can stop it.*

The ad plays on the intuitive idea that little things add up. They can add up for worse (polluting) or for better (cleaning pollution up). If each of us just takes responsibility for our tiny corner of the world, then and only then will we fix the collective messes we've made.

As natural as this logic is, the message is catastrophically misleading. So was the ad. It might have helped reduce roadside litter, but that wasn't its real purpose.

Disciples of Disposability: The Big Business of Blaming Individuals

In the years before his death at age ninety-four, Cody spent much of his time giving talks to Native Americans, often admonishing them about gambling and alcohol. That he spent his twilight years telling Native Americans how to improve themselves is perhaps the bitterest of Cody's ironies. Because Cody wasn't Native American. His given name was Espera Oscar de Corti, and he was second-generation Italian American. His parents were not Cherokee and Cree; they were Sicilian. He was raised in Gueydan, Louisiana, with three siblings, two of whom, oddly, also went on to play Native Americans in film.

American history is full of frauds and con artists, from Frank Abagnale to Bernie Madoff. What makes Iron Eyes Cody's lifelong con particularly interesting, however, is that it's tied to another one, a fraud reaching far beyond Hollywood.

According to its website, Keep America Beautiful—the group that made the PSA—was formed when "a group of corporate and civic leaders met in New York City to bring the public and private sectors together to develop and promote a national cleanliness ethic." Among those civic-minded founders so very earnestly concerned with national cleanliness were executives from beer, can, bottle, soft drink, chewing gum, candy, and cigarette companies. The group's chairman was himself president of the American Can Company.

Keep America Beautiful was formed when disposable containers were relatively new and increasingly popular. People in postwar America were trying to figure out how to solve the problems those disposable containers caused. One of those problems was that broken bottles cut cows' feet and damaged farm equipment. In response, the Vermont Supreme Court had upheld a law banning the sale of beer or ale in nonreturnable glass containers just six months before Keep America Beautiful was formed. This kind of law cut directly into the profits of the so-called "disciples of disposability"—the CEOs of beer, bottle, soft drink, candy, gum, and cigarette companies.

The CEOs decided that something had to be done. Their task was to stop more of these laws from being passed. The strategy they adopted was to steer people away from lobbying their state representatives to ban single-use containers. Instead, they aimed to convince people to take personal responsibility for the problem. The Crying Indian ad was their masterstroke.

Blaming individual people didn't stop with bottles and cans. Keep America Beautiful collaborated with the American Ad Council, which created Smokey the Bear ("Only *you* can prevent forest fires!"), McGruff the Crime Dog ("Take a bite out of crime!"), and aphorisms like "friends don't let friends drive drunk." They invented the term "litterbug" too.

All these campaigns take a social problem and make it about personal responsibility. The Ad Council Archives at the University of Illinois contains a zinger that displays the logic behind these PSAs with remarkable clarity. It's from a 1994 message about water pollution: "There are toxic chemicals in our water. Such as oil. And pesticides. You might think industry is to blame. But they're only part of the problem. You and I, in our everyday lives, are also responsible for a tremendous amount of water pollution."

As with the Crying Indian ad, this one plays on two very powerful feelings: guilt and empowerment. First, you're made to feel guilty for doing ordinary things, like watering your lawn. Second, you're made to feel responsible in a way that's empowering: you can do something to help!

The insidiousness of this is that you're not being told to shut up and deal with it. But the way you're being invited to help also doesn't threaten anyone's bottom line. So long as everyone is busy with anti-litter campaigns, the Ad Council accurately predicted, we won't bother passing restrictive laws. That's why these messages have had catastrophic effects. They take one important thing—it *is* good to clean up after ourselves—and use it to distract us from something even more important: holding big businesses and governments to account for tackling pollution head on.

Your Footprint, Your Responsibility

The more recent notion of everyone having a "personal carbon footprint" has similar roots in the dark arts of corporate PR. The oil giant BP popularized the term and bent it to its own purposes (figure 1.1).

BP worked from the same playbook as the Ad Council. After acknowledging that climate change exists, the company makes you feel responsible for it. And then they give you something to do that helps you *feel* like you're part of the solution. Meanwhile, BP continues pumping away, enjoying massive federal subsidies and outlandish profits while avoiding any new, restrictive regulations.

The strategy was popular. One analysis of decades of ExxonMobil's public communications found that the corporation framed climate change in terms of consumer energy demand when speaking publicly. But in internal company documents, ExxonMobil recognized that it could not continue to supply fossil fuels without disastrous consequences to the environment. They knew they were causing the problem (supply) but put the blame on us (consumer demand).

ExxonMobil even conducted its own secret research on climate change in the 1970s. The results were consistent with scientific predictions. The corporation's in-house models predicted that global temperatures would rise to within 0.2°C of what they have in fact risen to since. While it publicly claimed in 1997 that "some of today's prophets of doom from global

$\longrightarrow$

Figure 1.1
BP advertisement. Screenshot of advertisement appearing in various publications from 2004 to 2006.

What on earth is a carbon footprint?

Every person in the world has one. It's the amount of carbon dioxide emitted due to our daily activities—from washing a load of laundry to driving a car load of kids to school. Find out the size of your household's carbon footprint, learn how you can reduce it, and see how we're reducing ours at bp.com/carbonfootprint. It's a start.

bp

beyond petroleum®

bp.com

warming were predicting the coming of a new ice age," in the 1970s, Exxon's own scientists had privately been in agreement all along with the overwhelming majority of published science on climate forecasting.

Once you know what to look for, you start to see the message of personal responsibility everywhere. Worried about retirement? Start saving more. Have a gambling problem? Exercise some willpower and stay away from the casino. Worried about obesity? Fix your lifestyle. From 2008 to 2010, 87 percent of all alcohol ads in magazines told consumers to "drink responsibly."

While it was becoming clearer that Americans consume too much sugar, Coca-Cola fought back by subsidizing research arguing that the problem was not calories in but calories out: "Americans are overly fixated on how much they eat and drink while not paying enough attention to exercise." The central plank of the food industry's lobbying has been to frame discussions about eating habits in terms of personal responsibility (e.g., "portion control").

What these messages minimize are all the social, structural, and systemic drivers of health problems like diabetes. In one *New York Times* article, Dr. Dean Schillinger explained how "our entire society is perfectly designed to create Type 2 diabetes." There is no amount of scolding about sugary foods and exercise, he explains, and "no device, no drug powerful enough to counter the effects of poverty, pollution, stress, a broken food system, cities that are hard to navigate on foot and inequitable access to health care, particularly in minority communities."

Yet these companies have devoted enormous amounts of money to teaching the public to focus on the symptoms rather than the underlying system. They have taught us to track what we buy, and take responsibility for what we do with the stuff we buy, so that they won't have to stop making and selling the stuff we buy from them or deal with laws regulating how they do it.

A Too-Convenient Model for Facing Inconvenient Truths

Whole social movements have been built around this individualist, little-things-add-up ethos. An iconic poster from the early days of the modern environmental movement mirrors the Ad Council's claim that personal choices are both the cause of and the solution to pollution (figure 1.2).

This individualist thinking prevailed all the way from the 1970s environmental movement to May 2006, which marks one of the biggest box office

Figure 1.2
Earth Day poster created by Walt Kelly, 1970.

events in documentary history: the release of Al Gore's *An Inconvenient Truth*. The documentary reached millions of people around the world. Its vivid depictions of solar rays pelting the atmosphere and glaciers melting raised public awareness of climate change to new heights and ignited collective fervor about the environment like never before. It demanded action.

Widely and deservedly lauded, *An Inconvenient Truth* presented the facts in a way that was hard to argue with. It also presented solutions:

Each one of us is a cause of global warming, but each one of us can make choices to change that with the things we buy, the electricity we use, the cars we drive; we can make choices to bring our individual carbon emissions to zero. The solutions are in our hands, we just have to have the determination to make it happen. We have everything that we need to reduce carbon emissions, everything but political will. But in America, the will to act is a renewable resource.

The general template should sound familiar. What causes climate change? We do. How? Driving gas guzzlers, leaving on the lights, and buying unrecyclable plastic. What's the solution? Stop doing these things. Consume better.

This is another effect of the long history of corporate-funded individualist messaging: the first thing that comes to mind for many of us when we ask "what can I do?" is a series of thoughts about *stuff*. What should I buy? Where should I buy it from? What should I do with it? Even leaders in the fight against climate change have perpetuated our preoccupation with consumption.

As the credits of *An Inconvenient Truth* roll, the film offers concrete suggestions for how to make a difference, stating, "The climate crisis can be solved. Here's how to start." Here are the first five items in the list:

- Buy energy-efficient appliances + lightbulbs.
- Change your thermostat . . . to reduce energy for heating + cooling.
- Weatherize your house, increase insulation, get an energy audit.
- Recycle.
- If you can, buy a hybrid car.

These are good things to do, though energy-inefficient incandescent lightbulbs are basically illegal now and hybrid cars may be on their way to being old news. But *An Inconvenient Truth* exemplifies a whole world of books, TV, and academic research that looks at climate change through the lens of our personal consumer choices. Even academics have gotten in on the act. One widely cited study examined and ranked nearly 150 personal lifestyle choices by their effectiveness in reducing personal carbon footprints. The four most impactful options, it found, are having one fewer child, living car-free, flying less, and eating a plant-based diet.

Eventually, further down the list of action items, *An Inconvenient Truth* also tells viewers to do the following:

- Vote for leaders who pledge to solve this crisis.
- Write to congress.
   - If they don't listen, run for congress.

- Speak up in your community.
- Insist that America freeze CO_2 emissions + join international efforts to stop global warming.

These suggestions head in a different direction, away from what we buy. They gesture toward our political choices and our communities' values. This is promising, and we'll talk a lot more about why in the coming chapters. For now, notice how vague they are. "Speak up in your community" sounds empowering, but what does it really mean? Speak up to whom? Say what? "Join international efforts" sounds good too. But your average moviegoer may be forgiven for thinking, "Yeah, I'll get right on that." Most viewers likely walked out feeling alarmed, maybe intending to buy better lightbulbs. After all, lightbulbs were first on the list!

It turns out audiences did become both more knowledgeable and more concerned about the climate crisis. But this newfound knowledge and concern doesn't appear to have amounted to much, at least in the short term. One study found that a month after seeing the film, viewers had done next to nothing to put their newfound climate knowledge into action. Not one of them had examined their carbon footprint or written a letter to their senator.

Another study found that framing solutions in terms of individual consumer choices *decreases* people's willingness to take other forms of action to fight climate change. Maybe people feel like they're being blamed for a global crisis beyond their control. Maybe they resent being asked to respond with what to them look like merely symbolic, even futile, changes to their personal behavior. The danger, then, is not just that such messages don't help. It's that they might be making things worse.

System Change, Not Climate Change

Some people have started to get wise to this long history of corporations laying problems at the feet of individuals. The backlash it's helped create has produced slogans now found on fridge magnets, protest posters, and newspaper headlines. The most common ones suggest a different kind of thing to do: stop worrying about personal choices, and start focusing on changing the system. The news site *Vox* published an article in 2019 whose headline perfectly expresses this idea: "I Work in the Environmental Movement. I Don't Care if You Recycle."

The Sunrise Movement, a decentralized, youth-led group at the forefront of progressive climate politics, advocates system change: "to abolish or reimagine institutions that degrade our communities and our climate." This marks a generational sea change in climate activism. Abolishing or reimagining institutions was most certainly not on *An Inconvenient Truth*'s list. Writing for the *New Yorker*, Andrew Marantz recounts a telling experience with a Sunrise group in Philadelphia:

> The organizers were scanning the menu of a Middle Eastern restaurant on Uber Eats. Aru Shiney-Ajay, Sunrise's training director, sat at a laptop, taking orders. "Can you get me a beef kebab?" Dejah Powell, an organizer from Chicago, said. "Or, no. Beef is the worst, right? Maybe chicken. Or falafel?"
>
> "Dejah," an activist named John Paul Mejia said, in a mock-scolding tone. He started reciting a movement adage, using the singsong rhythm of a call-and-response: "The biggest driver of emissions is . . ." The others joined him, in unison: ". . . the political power of the fossil-fuel industry, not individual behavior." In other words, if you want the beef, get the beef.

One way to think about Sunrise's system-over-individual logic is to recall Iron Eyes Cody. We called him a fraud, but looked at another way, his personal deception obscures the bigger story. A first-generation Sicilian American was able to play some of the most iconic Native American roles in Hollywood because the movie industry excluded actual Native Americans from taking those roles. The biases woven into cultural norms and movie business practices allowed, and incentivized, Cody's personal fraud. Too much focus on what he should or shouldn't have done, as a single person, makes it easy to overlook the system that structured his options and made his personal choices possible in the first place. Coming to appreciate the significance of systems can be disorienting, but keeping that significance firmly in view is crucial to understanding the bigger picture. The little-things-add-up take on individual responsibility is too easily weaponized by corporations advancing their own interests. When it comes to climate change, they have long pushed a picture where "taking action" means tweaking our shopping choices. It's this history that Sunrise and other progressive climate activists are rightly standing athwart, yelling stop.

But even if we accept this change in perspective, it's not at all obvious what we should do next. To take that step, we'll look at another area of life where a loud chorus is rightly demanding structural change.

2 Structural Injustice: Why Conversations About Racism Become Conversations About Real Estate

The Accumulation of (Dis)advantage

Everyone gets to make choices, but we don't all get the same options. The differences between people's options are shaped by social structures.

Imagine 100 people have fallen behind on rent. They receive an ominous notice from the city about a court date to attend or else they'll be evicted. Of these people, 50 are Black, and 50 are white. Each wants desperately to show up and contest the eviction. Let's say a few from each group oversleep. So we're down to 48 left in the running to make their court date in each group. What else might prevent these people from making it?

In many places, neighborhoods with more Black Americans suffer more power outages than predominantly white neighborhoods. So maybe while some of our 100 people made a mistake setting the alarm, one or two more Black people oversleep when their unpowered alarms don't wake them up. We're down to 47 Black people and 48 white.

Some of these people work at fast-food restaurants. Unfortunately, over half of service sector workers, and three-quarters of fast-food workers, get their schedule less than two weeks in advance. So some of our remaining 95 people won't have received their schedule in time to get the day off. They'll have to make a terrible choice: go to court or keep their job. Black people are much more likely than white people to work in service, so let's say 5 Black people opt to skip court to go to work, while only 3 white people do. We're down to 42 Black people versus 45 white.

Among our remaining 87, a bunch will need childcare. For some, a friend or family member can help out. Others are lucky enough to live near affordable daycare or free pre-K. But the breakdown won't be equal here either.

Black Americans have less access to quality preschool. Speaking of kids, if one of them gets hurt or sick, they'll face longer ER wait times and receive less pain meds than white kids. So let's say another 5 Black people don't make it to court because their daycare provider called in sick or they spent the whole night in the ER, whereas 3 white people face the same problems. We're down to 37 Black people and 43 white.

Those who can't appear at the hearing may try to contact the court about rescheduling. Those with stereotypically Black-sounding names, though, are less likely to get a response. Research finds that government officials, including sheriffs, librarians, and school district reps, respond less to emails from DeShawn and Tyrone than from Greg and Jake.

How about physically getting to the courthouse? In most of the US, driving is the default option—for those with a car. Yet while just 6 percent of white households lack access to a car, 18 percent of Black households are carless. This disparity is not just because Black Americans have, on average, less money than white Americans. Even white and Black people with similar finances have dissimilar access to vehicles. For example, used car salespeople offer higher initial prices to Black consumers and are less willing to negotiate.

Among our remaining 80 people who do have a car, some are less likely to get to the courthouse without being stopped along the way. Black drivers are stopped 20 percent more often. We're down to 34 Black people, 44 white.

If you're skeptical, you might be wondering something like, "well what if Black people speed more?" It's possible. But using data from the rideshare app Lyft, researchers found no differences in driving speeds by race. Nevertheless, Lyft drivers of color were 24–33 percent more likely to get pulled over than white drivers, and they paid 23–34 percent more in fines.

Other commuters rely on public transportation. But neighborhoods with more Black residents tend to have fewer public transit options. These neighborhoods are also farther from business districts, city centers, and courthouses. Research finds that a one-hour increase in transit time doubles people's rate of eviction. In a segregated world, this disparity, like the others, falls along racial lines. (Things could be structured differently. During the COVID-19 pandemic, eviction proceedings were held virtually on Zoom. Showing up to court suddenly got much easier. One Philadelphia study found that this structural change eliminated the impact of distance from the courthouse on eviction rates.)

Of the public transport takers, a few of our remaining 78 people realize at the bus stop that they forgot their fare cards. It's a mistake nearly everyone's made, yet they won't all face the same consequences for that same mistake. One experiment found that bus drivers, wittingly or not, were two times more likely to allow white people to ride for free than Black people. Let's say 4 Black people fail to make it because the bus driver won't let them on, or the bus fails to arrive at all, whereas only 2 white people miss the hearing for the same reason. Now we're down to 30 and 42.

And for those who finally do make it to the hearing? They'll meet judges who dole out harsher judgments to Black people than white.

The above describes *structural racism*, which is one species of *structural injustice*. Disadvantage accumulates when one group of people faces more obstacles than another. The question is not whether Black people can overcome all these obstacles if they try hard enough. The injustice here is precisely that they have more obstacles in their way. They face a different set of choices, and different consequence for the choices they make. That's unfair.

Choices are shaped by *social structures*, which include laws, norms, history, and culture. Social structures also include the way neighborhoods, police jurisdictions, congressional maps, and economies are laid out. Pick any one part of life—like going to school—and there are umpteen social structures organizing it, from what time the bell rings in the morning (affecting how much sleep kids get) to the number of kids in the classroom (shaping how much attention they get) to the grades they receive (influencing what kinds of opportunities they'll have in the future).

There's plenty of scholarly debate about the best way to understand social structures. We'll define them as the more or less stable features of our shared, external social worlds. These features contrast with what's inside people, like their beliefs, goals, and personality traits. Some kids are eager beavers ready to start school at 8:10 a.m., and others are night owls who have to be dragged out of bed at noon. Differences in such internal traits can lead kids to react to a shared social structure—in this case, the time school starts—differently.

To get a more complete view, we need to take a closer look at how racial inequity is woven into our neighborhoods, cities, and cultures—why conversations about racism quickly become conversations about real estate.

Residential Racial Segregation and the Maneuvering of People into Poverty

If you happen to own an old home in Seattle, the language of racial segregation may still linger in your house's deed. Two hundred and eighty parcels of the Roxbury Heights subdivision, for example, formed in 1942, were subject to the rule that "No person of any race other than the white race shall use or occupy any building or any lot, except this covenant shall not prevent occupancy by domestic servants of a different race domiciled with an owner or tenant." Deeds like this aren't rare. The University of Washington keeps a list of racially restrictive covenants. By now they're legally voided, but they're still available for anyone to see. The list is depressingly long, and it's just for Seattle.

Policies like these represent one move in the long history of American racial oppression. Many of them were responses to the Great Migration, the movement of about six million Black Americans out of the South over the twentieth century. Across the country, white Americans did just about everything possible to preserve segregation, not just against Black Americans moving out of the South but also against immigrants and other non-white groups. And the segregationists have been winning. Eighty percent of American cities are more segregated today than they were in 1990, and the trend is continuing in that direction.

Some say residential racial segregation is the "linchpin" or "structural ground" of contemporary racial inequality. They point to segregation's power to lock other racial injustices in place. Malcolm X explained it with characteristic verve in 1963:

> Our people are scientifically maneuvered by the white man into a life of poverty. Because we are forced to live in the poorest sections of the city, we attend inferior schools. We have inferior teachers and we get an inferior education. The white power structure downtown makes certain that by the time our people do graduate, we won't be equipped or qualified for anything but the dirtiest, heaviest, poorest-paying jobs. Jobs that no one else wants. We are trapped in a vicious cycle of economic, intellectual, social, and political death. Inferior jobs, inferior housing, inferior education which in turn again leads to inferior jobs. We spend a lifetime in this vicious circle.

Historian Thomas Sugrue put it succinctly: "geography is destiny." "Zoning" is the term used in the US for the methods and laws that municipalities and other local governments use to divide land into different zones (e.g., residential, commercial, industrial) and regulate how those different zones can be developed. While seemingly banal, it remains among the most significant causes of race- and class-based injustice. In 1922, then Secretary of State Herbert Hoover pushed for the Standard State Zoning Enabling Act, which delegated decision-making about land use to local communities. Now that cities couldn't pass laws explicitly excluding Black people, they turned to zoning rules. In one example among many, Ford moved a factory—including all 1,400 employees, of which about 250 were Black—from Richmond, Virginia to the outskirts of Milpitas, California. Milpitas quickly moved to incorporate the new factory within its city limits and then to ban apartment buildings and ensure that only "qualified buyers" (i.e., white people) could secure a mortgage for a home.

This maneuvering spilled over into the nefarious practice known as redlining, which began in the 1930s and wasn't outlawed until 1968. The term comes from the practice of financial institutions using color-coded real estate maps to rank neighborhoods by the likelihood that homebuyers there could pay off their mortgages. Neighborhoods deemed "too risky" for housing loans were colored red. Mortgage lenders stayed away, making it extremely difficult for residents of those neighborhoods to purchase their own homes or sell them to new buyers. Redlining systematically shut people out of the American Dream.

How was a neighborhood's "risk" level determined? Rather than say the quiet part out loud—that loans shouldn't be given to Black families—agencies like the federal government's Home Owners' Loan Corporation based their ratings on proxies for race.

Mortgages, it is said, are like time machines: They allow you to have the future you want but today. But thanks to redlining, not everyone got the time machines. The invention of the modern mortgage was integral to one of the greatest periods of intergenerational wealth building in US history, but the boom was largely restricted to white people. Over the course of more than three decades, from the mid-1930s to the late 1960s, non-white applicants received just 2 percent of federally approved loans. In some places, the only option available to aspiring Black homeowners was to accept unorthodox loans from predatory "contract sellers." These involved large down payments and high interest rates. Buyers would only be granted ownership of the home after the contract was paid in full and so garnered no equity while making monthly payments. One estimate found that in the 1950s and 1960s, Black families in Chicago alone lost $3 to $4 billion to contract sellers.

The Cycle Is the Story: The Cascading Effects of Injustice

None of these racist housing maneuvers happened in isolation. The GI Bill that sent a generation of World War II veterans to college was de facto unavailable to Black soldiers. Using the same tactics that worked to restrict the benefits of the New Deal to white people, Southern members of Congress insisted the GI Bill be administered at the state level, and Jim Crow laws made it nearly impossible for Black veterans to take advantage of it in many states.

There were countervailing victories, of course. The 1968 Fair Housing Act outlawed new forms of explicit housing discrimination. Probably as a result, residential segregation declined during the 1970s. But the law did little to counteract manipulations of zoning laws and mortgage lending practices.

Other putative victories ended up yielding mixed results too. When *Brown v. Board of Education of Topeka* outlawed racial segregation in public schools in 1954, redlining and other forms of residential segregation became popular tools for keeping white schools white. They appear to have worked. In 2021, about 40 percent of American public school students attended racially segregated schools, and currently, four out of five students at low-income schools are Black or Hispanic.

The story of residential racial segregation not only highlights the structural features of racism in the United States. It also illustrates the cascading effects of these arrangements. When public schools are financed through local property taxes—as they overwhelmingly have been in the US—poorer areas will have poorer schools. If Black Americans live in segregated poorer neighborhoods, then Black kids will get a worse education. What's more, children living in predominantly Black neighborhoods are exposed to more environmental toxins like lead, whose harmful influence on cognition can be detected in math and reading scores.

The cascading effects of segregation don't stop there. Residents of impoverished neighborhoods also have less access to banks (as opposed to payday lenders), public transportation, decent grocery stores, and jobs offering better pay. Researchers call this "spatial mismatch": poorer people don't live near the services and opportunities that would benefit them.

Residents in segregated neighborhoods also have longer and more difficult commutes, increasing their transportation costs and the "time tax" they pay to get to work. Segregation also "taxes" people by limiting their social networks. "It's not what you know but who you know" is one of life's great truths, and it drives home how important it is to *have the opportunities* to know the right people. Missing such opportunities because of where you live is yet another cascading effect of segregation.

This last example highlights a particularly important aspect of structural racism. The cycle is the story. Segregation leads to unequal schools, which leads to unequal opportunities, which leads to unequal wealth, which leads to more segregation.

Once set in motion, the whole cyclical process can keep chugging along, without anyone at the wheel. Imagine you're hiring for a company you work for. Wouldn't you be grateful for a tip from someone you trust about a well-qualified candidate? Giving a special look to someone with a personal reference surely isn't racist, or even wrong. We help friends out all the time. Nevertheless, in a racially segregated society where white people are overwhelmingly likely to have mostly white friends, the practice of favoring friends perpetuates injustice. As the philosopher Elizabeth Anderson puts it, "segregation along lines of social inequality is the key feature that turns otherwise innocent [choices] into vectors of . . . injustice."

There are plenty of intentionally and unintentionally biased people contributing to segregation. But focusing on individually biased people leaves the structural drivers of unfairness out of the story. Even if someone could snap their fingers and eliminate every racist idea in every human's head, racial injustice would persist. People of color would still wake up the next morning, and the morning after that, in neighborhoods with worse schools, fewer jobs, more pollution, and less justice. Because of how social structures organize our world, people of color face unfair obstacles even when other people aren't treating them in prejudiced ways.

Many companies today say they're trying to root out the biases in their hiring practices and recruit people from different walks of life. They're not always genuine but sometimes they are. Even then, residential segregation and spatial mismatch create formidable challenges. The people these companies want to hire don't hear about the job openings, and employers don't know how to find them. And even if employers and employees find each other, segregation might make a Black recruit's commute to work double the distance of their white colleague's. Hence the saying about (and by) Black strivers in the United States: you have to be twice as good to get half as much.

If simply making people less prejudiced won't uproot structural racism, what will? The overturning of exclusionary zoning laws would be a good start. Maybe we need a massive social movement too. Either way, how do we do these things? In the last chapter, we explored how the dark arts of corporate PR shifted blame for problems like climate change off companies and governments and onto individuals. These PR campaigns created "litterbugs" and "personal carbon footprints" to distract people from more impactful collective action. It turns out that similar tactics have stymied the collective fight against structural racism.

How Not to Resist Structural Racism

Seventeen-year-old Darnella Frazier could not have known what she was about to set in motion when she pulled out her cellphone on May 25, 2020, outside a convenience store where George Floyd had just been arrested for attempting to use a counterfeit $20 bill to buy cigarettes. During the arrest, officer Derek Chauvin pinned Floyd to the ground, pressing his knee to Floyd's neck. Floyd pleaded and called out for his mother for over eight minutes. While other officers either knelt on Floyd's back or stood by and did nothing, and a growing crowd of onlookers begged for them to stop, Frazier started recording. Floyd was eventually taken to a hospital but died due to injuries from the arrest.

Frazier's video helped spark what became known as the Black Lives Matter (BLM) protests, which peaked on June 6, 2020, with over half a million people marching in at least 550 cities. Over the course of about a month, between 15 and 26 million people participated in the demonstrations—the largest in US history.

The protests demanded justice for Floyd, and much more. They insisted police stop using excessive force on Black Americans. They called for profound transformations of the entire criminal justice system. They demanded the end of cash bail. They demanded alternative responses to people experiencing mental health crises. They demanded community oversight of police departments. BLM has come to stand for a whole set of ideas, ways the system needs to change to treat Black and brown people with respect and dignity.

One effect of the protests was immediately noticeable: a hiring spree. In the three months following Floyd's murder, the largest publicly traded companies in the United States tripled their hiring of chief diversity officers. Job openings focused on diversity, equity, and inclusion (DEI) surged by 50 percent in June 2020. This response increased the growth of what had already become big business. According to some estimates, US companies spend around $8 billion a year on diversity initiatives, most prominently on paying consultants for diversity and antibias training. By 2021, the DEI industry was projected to continue to grow dramatically, surpassing $15 billion a year by 2026. (These projections may have been too bullish, however; the hiring spree has cooled since 2021, and has even been reversed at some corporations and universities.)

This was not, to put it gently, on BLM's list of demands. It's hard to imagine protestors passionately chanting "No justice, no peace! Hire more diversity chiefs!" The diversity hiring boom was exactly the kind of Band-Aid response to racial injustice the BLM movement was criticizing. Diversity workshops, racial sensitivity trainings, and courageous conversations have been common practice, even in police departments, for decades.

Suspicion of the true motives behind the boom in DEI hiring came nearly as immediately as the boom itself. In an article titled "Workplace 'Anti-Racism' Trainings Aren't Working," for the socialist magazine *Jacobin*, J. C. Pan wrote, "workplace antiracism training isn't a practice that anyone invested in the well-being of workers of any race should defend. The problem with such trainings isn't that they push 'un-American propaganda' or 'neo-Marxist' ideas in the workplace as the Right has fretted, but rather, that they increasingly allow employers to consolidate their power over employees under a veneer of social justice."

All this hiring *is* good for at least one thing: preventing lawsuits. An unironic article on the Leaders' Choice Insurance website, for example, is titled "Conduct Diversity Training to Head Off Potential Lawsuits." When a business or a school demonstrates that it required everyone to complete a DEI event, it can say it took proactive action to prevent discrimination. The implication—left unspoken—is that nothing further in the institution's culture or policies needs fixing. After the organization "checks the box" saying that everyone completed the training, they can blame future discriminatory actions on misbehaving individual employees. Pan gets at the economic sense of this: "a weeklong anti-racism workshop that costs an employer tens of thousands of dollars is still cheaper than a discrimination lawsuit (or raising workers' wages)." As *Jacobin's* founding editor Bhaskar Sunkara put it, "Inclusivity seminars . . . protect power; they don't challenge it. We're being hustled."

Although there's more to (some) diversity trainings than these critics allege (see chapter 5), nobody who's seeking progressive change should want to be a mark for forces like these. Structural racism is an "everything problem" like climate change. In both cases, the forces defending the status quo have roots hundreds of years deep and tendrils in nearly every part of daily life. They won't be undone by shopping better or one-hour diversity trainings alone. We need to set our sights on structural change: what it is and how to create it.

3 Change Against the Machine: Structural Change in the Public Mind

Big Structural Change

We've seen that too much focus on what individuals can do in their own little corners of the world diverts attention from the real action: the pursuit of transformative, structural change. But what is structural change, and how does it happen?

Structural changes promise to be big. They're significant and far-reaching, in contrast to the itty-bitty changes individuals can make on their own. Senator Elizabeth Warren built her 2020 presidential campaign around the demand for "Big Structural Change." Her proudest example of "a structural fix" was the creation of her brainchild, the Consumer Financial Protection Bureau, a "new government agency whose sole mission was to look out for consumers." The agency set out to fight banks and other companies on behalf of bilked citizens.

Also in the 2020 Democratic primary, Pete Buttigieg backed "structural democratic reforms," including the dissolution of the Electoral College and statehood for Washington, DC. Cory Booker campaigned on ending "structural inequality and institutional racism," through, for example, a "baby bond" bill that would give every child born in the US $1,000, with more funds given each year, especially to poorer children. Bernie Sanders promised "to treat structural racism with the exigency it deserves" by, for example, ending the "war on drugs"; abolishing cash bail, capital punishment, and private prisons; guaranteeing every American a job; automatically registering every eighteen-year-old to vote; and granting free, high-quality healthcare to all.

Others have focused beyond law and policy, on versions of structural change that don't go through government. In January 1969, the Black

Panther Party worked with a local Oakland priest to start offering free breakfast to children at a church. Funded through donations and staffed with volunteers, the program rapidly expanded nationwide, serving thousands of children in twenty cities by the end of the year. Eventually, this did provoke government action. The federal government passed its own permanent breakfast program in 1975, which to this day feeds nearly 15 million children every morning. (The federal government stepped in only after systematically dismantling the Black Panther Party, murdering several of its leaders, and discrediting their free breakfast program, which Federal Bureau of Investigation [FBI] Director J. Edgar Hoover called "a front for indoctrinating children with Panther propaganda.")

Whenever people make it easier or harder to eat breakfast, vote, cross national borders, access unemployment insurance, buy a gun, or get a gas-guzzler or an electric car, they're changing the structures that shape everyday life. These background structures act like fuel or friction for our personal choices. They make some options easy and obvious and others hidden and arduous.

Many people think that seriously tackling "everything problems" like climate change and racism will require a revolutionary transformation to a new global order, on par with the transitions from hunter-gatherer societies to farming economies and from feudal kingdoms to capitalist democracies.

One of the biggest transformations was what the Nobel laureate economist Angus Deaton calls humanity's "Great Escape." For almost all the roughly 300,000 years that modern human beings have existed, the average lifespan was about thirty-five years. Child mortality held the average down; roughly one-third of children died before puberty. Aside from small fluctuations around big harvests or disease outbreaks, these numbers remained the same until about the middle of the eighteenth century. Change came slowly at first and mostly in Europe. But the escape from truncated life started to take off with astounding speed and reach at the end of the nineteenth century, eventually achieving a global average of seventy-three years by 2019. To put that in perspective, in the last 0.05 percent of our species' existence, the typical human life has *doubled* in length.

This is astonishing, but it's only part of the truly transformative changes human beings have experienced over the past 200 years. Suppose the world consisted of 100 people:

In 1820	In 2020
—88 people were illiterate, while 12 could read.	—14 people were illiterate, while 86 could read.
—83 people received no formal education, while 17 received at least a basic education.	—14 people received no formal education, while 86 received at least a basic education.
—99 people didn't live in a democracy and only 1 did.	—44 people didn't live in a democracy, while 56 did.
—84 people were living in extreme poverty and 16 were not.	—9 people were living in extreme poverty and 91 were not (though 76 were still poor).
—Nobody was vaccinated against anything.	—14 people weren't vaccinated against anything and 86 were.

Dramatic changes like these have many causes. They include revolutions overthrowing governments, important laws being passed or repealed, progress in science and technology, and cultures adopting norms that spread from the margins to the mainstream. Some such changes are unintended, like the US military experimenting with networked computers, which became the internet, which became "Distracted Boyfriend" memes and Tik-Tok. Others have been driven by disasters, like the 1666 Great Fire of London that gave rise to modern city planning. Others still have been driven by invention: vaccines and antibiotics, planes and trains, nuclear fission, and maybe next artificial intelligence.

It's rarely the case that things simply get better overall. For all the tremendous advances of the last 200 years, the biggest societal challenges we face today—inequality, biodiversity loss, democratic backsliding—are in some ways products of the very things that made those changes possible, like cheap fossil fuels and racial exploitation.

Structural change also happens piecemeal and unevenly. Many people live in abject poverty even as the world as a whole grows richer. Some children—especially in marginalized communities of color—continue to die young despite rising averages in lifespan. A 2023 California study found that for every 100,000 births, 173 babies born to wealthy white women die before they turn one, whereas 653 born to poor Black women do.

There's plenty of room to disagree about which social structures we ought to try to change and how we ought to do it. Even among advocates for change who agree about structural goals—decarbonization, racial equity, ending poverty—there's ongoing, complex, and reasonable debate about what to do. For example, staving off the climate crisis requires scaling up the extraction of minerals for "clean" technology, like batteries to power electric cars. Many of these mining efforts have disproportionately harmed indigenous and marginalized communities. But the solution to climate change can't be a strategy that poisons the least well-off and tramples their ways of life. The steps to decarbonization have to be fair, safe, and democratic.

Maybe global warming can't be reversed without a world-historical transformation, like the death of capitalism. Or maybe it can. It's possible that multifaceted incremental progress through a hodgepodge of less radical reforms, from tax rebates for induction stoves to new ways to sequester carbon pollution in concrete, can get the job done. We don't know. For the rest of the book, though, we'll take "structural change" to include all the above.

Either/Or Thinking

Otherwise commendable demands for structural change too often slip into either/or thinking. People demand structural change *instead of* individual change. In the coming chapters, we'll make the case that changing people and changing systems are interconnected and mutually reinforcing. They're complements rather than competitors. Either/or thinking can be deceptively appealing, though, so a key step in escaping it is getting a clearer picture of what it is and how it works.

Start with what social psychologists Keith Payne and Jason Hannay predict are among the best ways to tackle racial injustice: "policies that directly increase racial equality and participation, such as voting rights legislation and affirmative action policies, are likely to have more impact than changing attitudes." In another essay, Payne and Heidi Vuletich insist that "solutions need to focus on structuring the social context, rather than changing the beliefs or values of individuals." Claims like these don't just portray changing individual attitudes as *insufficient* for combating racial inequality and bias. They're not advocating that we change both attitudes and structures. They're saying we can't have it both ways.

Historian Ibram X. Kendi draws out this line of thinking in vivid, autobiographical detail. He describes his own escape from the more individualist view he held at an earlier time in his life: "I became a college professor to educate away racist ideas, seeing ignorance as the source of racist ideas, seeing racist ideas as the source of racist policies, seeing mental change as the principal solution, seeing myself, an educator, as the primary solver."

Over time, however, Kendi came to see things exactly the other way around, believing that racist "policies"—such as slavery, segregation, and mass incarceration—are the source of racist ideas:

> I was taught the popular folktale of racism: that ignorant and hateful people had produced racist ideas, and that these racist people had instituted racist policies. But when I learned the motives behind the production of many of America's most influentially racist ideas, it became quite obvious that this folktale, though sensible, was not based on a firm footing of historical evidence. Ignorance/hate → racist ideas → discrimination: this causal relationship is largely ahistorical. It has actually been the inverse relationship—racial discrimination [that is, large-scale racially discriminatory policies and structures like segregation] led to racist ideas which led to ignorance and hate. Racial discrimination → racist ideas → ignorance/hate: this is the causal relationship driving America's history of race relations.

On this view, racist ideas are what philosophers call "epiphenomenal"—they're a by-product, not a cause. If racist ideas are mere by-products of racist policies, then we ought to focus on changing the policies rather than the ideas. To borrow a concept from the economist Douglass North, we should work to change the "rules of the road" that structure individual choice. Systems and structures are the problem, Kendi and Payne and North would say, so changing them—rather than individual hearts and minds—is the solution.

There's something right about this, especially the insistence that we keep our sights set on structural change. But there's also something troublingly incomplete about it. What could it possibly mean to change racist policies "directly?" Without persuading anyone to do anything differently?

This either/or thinking isn't specific to fighting racism. There was a massive decline in carbon pollution in 2020 due to COVID-19 lockdowns, when so many people stopped driving and traveling. Nevertheless, carbon pollution rebounded after the lockdowns ended. Robinson Meyer concluded that "this extraordinary and painful trial should provide the final proof, I think, that climate change simply cannot be solved by changing our personal behavior. We have to change systems." You'll remember that distracting people from supporting regulations was exactly the goal of corporate PR campaigns like Keep America Beautiful. Meyer is rightly fighting back against that long history, trying to redirect attention toward important but obscured sources of the problem. But his use of either/or thinking again raises the question of how systems will change if nobody has to change their personal behavior.

Other times, either/or thinking is offered as a corrective against pernicious kinds of victim blaming, which happen when too much responsibility is foisted on individuals. Most of us have no choice but to live in a world powered by fossil fuels, so thinking that the climate crisis requires individuals to take personal responsibility for their carbon footprints seems akin to blaming those who aren't at fault. But even though it's wrong to blame victims, somebody should do something!

The fogginess surrounding the idea of what one person can do to change systems drives other instances of either/or thinking, too. Political scientist Matto Mildenberger writes, "Yes, it's great to drive an electric vehicle (if you can afford it) and purchase solar panels (if powerful utilities in your state haven't conspired to make renewable energy more expensive). But the point is that *interest groups have structured the choices available to us today. Individuals don't have the agency* to steer our economic ship from the passenger deck." Mildenberger goes on to talk about the importance of joining a social movement to fight climate change, and we'll say more about that later. For now, notice the framework here: bad systems have made it so that individuals don't have the agency to create change. It's moments like these when, we fear, necessary corrections become troubling overcorrections. The well-taken concern that people have been investing their efforts to fight climate change and racism in misguided and individualist ways drifts into despair. If no one has agency, well then, I guess we're done here.

Individual Change or Structural Change: Which Comes First?

Besides the motivational morass that comes from being told "personal behavior doesn't matter," the obvious problem with either/or thinking is that *someone* is going to have to make change. Civil rights activist Bayard Rustin once posed the question: "What is more important to bring about change as a society, changed individuals or a changed social structure? The answer to that is very simple because if you don't start out with individuals who are determined to change something, you will never get a political consensus." Rustin takes for granted that both individual change and structural change are necessary. He avoids the pitfalls of simplistic little-things-add-up individualist thinking. As one of the main organizers of the 1963 March on Washington, he knows as well as anyone that antiracist responsibilities can't be met simply by overcoming private prejudices.

Nevertheless, Rustin is, quite explicitly, still posing an either/or choice, about which kind of change to pursue first. His view seems to go like this. Step 1: change the hearts and minds. Step 2: build a political consensus. Step 3: use that consensus to change the structures. This represents a subtler form of either/or thinking, and one with intuitive appeal.

Rustin's approach raises problems. You'll remember that DEI workshops have largely failed to move the hearts-and-minds needle in meaningful ways. Part of the problem is that these workshops are embedded in and serve the lawsuit-dodging aims of organizations. Maybe, then, the work of changing hearts and minds should take place outside corporate contexts, within alternative structures. The new question becomes, What kinds of social structures must be in place to change individuals so that those individuals go on to build a consensus and change social structures?

Another common and plausible position is that both individual and structural change are important but structural change is more important. In "What 'Structural Racism' Really Means," Jamelle Bouie brings us back to a 1948 book called *Class, Caste, and Race: A Study in Social Dynamics*, by the Trinidadian sociologist Oliver Cromwell Cox. Cox ties racism to economic exploitation, positioning his framework as an alternative to the more familiar way of thinking of racism in terms of false beliefs about group differences or tribal animus (i.e., bad hearts and misled minds). Building on Cox, Bouie writes, "We must remember that the problem of racism—of the denial of personhood and of the differential exposure to exploitation and death—will not be resolved by saying the right words or thinking the right thoughts. That's because racism does not survive, in the main, because of personal belief and prejudice. It survives because it is inscribed and reinscribed by the relationships and dynamics that structure our society, from segregation and exclusion to inequality and the degradation of labor."

Bouie is careful to say that racism doesn't survive "in the main" because of individual prejudice. He's not fully either/or. He acknowledges that individual prejudice contributes to the problems of racism rather than dismissing it as a mere by-product. On the other hand, Bouie also holds that individual prejudice can only be fully understood in terms of how it's inscribed into "the dynamics that structure our society." Those dynamics are the most important thing—they take priority.

This is puzzling. Consider what Bouie says when describing what to do to change structures of racial exploitation. He continues:

> The solution, as the Rev. Dr. Martin Luther King Jr. wrote in the year of his assassination, must involve a "revolution of values" that will "look uneasily on the glaring contrast of poverty and wealth" and see that "an edifice which produces beggars needs restructuring. If democracy is to have breadth of meaning," King declared, "it is necessary to adjust this inequity. It is not only moral, but it is also intelligent. We are wasting and degrading human life by clinging to archaic thinking."

Truly addressing structural racism would require a revolution in values and abandoning archaic thinking. Bouie endorses this here but also says earlier in the essay that racism will not be solved by getting people to think the right thoughts.

What he most likely means is that racism will never be solved if *all* we do is think different thoughts. It's difficult to disagree. But which values and thoughts? And more importantly, which values and thoughts lead to guilt-absolving insignificant choices and which lead instead to system-changing action?

Toward a Both/And Picture of Social Change

We're equal opportunity skeptics when it comes to "most importants" and first movers of any kind. What happens in hearts and minds surely matters, but what causes those changes in people's hearts and minds is often . . . changes to systems and structures. What causes changes to those systems and structures is often . . . people with conviction in their hearts and new ideas in their minds.

Instead of dichotomies and linear sequences and first movers, we favor an alternative picture, one featuring constant feedback between people and systems. As we'll explore in the coming chapters, norms and expectations, culture and hierarchies, and institutions and laws are the very things that cause us to make the individual choices we do.

When people get motivated to fight climate change because a hurricane or heat wave affects them personally, they're acting as structurally situated individuals. They're not heroic loners springing into being ex nihilo. Their choices and aims are shaped by the effects of the literal, physical structure of the city they've been living in, perhaps one with crumbling climate-vulnerable roads and buildings. Similarly, when indigenous people in Ecuador rise up to resist the exploitative and toxic practices of resource extraction in their communities, they're *reacting* to and resisting the unjust structures that oppress them. Whenever someone says "change comes first from within," we say "but what change causes that?" Their supposed first mover, the individual, has to be moved.

Individuals aren't prior to structures because structures motivate or demotivate, incentivize or prohibit, provide fuel or friction to individual action. Structures aren't prior to individuals either. Whether those structures last or crumble depends inevitably on what people think and feel about them. Frederick Douglass knew this well: "Power concedes nothing without a demand. It never did and it never will. Find out just what any people will submit to, and you have found out the exact amount of injustice and wrong which will be imposed upon them; and these will continue till they are resisted with either words or blows, or with both. The limits of tyrants are prescribed by the endurance of those whom they oppress."

Resistance to injustice can't be understood in either/or terms. It exists both inside people (in their willingness to resist) and outside them (in the institutions they're rejecting). So how can we avoid slipping into either/or thinking, and what do we put in its place? Moving forward requires looking back. So we begin with two lessons from history.

II   A Better Picture of Social Change

4   Hidden Histories of Social Change: People Who Change Systems That Change People

It's Always a Duck and It's Always Also a Rabbit

One of the world's most famous visual illusions was first published in the German humor magazine *Fliegende Blätter* in 1892. It will be familiar to anyone who has taken an intro psychology class (figure 4.1). Some people see a duck facing to the left, while others see a rabbit looking to the right. Most people assume there's only one way to see it until something prompts a second look. The illustration serves as a reminder that the very same thing can be understood in completely different ways.

Researchers showed this image to hundreds of people, from ages two to ninety-three, entering the Zürich Zoo in Switzerland. When they conducted the exercise on a random Sunday in October, most zoo-going Zürchers saw a bird of some kind, like a duck or a stork. When they conducted it

Figure 4.1
The duck-rabbit.

on Easter Sunday, though, a large majority (including 90 percent of young children) saw a bunny.

"But when you get down to it, taking away the influence of Easter or whatever," someone might ask, "what is it *really*—a duck or a rabbit?" The answer is that it's both. The image is not really a duck. And it's not really a rabbit. It's a duck-rabbit. A single picture can be interpreted in more than one way. So when we (Michael, Alex, and Dan) see a duck-rabbit, we see a reminder to reject false choices. We see a reminder to question the way a problem, or a history, or a program for changing the world, is framed.

Social events can also be interpreted in different ways. Depending on how they frame it, one storyteller can make an event look like a vindication of the importance of individual action. Another storyteller can make the very same event look like a demonstration of the priority of structural change. Consider the following:

E-scooters: Italy awards 500€ grants to city dwellers who purchase bicycles or e-scooters. These awards can be framed as an individualist reform because they aim to encourage citizens to reduce their carbon footprint by reducing their personal use of automobiles. They can also be framed as a structural reform because they're made possible by a far-reaching nationwide public policy that aims to change the financial incentives that structure individuals' choices.

Phone banking: You volunteer with an organization to make phone calls to persuade voters in your town to reform the racist and classist cash bail system. This effort can be framed as individualist because you're trying to persuade other people to change their votes one by one. This action can also be framed as structural because it is part of a collective action movement seeking to change laws and ultimately to change the structural conditions for poor people who end up entangled with the criminal justice system.

COVID-19: The economic slowdown caused by the coronavirus pandemic reduced global carbon pollution by over 6 percent in 2020 as compared to 2019. This was the largest single-year drop in modern history. The temporary reduction in emissions was framed by some as vindicating the power of individual action, because it showed the enormous changes people can make if they choose to alter their behavior. It was framed by others as vindicating the importance of larger structural forces because the individual behavioral changes resulted from a profound "shock to the system" that was enforced by emergency, top-down, state-based policy.

Which lesson someone comes away with depends a lot on how the story's told. One journalist pitches the pandemic-based drop in pollution as a story about the power of individual behavior change, while another highlights the need for structural reform. We ask, Why not both?

Each example above involves individuals who help initiate change. Somebody in Italy has the idea for e-scooters. Somebody in the activist organization sets up the phone bank. Each example also requires individual people to implement the change after it's set in motion. Somebody needs to advertise the e-scooter rebates; somebody has to cut the checks. And each change will wither away if people don't persist in their efforts to sustain it: Italians need to buy the scooters, ride them, and pester their friends and neighbors to do the same. Phone bankers have to make call after call after call. Motivated individuals are crucial to initiating, implementing, and sustaining change.

But none of this happens in a vacuum. Each individual action occurs within a set of social structures, a broader cultural and physical landscape: roads to ride the scooters on, phone networks, neighbors willing to take calls. Individual actions are predicated on structures like these. What's more, the individuals in these cases are trying to make changes to the structures in which they operate. Some aim to spread new norms for a low-carbon lifestyle, others to end cash bail. These structures are not easy to keep in view. Individualist cultures like the US often relegate social structures to the unnoticed background, like the duck on Easter Sunday. Instead, most Americans are almost inevitably drawn to individual people, much as one's eyes are drawn to the figure in the center of a photo.

Resisting false choices is an important step forward in seeing ourselves in structural change. Before the rest of this book makes the case for a both/and approach to repairing contemporary injustices, this chapter explores two historical case studies. In each, we tease out overlooked features that are hard to notice when too much attention is given to individuals in isolation or to social structures in isolation.

Getting MADD

On May 1, 1980, Clarence William Busch was arrested for drunk driving, his fifth DUI in four years. His car was impounded, but he was released on bail the next day and allowed to keep his driver's license. After taking his wife's car to a bar, Busch, drunk again, veered into a bike lane and killed thirteen-year-old Cari Lightner.

This was the worst, but not the first, of the Lightner family's horrendous encounters with reckless drivers. A drunk driver had crashed into and injured Cari's grandmother and sister Serena, and her four-year-old brother Travis spent four days in a coma after being hit by a driver impaired by tranquilizers. With Cari's death, her mother Candace had had enough, and four days after the funeral she started MADD.

MADD stands for "Mothers Against Drunk Driving," and it's a remarkable organization. A 2005 Gallup poll found that an amazing 94 percent of Americans were familiar with it. MADD is an exemplar of the many citizen activist groups that flourished in the 1970s and '80s, and it may be one of the most successful. From 1980 to 2004, alcohol-related traffic deaths decreased from an estimated 30,000 per year to 16,694. For individuals under twenty-one, these deaths had decreased by 83 percent by 2021.

Nobody knows for sure how instrumental MADD was in creating these changes, but there's reason to think the group was influential. Media coverage of alcohol-impaired driving shot up in the '80s, often featuring representatives from MADD. The group lobbied state legislatures to increase the penalties for impaired driving, and MADD leaders were typically present at the signing of these bills. Candace Lightner was involved in, and present at, the signing of the National Minimum Drinking Age Act of 1984, which compelled states to raise the drinking age to twenty-one. Good evidence suggests that enacting this law was a structural change that effectively reduced drunk driving.

One way to tell this story focuses on Lightner herself, the charismatic individual who inspired many more individuals, starting a crusade that went on to make a big difference. Her efforts led to a shift in popular attitudes about drunk driving, changing the way people think, feel, and act. In addition to the official laws, social norms around drunk driving have also transformed since the 1970s, in part because of Lightner and MADD's efforts. It's now widely understood that driving drunk is shameful and friends and family, bartenders, and bystanders share the responsibility to intervene and prevent it. A full accounting of the decline of drunk driving would have to note how one individual sparked a movement, inspiring other individuals to change a whole lot more individual hearts and minds.

These successful efforts to change widespread perceptions and norms around drunk driving were in turn integral to getting all those bills passed. Building a new consensus helped Lightner and other activists persuade individual policymakers to introduce pivotal legislation. It made it easy for legislators who had been on the fence to vote in favor of the new bills without hurting their chances to get reelected. It also helped motivate agents of the state to carry out all the new rules and regulations.

Newly passed and enforced laws then fed back into and reinforced evolving perceptions and norms around drunk driving. All this gradually coalesced into a new facet of the background structure of American life. This is precisely the pathway to change that Margaret Mead had in mind when she reportedly said, "Never doubt that a small group of thoughtful, committed citizens can change the world. Indeed, it's the only thing that ever has."

But there is always more to the story. How, for example, was Lightner able to persuade so many people? To understand how her message broke through, it can't be examined in isolation. The broader culture and network of social structures in which Lightner was operating must be taken into account, as they provided the conditions for her message to take root and thrive.

Mothers Against Drunk Driving wasn't the group's original name. When Lightner started the group, it was "Mothers Against Drunk *Drivers.*" Lightner herself didn't think the fundamental problem was the drinking age or that the solution was Big Structural Change. She unrepentantly blamed drunk driving on reckless individuals. "This was not an 'unfortunate accident,'" she told *People* in 1981, "Cari was the victim of a violent crime. If my daughter had been raped or murdered, no one would say of the killer, 'There but for the grace of God go I.' Death caused by drunk drivers is the only socially acceptable form of homicide."

It's likely, then, that part of MADD's success derived from the ways Lightner tapped into the shared culture of individualism we've explored in previous chapters. Her emphasis on individually irresponsible drivers resonated with the general law-and-order stance of a then very popular President Reagan, who endorsed the organization. While the Crying Indian ad said that people start pollution and people can stop it, Lightner was saying that (drunk) people cause accidents, and (sober) people can stop them. The case of Candace Lightner getting MADD shows how movements gain a foothold when their messages harmonize with their cultural moment.

While the Ad Council and Keep America Beautiful invoked personal responsibility to block structural change, Lightner's appeal to personal responsibility brought structural change. The American culture of individualism itself formed a key element of the structural background that empowered her committed group of individuals to bring about changes to norms and laws. By playing to the ambient individualism humming in the background of American minds, Lightner was able to get her hands on the levers of power.

Even the campaigns created by the Ad Council and Keep America Beautiful—the campaigns rightly criticized for placing the blame for litter on individuals rather than companies—did some good. It's nice to live in a country without roadside litter, which declined dramatically in the '70s. More important, it's difficult to imagine the creation of landmark laws like the Endangered Species Act and the Clean Air Act outside the context of the early days of the environmental movement, even with its worrying focus on personal responsibility. The United States has some of the cleanest air in the world today.

Of course, there are plenty of ways to promote structural change without demonizing individual people the way Lightner did. Hers is not the only roadmap to social change. Rather than using persuasive strategies that exploit a prevalent culture of individualism, many social movements in the US and abroad have sought to resist that very culture. One way people have tried to do this is by building—literally, physically building—new spaces for communal culture to flourish.

Go Down, Moses

Modern-day Copenhagen is a haven for pedestrians and cyclists (figure 4.2). Each day in the city, half of all commutes to school and work are taken by bicycle. Copenhageners are happy with it too, with 97 percent saying they're satisfied with city cycling conditions. But Copenhagen wasn't always like this. Figure 4.3 shows the same square in 1960; figure 4.4 shows similar pictures from Amsterdam in 1971 and 2020.

What happened? European cities like Copenhagen and Amsterdam faced pressure in the 1960s to modernize. Big US cities, with their freeways, wide roads, and suburbs, were seen as the future. In Great Britain, large parts of Birmingham were demolished to build a ring road, turning footpaths into underpasses. In 1966, Stockholm city planners sought to connect the islands of the city with the six-lane Essingeleden highway. It remains an auto-dense city. Copenhagen was headed the same way. In 1958, the city

Figure 4.2
Copenhagen, 2018.

Figure 4.3
Copenhagen, 1960.

Figure 4.4
Amsterdam, 1971 and 2020.

proposed a twelve-lane highway that would cut across the city center and pave over parts of its urban lakes, with plans to raze the Vesterbro neighborhood for motorways.

Fortunately, a small but developing group of urban planners in the "livable cities" movement agitated for a different approach and advocated organizing the city around bikes and buses. Shopkeepers pushed back, arguing they'd lose customers without car traffic. It wasn't obvious which way things would go until an unexpected shock to the system: the 1973 global oil crisis. Gas became sharply more expensive, car culture suddenly looked much less appealing, and cycling took off. It's been growing ever since.

Overhauling major cities in this way may sound a bit like magic to people living in places with dysfunctional politics. But similar triumphs have happened elsewhere. For example, Washington Square Park in Manhattan used to be a parking lot (figure 4.5). It was also nearly turned into a highway. The indomitable Robert Moses wanted to remove the park's fountain and run what he dubbed the Lower Manhattan Expressway right through the middle. At the time, Moses seemed to have the power to do anything. Despite having never been elected to office, he held twelve official public titles simultaneously. He also controlled construction for all of New York City's Housing Authority, built the Triborough Bridge (now the Robert F.

Figure 4.5
Washington Square Park, Manhattan, circa 1960–1969. Image via NYU Local.

Kennedy Bridge), most of the city's pools, and basically created suburban Long Island. Robert Caro's Pulitzer Prize–winning biography *The Power Broker* is a 1,200-page display of Moses's influence, ego, and racism. Caro recalls watching Moses hang up his office phone and say, "They expect me to build playgrounds for that scum floating up from Puerto Rico."

But Moses failed to pave over Washington Square Park. He met his match in one Jane Isabel Butzner from Scranton, Pennsylvania. By that point, Jane Butzner had become Jane Jacobs, journalist for *Architectural Forum* magazine. A social change entrepreneur, Jacobs would end up writing ten books about city life, inequality, and self-government, including *The Death and Life of Great American Cities* (1961), an influential critique of urban renewal programs. At the time, "urban renewal" was one of those code words like "redlining," a bland euphemism for razing Black and brown neighborhoods to build more highways, pools, and parks, predominantly for white people.

In opposition to Moses, Jacobs formed the catchily named Joint Emergency Committee to Close Washington Square to Traffic. The name was her idea, and she took pride in it. "Always put what you are trying to achieve in the name of the committee," a friend recalls Jacobs saying, "because most people will read no further than that." Jacobs pieced together the labyrinthine relationships between New York City agencies and managed to halt Moses's plans. Her efforts culminated with a successful petition of the "Board of Estimate" to direct the traffic commissioner to create a three-month trial of closing the park to traffic. The trial was a hit, too popular to reverse. On June 25, 1958, the city closed Washington Square Park to traffic for good. They held a ribbon *tying* ceremony to celebrate.

One lesson from these histories is that good urban planning matters. The built structure of a city can make the difference between a pedestrian utopia and gridlocked traffic-choked streets. Two waterfront urban hubs as culturally and historically similar as Stockholm and Copenhagen can be worlds apart when it comes to city cycling. (That said, both cities have extensive public transportation networks of subways and buses, which makes them both worlds more livable and accessible and less polluted than, say, Los Angeles.) The right kinds of urban design and built environments, in turn, promote a stronger sense of community and discourage a culture of individualist isolation. No wonder that, by some measures, Denmark has the highest levels of social trust, fellow feeling, and happiness in the world, whereas the US is at best in the middle of the pack.

Given the power of urban planning to shape the quality and community of city life, score one for structural reform. But also note that committed individuals had to put these structures in place and fight to preserve the ones they already had. You might have paid for parking in Washington Square Park on your last trip to the Big Apple if it hadn't been for Jane Jacobs.

From Either/Or to Both/And

Suppose you too are passionate about making cities and neighborhoods more livable, safe, and healthy. You've recently visited Copenhagen and you're fired up to promote bike commuting in your hometown. You talk to some friends—maybe older, liberal friends—and they tell you:

> Change begins within. Focus on your own choices and what you can control. Start riding a bike to work. Join a cycling club! Never doubt that a small group of thoughtful committed individuals can change the world! Vote!

But then you talk to some other friends—some younger, more radical friends —and they tell you the opposite:

Ride your bike if you feel like it, but don't mistake it for activism. What you do on your bike is just a drop in the bucket. It's dangerous without protected bike lanes anyway. City planning is a structural problem, and structural problems require structural solutions. Don't focus on yourself, change the system!

This kind of debate between your two groups of friends succumbs to the either/or error. It's also an instance of what philosophers call a "category mistake," which is just a fancy way of saying your friends are comparing apples to oranges. If you, an isolated person, decide to ride your bike to work every day, chances are this will have a small impact on the course of human history. If a city government—a legal entity empowered to build roads, enforce laws, and determine where people live—decides to reduce street parking in favor of promoting bike lanes, this will likely have a bigger impact. If all the nations of the world come together to sign an enforceable treaty to plaster every country with bike lanes, then the impact, presumably, would be bigger still. But these are comparisons between a small thing an individual can do, a bigger thing a city government can do, and an even bigger thing that nations can do together.

We could just as well draw the contrast differently. If you, a single person, decide that biking to work is not enough and instead dedicate your life to criticizing "urban renewal" projects, and you write ten books about it, study the unnoticed levers of power in your city, and enlist influential friends to your cause, then you, an individual, will have a better chance—like Jane Jacobs—of making a bigger impact. Meanwhile, if a government is feckless and stymied by infighting or partisanship, or staggers from bankruptcy to bankruptcy, chances are that its "big," "structural" urban planning will have a small impact. The best-laid plans of social institutions often go awry (or go nowhere).

More useful comparisons avoid these category mistakes. Rather than engaging in an unanswerably abstract debate about whether individual change matters at all, someone could compare one specific thing an individual might do to another specific thing that individual might do. A person moving to a new place might consider the many pros and cons of living close to work and commuting by bike, or living further away and commuting by bus, or living even further away and taking the money saved on housing to buy an electric car.

Meanwhile, people can compare, say, one urban plan to another. Given limited financial resources, should a town trying to go green focus on building more sidewalks, or more bike lanes, or more public transportation, or more electric vehicle (EV) charging stations? Or perhaps the town can drum up the resources to pursue all these by hiking taxes on its wealthiest residents and cutting spending elsewhere, say, by skipping next year's purchase of militarized police gear?

These kinds of comparisons—between tangible individual changes or between tangible structural changes—avoid pitting apples against oranges. We have to start with comparisons that make sense. Once we do that, we can start bringing more nuance on board. Comparing tangible things individuals can do requires paying attention to the structural background, and comparing tangible structural changes requires paying attention to the individuals in the foreground.

For example, the promise of any policy proposal for a town deliberating about how best to go green will depend on what individual citizens think about the policy. People with specific values and viewpoints—design planners, engineers, voters, government officials, activists, lobbyists—will have to initiate, implement, and sustain the change it specifies. All these individuals have a say in which structural reforms, if any, get made.

And for every structural change to promote, there are actions that individuals should take to promote that structural change. Which actions any particular person might take will depend on which roles they occupy (urban designer, parent, voter) and how much bandwidth, money, and time they have to devote to the cause. If the community settles on more bike lanes, then individuals who support that decision could, for example, start buying and riding bikes, inviting their friends on Sunday morning group rides, handing out pro-bike lane flyers, opening up a used bike shop, and so on.

The vice versa is equally vital: for every individual behavior change to pursue, there will be structural changes to put in place because they enable individuals to make those changes. What kinds of structural changes will get people to buy and ride bikes? Cash incentives would probably help (see Italy's rebates for e-scooters). Maybe the town, or a group of volunteers, starts offering free cycling lessons or local tours for children and adults. Maybe teachers at the school redesign their curricula to ensure that kids are learning about the virtues of bike lanes in class. Schools can start "bike buses," morning group rides making it safer for little kids to pedal to class. Maybe residents donate money to the school to start an afternoon cycling club for students. Maybe they take field trips to go mountain biking or watch a race.

The mistake is to compare an individual change to a structural reform (one person taking up cycling versus a whole town creating bike lanes). The solution is to compare various individual changes to each other, some of which have better potential to scale up to structural change, and to compare various structural reforms to each other, some of which have better potential to be implemented and sustained by individual people.

Another way to put this is to think in terms of bundles. What is the bundle of individual changes that people can make to promote the right kinds of structural changes that will in turn enable individuals to make the most impact? The best bundles will be those that are sensitive to the culture of the communities they are designed for. They'll aim to create feedback loops between individual and structural reforms.

The Real Remaining Trade-Offs: Effort and Attention

When we say there's no sense to be made of choosing between changing individuals or changing structures, it might sound like we're denying that there's any meaningful distinction between individuals and social structures at all. We're not. There is a difference between them, just like there is a difference between figure and background in a photo. Both are real, both are present, and both are essential. That said, people can't focus on everything everywhere all at once. There are only so many hours in a day, and everyone has to set priorities. They have to choose what to pay attention to, and that might mean sometimes paying relatively *more* attention to individuals or to structures.

In some cases, people might be able to focus on how best to design social systems without worrying too much about the details of individual psychology. Say a policymaker wants to make it as easy as possible for people to show up for court. They don't need a doctorate in neuroscience to predict that offering people multiple attendance options (e.g., online via Zoom or in person, morning or night, weekday or weekend) will boost attendance rates.

Other times, it's important to let the structures remain in the background and keep specific individuals front and center. Say someone hears their white friend ask about touching a Black stranger's hair. They don't need a PhD in ethics to know this isn't OK.

Examples like these show the importance of being able to shift focus between individuals and structures as the situation demands. Seeing when to focus on one or the other requires understanding how they're related, just like a songwriter knows when the melody or rhythm of a song needs to be changed by appreciating how they're related.

People can't get policymakers to sign off on allowing multiple court attendance options without persuading them to do it. Likewise, people can't understand everything wrong with asking to touch Black people's hair without knowing the history of racist Europeans treating Black bodies as exotic oddities to put "on display." The full meaning of an individual action depends on the history and structures shaping it, and the possibility of structural change depends on the individuals creating and sustaining it.

We next turn from the past to the present and future. We'll offer a novel take on what many hold up as the Most Distractingly Individualist Approach of them all: diversity trainings.

5 Unlearning the Habit of Racism

The Racialization of American Politics

President Barack Obama took a risk in 2009 when he decided to make healthcare reform the top priority of his first term. He had to choose between several deserving ways to spend his political capital. Climate change? Immigration reform? His healthcare initiative also followed in the wake of recent Democratic failures. Hillary Clinton's efforts to reform medical insurance in 1993 were still remembered as a political debacle. The system remained untouched, and Democratic strategists came to think healthcare was a political minefield. Insurance companies were too powerful and Americans too attached to their doctors to risk attempting an overhaul of the system.

But Obama was taking another risk, less obvious at the time. He knew well that American politics had become increasingly polarized, with "blue states" and "red states" far apart on many issues, including healthcare. What Obama did not see coming was just how much American politics had become racialized. As it turned out, he was betting the success of healthcare reform on navigating the tricky waters of American attitudes about race.

This story and others like it foretell that the prospects of overhauling entrenched American systems hinge on the prospects of uprooting entrenched American prejudices. One lesson from chapter 2 seemed to be that common efforts to reduce prejudice—through diversity training and antibias workshops—are ineffective. They're often individualist distractions from deeper structural problems. But if there's no way to reform big structures like healthcare without reducing prejudice *and* there's no effective way to reduce prejudice, does that mean we're doomed? Fortunately not.

Under the right conditions, real prejudice reduction is possible. And prejudice reduction is necessary.

Everything Is Two Degrees from Race

The political scientist Michael Tesler studies how people's attitudes about race shape their views about politics, culture, and public policies. Through a series of studies, Tesler showed that white Americans' thoughts about Obama's Affordable Care Act (ACA) were predicted by their racial attitudes. As Obama himself became the face of healthcare reform—even embracing the branding of it as "Obamacare"—the influence of those racial attitudes became stronger and stronger. The racial divide between Black and white Americans' support for healthcare reform ballooned by 20 percentage points between Clinton's plan in 1993 and Obama's in 2009.

Why? Tesler had a hunch, as he said in one interview, that race was "simply more on the top of people's heads when it comes to Barack Obama." In 2009 the president was asked on *Meet the Press* about the possibility, expressed by former President Jimmy Carter and members of the Congressional Black Caucus, that racism was behind the growing hostility toward the ACA. Obama acknowledged that race could be a factor: "Sometimes they vote for me for that reason, sometimes they vote against me for that reason." But he tried to assure anxious voters that "this debate that's taking place is not about race."

Try as he might, Obama failed to keep race out of people's minds when it came to healthcare reform. Tesler and his colleagues looked closer and found a causal connection between racial resentment and people's support for the ACA. In one experiment, they described the details of the ACA to one group of voters as part of Obama's proposed reforms, to another group as part of President Clinton's 1993 reform efforts, and to a third group as simply being proposed by "some people." The most racially resentful white voters opposed healthcare reform in all three cases, but they were almost twice as likely to dislike elements of the ACA when they associated them with Obama instead of Clinton.

The racialization of American politics isn't new, but its strength and scope have grown dramatically since the 1980s. In some cases, the link between people's racial attitudes and their political beliefs is unsurprising. Take views about welfare and crime. It's relatively easy to see how pernicious racial stereotypes about certain people being more prone to violence or less willing to "try hard" could increase support for harsher crime and welfare policies. It's more surprising that racial attitudes inform people's beliefs about things like Social Security, tax policy, and the Iraq War. According to some scholars, race has "eclipsed class as the organizing principle of American politics" since the 1960s.

There's a similar story to tell about race and climate change. Most people know that Republicans tend to be less concerned about climate change than Democrats. What most people don't know is how big a role race plays in this disparity. Among the least racially resentful white Republicans, only 7 percent deny that climate change is happening. Among the most racially resentful, the percentage jumps to 26. What about the reality that climate change is caused by humans? A full 84 percent of white Republicans high in racial resentment do not believe that human activities are driving climate change. Put it this way: if you wanted to guess someone's view about any randomly chosen political topic, and you could only ask them one question, what they think about race would be a good option.

The powerful influence of race on politics didn't end with Obama's presidency. Probably the most spirited debate around Donald Trump's political rise in 2015 and 2016 was whether his support was driven more by economic factors or racial resentment. During the campaign, Trump's speeches were full of racist, sexist, xenophobic, and otherwise incendiary comments. He demanded, for example, "a total and complete shutdown of Muslims entering the United States until our country's representatives can figure out what is going on."

Were voters supporting him because of or in spite of this talk? Many pundits and politicians argued for the latter, claiming voters were so concerned about pocketbook issues and the trajectory of the economy that they were willing to hold their noses and vote for Trump despite all the bigoted bluster. As US senator and presidential hopeful Bernie Sanders said, "Many of Trump's supporters are working-class people and they're angry, and they're angry because they're working longer hours for lower wages, they're angry because their jobs have left this country and gone to China or other low-wage countries, they're angry because they can't afford to send their kids to college so they can't retire with dignity."

But the truth is that this either/or framing—either economics or racism—presented a bogus choice. The economic grievances were *themselves* shaped by racial resentment. Trump supporters perceived themselves, and their peers, to be at greater economic risk than did non-Trump supporters, even when their economic positions were basically secure. In 2017, 86 percent of pro-Trump white millennials were employed, and they were less likely to be low income than anti-Trump white millennials. Whether or not a person described themselves as feeling economically anxious was better predicted by measures of their racial resentment than by any objective economic indicators.

Race is nearly everywhere in the United States. This is one reason why slogans like "policy change over mental change," which imply a choice between changing systems or changing hearts and minds, are misleading. When Americans try to figure out what to believe about some issue—whether to support healthcare reform or whom to vote for or what to think about climate science—their racial stereotypes and prejudices are right there, part of every decision. If prejudice drives economic anxiety (and economic anxiety reinforces prejudice), then it makes little sense to debate whether support for far-right politics is really driven by one or the other.

What this piece of either/or thinking misses is that for nearly any systemic problem in American political life, race sculpts public opinion about it. If there are six degrees of separation between each of us, there are at most two between race and everything else. The upshot of this, which we can call *two degrees of separation from race*, is twofold. On the one hand, critics of individualist approaches to racism are right to call for changes to the basic norms, laws, and structures maintaining inequalities between white and non-white people. On the other, the pursuit of those structural changes is no alternative to trying to change people's prejudices. Rather, those prejudices are themselves a central source of resistance to systemic change. The route to changing systems goes through, not around, biased minds.

Devine Intervention

But what if American hearts and minds can't, or simply won't, change? What if American racism is a habit too well inscribed in prevailing social structures to dislodge? As we explained in chapter 2, most antibias DEI workshops are thinly veiled attempts to insulate organizations from lawsuits and maintain the status quo. But not all of them. Some really do change minds.

Patricia Devine—who runs the Prejudice and Intergroup Relations Lab at the University of Wisconsin-Madison—isn't interested in helping people check "do something about racism" off their to-do list. "If we're just making white people feel better," she says, "who cares?" Devine is the kind of person who commands an audience's attention. When she runs antibias workshops, she paces the room, making eye contact with each participant one by one. "I submit to you," she is known to say, "that prejudice is a habit that can be broken." This kind of statement, said with conviction, can contribute to its own truth. Believing that you can break a habit is part of breaking a habit.

Devine has been refining her habit-breaking approach to prejudice for over thirty years. Her work flies under the radar. It's not flashy. Yet real, repeatedly replicated evidence suggests it works. It empowers people to make meaningful changes to their daily lives—and even, as we'll eventually see, their institutions.

Devine focuses on three things: belief, desire, and know-how. First is getting people to accept that there's a problem. They need to understand that they might be biased when they interpret someone on the street as looking dangerous or when they choose a partner for a class project.

Second, people need to be motivated to change. Devine aims to engage people who already want to be unprejudiced. She's not out to convince avowed racists of the wrongness of their ways. But even people who personally disavow racism may not be motivated to do much about it. They might think it's not *their* problem and that as long as they're cordial with everyone they meet, they're doing their part.

Devine's way of getting people to care is to convince them their biases aren't their fault—but that those biases cause harm nevertheless. Since stereotypes are peppered throughout American culture, everyone, including children, are repeatedly exposed to them. They're picked up early, like an accent. "Biased responses become the default, automatic, and habitual reactions to members of stereotyped groups," Devine writes, with her frequent collaborator William Cox. Putting it this way helps her tap into people's motivation because it defuses their defensiveness. The message is that people are not prejudiced because they have bad hearts. People are prejudiced because they live in a prejudiced world.

Conveying this message requires a subtle balancing act. Devine wants to get past her audience's defensiveness but also wants them to feel a little uncomfortable. The aim is to create a kind of tension—or "cognitive dissonance" as psychologists call it—as people recognize that their behavior is out of alignment with their values. Once they feel this kind of conflict—one inner voice saying that stereotyping is wrong, another saying that they, like everyone, are prone to stereotyping—people basically have three options. They can change their values, essentially saying "well if I act biased, it must be for a good reason. Maybe some of these so-called prejudices are justified." Or they can reject the evidence: "maybe some people act in prejudiced ways but not me." Or they can try to be less biased. Devine's goal is to guide participants toward this last option.

The third part of Devine's trainings imparts evidence-based lessons about how to change and how not to. For example, attempting to be "colorblind" doesn't work. Trying to "not see race" just makes race take up more attention. It's the analogue of an old experiment from social psychology, itself inspired by the novelist Fyodor Dostoevsky. If you're told "don't think about a white bear," guess what you just thought about? Instead, Devine teaches people to use strategies like "individuation," where they focus on thinking about of a person in terms of their individual characteristics, not stereotypes about their social group. Participants learn what to attend to rather than what to ignore.

This "Devine intervention" isn't going to change the world by itself. But carefully designed studies find that her participants become more aware of their biases, more concerned about discrimination, and more empowered to take action, even years after the training. One study followed up with a group of Wisconsin undergrads two years after they completed Devine's program. Researchers posed as reporters for the school newspaper, *The Badger Herald*, and said they were testing a new editorial format: one student writes an opinion piece and another responds. The first opinion piece, "Racial stereotypes are useful tools," was already written. It argued that stereotypes were harmless and had only gotten a bad rap because of "PC culture."

The researchers asked the students, including one group who had completed Devine's program and a control group who hadn't, what they thought of the article. Were they interested in publishing a response? Pretty much everyone disagreed with the pro-stereotyping op-ed. Yes, stereotypes are bad. No, we shouldn't promote them. But while just 48 percent of the control group opted to publish a response, a full 79 percent of Devine's former participants did.

What's the secret sauce to the Devine intervention, when so many other approaches to prejudice reduction come up short? There's more than one ingredient. Her workshops give participants strategies they can adapt to their own situations, are based on well-established theories in cognitive and social science, and encourage people to become self-driven agents of change rather than simply telling them what to do. This is a far cry from Leaders' Choice Insurance (see chapter 2), where the cynical point of workshops is heading off lawsuits.

It's crucial to distinguish good from bad workshops and effective from ineffective leaders. Many antibias workshops *are* superficial, ineffective, and implemented for the wrong reasons. But acknowledging this doesn't lead to the conclusion that all forms of antibias education are a waste of time. Thinking otherwise would be like refusing to see any doctor because some doctors are on Big Pharma's payroll.

Mindsets That Matter

Critics say antibias workshops don't work. We agree they're right to worry, but the correct conclusion is that *poorly done* workshops don't work—and trainings implemented for cynical reasons are usually poorly done. When Trish Devine and like-minded scientists, teachers, and activists base their antibias efforts on solid science, keep at it for decades, and wear their genuine motivation on their sleeve, they can make a real difference. Given how racial bias colors people's perceptions of all aspects of modern life, this evidence for the malleability of the American mind is marvelous news. Getting more out of antibias education, however, requires seeing it from a both/and point of view.

An especially important lesson that good antibias workshops teach is that change is possible. In doing so, they foster in their participants a "growth mindset" toward prejudice reduction. Good workshops, in other words, emphasize the possibility of continuous incremental improvement, much like parents, counselors, and coaches often do. Whenever a coach says, "We're just trying to get a little bit better every day," they're invoking a growth mindset. The opposite is a "fixed mindset" that is centered on the idea that, for any kind of capability—musical talent, athletic potential, reasoning ability—people have what they have and not much is going to change.

Some worry that too much focus on people's "mindsets" is another form of victim blaming for larger structural problems. Others are skeptical that the effects of growth mindsets are as large as proponents claim. They suspect that structural factors affecting skill development like wealth, health, and racial privilege are much more important than individual mindsets. Their skepticism is buttressed by the finding that growth mindset interventions seem to work in some contexts but not in others. When researchers average across all the experiments, they get muddled results.

Fortunately, the next generation of studies is un-muddling the mess. One consistent finding is that teachers' mindsets matter too. The message of growth takes root when it's planted in the right soil: supportive teachers who genuinely believe their students can grow and who structure their classes in ways that encourage their students to prove them right.

When Devine looks workshop participants in the eye and insists that "prejudice is a habit that can be broken," she means it. Compare that to different experience: your company mandates a DEI training, but your boss says, "I know this training is a pain, but we just have to do it to get HR off our back." So much for getting a little bit better today!

Studying and promoting growth mindsets is in no way inconsistent with focusing on the structures and environments in which people's mindsets are embedded. The fact that teachers' mindsets matter shows the opposite, that changing minds *requires* the right environment. The ways that teachers think, act, and structure their classes are vital parts of students' environments—as anyone who has ever had an inspiring mentor knows.

Duck-Rabbiting Social Change

Promising as all this is, thinking of bias as a habit of mind might nevertheless seem trivializing. Racism is a caste system, sustained by social structures like segregation. It's baked into nearly every aspect of American life. In comparison to overthrowing white supremacy, an experiment that nudges a few more undergrads to clap back at a racist op-ed might look trifling. Is this a mere drop in a gigantic, structurally racist bucket?

We think this is a bad question. There's no contradiction in thinking of racial bias as a habit and acknowledging its rootedness in social structures. Nor is there any conflict between trying to change biases in individual minds and trying to abolish the structural conditions that spur them on.

Think about another bad habit: smoking. It can be tempting to frame smoking as a simple matter of individual vice, but it can also be understood as a structural problem. Cigarette companies lied for decades about the dangers of smoking. Dedicated sections in airplanes and restaurants normalized it. Studies suggest that nicotine addiction is driven more by poverty than weakness of will; people living below the poverty line smoke nearly twice as long as those above it. Acknowledging that smoking is a habit doesn't invalidate any of these points. And it doesn't preclude paying attention to the structural factors that shape people's habits.

Smoking is also a product of social networks. Kids start smoking when their peers do. As the economist Robert Frank has put it, the biggest danger of smoking in public isn't secondhand smoke. It's creating more smokers by making smoking seem normal and cool.

The good news is that the same social logic applies to quitting. The odds that people keep smoking drop by 25 percent when a sibling quits, by 36 percent when a friend quits, and by a whopping 67 percent when a spouse quits. Rates of smoking have plummeted from their peak in the 1960s and '70s in large part because "whole groups of people were quitting in concert."

Habit breaking, just like habit forming, is socially contagious. This is one of many phenomena that connect individuals to wider structures. It's true that Trish Devine is trying to reduce prejudice one individual (or at least one workshop) at a time. It's also true that one undergrad publishing one response to one racist op-ed isn't the same as toppling the racial hierarchy. But Devine's approach also leverages the fact that every workshop participant is a node in numerous social networks. Habits like smoking and prejudice spread through those networks and quitting them does too. Participants in the Devine intervention regularly report sharing what they've learned with others. And it looks like they can have a genuine impact on their peers. One study found that university professors who had not attended the training but worked closely with professors who had also became more likely to work for social change in their academic departments.

Thinking in a both/and way makes salient all sorts of external conditions that are important factors in change. The right teachers with the right mindsets, the right peers in the right networks, the right institutions with the right material and emotional support—these are all essential ingredients of individual change.

But even if these trainings can, under the right conditions, reduce bias, what if there are other more impactful ways for people to direct their efforts to fight racial injustice? We turn now to what many critics of individualist approaches to racism take to be a leading alternative to DEI workshops. As Bhaskar Sunkara, president of *The Nation* and founding editor of the socialist magazine *Jacobin*, says, "We do know, for example, of a tool far more useful than unconscious bias trainings in creating respect and equality: unions."

Labor Organizing and Prejudice Reduction

Sunkara and others are onto something. Unions have a long history of promoting structural change. But these champions of unions are thinking about them too narrowly. Far from being competing alternatives, unions and antibias education are better understood as two mutually supporting pieces of broader struggles for justice.

Sunkara is right that unions do much more than advance their members' financial interests. In some places, labor organizing has been integral to the struggle for racial justice. Martin Luther King Jr. saw the full threat of so-called "right-to-work" laws, for example, but put them in a broad context. These laws mandate that unions negotiate on behalf of nonunion members while prohibiting unions from requiring that those nonmembers pay dues. Right-to-work laws are part of the decades-long dismantling of labor power in the US. Anticipating their disastrous effects on economic and racial justice, King said, "In our glorious fight for civil rights, we must guard against being fooled by false slogans, such as 'right to work.' It is a law to rob us of our civil rights and job rights. Its purpose is to destroy labor unions and the freedom of collective bargaining by which unions have improved wages and working conditions of everyone. . . . Wherever these laws have been passed, wages are lower, job opportunities are fewer and there are no civil rights."

King was prescient. In unions, people from varied walks of life can collaborate side by side as equals. This is one of the best ways to reduce prejudice. Social scientists have incorporated this insight into what they call the theory of intergroup contact. For people from different backgrounds— different politics, races, or religions—to form real bonds, they can't just be thrown together in the same room. Anyone who's seen a middle school cafeteria knows how easily we self-segregate. But when different kinds of people work alongside each other, doing something meaningful, on relatively equal status, their prejudices tend to lessen.

It's not just unions. Sports teams, first-year college roommates, and even Mormon missionaries have all been shown to reduce prejudice through intergroup contact. Unions are distinctive, though, because they're not only places where workers have interracial interactions on relatively equal footing but also where collective bargaining creates incentives for union members to create strategic coalitions and cooperate across racial lines.

Consider again Sunkara's claim about unions, antibias training, and prejudice. He's right about the power of unions to reduce prejudice, but he's wrong to promote unions rather than trying to change biases through workshops. What's a good context for educating people about the importance of unions? One place is antibias workshops! Some—like the ones Alex and Michael lead—already do. Dedicating time in antibias workshops to the importance of unions is just one example of how these trainings can be oriented toward changing social structures. Workshops don't have to only focus on our individual feelings and workplace interactions. They can also be *structure facing*. They can explain how individuals' choices are shaped by social structures and guide participants toward ways to change them.

Structure-facing features are a centerpiece of Devine's workshops. She begins by explaining how individuals' prejudices result from growing up in a structurally prejudiced world, and then explores how to reconfigure those structures. For example, workshops with academic faculty consider different procedures for hiring and promotion. Participants learn about strategies like developing clear and consistent criteria for evaluating candidates ahead of time and sticking to them even when it's difficult. Too often the alternative is that faculty fit the criteria to the candidates they like, who often happen to be a lot like the faculty themselves. As a result, successful candidates often end up being a lot like the white men who hire them. Devine's workshops challenge these long-standing practices and encourage people to think through how to improve them.

Another of Devine's experiments, one that explores ways of overcoming gender discrimination, brings this point to life. Researchers worked with a range of science, engineering, math, and medical departments, again comparing departments that hadn't undergone her antibias training to those that had. Two years before the intervention, both sets of departments were hiring men over women at a rate of two to one. Two years afterward, the gender hiring gap was unchanged in the nonparticipating departments but had all but evaporated in the participating ones. What's more, faculty in the participating group (men and women alike) reported feeling that they "fit" better in their department, that their work was more valued, and that they were more comfortable talking about family obligations with colleagues.

Another way to put this is that people can learn to adopt growth mindsets about institutions themselves. Critics worry that promoting growth mindsets risks turning participants' gaze inward, to the thoughts in their heads rather than the systems that surround them. But there's nothing stopping workshops from also helping turn peoples' gaze outward. We can come to see the systems around us as malleable, not fixed in stone. The belief that the system can change contributes to its own truth.

Of course, just as antibias workshops are not inherently individualist, unions are not inherently prejudice reducing or structure changing. For example, some trade unions have histories of virulent racism and sexism. Police unions have blocked criminal justice reform and defended officers even in the worst cases of abuse. Mining, drilling, and fracking unions have been adamant forces standing against clean energy. Sometimes unions reduce prejudice and help upend the status quo and sometimes they don't.

When they do, what seems to make the difference is how comfortable their members feel talking about race and politics, particularly around members of other racial groups. Acknowledging and confronting the issues helps; pretending they don't exist doesn't. The punditry seems increasingly convinced that antibias workshops are bullshit and that stubbornly racist unions won't improve without some kind of heavenly intrusion or deus ex machina. But maybe they just need a Devine intervention.

The Return of the Allegedly Irrelevant

If someone tells you to support unions rather than antibias workshops, suggest to them that better antibias workshops could strengthen unions. Unions thrive when members learn how race and racism are used to divide the working class. If someone tells you that the right way to fight racial inequality is universal healthcare instead of worrying about mere feelings and beliefs, remind them that prejudice stands in the way of universal healthcare. Years of racist backlash to Obamacare very nearly led to its undoing.

Similarly, if someone tells you that electing Democrats or turning back the climate crisis or increasing the minimum wage or ending capitalism is what it will take to conquer racism, remind them that reducing individual prejudice will be integral to each of these goals, too. Race and racism are as much causes of other social ills as they are effects.

We call this the Return of the Allegedly Irrelevant. Over and over again, we're told that efforts to make change, like attending an antibias workshop, are individualistic wastes of time, irrelevant to social change. We're told that the real, structure-changing action lies elsewhere, like in building unions and social movements. What we're not told, however, is that the allegedly irrelevant efforts often end up being vital for the supposedly relevant ones. The bridge-building needed for structure-changing unions and social movements goes through effective antibias workshops, or something a whole lot like them.

6 A Both/And Picture of People

Human Nature and Social Change

The impulse to frame problems and solutions in either/or terms is deeply rooted. It involves assumptions about human nature itself. To see how it's always both—changing systems is always a matter of changing people, and changing people is always a matter of changing systems—those assumptions need to be dragged into the light of day. Thankfully, a whole nexus of researchers from anthropology, biology, evolutionary science, and cognitive science has coalesced in recent decades around the idea that human beings are uniquely and spectacularly interdependent creatures. The social world permeates our inner worlds more than we realize. Far from being isolated individuals, detached from one another like solitary atoms, human beings are enmeshed in the wider world and with each other in surprising ways.

Similar ideas can be found in rich intellectual, spiritual, and political traditions from around the world, including forms of Buddhism, Confucianism, feminism, environmentalism, and numerous indigenous ways of thinking, as we discuss below. Although there's not enough exchange, these schools of thought converge around a shared both/and picture of people.

WEIRD Culture

At least for Americans like us, one reason it's so easy to forget that it's always both is that we've been raised in what is probably the most individualist culture of all time. We recounted the history of corporate PR that taught us to think of social problems like climate change and racism as matters of personal responsibility in chapters 1 and 2. A big part of why this PR worked is that American minds were primed for it. Think of macho John Wayne riding off into the sunset. Or Horatio Alger's fourteen-year-old hero pulling himself up by his bootstraps in *Ragged Dick*, aspiring "to turn over a new leaf, and try to grow up 'spectable.'"

The now familiar expression "rugged individualism" was coined by President Herbert Hoover in a 1928 campaign speech when he told voters they faced an either/or "choice between the American system of rugged individualism and a European philosophy of diametrically opposed doctrines of paternalism and state socialism." Hoover himself was appealing to an ethos powerfully articulated by Ralph Waldo Emerson nearly a century earlier in his essay "Self-Reliance." Emerson urged people to trust and stay true to themselves, to follow their own instincts and intuitions. He depicted social life as demanding conformity at the expense of authenticity, and counseled resistance: "Insist on yourself; never imitate."

Yet American individualism is just an extreme outgrowth of a much longer and more widespread set of cultural traditions. In a pathbreaking paper published in 2010, cultural evolutionists Joseph Henrich, Steven Heine, and Ara Norenzayan coined the acronym "WEIRD" to describe cultures that are Western, Educated, Industrialized, Rich, and Democratic. The idea was that such cultures—especially in the United States—produce individuals with an idiosyncratic psychological profile. People in WEIRD cultures have come to associate rationality with thinking for oneself, for example. The motto of the Enlightenment, according to Immanuel Kant, was "Have the courage to use your own understanding."

WEIRD cultures also generate an image of people as egoists, driven by their own needs and desires. Governments are needed, in this picture, to keep human selfishness in check. "Government is necessary, not because man is naturally bad," Thomas Hobbes wrote in 1651, "but because man is by nature more individualistic than social." WEIRD cultures also tend to instill the belief that individuals know themselves better than they know others. Each person has privileged access to their own minds, and it's a typical WEIRD value to treasure authenticity—being your true self, whom only you truly know.

WEIRD minds are molded by WEIRD cultures, especially their norms, ideals, and institutions. The "nuclear family" is a good example. Picture a stereotypical suburban home, separated from the houses around it by a series of manicured lawns. Every kid in this home (all one or two of them, that is) has their own room, a private kingdom to personalize in whichever ways they choose to express their unique, authentic selves. Their house is tucked away in the urban outskirts, far from shared spaces like parks and libraries and Main Streets. Forget about bike lanes—the streets out here don't even have sidewalks, so cars rule supreme. The parents drive off in separate vehicles to pursue their personal "callings," which is a romantic spin on the fact that their job has become the all-consuming center of their lives. They spend whole days isolated in their office, often working through lunch. When they drive home again, they insist the household sits down together for fifteen to twenty solid minutes' worth of the Family Meal. Before long, each WEIRDo retreats to separate rooms and separate screens, settling in to spend the rest of the evening curating their smartphone experiences, scrolling alone.

Of course, many American families don't get to live this supposedly idyllic suburban life, but it's incredible how many want to. Some version of this has been the American Dream since at least the 1950s.

As familiar as they might be, WEIRD minds, norms, and institutions are . . . weird. A wider look at familial, social, and cultural arrangements around the world, as well as back into our evolutionary past, shows that human beings are extraordinarily social animals. People are not at bottom isolated and egoistic; they're gregarious and groupish. People are, and have evolved to be, thoroughly enmeshed with one another, saturated by the influence of other people, institutions, and culture. The old saw about "nature versus culture" is misleading. For human beings, our nature is cultural.

Human minds don't start out as completely empty vessels, but a lot of what they end up containing is absorbed from their cultures and communities; it originates outside of them. In this way, we're uniquely "outside-in" creatures. We soak up social structures exactly because we're so thoroughly reliant on them, and our social worlds become woven right into the fabric of our minds and selves. The flip side of this is that while social influence is the air we breathe in, we're always exhaling it too. Whether we realize it or not, we're all already equipped to be agents of social change.

People Who Need People Are the Only People in the World

Henrich begins his book *The Secret of Our Success* with this thought experiment:

Suppose we took you and forty-nine of your coworkers and pitted you in a game of Survivor against a troop of fifty capuchin monkeys from Costa Rica. We would parachute both primate teams into the remote tropical forests of central Africa. After two years, we would return and count the survivors on each team. The team with the most survivors wins. Of course, neither team would be permitted to bring any equipment: no matches, water containers, knives, shoes, eyeglasses, antibiotics, pots, guns, or rope. To be kind, we would allow the humans—but not the monkeys—to wear clothes. Both teams would thus face surviving for years in a novel forest environment with only their wits, and their teammates, to rely on.

Who would you bet on, the monkeys or you and your colleagues? Well, do you know how to make arrows, nets, and shelters? Do you know which plants or insects are toxic (many are) or how to detoxify them? Can you start a fire without matches or cook without a pot? Can you manufacture a fishhook? Do you know how to make natural adhesives? Which snakes are venomous? How will you protect yourself from predators at night? How will you get water? What is your knowledge of animal tracking?

The smart money's on the monkeys, Henrich argues, "despite your team's swollen crania and ample hubris."

Even bringing along a boatload of equipment wouldn't guarantee survival in an unknown environment. In 1845, Sir John Franklin of England led the HMS *Erebus* and the HMS *Terror* in search of the Northwest Passage, a fabled waterway between Europe and Asia. Franklin's ships were state of the art, field-tested, reinforced icebreakers with steam engines and detachable rudders. They had coal-fired heaters, desalinators, and five years' worth of provisions. He expected to get locked in the ice in their first winter, which he and his crew did. They waited it out, as planned, and then moved south. Their second winter of being ice-locked was not planned, however. After nineteen months on the ice, the ships were abandoned in April 1848. Everyone on the voyage eventually died.

Henrich contrasts the fate of Franklin's crew to the indigenous Netsilik population who had been living in the area for tens of thousands of years. The comparison is apt. Netsilik communities were about the same size as Franklin's crew (around 100 people, though that includes children, whom Franklin didn't need to worry about).

What the Netsilik had and what Franklin's men lacked was the relevant cultural knowledge. The Netsilik built tents and kayaks out of driftwood in the summer and built snow houses on the ice during winter. They hunted reindeer and birds with sophisticated bows. They caught fish with three-pronged spears and seals with harpoons. In fact, there were so many big seals to hunt by the island's harbor that the Netsilik named it *Uqsuq-tuuq*, or "lots of fat." In short, they found the same area—the one Franklin's crew found to be desolate and deadly—"rich in resources for food, clothing, shelter, and tool-making."

The Netsilik's cultural knowledge embodies what Henrich believes is the secret of human success in the animal world. The secret "resides not in the power of our individual minds, but in the *collective brains* of our communities." These collective "brains" are fundamentally social—made up of big groups of people knit together by a complex set of norms and practices— and fundamentally cultural too—containing centuries' worth of know-how passed along from one generation to the next.

Henrich and others argue that this feature of human nature, more than any other, enabled people to spread across the globe to inhabit virtually every land-based ecosystem—from deserts to rainforests to the arctic, from Polynesia to the Americas—long before they invented agriculture, cities, or writing. The human community has thrived despite its many comparative weaknesses to other animals: "Any adult chimp can readily overpower us, and any big cat can easily run us down. . . . Compared to other mammals of our size and diet, our colons are too short, stomachs too small, and teeth too petite. Our infants are born fat and dangerously premature, with skulls that have not yet fused." Likewise, human beings lack the kind of innate knowledge that allows other animals to instinctively meet survival needs. People need to learn, for example, which plants are poisonous and how to make fire and cook food.

What we're good at—when we act together rather than alone—is teaching, learning, and expanding our cultural store of knowledge, the information stored not in genes but in communities and practices. How this cultural knowledge grows and changes is at the center of an emerging scientific image of human beings. It's a profoundly different image from the individualist one many of us grew up with.

The Cultural Evolution of Human Nature

Aristotle was so impressed by our species' sociality that he claimed in his *Politics* that we are "by nature a political animal." "No quality of human nature is more remarkable," the Scottish philosopher David Hume wrote, "both in itself and in its consequences, than that propensity we have to sympathize with others, and to receive by communication their inclinations and sentiments, however different from, or even contrary to our own." Charles Darwin deserves a spot at the top of any list of towering precursors to the modern scientific image of our species too.

Similar themes are found in the work of feminists like Audre Lorde, Barbara Smith, and other authors of 1977's Combahee River Collective statement; Gloria Anzaldúa, Cherríe Moraga, and other self-described "third-world women" in the 1981 *This Bridge Called My Back: Writings by Radical Women of Color*; and many more. These scholars have long rejected the isolated, atomic view of the self, defined in terms of the private inner workings of the rational autonomous mind. In its place, they've described a dynamic and relational self, one constituted by its relations with other people.

Our relationships to others are literally part of what makes us who we are. Gertrude Stein put it beautifully: in lieu of Descartes' claim that "I think therefore I am," she wrote, "I am because my little dog knows me." The Zulu and Xhosa notion of *ubuntu* captures a similar idea; often translated as "humanity toward others," it suggests that "I am because we are." Nelson Mandela praised ubuntu philosophy for capturing "the profound sense that we are human only through the humanity of others."

These ideas also anticipate much of what's emerging from contemporary work on human psychology and cultural evolution. Human beings are distinctively and completely reliant on each other: natural born social learners, eager collaborators, and cooperative norm followers. Emotionally, people crave togetherness and belonging. Cognitively, human beings are equipped with sophisticated capacities that allow them to navigate across many overlapping social worlds and find meaning in attachments and collective activities. People easily and instinctively thrive in dynamic networks of social relationships because human minds are built for it.

Like other species, *Homo sapiens* is a product of evolution. But in addition to the process of natural selection acting on genes, people are also shaped by various forms of cultural selection. The term "culture" has a technical meaning in this context. It picks out a class of information, namely information that is transmitted socially. The concept provides a useful contrast with the genetic information that is transmitted via genes. A bit of information counts as cultural when it is passed from one organism to the next not by genetic means but by social processes. All living things are endowed with a genetic inheritance, but human beings enjoy an extensive cultural inheritance as well.

Cultural information can be stored in brains but also outside of them: in artifacts, technologies, stories, books, traditions, institutions, built environments, and social structures. Culturally acquired traits like the desire for the American Dream aren't innate. They develop over time, piece by piece, with improvements and additions made by many people dispersed across space and time.

Socially transmitted information accumulates, allowing later generations to retain and build upon the knowledge, skills, and traditions of previous generations. Think about architecture, animal husbandry, or cooking—all are the product of slowly evolving and accumulating cultural knowledge.

Less useful ideas and behaviors are forgotten, discarded, or otherwise fall out of circulation, and as more useful ideas and behaviors are adopted by more individuals, they spread and develop over time. This is what the Netsilik had that Franklin's crew did not: a cultural inheritance that, over the course of generations, had slowly accumulated knowledge and skills and technologies that were specifically adapted to the challenges of surviving in the tundra.

Another idea central to this picture of human nature is that the two inheritance systems—the genetic and the cultural—came to interact with each other in an increasingly complex system of feedback loops known as "gene-culture coevolution." A classic example is lactase persistence in adults, which is what allows some adults to be able to digest milk. Milk contains a sugar called lactose, and digesting it requires the presence of an enzyme called lactase in the intestine. Almost all babies have lactase, while many adults don't. So what explains lactase persistence in other adults?

Evolutionary geneticists have traced this trait to ancient cultures that used milk for sustenance. It developed separately in distinct regions, including sub-Saharan Africa, Europe, and the Middle East, between 8000 and 4000 BCE. Descendants of people from these areas are now genetically disposed to be able to drink milk as adults, while those descended from areas that didn't use milk, including much of East Asia, the Americas, and Southern Africa, are not. In short, the cultural evolution of dairy farming drove the genetic inheritance of lactase persistence. Culture changes genes. But gene-culture coevolution is a feedback system. The genetic ability to tolerate milk as an adult in turn shapes cultural practices, which bring you

Parmigiano-Reggiano and the shmear of cream cheese on a bagel. Just as people shape systems and systems shape people, genes shape cultures and cultures shape genes.

Gregariousness

Earlier we noted how, if dropped off in a tropical forest, a group of fifty capuchin monkeys would be more likely to survive than a group including you and forty-nine of your best friends. But in other circumstances, the odds flip. Consider the primatologist Sarah Hrdy's thought experiment, which she called "apes on a plane":

> Each year 1.6 billion passengers fly to destinations around the world. Patiently we line up to be checked and patted down by someone we've never seen before. We file on board an aluminum cylinder and cram our bodies into narrow seats, elbow to elbow, accommodating one another for as long as the flight takes. With nods and resigned smiles, passengers make eye contact and then yield to late-comers pushing past. When a young man wearing a backpack hits me with it as he reaches up to cram his excess paraphernalia into an overhead compartment, instead of grimacing or bearing my teeth, I smile weakly, disguising my irritation. Most people on board ignore the crying baby or pretend to. . . .
>
> I cannot help but wonder what would happen if my fellow human passengers suddenly morphed into another species of ape. What if I were traveling with a planeload of chimpanzees? Any one of us would be lucky to disembark with all 10 fingers and toes still attached, with the babies still breathing and unmaimed. Bloody earlobes and other appendages would litter the aisles. Compressing so many highly impulsive strangers into a tight space would be a recipe for mayhem.

Individualist cultures depict human beings as fundamentally self-interested, predisposed to be on guard against one another. But in reality, while people are sometimes selfish and suspicious of each other, these disruptions of trust occur against a backdrop of otherwise massively well-organized, unthinkingly efficient, and stunningly smooth cooperation.

Human beings in general are not just social but also abnormally socially tolerant. We're temperamentally more docile and less aggressive than even our most closely related species. There's a lot of variability, of course. Some people are bookworms, while others are the life of the party. Most are peaceful, but some are aggressive and violent. On the whole, though, human beings have a unique and unparalleled capacity for cooperation. People tolerate strangers, trade with rivals, and usually go about their business without confrontation, even when others are annoying, insulting, or threatening.

This thinning out of aggression from human nature, sometimes called "self-domestication," is tied to our species' uniquely deep entanglement with culture. In so many ways, people's access to what they need—from resources to recognition—depends on playing nicely with others. They've got to read the room. This gregariousness permits individuals to get and stay close to each other, to knit together into families, bands, and larger and more complex communities. These social arrangements in turn require more and more ability to collaborate, keep track of social networks, and understand each other's minds. In many ways, the story of human evolution is the story of culture and cooperative psychology ratcheting each other up in a feedback loop.

People *are* sometimes selfish or vicious, but these are not humanity's fixed, core traits. Human beings are outfitted with altruistic emotions like empathy, sympathy, love, and compassion. We're also equipped with more evolutionarily recent, distinctively human social emotions: shame, guilt, embarrassment, social anxiety, and moral disgust. These emotions help keep people obsessed with rules and norms, closely monitoring who's following them and who's breaking them. Gratitude, respect, team spirit, group pride, and patriotism are all affiliative too, even if they sometimes have dark sides. Even experiences like confusion, boredom, and curiosity help guide people through the enormous flow of cultural information they encounter every day.

The individualist view that self-interest is the fundamental motivational core of human nature isn't just misleading but also drearily flattening. Mountains of evidence tell us that it's time to replace this oversimplification with a picture of human nature that is richer, more complex, and more outside-in, highlighting the relationships that connect and shape us. So think twice the next time someone suggests that "change begins within." The changes within us are inseparable from the people and structures around us.

Interdependence

Imagine showing a four-year-old kid a puzzle box with a sticker inside. Opening the box requires a series of steps. There's a tool that allows you to move a bolt, which allows you to slide the tool into a hole, which allows you to open a door, and so on. You tell the kid that they can try to open the box however they want. Then you demonstrate how to open it and then leave the room. A hidden video camera records what the kid does.

It's no surprise that most kids imitate the steps they were shown to open the box. But there's a twist. When demonstrating, you've slipped in a couple unnecessary steps, like tapping the tool against the side of the box. Do the kids imitate these unnecessary steps too? You bet. They're doing what's called "over-imitating." It might sound cute (and it is), but it's also a window into something distinctive and deeply important about us.

In a famous study of over-imitation—the one we've just described—most four-year-old kids copied all the researcher's steps no matter whether the box was transparent or opaque. When the box was see-through and they could tell that tapping its side did nothing to help them open it, the kids still copied the unnecessary steps. This is the "over" part of over-imitation, and human children appear wired up for it. Over-imitation has been found all over the world, even in the Bushmen of Africa's Kalahari Desert, a culture with little tradition of explicit teaching. There, kids follow their elders around, soak up what they see, and build skills through trial and error. Still, researchers have found that they over-imitate the adults around them.

Even more striking, in this study and others, is the comparison between how kids and nonhuman animals perform. In an experiment comparing four-year-olds to chimpanzees, both the kids and the chimps were shown necessary and unnecessary steps for opening the box. In contrast to the kids, the chimps skipped the unnecessary steps when they could see that they didn't do anything. "Animals focus on getting the job done," as Mark Nielsen, a psychologist who studies comparative cognition put it, while "humans seem to almost forget about the outcome and copy everything we see."

Research like this—comparing imitation in human and nonhuman animals—can make human beings look silly. Chimps, dogs, and elephants have been shown to solve certain tasks more efficiently than human children, who will go through all kinds of elaborate needless steps if that's what they've seen other people do. But while examples of over-imitation can seem mindless in isolation, this tendency for conformity has a good rationale.

Viewed from the perspective of the cultural evolution of human nature, over-imitation is a feature, not a bug. It functions to help ensure that people make efficient use of the vast wisdom found in culture, all those complex skills and technologies and institutional procedures pieced together and refined by generations of forebears. The instinct to copy is so strong because learning too much from others is a "better" mistake than copying and learning too little—especially for a species that relies so heavily on culture. Following the wisdom of the collective is usually a better bet than relying on the intelligence of the individual.

Reasoning like this can recast other aspects of human psychology. A "conformity bias" makes it feel sensible to do what seems normal, and a "prestige bias" inclines people to copy those who have found success. People tend to be relentlessly interested in what others are thinking and have a unique set of tools for "mentalizing"—predicting what others will do and trying to understand them. Instincts like these make it easier to learn from others, to learn the right things, and to execute what's been learned correctly. They allow better and smoother access to the cultural inheritance system.

All these instincts lead groups of people to accumulate cultural knowledge over time, even when the individuals who use it don't know exactly what it's doing. Leading up to the Viking Age, sturdy iron was hard to find in the Scandinavian bogs. So warriors sought out another way to compensate for the weakness of their iron swords: infusing weaponry with the spirits of the dead. They mixed in the bones of their ancestors and animals. What they were also doing—unknowingly—was turning iron into steel. Much like making charcoal out of wood, burning bones in oxygen-poor conditions creates "bone coal." Their swords, axes, and arrowheads became much stronger but not for the reasons they thought. It wasn't individual rational problem-solving that led to the creation and persistence of this ritual; it was cultural evolutionary processes that involved over-imitation, conformity bias, prestige bias, and social interdependence.

Interdependence for Social Change

Compared to the individualist image of human nature that holds so much sway in the WEIRD world, this alternative culture-centered image is good news for anyone interested in social change. It softens the perceived boundaries that separate people from each other as well as those between people and the systems they live within. Human beings are designed by evolution to inhabit their world but also to shape and reshape the structures that organize it.

This image of individuals and structures as deeply interwoven is a key piece of a difficult puzzle, the puzzle of figuring out how to see ourselves as part of "big structural change." People are more influenced by their surroundings than we notice, but there's also a flip side to this insight. We're not just the over-imitators; we are the over-imitated.

7   We Are Each Other's Situation

Recycling Revisited

"I work in the environmental movement. I don't care if you recycle," wrote the climate justice activist and journalist Mary Annaïse Heglar in 2019, "Stop obsessing over your environmental 'sins.' Fight the oil and gas industry instead."

Individual actions like recycling can indeed seem trivial when they're stacked up next to taking down the fossil fuel industry. But from a both/and perspective, recycling turns out to be an excellent case study of how we can use our radical interdependence for good.

People are used to thinking that what matters about their actions are the immediate material consequences, like how many bottles and cans they throw in the blue bin and how big their overall carbon footprint is. But climate scientist Katherine Hayhoe points to another kind of consequence: "our personal actions do matter, but they matter because they can change others." This chapter unpacks Hayhoe's idea. Our actions affect other people in lots of ways, including by shaping social norms. What's more, one of the "other" people your personal actions can affect is yourself—that is, yourself in the future. Little things you do now can put you on the path to doing more and bigger things later.

It's odd that so many people's first inclination when they think about fighting climate change is to get serious about recycling. Landfills do contribute to global warming, but they're one cause among many. Recycling owes much of its outsized prominence to the corporate PR campaigns about individual responsibility we saw in chapter 1. Recycling was also emphasized by the environmental movement in its focus on wastefulness.

When it comes to plastic waste, there really are reasons to worry. Plastic waste is contributing to species extinction, ecological devastation, and numerous health problems. Microplastics are found in the Pyrenees Mountains over 100 miles from the nearest town, in fields where food is grown, in virtually all brands of bottled water, and in our bodies. Plastics contribute to climate change more directly, too. Ninety-eight percent of them are made from fossil fuels, and as energy production shifts to renewable sources, corporations are using more and more fossil fuels to make plastic. If every other source of carbon pollution in the world was cut to zero tomorrow, plastic production alone would heat the Earth 1.5°C as early as 2060.

Given all this pollution, it's reasonable to try to recycle. In the US, about 68 percent of paper gets recycled, and Americans recycle a lot of metal and glass too. Unfortunately, plastics recycling is a disaster. As one set of experts put it, when it comes to plastic, "recycling does not work and will never work." There are thousands of types of plastic, each requiring a distinctive recycling process. And unlike glass and paper, plastic isn't inert. It absorbs all kinds of dangerous chemicals, which limits the uses of recycled plastic. Even the process of recycling plastic is wasteful and expensive.

As a result, only about 8 percent of American plastic overall gets recycled. Americans used to ship vast amounts of it to China, where it was "recycled"—which usually meant it just got burned or buried. Then in 2018, China prohibited most plastics importing. In response, the US started shipping tens of thousands of containers of plastic to Malaysia, Thailand, and Vietnam instead. Those countries quickly banned plastic waste imports too, in part because burning it contaminated water, killed crops, and inflamed respiratory illnesses. So the US turned to Bangladesh, Cambodia, Ethiopia, Ghana, Kenya, Laos, and Senegal.

The US does its fair share of plastic incineration as well. Americans burn six times more plastic than they recycle. Where, you ask? Once again, everything is two degrees separated from race. The United States' most marginalized communities, the ones with more poverty and fewer white people, house the overwhelming majority of plastic incinerators (nearly eight out of ten, according to one 2019 report). The proliferation of these incinerators is a catastrophe as well as an injustice—in this case, what has become known as environmental injustice.

For all these reasons, when a company like Starbucks pats itself on the back for transitioning to "recycl*able*" lids, they're doing little more than buying themselves a bit of good publicity. Only 5 percent of polypropylene—or the number 5 plastic making up Starbucks's lids—was recycled in 2015. (Alex's sunny Southern Californian city of Claremont doesn't even pretend to recycle any plastic higher than number 2.) Nearly all the lids end up in the same places as most other plastic: in the ocean, the sky, our food, your lungs.

With all this in mind, should you bother recycling? In public discussion of this question, the answer has a standard—and by now familiar—format. It goes something like this:

Expert: Individuals can't fix this problem. We need to change the system.

Journalist's silent plea: But we have to give the reader something to do.

Expert: Here are some small steps you can take to feel like you're doing your part.

There *are* structural fixes for this problem. One approach—familiar from the early days of the American Can Company and its fight against disposable bottle bans—uses "producer responsibility" laws. Like a carbon tax, these laws shift the cost of recycling to manufacturers by taxing products with high environmental impacts and offering incentives to those who produce "greener" items. By 2022, Maine, Oregon, and California had all passed laws like these. When there's a market for recycled goods, manufacturers themselves can end up supporting such laws.

How do we get from here, where plastic is a disaster, to there, a place where the markets for recycled goods are large, single-use plastics are no more, and producer responsibility laws are common? Another duck-rabbit shift in perspective will be valuable in finding a way. Individual actions like recycling can be measured not just by their material consequences—how many bottles you save by doggedly sorting the trash—but also by their social consequences.

The Power of Moral Charisma

Understanding social influence requires flipping the script on a long-standing psychological debate. For decades starting in the 1960s, psychologists studying personality and behavior were locked in an argument. One side took what seems like the obvious position: people have personalities, and those personalities matter. Traits like being funny or shy or optimistic are real and contribute to people's character. "Personality psychologists" measured traits like these and used those measurements to make predictions about people's behavior. If a person is shy, they'll be less likely to start a conversation with a stranger. If someone is funny, they'll tend to tell jokes and make people laugh.

This seemingly uncontroversial line of thought ran into problems. When personality psychologists measured traits of character and then tried to predict actual behavior—starting conversations, telling jokes—the measurements didn't do a stellar job. Someone who scored high on a test of honesty wasn't much more likely to avoid telling a convenient lie than someone who scored low on a test of honesty. Ostensibly stingy people donated just as much money to a stranger in need as the ostensibly generous.

A rival view, which came to be known as "situationism," emerged to explain these surprising results. Proponents of situationism argued that personality is basically a myth. People aren't carrying around within themselves stable traits like generosity and honesty. Instead, the situation we're in largely determines what we do. In some situations—say, when the penalties for getting caught lying are steep—people tend to be honest regardless of who they are. In other situations where the stakes are low, people of all putative personality types tend to fudge the truth.

The situationist view has its own intuitive appeal. It too has a claim to being rooted in common sense, where it's expressed in ideas like "peer pressure" and platitudes like "power corrupts." Put most people near enough to power and they'll lie, cheat, and steal. On a more day-to-day level, people can be honest with their boss but not their kids, or be kind right after getting a compliment but grouchy after getting insulted. The situationist charge was that people's behavior is so fluid, so context-bound, that it's wrong to think of behavior as driven by internal character traits at all. People are much more like grass blowing in the wind than personality psychology suggested.

The academic debate cooled off after a few decades when it became clear that both sides were kind of right. There's little doubt that many popular ways of measuring personality are at best entertainment and at worst pernicious scams. The Myers-Briggs Type Indicator (MBTI), which divides personality into sixteen types, is exhibit A in the courtroom of bullshit. It's as scientific as zodiac signs or a Hogwarts House Test. But improvements in the actual science of personality, along with new statistical techniques for measuring personality over time, have produced better results.

Scientifically validated traits include the Big Five, which go by the acronym OCEAN: Openness, Conscientiousness, Extraversion, Agreeableness, and Neuroticism. Openness, for example, stands for "openness to new experience," and people who rate high in it are more likely to try exotic foods, travel on adventures, and feel comfortable talking to randos. Conscientious people tend to be self-disciplined, preferring plans to chance encounters and rule following to rule breaking.

There is a legitimate (albeit imperfect and ever-evolving) science to personality. But even using these newer, well-validated measures, nobody is open to new experience or conscientious or anything else all the time and independently of context. Even those very open to new experiences might not like spicy food, so when their friends suggest trying the new Thai restaurant down the street, they decline. They can have the stable trait of being closed to new experiences with spicy food but have another stable trait alongside it: openness to nonspicy foods.

The name for this view—that personality is both real but also highly situation dependent—is "interactionism." Traits of character are the product of interactions between features of persons—things that people are born with or take shape in early childhood—and features of the environment—that situational "wind" blowing us around.

Even with this advance, something was still missing from these discussions about personality. Hagop Sarkissian, a philosopher who studies both social psychology and classical Chinese ethics, noticed in the early aughts that acknowledging the power of situations seemed to leave little room for individual freedom. People talked about "the situation" like it was some kind of faceless force outside individuals, controlling their choices. But Sarkissian stressed that one of the most important elements of the situations shaping people's choices is other people. We are each other's situations.

Recall, for example, that the best way to predict whether someone will become a smoker is by looking at how much time they spend around other smokers. The power of situations, as Sarkissian put it, is reciprocal. It creates a looping effect. If you're part of my situation, shaping my choices, then I'm part of yours too. The fact that smokers help make other smokers shows how we're all social influencers.

As Sarkissian put it, "we do not simply *react* to external situations, but we also *shape* our situations through the variables we ourselves introduce." His work develops this insight by connecting it to the virtue of *de* (德) in classical Confucian ethics, which is a kind of moral charisma. Individuals who cultivate it influence others by shaping their shared situations.

Confucian ethics sweats the small stuff. It directs people to pay meticulous attention to their mannerisms, tone of voice, posture, and expressions. The *Analects of Confucius* is packed full of instructions about how to bow to this person or that, what color clothes to wear for one occasion or another, and so on. For example, Confucius's ideal leader "wears a black robe over a lambskin coat; a white robe over a fawn fur coat; and a yellow robe over a fox fur coat."

Confucius compiled a cookbook for using human interconnectedness for good. Many of his recipes, like the one prescribing which fur to wear for which occasion, are specific to his place and time, but they're easy enough to translate. Minding our manners is another way we influence each other, making etiquette a vital part of moral charisma. Sarkissian's spin on the Confucian virtue of *de* points to the potential for change rooted in humanity's outside-in nature (chapter 6). Each person is the powerful outside to someone else's inside. The same is true when it comes to helping each other change systems and structures.

Social Norms for Social Influence

We all help make up each other's situations. This means that even seemingly individual choices aren't so individual. There are also better and worse ways to be someone else's situation. A recent explosion of research on social norms is helping to distinguish the better from the worse.

Social norms are unstated rules about "what we do." They're everywhere, telling Americans to shake hands but Japanese people to bow. The norms of other places and times can seem strange when viewed from afar, like the Victorian norm to never ask a direct question. (A polite person would say, "I hope you're doing well" but never ask "how are you doing?") Norms are also often imbued with prejudice and stereotypes. Women in the 1950s were instructed to avoid letting their hands hang at their sides "like dead fish," as it would detract from the silhouette of their figure and make them look "lifeless" (figure 7.1).

"Dead Fish"

Figure 7.1
"Dead fish" hands.

Norms aren't just ubiquitous; they're powerful. Far from merely inform-
ing people about, say, which fork is for the salad, they're essential for the
kind of cooperation we explored in the last chapter that makes the human
species so distinctive. Norms help people solve collective action problems,
situations where it's in everyone's collective interest to cooperate but no
one's interest to do so alone. They're indispensable to the effectiveness of
governments, affecting how policies and laws are actually implemented.
Which norms prevail in a polity can make the difference between tolerating
corruption and uprooting it.

Knowing the norms of a community is part of what it is to be a member
of one. In the evolutionary past, in order to build things together, trade,
and intermarry, people needed to know what to expect from one another
without relying on governments to lay down the law (since governments
didn't yet exist). Norms provided this information.

But norms don't *just* provide information. They don't merely encode
what "people around here do." They come with a complex motivational
oomph. In grasping norms—internalizing a community's unwritten rules—
we become motivated to follow them. We also become ready to enforce
them and to accept it when others enforce them on us. Have you been stuck
in line at the supermarket behind someone talking loudly on speakerphone?

There's no law against this, but that person is apt to get a lot of side-eye. That's norm enforcement in action.

Research on children shows that the motivation to learn, follow, and enforce norms emerges at a remarkably young age. As soon as most children learn "a blickett is for twisting" (or whatever norm for using a new toy the researcher teaches them), they're ready to lay down the law against would-be renegades who try kicking their blicketts. They'll start to internalize the norm straightaway, and once they do, they won't need encouragement to follow it anymore. Nor will they need encouragement to convey their disapproval to anyone else who fails to comply.

Even when norms are arbitrary—like "twist blicketts," "use the small fork for salads," and "don't ask direct questions"—following and enforcing them becomes, psychologically, something like an end in itself. Those people in the supermarket line are monitoring your behavior, ready to react negatively if, say, you're chatting away on speaker instead of putting your food on the conveyor belt. You may not always realize it, but you're doing the same to them. You might not love it when others "police" your checkout etiquette, but you've almost certainly policed someone else's. This can seem trivial and annoying, but social norms are what allow us to Live In A Society.

Putting all this in the context of creating social change, Michael Grunwald returns to the iconic Pogo poster, which announced that "we have met the enemy and he is us." The poster served the interests of industry, but it also "helped make littering extremely uncool." Grunwald continues:

> Carbon emissions are atmospheric litter. Every gram of carbon makes global warming a bit worse. But carbon litter is invisible, while normal litter is ugly, which helps explain why carbon litter, though much harder to remove than normal litter, is not yet uncool.
>
> As solar goes mainstream, fossil electricity could become as uncool as littering; as electric cars get cheaper, the same thing could happen to internal combustion engines. The Crying Indian illustrated how an individual ethic can be as contagious as a virus, inspiring people to do things because they just seem like the thing to do.

We think Grunwald is spot-on. Researchers from across academic disciplines have explored ways to take his ideas further, to use our position as each other's situations to scale up the potency of personal choices.

Putting Norms to Work

It can be pretty tempting to join in when "everyone's doing it," whatever "it" is. This pull drives social change. According to some estimates, nothing moves us to get involved more than comparing our choices to others' choices. Likewise, people who get involved in collective movements—as we'll dig into in the coming chapters—tend to feel highly motivated to follow the movement's norms.

This is especially true when people get a sense that things are changing, that what "we normally do around here" is in flux. Researchers think about trends on the brink of catching on in terms of "dynamic" norms. Early adopters of dynamic norms can enjoy the pleasure of getting to say "I was onto that before it was cool" rather than being the last to hop on the bandwagon. Take a headline from *The Hill*: "Vegetarianism Is on the Rise—Especially the Part-Time Kind." Telling readers how "more and more" people are reducing meat consumption can be a more powerful driver of norm change than describing the stats as static (i.e., simply stating how many people avoid meat at a snapshot in time).

This kind of messaging is particularly helpful for promoting new norms when they haven't yet managed to go mainstream. Political scientists have documented many cases of tipping points and "norm cascades," when early uptake of a new norm is slow but then a critical mass of support is reached, triggering a sudden and rapid spread. (An unparalleled pandemic example from the beginning of the COVID-19 years: "masks on!" Then, "masks off!") Again, much of the power of norm-based approaches to social change is that learning norms involves more than gaining information about what people are up to. Even just learning about an emerging norm can galvanize action.

There are also benefits to talking about the importance of a norm out loud, to consciously and explicitly announcing one's embrace of the norm, both to oneself and to others. It's one thing to silently intend to go to the gym and another to stake one's reputation on being a gym person by talking with friends about how good it feels to exercise. In conspicuously supporting a norm in public, people help spread it through the community. They become norm entrepreneurs.

Central to the power of norms is how they are enforced by the community, but norm enforcement doesn't only take the form of punishing violations. Praise is critical to norm change too. People help promote new norms—like bicycle commuting and getting vaxxed—when they applaud others for adopting them. In return, the people who express praise feel good about supporting other members in the growing club. Praise offers the praiser a little do-gooder booster shot.

Social Influence on Your Future Self: How Each Choice Affects the Next

To summarize: the power of individual action goes beyond tallying up material consequences, like how much less gas gets guzzled when one driver switches to an EV. It also includes social consequences, like the way a single norm entrepreneur can shape others' situations. But the power of individual action goes further still. There are consequences for our future selves. The choices we make today affect the person we become tomorrow.

There's a familiar and depressing version of this: people sometimes do good deeds to get away with bad ones. Some of the most famous examples are the most atrocious. In the late 1800s, while oppressing, mutilating, and massacring African colonial subjects in what today is the Democratic Republic of the Congo, the Belgian King Leopold II won acclaim for his philanthropic work. The International Stalin Prize for Strengthening Peace Among Peoples (aka "The Lenin") was created not long after Stalin starved 3–5 million Ukrainians with his agricultural collectivization plan. In 1988, Bill Cosby donated $20 million dollars to Spelman College, the most prestigious historically Black college for women in the country, at the same time as he was well on his way to allegedly raping sixty women. "The great mystery of evil," Jelani Cobb wrote, "is not that it persists but, rather, that so many of its practitioners wish to do so while being thought of as saints."

Non-evil people are susceptible to a more banal form of the same dynamic, making this susceptibility a cause for alarm about individualist approaches to social change. What if doing a good deed now—say, buying solar panels—makes a person feel "licensed" to do less for the climate going forward? What if people think they can "make up" for their political inaction through superficial gestures toward personal improvement?

It's an understandable problem. Take someone who cares deeply about the environment. They believe the most impactful personal changes include flying less, driving less, and eating less meat. Now suppose they've just taken a twelve-hour overnight train ride to visit family, foregoing what would have been a two-hour flight for a comparable price. They walk in the door to the smell of sizzling bacon in grandma's kitchen. They've been keeping things pretty plant-based at home, but, hey, what's the harm in eating a few strips? After all, they just did their part to curb carbon pollution by taking the train. Doing all that good gives them license to get away with a peccadillo or two, especially if they wait to eat that bacon when no one else is looking.

What's happening here is that one choice has downstream influence on another, with the first choice spilling over to affect the next. After making one climate-friendly choice, a person might feel less guilty about a subsequent climate-unfriendly choice. This is called "negative spillover," when doing something good makes people more likely to turn around and do something bad.

Critics of individualist approaches to climate action often invoke the threat of negative spillover (even if they don't use the specific term). There are two distinct but related concerns. One is that people's efforts to make green choices are sometimes canceled out because they feel permitted to engage in even more carbon-intensive behaviors. For example, studies have found that people who weatherize their homes tend to raise their thermostats, ironically resulting in decreased energy savings and increased pollution.

The second concern is that expending energy on things like flying less or weatherizing one's home is a diversion. Critics say that individual sacrifices like these are a misuse of time, energy, and resources better spent on more important opportunities to effect larger-scale structural change. Mary Annaïse Heglar writes, "The belief that this enormous, existential problem could have been fixed if all of us had just tweaked our consumptive habits is not only preposterous; it's dangerous. It turns environmentalism into an individual choice defined as sin or virtue, convicting those who don't or can't uphold these ethics."

The idea is that tweaking our individual consumption habits takes away from more important—political, impactful—things we could be doing. It can also lead us to blame people for problems that aren't really their fault. As we detailed in chapter 1, the whole impetus behind corporate campaigns against littering and for carbon footprint monitoring has been to keep the public complacent and distracted from big business' much larger contributions to ecological devastation and the climate crisis.

But does it follow that people should focus their efforts on making these big projects happen *rather than* worrying about personal consumption? Is the personal stuff a counterproductive distraction from joining the larger battle?

No, or at least not always. Spillover can also be positive. Start with some simple, smaller-scale examples at the personal level. Hotel guests who make a commitment to reuse their towels are more likely to turn off the lights when they leave the room. Californians who start composting go on to save more energy and water.

In these examples of positive spillover, the values expressed in one decision carry forward and positively reinforce decisions about other things in the future. One good deed for the climate can beget the next. In at least some cases, the effect here looks genuinely causal: the first choice drives the second. Reusing towels causes people to turn off the lights, and composting makes people more likely to save energy and water.

One might worry, though, that these examples of positive spillover all happen between similar kinds of choices. They all have to do with personal consumption choices. What about positive spillover from the personal to the political?

In research on voters in Maine, John Thøgerson and Caroline Noblet found that personal behavior changes, including buying energy-efficient products and, yes, even recycling, made people more supportive of wind power projects. Their findings suggest that small personal steps can springboard people into backing substantive structural change. Taking action may have helped shape people's policy preferences over and above how committed they already felt to environmental issues. So it wasn't just that people who cared about the environment were more likely both to be "green consumers" and to support wind power. It looks like people who acted like green consumers *became* more concerned about the environment—and also more supportive of wind power.

Studies like this give reason to think that personal behavior changes don't necessarily crowd out actions focused on structural change. They can crowd them in too. Thøgerson and Noblet think of positive spillover as a kind of catalytic conversion, where seemingly small, inconsequential things have the potential to catalyze interest in doing other, more potentially impactful things.

Research on positive spillover is young but suggestive. One working paper for the National Bureau of Economic Research finds that German households that put solar panels on their roofs become more likely to vote for the Green Party. It's not just that people who put up panels are already likely to vote Green. There seems to be a causal effect: installing the panels subsequently affects how they vote. The authors suggest that the catalytic process works in much the same way that Trish Devine thinks people overcome the habit of prejudice, as we described in chapter 5. People sense a conflict between the values expressed in the different decisions they make—they feel the dissonance—and are driven to find a way to resolve it. Putting panels on the roof resolves the conflict by signaling "I'm the kind of person who supports renewable energy." Positive spillover is more likely when it helps people see themselves as good.

There are a lot of caveats, of course. Negative spillover is a live threat, and plenty of experiments predict positive spillover only to find zilch. A spillover effect is only so strong, and the second action might be costly enough to quash it.

One way to think about the findings so far is as a proof of concept: small acts can add up, but not only in the way that votes add up or plastic bottles in a landfill do. Instead, they add up by affecting other, more consequential choices. Buying the right thing can seem like a trivial form of activism, but if it leads people to vote differently or join a movement, then it's not so trivial after all.

Scaling Up

We began this book talking about how corporate PR directed attention to energy-efficient lightbulbs, litter, and recycling in order to distract attention from more impactful solutions. You might be wondering why we're now defending some of those very same, much maligned consumer choices. The reason is *not* because we think human beings are going to recycle their way out of the climate crisis. Rather, we think that even these seemingly trivial acts have the potential to lead to big—often surprising—payoffs. Reshaping the energy grid is more important than recycling, but recycling might help us reshape the energy grid. The next chapter is about all kinds of different ways that little things—all the allegedly irrelevant goings-on at the individual level—can combine and grow and cascade into revolutionary change.

8 Cascades, Loops, and Tipping Points

From Agents of Change to Agents of Transformative Change

Small acts can have large effects. Sometimes the effects are personal, influencing one's future choices, while other times they are social, affecting other people's choices. Sometimes effects combine, and combine again, and combine again, and suddenly small acts become big cascades that change the world. When this happens, slowly at first and then seemingly all at once, a tipping point's been crossed.

Tipping points are all over the place. Novel viruses and dance crazes initially appear in isolated locations and then are suddenly everywhere; electric bikes and mobile phones remain niche luxury goods, and then overnight everyone has one; rumors and misinformation simmer at the fringes of society until a social media post goes viral.

Tipping points in social change are difficult to see coming. Everything seems stably arranged just before the quantum leap. There are lessons here for would-be changemakers, if we look in a both/and way.

The Great Escape

Back in chapter 3, we described humanity's "Great Escape" from abject conditions and poor health over the past 200 or so years. In 1820, four out of every five people lived in poverty, almost none lived in a democracy, and the vast majority spent their whole lives without learning to read. This had been the status quo for most of the 300,000-ish years that human beings had been around. The rate of change between what happened in the past 200 years and the rest of our species' existence is jaw-dropping. For 99.95

percent of that time, we lived on average about thirty-five years. The typical human life doubled in length in the last 0.05 percent of our species' existence. This didn't change at a continuous pace; it was a radical shift.

Even the most breathtaking tipping points like the Great Escape have their origins in countless smaller acts and events. Consider, for a moment, the problem of milk. Life expectancy in the United States in 1880 was barely above the global average, about forty years. The overall average lifespan was kept low by a gruesomely high infant mortality rate, which at the time was trending in the wrong direction. In the middle of the nineteenth century, 60 percent of all deaths in New York were children under five, which was *up* from 30 percent in 1815. Life expectancy overall had also gone backward, declining by thirteen years from 1800 to 1850. The main culprit at the time appeared to be industrialization and the rapid growth of crowded cities.

One effect of this growth was to push farms further away from urban centers. An effect of that, and one of the reasons big cities became dangerous, was that milk now had to travel much farther from a cow's udder to a kid's lips—sometimes upward of hundreds of miles. All milk at that time was raw, and it spoiled fast.

Milk had already been a cause for concern because of the "swill milk" scandals of the 1850s, when dairies started feeding their cows residual mash from distilleries to save money. A *New York Times* editorial said swill milk was a "bluish, white compound of true milk, pus and dirty water, which, on standing, deposits a yellowish, brown sediment that is manufactured in the stables attached to large distilleries by running the refuse distillery slops through the udders of dying cows and over the unwashed hands of milkers." Some dairies were caught faking the look of cream at the top of milk bottles by adding a layer of pureed calf brains. Apparently the illusion was pretty convincing, right up until you poured the brains into a cup of coffee.

Both swill and ordinary milk were brimming with microorganisms, exposing babies to tuberculosis, typhoid, scarlet fever, diphtheria, and other diseases. Older kids who drank it were vulnerable as well. Contaminated milk contributed to the fact that about one in four American kids didn't make it out of childhood in 1890. One reporter at the time alleged that "the deaths of two-thirds of the children in New York and Brooklyn could be distinctly traced to the use of impure milk."

On a common telling, the invention of pasteurization saved the day. The story usually goes like this: the great French chemist Louis Pasteur was helping local distilleries solve problems with souring wine in the 1850s, which led him to discover that airborne microorganisms caused fermentation and . . . yadda yadda yadda . . . Pasteur came up with the germ theory of disease. At the request of Napoleon III in 1863, Pasteur began looking for solutions to wine contamination and discovered that heating it to about 130 degrees killed the microorganisms. He saved the French wine and beer industries before applying the process to milk.

The impression created by this story is that Great Man Genius Inventor Pasteur came along, discovered germs and pasteurization, and thus saved countless babies. It's not totally wrong. The process *did* save thousands upon thousands of lives. Infant mortality plunged to 7 percent in New York City in 1900, for example, thanks in part to the city's early adoption of pasteurization. But notice the dates. Pasteurization didn't become standard practice in the United States until a full half-century after Pasteur discovered it. The first state-wide requirement to pasteurize milk wasn't passed (by Michigan) until 1947!

Why did it take so long? Why wasn't pasteurization accepted or required by law right after Pasteur's discovery? Unsurprisingly, there were a lot of social barriers. Dairy farmers didn't want to foot the bill to install pasteurizers. Some worried that "cooked milk" wouldn't sell, and they might not have been wrong. Many people preferred the taste of raw milk, and folk theories about "good bacteria" being killed by pasteurization were common. The "sour milk cure," for example, was the idea that spoiled milk would "overcome" the bacteria in your body that was making you sick. (Ideas like these never went away. The website "goop" still recommends cleanses of raw goat milk to eliminate "parasites" in your gut.) Even the American Pediatric Society was disastrously late to the game, warning parents in 1899 that feeding pasteurized milk to their kids could give them scurvy.

It was a messy, decades-long battle, and the fighting wasn't just over pasteurization. Milk was one front in a larger war about consumer safety and the growth of the regulatory state. In 1906, Upton Sinclair's *The Jungle* was published, a searing exposé of Chicago meatpacking factories. That same year, the country took a big step forward in food safety as the federal Pure Food and Drug Act was passed into law.

An incredible change in human existence—the doubling of the average lifespan—was not due to scientific discovery alone. It required all sorts of people to fight for it, from journalists like Sinclair to philanthropists like

Nathan Straus, who opened a series of milk distribution depots for poor children in New York City. These remained open for decades, helping to pave the way for normalizing pasteurization. They served many further purposes too. During the economic panic of 1893, the depots gave coal away to people who couldn't afford it, and in 1914–1915, they served 1,135,731 penny meals to the unemployed.

There's no telling what fraction of credit Straus deserves for popularizing pasteurization. Countless other overlooked figures contributed as well. Take Alice Evans, who rose from a rural Pennsylvania farm to become the first woman ever elected president of the American Society for Microbiology, in 1927. Her pioneering work on the *Brucella abortus* bacteria helped build scientific consensus about the dangers of unprocessed milk.

The Personal and the Social: Interacting Origins of Tipping Points

In the early twenty-first century, extraordinary changes in what it's like to be a gay person rippled through the US. Through most of the previous century, gay Americans often stayed in the closet. Those who came out risked being openly disowned by their families, exiled from their religious communities, fired from their jobs without legal recourse, mocked in popular culture, and regularly threatened with violence.

These risks remain, but they have lessened. Both institutions and individuals have changed. Institutionally, in psychiatry, same-sex attraction is no longer pathologized, nineteen states have banned conversion therapy, and hate crime laws have been expanded to include discrimination on the basis of gender, sexual orientation, and gender identity. The Department of Defense abandoned "Don't Ask, Don't Tell" in 2011, and it was not long before marriage equality became the law of the land with the Supreme Court's *Obergefell* decision in 2015 and the federal Respect for Marriage Act of 2022. Meanwhile, more churches than ever before are welcoming gay congregants and allowing them to become ministers.

Alongside these changes in laws, policies, and institutions, people's minds changed too. In 2001, just 35 percent of American adults favored same-sex marriage; by 2019, that percentage rose to 61. Both the scale and the breadth of these changes in attitude have been remarkable. Although not completely even, the direction of change is the same for Democrats and Republicans; whites, Blacks, Asians, Hispanics, and Native Americans; men and women; and millennials, Gen Xers, baby boomers, and the Silent

Generation. There's still much further to go, and progress has been full of fits and starts and setbacks, but the US has come surprisingly far, surprisingly fast.

The institutional and individual aspects of this change are interlinked. As gay people gained visibility in culture, politics, and media, more and more gay people came out of the closet. One result of this was that more and more Americans came to understand that they already knew and loved people who were gay. More and more people's attitudes changed, and the market grew for positive representations of gay people in culture, politics, and media. More fictional characters in film and TV started coming out too.

This kind of self-reinforcing cycle is a positive feedback process. A change in the system—public representations of gay people—pushes other elements of the system to change—people's attitudes—which in turn creates more change in that first element—public representation. These spiraling changes in systems, attitudes, and representations eventually rippled out beyond the struggle for LGBTQ justice, inspiring activists in other social movements. These included migrants without documentation and people with mental health disorders who initiated campaigns to "come out" to the wider world as well.

There's no "first element" in any of this, just like there's no point where a circle "begins." We could have reversed how we described the elements in this example, with changes in attitudes causing changes in representations that in turn create more changes in attitudes. But that's just a matter of how we decided to tell the story.

Feedback Loops Defined

Going forward, how can we identify potential cascades and tipping points and nudge social change along? It's easy to see in hindsight that Nathan Straus and *Will & Grace* were pivotal, but examples like these aren't easy to translate into guidance here and now. "Make a fortune and create a highly effective charity to promote pasteurized milk" or "write a hit TV show that empowers people to come out" is a bit like the advice to "buy low and sell high": not wrong, just too abstract to be useful.

One step is returning to basics to understand the underlying processes—like feedback loops—that drive these kinds of cascades and tipping points. A feedback loop is a process where the output of one part of a system feeds back and becomes part of the input to another part. Take audio feedback.

When someone speaks into a microphone, the sound runs through the system, which then outputs it, amplified, from a speaker. But what if the sound from the speaker gets picked up by the mic because they're too close together? Then that louder sound entering the mic gets run through the system and ultimately becomes even more amplified when it's pumped out of the speaker . . . and can't you just hear that screeching pitch now?

Musicians and public speakers do everything they can to prevent these escalating audio feedback loops, though even seemingly uncontrollable spirals of noise can be harnessed—Jimi Hendrix was a pioneer and master at using feedback intentionally. Positive feedback is usually what people have in mind when thinking about tipping points and social change. The Great Escape and viral pandemics are examples of positive feedback.

"Positive" here doesn't mean "good." A process counts as a positive feedback loop when the input pushes it to continue in the same "direction" as the previous state. In the audio example, each cycle of sound through the system makes it louder, amplifying and amplifying until it reaches as high of a volume as the system can sustain.

Unchecked, positive feedback loops are intrinsically unstable. The previous equilibrium is disrupted, changes build upon themselves, and an earlier state of the system is left behind. The changes will continue until the feedback loop is disrupted by some external factor, with the screech growing louder and louder until the sound system reaches its capacity—or someone pulls the plug. Think population explosions, inflation, the proliferation of cancer cells, and economic boom-and-bust panics.

So too are some of the more terrifying courses that climate change could take. One likely contributor to a positive feedback loop of planetary heat is the thawing of permafrost. Around 20 percent of the Northern Hemisphere is permafrost, where the "perma" indicates that it's so cold the soil stays frozen for at least two years straight. Permafrost stores gargantuan quantities of carbon. When it melts—which it is doing at alarming rates now thanks to warming global temperatures—soil microbes in permafrost could turn all that long-buried carbon into CO_2 and methane (which traps 25 to 86 times more heat than CO_2, pound for pound). The release of these gases and microbes could then further accelerate the planetary rise in temperature, not to mention risk unleashing another pandemic or two.

The other kind of feedback is negative. Again, "negative" here doesn't mean "bad." Negative feedback loops still involve processes in which the outputs of one cycle become the inputs of the next. But here the new input is subtracted from the previous output. Rather than amplifying a change, negative feedback processes often work to stabilize a system.

Thermostats illustrate this point. When a change is detected—heat or cold seep in from outside—a thermostat takes that input and produces an output that will counteract it to keep the room's temperature steady— activating the AC or turning on the heat. The level of water in toilets, cruise control in cars, flight control systems on airplanes, and the regulatory systems in the human body use negative feedback processes, too.

In contrast to the inherent instability of positive feedback, negative feedback keeps things at a steady state as outside influences push it to change. The system aims to maintain equilibrium, "absorbing" and adjusting to whatever the world throws at it.

Positive feedback is the more familiar image when it comes to social change, as activists often want to kickstart tipping points. But maintaining some equilibria and preventing the wrong kinds of spiraling positive feedback can be just as worthy goals. Certainly, this is the case when it comes to physical systems like the Earth's climate. The more humanity can do to subtract from the escalating climate catastrophe, the better.

Preventing the worst excesses of positive feedback is no less crucial in some social systems. Stabilizing democracy and reproductive rights spring to mind. Political scientists and historians have been sounding the alarm that the institutions protecting practices like these are far more difficult to create than they are to destroy.

Perhaps nothing puts the power of negative feedback into sharper relief than the threat of nuclear holocaust. The Cold War spiraled through a terrifying positive feedback loop in the latter half of the twentieth century, as the US and the Soviet Union strove to outdo each other with bigger and better ways to blow up the world. But some combination of restraining forces and dumb luck have prevented nuclear holocaust (so far). There's a both/and lesson here too.

Some of these restraining forces were people. Vasily Arkhipov was a Soviet officer in October 1962 when his submarine was stationed near Cuba. The sub had gone days without hearing from Moscow when the US Navy discovered it and began releasing depth charges to draw it to the surface. The sub captain quickly concluded they were under attack and that World War III was underway. He needed two more officers to agree to authorize launching their nuclear torpedoes, but he only persuaded one. The other was Vasily Arkhipov. He talked the captain down, and the sub came up. Arkhipov's stabilizing efforts may have literally saved the world.

Some systems need to be destroyed, others reconfigured, and still others stabilized. The rapid change in attitudes toward gay people and marriage equality in the US show we have the power to create progressive, not just positive, feedback loops. Vasily Arkhipov's story shows that there are even rare occasions when individual people find themselves with the power to stabilize an entire system and prevent the worst of all possible disasters.

Learning from Loops

There are no surefire ways to hasten or smother cascades of social change, but there are lessons to learn. Here are a few.

We May Be Very Far from Transformational Change; Then Again, We May Be Very Close

Working to create big structural change can be a lot like navigating a foreign land without a map. Would-be changemakers don't have landmarks to indicate how close or far they are from achieving their goals. Without a clear point of reference, even small increments of improvement can seem inconsequential, making it dispiriting to "settle" for them. This likely contributes to what many people experience as "climate anxiety." The problem feels enormous, and the proposed solutions are mind-stretchingly complex. Even when big victories are won, it's hard to be sure of their real impact. In 2022, the US passed the Inflation Reduction Act (IRA), which, despite its name, is less about inflation than about climate. It's the most significant piece of climate legislation the US has ever passed, and yet from a global perspective, even this can look like a drop in the bucket.

On the other hand, being in the dark about how far we are from a tipping point implies that truly transformational change may not be that far off. Many people dedicate their lives to making change, finding their efforts thwarted over and over until a hidden tipping point is crossed. Ignaz Semmelweis, the "savior of mothers," discovered in 1847 that women's odds of surviving childbirth dramatically increased if doctors washed their hands. His research was roundly ridiculed for decades and hadn't been accepted yet when he died in 1865. That was right around the time Louis Pasteur discovered germ theory and . . . yadda yadda yadda . . . now doctors wash their hands dozens of times every day and (almost) all the milk is pasteurized. We're often largely in the dark about how far away big changes are. For all we know, there might be one right around the corner.

Flapping Your Butterfly Wings: The Unpredictability of Social Phase Changes

June 17, 1972, seemed like just another Saturday night of making the rounds for security guard Frank Wills. Then he noticed some duct tape on a door and realized it was preventing the latch from locking. Wills ripped it off and resumed his rounds, only to find another piece of tape on the same lock when he circled back a half hour later. He hustled up the stairs to the lobby of the office building, the Watergate, and called the cops. Without realizing it, and just by doing his job well, Wills had discovered agents of the Nixon administration trying to break into and bug the Democratic National Committee office. Wills's phone call started a sequence of events that would lead to President Nixon's resignation two years and two months later.

Minor actions can set off cascades that lead, in a surprisingly short time, to major structural outcomes. This reflects a general feature of complex systems. Causal effects in such systems don't always build on each other in a smooth or continuous way. Sometimes they build nonlinearly, allowing seemingly small events to produce disproportionately large changes.

This is another reason that, as strong as it is, the temptation to compare the effects of individual actions to drops in a bucket can be profoundly misleading. When filling a bucket of water, each drop contributes the same amount. But interventions in complex systems don't work that way. Luckily, there's a better analogy nearby: when heating a bucket of water, not every degree of temperature change has the same incremental effect as the one before it. Some are transformational. For example, freezing and boiling reflect chemical tipping points. When one of those is crossed, a phase transition happens, and the properties of the entire bucket of water shift quickly and dramatically.

Like water, the social world is a complex system rife with tipping points. However, unlike water, we rarely know where the tipping points in the social world are. As a result, there's no recipe for creating cascades of change in complex social systems. But once again, there's another way to look at this. Like the storied butterfly that flapped its wings and caused a tornado halfway around the world, any of us could be on the brink of doing something that will change the world, even if we don't know where or when.

Being Conservative About Being Conservative About Social Change

Human beings have a long track record of earnestly trying to engineer incredibly complex systems to improve them, only to make things worse. The economist Horst Siebert gave a catchy name to these kinds of unintended consequences: the *cobra effect*. The story goes that the colonial British government in Delhi was fed up with the proliferation of venomous cobras, so it offered bounties to hunters who brought in cobra skins. The bounty program seemed to be going great, right up until the Delhiites figured out that they could just breed the cobras themselves instead of hunt them. Once the Brits realized that the bounty had become a perverse incentive, they canceled the program, at which point people released the cobras that they had been breeding, making the population of wild cobras even larger than it had been before the bounty.

The cobra effect sharpens the bind we're in. There are big problems. We have to do *something* and probably something big. But the big things we have to do risk unintended consequences. Should people bioengineer mosquitoes so that they can't carry malaria? Should we research ways of spraying sulfur dioxide into the stratosphere to reflect sunlight in hopes of cooling the overheated Earth?

The philosopher and economist Friedrich Hayek spearheaded modern libertarian skepticism about human beings' ability to understand and control complex social systems. Hayek argued that people understand their social systems far less than they think. As a result, he recommended caution. Since no one has a comprehensive grasp of how large complex social systems work, if people enact reforms too recklessly or hubristically, they can make things worse rather than better.

We agree with Hayek in one sense. Aspiring changemakers can be honest about what they don't know. This is especially true when pursuing structural change. One good way to grapple with that ignorance is by using the best tools available to investigate the likely effects of different proposals for change. That investigation should be informed, ideally, by empirical findings, modeling results, and detailed histories of relevant successes and failures. It's easy for all of us to breezily assume we know what works. But would-be changemakers should keep an open mind and be willing to adopt an experimental mindset that is sensitive to what data suggests about the downstream effects of their work. "Data" here can range from formal scientific studies to informal check-ins, with others and oneself, about whether a new policy seems to be helping, hurting, or doing nothing at all.

There is a duck to this rabbit, though, and a point where we think it's reasonable to get off the Hayek bandwagon. Yes, intellectual humility makes sense when it comes to intervening in complex systems. The effects of any specific effort to create change are difficult to predict. But so too are the effects of inaction, of not doing anything. There's no guarantee that our current course isn't heading into a cascade of looping effects that lead to disaster (and plenty of reasons to think it might be). We can't sit back and count on the world's negative feedback loops to keep things stable.

The consequences of action and inaction are both unknowable. This isn't to say they're the same. The status quo is more familiar than some hypothetical changed world. Elizabeth Kolbert's book *Under A White Sky* tells one tale after another of human beings falling prey to the cobra effect. A representative case: Central American cane toads were intentionally released in Australia in 1935 in hopes that they'd eat native beetles that were detrimental to sugarcane harvests. In the wild, the cane toads ignored the beetles but feasted on just about everything else. Today, there are about 200 million cane toads in Australia, and they're responsible for devastating populations of many native species, from northern quolls to goannas. (Quolls, goannas, and other animals get sick and die when they eat the toads, which are poisonous.) Before they released boatloads of imported cane toads into the outback, Australians had a pretty good sense of what a cane-toad-less future world would be like. (Pesty.) But they didn't have a good sense of what a future with them would be.

In the sorts of cases like racism and climate change that we've been concerned with in this book, expecting the future to resemble the past is a tougher sell. The status quo isn't static in these domains. There's no going back to how it was, but there's also no "new normal" on planet Earth as long as it keeps getting hotter and hotter, artificial intelligence grows smarter and smarter, and so on. *Not* taking action involves uncertainty and risk as well. What lies on the other side of that uncertainty and risk may be worse than the unexpected outcomes we risk by acting.

Incrementalism and Anti-Incrementalism

There's a reason coaches have to convince kids who are learning sports that the best they can do is improve little by little. The slow grind of incremental improvement is as unsexy as it gets. It's frustrating, unpleasant, and bor-ing. Who doesn't wish they could have the program for Kung Fu instanta-neously downloaded into their brain like Neo in *The Matrix*? (Alex gets as close as he can by listening to podcasts at 3.3 times speed.)

Change is hard to see. Your hair grows at a constant rate but mostly seems the same length from one day to the next. (Then one random morning—boom—you're in dire need of a haircut, Dan, you hippie.) In the same way, progress is difficult to see as progress when it happens incrementally.

One neat psychological study put this idea to the test. Across fourteen experiments and almost 11,000 participants, who shared their thoughts on twenty-five different issues, it found that people tend to have an all-or-nothing bias in their perception of change. They were asked, for example, to compare two manufacturing companies that had set out to become more sustainable. Neither company reached their sustainability goals after one year, but one had gotten much closer than the other. While some partici-pants acknowledged that one company had done better than the other, many lumped both "failures" together as "all the same." Worse are the demotivating effects of this all-or-nothing bias. People tend to check out when they see all failures as the same. They become disenchanted and stop trying. They question the intent and commitment of those who didn't achieve "complete" change.

We need to find ways of countering this bias, and the stakes are high. If someone thinks surpassing 1.5°C of global warming is unavoidable—and as of 2025, it looks nearly inevitable they'd be right—they become more likely to think the game is up and there's no point in continuing to try to prevent further warming. They'd be disastrously wrong, though. Every fraction of a degree makes an enormous difference. But the salience of that clearly stated threshold has a psychological effect, making it seem like an all-or-nothing goal. It becomes all too easy to think that any efforts failing to limit warm-ing to 1.5°C are futile, that they don't matter and all is lost, but also that if we succeed in limiting warming to 1.5°C, we can declare "Mission Accom-plished" and the climate crisis solved; all the work is done. The first part is probably the most worrisome, though—once people set their sights on a goal, failing to meet it makes them susceptible to giving up.

We suspect that this anti-incrementalism bias reverberates widely. Reduc-ing infant mortality can feel like no progress at all as long as inequities in infant care related to race and poverty remain. Most people aren't aware that US carbon and greenhouse gas pollution has been declining since its peak between 2005 and 2007. Most people—across the political spectrum— think that Black incarceration rates have continued increasing since 2006, when they've actually declined by 35 percent.

These improvements are not nearly enough, but they're real and important. They're evidence that collective efforts to turn the tide can work. It's maddening when they go unreported and uncelebrated.

Incrementalism can be a real distraction, of course, like when fossil fuel companies—against all the best science and economics—try to convince us that we need to invest in natural gas as a "bridge fuel" before renewables are ready for prime time. Advocating incrementalism in the face of massive injustice can invite the often-fair criticism that "justice delayed is justice denied." But this shouldn't cloud serious assessments of what counts as progress or be taken as reason not to celebrate small victories. The takeaway here is not about defending incremental progress. It's about not getting defeated by it.

Onward to Organizing   Back in chapter 1, we cited evidence that the film *An Inconvenient Truth* raised awareness about the climate crisis but failed to inspire palpable changes in the public's behavior. (We speculated that its individualist recommendations for tackling the problem were partly to blame.) But the truth is we don't really know for sure what incremental long-term effects the film has had on inspiring people to take action. It could have seeded ideas that took a while to bear fruit, whether or not social scientists ever figure out how to measure the film's impact.

History has a way of defying expectations. In 2018, in the wake of yet another mass shooting, students in Parkland, Florida, walked out of their classes to demand gun reform. It might be tempting to see their efforts as just one more failure, and the effects their protests ultimately have on gun control will be difficult to say. But here's one effect we know they did have: inspiring a fifteen-year-old Swedish girl by the name of Greta Thunberg to start a school strike to protest climate change.

One way unexpected consequences are brought about is by one social movement spilling over into another. That's where we'll head next, to take a both/and look at the promise and peril of social movements. If we're going to light a fire for social change, it's going to need little things like sparks and kindling and oxygen to get lit.

III Putting It into Practice

9 Social Movements and Structural Change

Seeing Power in the Collective

"Tinkering is for mechanics, not racial justice advocates," writes Michelle Alexander in *The New Jim Crow*, "If we can agree that what is needed now, at this critical juncture, is not more tinkering or tokenism, but as King insisted . . . a 'radical restructuring of our society,' then perhaps we can also agree that a radical restructuring of our approach to racial justice advocacy is in order as well. . . . I argue that nothing short of a major social movement can successfully dismantle the new caste system." For Alexander, like Martin Luther King Jr. before her, real structural change is only possible through widespread collective action. Stop sweating the small stuff and start the revolution.

Social movements can be powerful and sometimes change doesn't happen without them. But their power doesn't come from refusing to tinker or sweat the small stuff. Their effectiveness is grounded not in some big magic power they have but in a million smaller interconnections that bind their members together. Social movement power comes from people speaking to and strategizing with each other—taking the *right* small steps—to organize, show up, and keep pushing to create structural conditions that allow these movements to thrive. As is often the case, the wrong kind of tinkering can be distracting, even damaging. The right kind can do wonders.

Social movements like this one are, for many people, what first comes to mind when they think about what brings about big structural change. There's good reason for this: social movements can and have achieved great things. Still, their odds of success are long, and they can go sideways in all kinds of ways.

Creating a social movement is like lighting a fire—both require essential ingredients. Fires need something flammable, like wood, and oxygen to burn. Without these background conditions in place, no fire would light. Background conditions must be in place for social movements to take off, too. They need public places where their message will be seen, and organizers need networks of social relationships to take advantage of. And money. They always need money.

But those are background conditions. Neither fires nor social movements start themselves. Fires need a spark to start burning. Social movements often need attention-grabbing, catalyzing events to make big leaps in their numbers and influence. And then those people already in the movement, who have already been showing up day after day and are committed to the cause, need to be able to capitalize on those events to fan the spark into real change. But how?

We'll explore this question by looking at two examples, one highlighting the individuals who create a spark and another highlighting the background conditions that enable and sustain the flames.

"My Kind of Trouble": How Troublemakers Make Movements

Chris Smalls (figure 9.1) sparked one of the most shocking and successful unionization movements in the twenty-first century. Growing up in Hackensack, New Jersey, he was an athlete good enough to have NBA aspirations. But he was hit by a car as a teenager, ending his basketball career. He tried community college in Florida but gave it up to make music in New York. Smalls wasn't doing badly in the hip-hop scene, even touring briefly with chart-topping rapper Meek Mill. But when his wife had twins, Smalls took jobs at Walmart and Home Depot and then added graveyard shifts at FedEx and Target warehouses. In 2015, he started working as a "picker" at an Amazon warehouse in New Jersey. By 2018, he had moved up to assistant manager at the JFK8 warehouse in Staten Island. Then things got interesting.

Smalls says he liked working at Amazon but began noticing what he describes as "deep systemic" problems with the company. Black and brown people weren't being promoted, caregivers with kids or family at home weren't given any help, and safety protocols were inadequate and ignored. On March 30, 2020, as COVID-19 ripped through New York City,

Figure 9.1
Chris Smalls. Brendan McDermid/Reuters.

Smalls collaborated with fellow JFK8 employee Derrick Palmer to arrange a walkout to demand personal protective equipment and better quarantine protections.

During this hellish first three months of the pandemic, about 20,000 New Yorkers died from COVID-19. According to the CDC, the average fatality rate in New York City during this period for anyone who contracted it was almost 10 percent, though that number was even higher for Black and Hispanic New Yorkers. Amazon's response to the walkout for better protection was callous; it fired Smalls that same day. The company's senior vice president for policy and press, Jay Carney (who was formerly press secretary for President Trump), offered as justification that Smalls had violated Amazon's social distancing guidelines.

Along with Palmer and a small group of dedicated coworkers, Smalls responded by organizing. They started The Congress of Essential Workers (TCOEW), which orchestrated May Day strikes and "Prime Day" protests.

They marched to Amazon CEO Jeff Bezos's mansion in Beverly Hills on Prime Day, demanding $2/hour raises in front of his $165 million home. Public support for Smalls and TCOEW exploded when an internal Amazon memo referring to Smalls as "not smart or articulate" was leaked to *Vice*. According to the reporting, the company's General Counsel David Zapolsky thought it would make good PR to paint Smalls—who didn't shy away from dressing "Black," wearing sweats, sneakers, and durags to meetings and public appearances—as "the face of the entire union/organizing movement."

All this caught the attention of New York's Attorney General Letitia James, who opened an investigation into Smalls's firing, ultimately finding it illegal. New York Mayor Bill DeBlasio commented on the case, as did Representative Alexandra Ocasio-Cortez. Eventually, nine US Senators sent a letter to Amazon demanding information about the firing of whistleblowers like Smalls.

Meanwhile, Smalls, Palmer, and other organizers focused on gathering signatures for a union authorization vote. The audacity of this effort is hard to overstate. Amazon is infamous for its aggressive and successful union busting. Even more impressive, Smalls and company did it without the affiliation of a national union, which one long-time labor organizer described to us as "bananas." Nevertheless, Smalls sat in a tent by the JFK8 bus stop day after day, providing workers information about the benefits of unionization. Palmer strategically sought out leaders of social cliques. "What I'll do is study a group of friends and go to the leader of the pack," he said. "Whatever the leader says, the rest of the group is going to do."

Angelika Maldonado was another early organizer. Since Amazon had a policy prohibiting workers from talking about the union on company time, she made sure someone was always in the break room to field questions. A chat group, on the mobile messaging app Telegram, grew with curious members, though as Maldonado put it, "to be honest, the chat wasn't that big a concern for us; the main thing was the face-to-face interactions. I think that's really what got the union going."

It took nine months, until January of the following year, to gather enough signatures to petition the National Labor Relations Board to hold a vote. On April 1, 2022, the workers at JFK8 voted 2,654 to 2,131 in favor of unionization, and with that vote, the first union at a US Amazon warehouse was approved. Smalls said, "We want to thank Jeff Bezos for going to space, because while he was up there we were organizing a union." At a visit to the White House a month later, President Biden told Smalls, "I like you, you're my kind of trouble."

This win didn't by itself overcome the systemic problems Smalls noticed when he started at Amazon, of course. Even replicating the group's initial success was difficult. Smalls's Amazon Labor Union helped to organize a unionization vote at another Staten Island warehouse, LDJ5, in May of 2022, but there the warehouse workers voted it down. Labor historian Janice Fine put it in context: "The history of unions is always about failing forward . . . workers trying, workers losing, workers trying again."

If they eventually succeed, unions can do a lot of good. They increase wages and benefits for workers, and as we saw in chapter 5, they can also be powerful locales for building trust and friendship across social differences like race or religion. They provide unique opportunities for people of different backgrounds to work cooperatively together toward shared goals. Diverse unions have acted like schools for cross-racial cooperation for a long time.

On top of reducing the racial biases of their members, unions can boost support for policies that promote racial equity in the workforce. When white waterfront workers decided to strike in post-Civil War New Orleans, they realized they needed to work across racial lines to prevent companies from simply turning to Black workers. Three Black and white unions formed a consortium—the Triple Alliance—that later shut down the Port of New Orleans and won major gains for workers. They also adopted a race-conscious policy called "half-and-half" that required crews to include equal numbers of Black and white workers.

Of course, unions aren't always forces for good (see chapter 5). Labor unions for mining, fracking, and harvesting fossil fuels have been some of the most powerful actors standing in the way of state and federal climate legislation for decades. They can also be internally corrupt. Trade unions have a long history of acting in racially and sexually discriminatory ways. Police unions reflexively defend members even in the most egregious cases of the abuse of power.

But at their best, unions can be fertile ground for promoting intergroup harmony, both/and thinking, and initiating and sustaining social change. Their influence has been in decline for the past couple decades, but there are signs that the decline is slowing. Indeed, 2022 was a banner year. Unionization efforts won more elections in the first half of 2022 than in any of the previous 20 years, with those 641 elections achieving a success rate of over 75 percent. And the share of Americans who say they approve of unions rose to over 70 percent, higher than at any time since 1965. Although the overall percentage of American workers in a union still declined slightly in 2022, there's room for optimism that more organizers like Smalls can start bending back the curve.

Sparks go out quickly without the right stuff to burn. But without any kind of spark to ignite it, there's no fire. Movements need the right people at the right place at the right time. Smalls, Palmer, and Maldonado were those people for JFK8.

Latin America's Green Tide and the Structural Preconditions of a Social Movement

Predicting those people and times and places is difficult, to say the least. It's hard to tell if the oxygen is there, ready to burn, until afterwards. Many sparks fail to start fires where conditions seem right, while others flare up into fires where nobody would have expected. Few movements in recent history provide as good an example of this as the Green Tide.

In 2021, Texas enacted what were then the most severe abortion restrictions in the United States, banning all procedures after six weeks of pregnancy. Shortly after, Mexican feminist activists sprang into action, sending abortion pills to Texan women and offering free advice over the phone about how to use them. These activists upend a long-standing image of the United States as more progressive on reproductive rights than its neighbors to the south. And they also represent just a sliver of an increasingly successful movement across Latin America. For example, Argentina's Congress legalized abortion in 2020, and Colombia's Constitutional Court and Mexico's Supreme Court decriminalized it in 2022 and 2023, respectively.

This Green Tide movement, named after the color of the bandannas worn by members, started in Argentina in the early aughts and has been spreading through Latin America since. Much of the Green Tide's success is connected to urbanization, as Latin American cities have grown quickly and the region is now 80 percent urban (by population). Movement activism there relies on interconnected, densely populated areas for public displays of messaging and meeting up. Political graffiti and murals are ubiquitous.

Shared physical space is easy to overlook, but it's a crucial ingredient. Much like union members who work side by side, people who live in the same city neighborhood have more opportunities to witness others in successful acts of resistance. As we discussed in chapters 5 and 7, these kinds of shoulder-to-shoulder interactions are vital both for reducing prejudice and for persuading people that resistance is alive and thriving. These are just a few of the key background structures that, when in place, provide wind to fan the flames of a growing movement.

Gains made in economic independence and social mobility were also key background factors. Many of these trends predated the stunning twenty-first-century growth of feminist movements in the region and so preceded the Green Tide. The size of these social and economic gains reflected how far many Latin American countries still had to go. Through the better part of the twentieth century, women's freedom to work was severely restricted. Legislation prevented them from opening bank accounts, signing contracts, and appearing in court. Men made the laws, holding more than 90 percent of lower or unicameral legislature seats through most of the 1990s.

Beginning in the 1970s, in part due to reductions in teen pregnancy, gains in education, and spikes in economic insecurity, more women joined the labor market. Movement organizing began to rise along with the number of working women. These changes reinforced positive feedback loops, like those we sketched in the previous chapter, where success begets success.

Women are taking more leadership positions, too. Improvements in education, reproductive justice, and labor power have corresponded with greater gender parity in legislative representation under both left- and right-wing governments. As of 2023, eleven countries in Latin America have passed reforms requiring gender parity, for example, among candidates for the legislature. Women comprise around half of at least one chamber of congress in Argentina, Bolivia, Costa Rica, Ecuador, Mexico, and Nicaragua. As Mexican Senator Adriana Díaz put it, "[it] is not making space [for women], it is not implementing a quota, it is sharing in decision-making so that together we [men and women] can be co-responsible in the true development and advance of democracy."

Changes in global economic conditions have pushed more women into urban centers and the labor market, which highlighted inequities in their political rights, which fostered organizing, which led to successful structural changes in political representation, which in turn gave women a greater voice in Latin American politics and culture. This greater voice feeds back into the process, inspiring more organizers to persist in the struggle for gender justice.

The Green Tide has its own charismatic fire starters, like Sibila Sotomayor Van Rysseghem, Daffne Valdés Vargas, and Paula Cometa Stange. Together, they make up the Chilean feminist, trans-inclusive collective LasTesis. After they performed their protest song, "Un Violador en Tu Camino" ("A Rapist in Your Path"), in front of a police station in 2019, the song went viral on social media. Soon, huge crowds of blindfolded women were singing and performing the coordinated dance in major cities like Santiago, Mexico City, and Bogotá.

All kinds of factors need to come together for a movement to grow and succeed. It requires the right leaders, where "right" includes personality traits like moral charisma and the creativity to bring people together. Those leaders also need to fit well into the structures and circumstances in which they operate. They have to possess the know-how that will allow them to align their strategies with the specifics of their situation. When it all comes together, social movements have the potential to rise in visibility very quickly.

Still, even when all these stars align, movements fail far more than they succeed. But there are lessons to be learned in those cases too.

Learning from Movement Failures

Social movements come up short for all kinds of reasons. But a common flaw is getting the relations between systems and people wrong. Consider a few examples.

#MeToo and the Perils of Overly Individualist Movements

#MeToo took off in 2017 after Alyssa Milano's tweet on October 15 (figure 9.2). The tweet appeared about a week after stories were published in the *New York Times* and the *New Yorker* about Harvey Weinstein's long history of sexual abuse. Within two weeks, 1.7 million tweets originating in over eighty-five countries had used the #MeToo hashtag.

A less well-known figure in the story of #MeToo is Tarana Burke, a Black organizer from the Bronx who had worked for decades fighting sexual violence. By 2017, she'd been leading what she called "Me Too" workshops

Alyssa Milano ✓
@Alyssa_Milano   ···

If you've been sexually harassed or assaulted write 'me too' as a reply to this tweet.

Figure 9.2

aimed at raising "empowerment through empathy" for eleven years. These created a safe space for survivors of sexual violence, a space where, as Burke puts it, "healing is a form of action" and "taking action helps us to heal." When Burke learned that #MeToo was exploding online, her first reaction was understandably frustrated: "This can't happen," I said through my tears. "Not like this! Y'all know if these white women start using this hashtag, and it gets popular, they will never believe that a Black woman in her forties from the Bronx has been building a movement for the same purposes, using those exact words, for years now. It will be over."

The minimization of Burke's role in #MeToo can be viewed as a parable about social movements in the age of internet virality. On the one hand, #MeToo was a powerful and progressive moment in American history. It educated the country about the pervasiveness of sexual violence and misconduct, much as Burke had set out to do eleven years earlier. It helped bring down serial abusers and rapists in high-profile positions, from producer Harvey Weinstein to New York Governor Andrew Cuomo. It proved how quickly an idea can catch on, precisely because we are all so tightly interconnected, making up the increasingly dense fabric of each other's situations.

But #MeToo was no unmitigated success. Although it led to the ousting of a handful of extremely powerful individuals, critics claim its impact on the lives of ordinary people has been small. Most of its victories, they say, were symbolic. For starters, rates of sexual harassment and assault have not declined. Some limited evidence suggests that while the targets and victims of these behaviors are a little more likely to report them, upticks in reporting have not corresponded with more perpetrators being held accountable. And those who report being targeted remain just as likely to suffer retaliation: further assaults, gaslighting, demotions, firings.

Recall how Angelika Maldonado downplayed the value of the virtual when she was organizing Amazon workers. What really "got the union going," she said, "was the face-to-face interactions." Maldonado's lesson puts in stark relief the contrast between the high-profile online discourse surrounding #MeToo and the near invisibility of grassroots activists like Tarana Burke, who had been working week after week on building in-person connections.

Genuine progress involves not just one-off takedowns of celebrity wrong-doers but also nationwide changes in the conditions of everyday people's lives. Assessing the overall effects of #MeToo will require nuanced and long-term study, but it's reasonable to ask how much #MeToo has moved from conversation and symbol to collective action and structural change.

In fact, there's some reason to think that things have gone in the other direction. In 1994, 58 percent of high school seniors disagreed with the idea that "it's usually better for everyone involved if the man is the achiever out-side the home and the woman takes care of the home and family." By 2014, that number had *fallen* to 42 percent. As of 2017, only 25 percent of millennial women, and 15 percent of millennial men, consider themselves feminists.

Jump ahead to 2022, five years after the spark of Alyssa Milano's initial tweet, and the needle didn't appear to have moved. A poll by the Southern Poverty Law Center found that 46 percent of Democratic men under fifty believed that feminism "has done more harm than good," and 60 percent of this same group believed that "men should be represented and valued more in our society." While just 10 percent of older Democratic women shared this dim view of feminism, the percentage more than doubled to 23 percent among younger Democratic women. The rise in support for Trump since 2016 among both young men and women of all racial and ethnic groups suggests tolerance for sexism is growing.

The public turn against feminism coincides with a broader trend of legal and political setbacks for gender justice that stretches back decades. Many laws and norms protecting the lives of women and pregnant people have been rolled back, the most notable (so far) being the US Supreme Court's 2022 decision in *Dobbs v. Jackson's Women's Health Organization* that rejected the Constitutional right to abortion. While *Dobbs* sparked plenty of out-rage, and 2022 voters in several states from California to Kansas responded by voting in support of reproductive justice, it is still too early—at the time we're writing this—to tell whether a sustained, organized, and effective resistance movement is emerging.

The overturning of *Roe* was not caused by inadequacies in the #MeToo movement. But it is still fair to ask whether #MeToo has (so far) helped stem the overall tide of setbacks—either in terms of individual attitudes or in terms of laws and structures. A common and not unreasonable view of #MeToo is that in its sudden rise, it became too white, too online, and too individualist. Some think it erred by focusing too much attention on celebrity villains and not enough on systemic change and that the solutions it offered were about overcoming personal traumas rather than creating collective action.

Some skeptics of #MeToo also criticized the movement for embracing a professionalized version of feminism associated with Facebook's former chief operating officer, Sheryl Sandberg. In her 2013 bestseller, *Lean In: Women, Work, and the Will to Lead*, Sandberg implored women to assert themselves to get ahead, but her critics noted that the details of her message indicated that it was mainly aimed at highly educated and otherwise privileged women. Like so many other examples we've explored in this book, *Lean In* has been criticized for foisting responsibility onto individual women to better "assert themselves" in response to sexism, rather than turning attention to the sexist people and structures standing in their way.

As Susan Faludi said in *The New York Times*,

> Pop feminism's Achilles' heel is a faith in the power of the individual star turn over communal action, the belief that a gold-plated influencer plus a subscription list plus some viral content can be alchemized into mass activism. The #MeToo campaign, as it evolved, was driven in no small measure by that faith—likewise Ms. Sandberg's "Lean In," a "movement" of free-standing C-suite aspirants, each of whom was instructed to defeat her "internal obstacles" to get ahead as an individual rather than organize to defeat external forces. That ethic made it attractive to the professional class but of little use to the great mass of working women.

Data seems to back up these observations. After the 2016 election, one poll found that only 20 percent of millennial women rejected the idea that feminism "is about personal choice, not politics."

We can't help but wonder whether a larger hurdle that #MeToo failed to overcome was the individualist mindset so entrenched in American culture. Indeed, Faludi's both/and diagnosis is that "the new individualist style of feminism so often cast itself as an alternative instead of as an aid to the old-fashioned communal activism."

From another perspective, #MeToo may not have been individualist enough, or at least it may not have paid attention to the right individuals in the right way. It failed to credit and celebrate hardworking organizers like Tarana Burke, who had been taking activism beyond hashtags for a long time.

Unintended Consequences

Social movements, like so much else in life, don't always go as planned. Sometimes their members pursue structural changes that sound great in theory only to see their efforts backfire when they run up against the complicated and conflicted minds of actual people. Even what seems like an obvious fix can make things worse. As we saw in chapter 8, sometimes a scheme to kill off cobras just creates more cobras.

A challenge for people in the United States who have spent time in jail is that many employers can, and sometimes must (by law), ask all applicants to "check a box" if they have a criminal record. As a result, formerly incarcerated people have a very hard time finding employment, which in turn makes them more likely to become desperate to make ends meet, re-offend, and then end up back in prison.

In one field study done in Milwaukee, the odds of getting a callback for an interview were 34 percent for white male applicants with no criminal record but only 17 percent for white men with a criminal record. The odds were 14 percent for Black male applicants without a record but only 5 percent for Black men with a record. Follow-up studies in New York City found much the same: people with a criminal record—especially Black and Latinx people—face a terrible challenge in landing a job. In the NYC studies, nineteen out of twenty formerly incarcerated people of color didn't make it past the initial screening, even just to land an interview, let alone secure the job.

An intuitive solution? "Ban the box." Restrict employers' ability to demand that applicants report their criminal records. This fix is typically construed as structural since it aims to increase racial equity without having to persuade anyone to be less prejudiced. It's changing the context of employer decision-making without requiring anyone to change their biases. As of October 2021, and as the result of a lot of movement organizing, 37 states and over 150 cities have adopted some form of ban the box policy.

These were celebrated as victories, but they may not have delivered what advocates hoped. One study compared employment rates in regions before and after banning the box and found that low-skilled Black and Latinx men were marginally *less* likely to be employed after banning the box than before. Banning the box in this case appeared to reduce discrimination against formerly incarcerated people but increase discrimination against applicants of color with clean records. Why?

A plausible hypothesis is that if employers aren't sure about whether a candidate has a criminal record, then that uncertainty provides an opening for racial bias to exert more influence on their decisions. Employers who cannot ask up front about criminal histories may (consciously or unconsciously) just assume that Black and brown applicants have sketchy backgrounds. Researchers point to "a growing literature showing that well-intentioned policies that remove information about negative characteristics can do more harm than good." As Michelle Alexander put it, "banning the box is not enough. We must also get rid of the mind-set that puts Black men 'in the box.'"

The social world is complicated, and the effects of even simple policies that seem like they can't miss are difficult to foresee. Banning the box inadvertently gives people's racial biases more room to operate. It provides another reminder that everything in the US is two degrees removed from race, that racial prejudice is never far from the scene.

Examples like this also illustrate once again the Return of the Allegedly Irrelevant. Some critics of individualist approaches to structural racism endorse "policy change over mental change" and for "policies that directly increase racial equality and participation" rather than "changing attitudes." They hold that the biases in our heads are irrelevant to creating bigger, far-reaching change. These critics might, we imagine, have advocated for ban the box campaigns in the following way:

> If we want to fight oppression against formerly incarcerated people of color, our movement shouldn't bother trying to change individuals' racial biases. These prejudices are irrelevant and are too hard to dislodge anyway. We shouldn't bother with moral persuasion. Instead, we should make simple and direct structural changes to our racist hiring procedures. The main obstacle to this isn't prejudice; it's the existing structures of power. So, we need a massive social movement to win power.

But the reality of banning the box shows otherwise. The allegedly irrelevant returns. Even "successful" efforts to change hiring procedures can make things worse when they fail to account for individual factors like psychological biases.

The critics might double down. Rather than grant that individuals' prejudices are relevant after all, they might offer a different diagnosis of the shortcomings of ban the box campaigns: they're just a tweak. They're a minor change and so are not structural enough. Real structural change, they might claim, is not just about which boxes people have to tick on a form. That's the sort of incremental tinkering Michelle Alexander thinks we should leave to the mechanics. Real structural change involves deeper and more wide-reaching transformations to prevailing social practices, like, say, passing a new amendment to the US Constitution. Surely that would do it.

Failed Successes

Americans used to drink *a lot* of alcohol. One reason was that drinking water often made people sick, and beer was generally safer because fermentation kills bacteria. This led the National Women's Christian Temperance Union to campaign in the late 1800s for structures making safe water easier to drink: public water fountains. So-called temperance fountains sprang up in cities across the country. The James Fountain in Union Square in NYC started off as a temperance fountain. In Washington, DC, a fountain simply known as *the* "Temperance Fountain" has a life-sized stone heron on top of a pair of carved dolphins, from whose snouts visitors drank water. But structural changes to the water supply weren't enough to stem the flow of booze. The temperance movement set their sights higher.

The Eighteenth Amendment to the US Constitution, ratified in 1919, made it illegal to produce, transport, or sell "intoxicating" liquors. Prohibition ensued. While it officially started in 1919, it was the result of a century of movement building and hard-fought political struggle. It's probably more accurate to say "movements" since the temperance movement that led to the Eighteenth Amendment was entwined with many strands of American politics, from progressive populism to religious revivals to racist nativism.

Some of the issues bringing this coalition together feel anachronistic—especially the moralistic ones about the inherent evils of any amount of alcohol—but others remain familiar. The Anti-Saloon League (ASL)—the group most focused on getting political results at the time—tied excessive drinking to domestic and sexual violence. In this it seems they were right: domestic abuse sharply declined during Prohibition. No surprise that women were disproportionate supporters of the movement.

But alcohol did not stay illegal for long. In 1933, the Twenty-First Amendment repealed the Eighteenth, a mere fourteen years after Prohibition began. It's the only amendment ever passed in the US that repealed another amendment. One reason for its unpopularity was that Prohibition fueled organized crime. Keeping a whole industry outlawed in the midst of the Great Depression was also terrible economics. Banning alcohol was effective in getting people to drink less, even leading to 20 percent declines in deaths from liver cirrhosis, but that wasn't enough to make Prohibition popular.

In fact, the Eighteenth Amendment never enjoyed popular support, even when it was initially passed. That legislative victory was the result of a highly mobilized and politically effective interest group. Their initial success provides an excellent example of the way a well-organized social movement can achieve its goals even when the democratic will of the majority opposes them. By forming coalitions with anyone who would sign onto their one single issue—from Klansmen to liberal internationalists—and by raising enormous amounts of money, the ASL was able to dictate terms to politicians. As one historian put it, they could say, "Are you with us or are you against us? . . . if you are against us we will defeat you. And if you are with us we will elect you."

But in the end, Prohibition turned out to be a colossal "failed success." It's notable because, for many Americans at least, nothing epitomizes the fantasy of "deep" and "durable" structural change like amending the Constitution itself. Think for a moment about how hard it is to even imagine the US passing an amendment in the twenty-first century about anything, let alone a momentous one that secured reproductive freedom for all or curbed the right to bear arms. On top of that, even if such an amendment were passed, if it was unpopular enough, or triggered a strong enough backlash, then it could also be repealed. When people don't support the changes they make, even amendments can be amended. And even if they are popular, it remains possible for nine unelected lifetime judges to reinterpret clearly written amendments in ways that eviscerate them.

The point is decidedly *not* that anyone should give up trying to make changes to the system. Rather, the point is that the pursuit of structural change is no alternative to the hard and grinding work of persuading our peers to support that change. Even momentous successes that are the culmination of decades of organizing can fail to stick when they get the people wrong. Change endures when it's etched just as deeply into our hearts and minds as it is into our most basic laws.

Prohibition didn't last long, and temperance fountains also went by the boards. Cities couldn't maintain them, and people found them unsightly. *The New York Times* called them "dismal and horrific effigies" and "crimes against . . . taste . . . and the common sense of mankind, warping the aesthetic instincts of babes unborn and perverting the ideas of infants." Few remained operational for long.

Of Minds and Movements

An important lesson of unsuccessful structural reforms is that even when they are achieved, they aren't guaranteed to last. Even the most apparently rock-solid changes to the founding documents of a country are durable only insofar as people support—or at least tolerate—them.

This is no vindication of the priority of individuals over structures. Even the power of the US president to enact reform is constrained in countless ways: by Congress's support of the president's agenda, by a Supreme Court that might overturn executive orders, by the staff who give the president information about what various policies will do, and so on. A justice of the Supreme Court might get outvoted by other justices. Even if you as an individual had the power to snap your fingers like the Avengers' nemesis Thanos and change social reality itself, someone else might change it all back. Some social changes do last longer than others, though. The next chapter looks to figure out why.

10 Lighting the Spark: Social Identity, Collective Action, and Making a Difference

A Movement Born of Murder

After getting out of school on March 3, 1931, Harlon Carter arrived at his home in Laredo, Texas, to find his mother in distress. She claimed to have seen three "Hispanic" boys hovering around their property. Could they be behind the recent theft of the family car? Carter, who was seventeen years old, grabbed his father's shotgun and went out to find them. The three boys he found at a nearby swimming hole—who may or may not have been the three his mother said she saw—were between the ages of twelve and fifteen. Carter insisted that they return with him to his house. The oldest, Ramón Casiano, refused and then reportedly pulled out a knife and told Carter to leave them alone. Carter responded by shooting Casiano in the center of his chest, killing him almost instantly. He was eventually convicted of murder and sentenced to three years in prison.

Sixty-one years after Carter murdered fifteen-year-old Ramón Casiano, the National Rifle Association named its most prestigious award after him. The Harlon B. Carter Legislative Achievement Award is given each year by the NRA to a politician who has most loyally worked to prevent gun restrictions from being enacted in the United States.

Despicable as he was, Carter deserves to be the award's namesake. He spearheaded the transformation of the NRA from a marginal hobby group for hunters into a major player in American politics. Carter took advantage of one of the deepest features of human psychology: people want—need—to feel like they belong. As we explored in chapter 6, it's human nature to be social. What Carter's story exemplifies is the power of using this part of human nature in the service of social change. Nothing lights the fire like appealing to "group identity," the sense of who *we* are and what *we're* all about.

Whatever one thinks about the NRA's values and aims (shocker: we're not fans!), it has been extraordinarily successful in its pursuit of them. It would be a mistake to not try and learn from their success.

The NRA's Remarkable Rise to Power

Not long after being released from prison in 1935, Carter joined the newly formed US Border Patrol. He rose through the ranks and by 1954 had taken control of an overtly racist and xenophobic federal deportation program named "Operation Wetback," which carried out the new-for-its-time idea of military-style tactics to remove Mexican immigrants from the US. Carter joined the national board of the NRA in 1951 and served as president from 1965 to 1967.

This was a transitional time for the organization. For decades, it had been a sportsman's association, focused on hunting, marksmanship, and recreational shooting. By the time Carter took over, the issue of gun control was gaining steam across the country. The murders of prominent leaders from John and Bobby Kennedy to Malcolm X and Martin Luther King Jr. led people to question whether high-powered weapons should be accessible to the public.

But many of the concerns about guns—and the concerns that got the most traction—became racialized. In the summer of 1967, American cities like Detroit and Newark had been wracked by waves of intense protests focused on racial discrimination. A 1968 federal report laid much of the blame for the violence on the easy availability of guns.

California's response was one of the first and clearest. It was set in motion on May 2, 1967, when thirty armed members of the Black Panthers approached the statehouse in Sacramento to demand justice. Before entering, Bobby Seale (who two years later would cofound the Black Panthers' Free Breakfast for School Children Program; see chapter 3) told the crowd of reporters, "Black people have begged, prayed, petitioned, demonstrated, and everything else to get the racist power structure of America to right the wrongs which have historically been perpetuated against Black people." To protect themselves "against this terror," the Panthers claimed the right to carry loaded guns in public. In response, California's overwhelmingly white legislature immediately created new gun restrictions.

On July 28, 1967, Republican Governor Ronald Reagan signed the Mulford Act, which prohibited carrying loaded firearms without a permit. Reagan said he saw "no reason why on the street today a citizen should be carrying loaded weapons" and that guns were a "ridiculous way to solve problems that have to be solved among people of good will." In a move that would be unimaginable a few decades later, the NRA endorsed the bill.

When the NRA also came out in support of parts of the federal Gun Control Act of 1968—which quickly followed California's law—Carter broke with the group. He wrote a letter to the NRA membership articulating ideas now all too familiar to twenty-first-century Americans. "We can win it on a simple concept," he wrote. "No compromise. No gun legislation." He opposed background checks for gun purchasers, arguing that the possibility of guns in the hands of "violent criminals" and the "mentally ill" is the "price we pay for freedom."

About a decade later, at an infamous all-night NRA membership meeting, Carter emerged victorious from what became known as the "Revolt in Cincinnati." He and his followers voted out the leadership and changed the organization's bylaws. Over the next few years, Carter led the Institute for Legislative Action, the NRA's lobbying wing, transforming it into a powerhouse dedicated to defeating gun control. NRA membership tripled during this time, and its budget and influence skyrocketed. Carter's villainy aside, it's hard to deny his success.

Before researching this, we had assumed the problem was just how deeply Americans love their guns. But this turns out to be too simple. A remarkable feature of the NRA's influence is how persistently unpopular its platform has been. Most Americans want more gun control. In 2019, 60 percent of Americans said that gun laws should be made stricter, while only 11 percent said they should be made less strict.

While there are partisan splits over guns, there is overwhelming bipartisan support for specific restrictions. Ninety-three percent of Democrats and 82 percent of Republicans favor making background checks mandatory for private gun sales and at gun shows. In fact, clear majorities of both gun owners in general (61.6 percent) as well as *Republican gun owners* (57.4 percent) believe that people should have to pass a safety course before buying

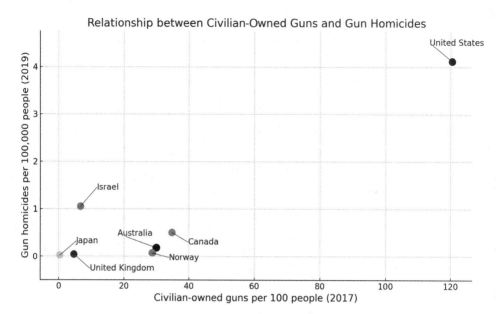

Figure 10.1

Gun ownership and homicide rates in developed countries. Small Arms Survey.

a gun. And yet restrictions like these have been repeatedly blocked. Compared to other countries, what gun laws the US does have on the books are weak. Their laxness is especially striking given how outrageously unparalleled gun violence is in the US (figure 10.1).

We had also assumed that the gun lobby was massively well-funded. But it turns out that much of the NRA's influence predates its political spending. Other interest groups spend far more than the NRA and come away with far less to show for it.

For years we also expected that the mounting number of tragic experiences with guns would eventually turn the tide. Had you offered us a bet that an event like the Sandy Hook massacre would be severe enough to finally push through significant gun control legislation, we would have taken it. We similarly would have guessed that victims of gun violence in the gun-owning community itself would make a difference. Gun owners remain far more likely to die from gun violence than non-gun owners, and the lion's share of gun-related deaths in the US are due to accidents, escalating fights, and suicide. An example: having a handgun in the house makes someone seven times more likely to be killed by their spouse or partner.

Women make up 84 percent of victims in these domestic partner killings. But the proximity of gun owners to tragic violence hasn't moved the needle.

The Rifleman: From Killer to Kingmaker

How has the NRA managed to hold the line with public opinion, tens of thousands of personal tragedies, and regular eruptions of mass outrage stacked against it? Matthew Lacombe, a political scientist at Case Western Reserve University, took a novel route to answering this question. He analyzed seventy-nine years of *American Rifleman*, the official magazine of the NRA, along with decades of letters written to the editors of four major newspapers by NRA members. He wanted to understand how the NRA framed discussions of gun control and used that framing to win power.

Lacombe concluded that the NRA succeeded by crafting and publicizing a specific social identity. Over and over, articles in *American Rifleman* emphasized the positive traits of gun owners and talked about them as a group of people who shared a distinctive identity. The articles also used the language of conflict, threat, and victimhood. Gun owners were depicted as a besieged group whose rights were at risk of being taken away by outsiders.

Lacombe traced this identity- and conflict-soaked language from the NRA's communications with its members directly into the opinion pieces those members sent to newspapers. *American Rifleman* was the source of four of the five most identity-related terms and phrases—including popular terms like "antigunner" and "freedom loving"—found in opinion pieces. Two-thirds of the editorials portrayed gun rights as under threat. Nearly all the editorials Lacombe analyzed—90 percent of them—discussed gun policies, and 75 percent discussed policy in identity-related terms.

However, the NRA did more than just work up a vocabulary of identity around guns. It also developed infrastructure in which that identity could grow. It built a community. A whole latticework of local organizations and events was created to cultivate and sustain that community. The national organization tied official membership to tangible benefits, from discount cards to life insurance. The NRA's investment in all this produced an increasingly cohesive group of motivated activists.

As members of the community grew to understand themselves as gun owners and advocates of gun rights, they increasingly became "single-issue" voters. A politician's stand on guns became the only issue that mattered.

The NRA transformed gun owners from people who would merely check a box on a survey saying that they supported gun rights to those for whom a politician's stance on gun rights was a dealmaker or a dealbreaker. Over 70 percent of Americans who prefer lax gun laws say they'd *never* vote for a candidate advocating stronger regulations. Compare that to people who favor stricter laws. Almost 70 percent admit they'd consider voting for a pro-gun candidate under some circumstances.

The first two essential ingredients to the NRA's success were creating an identity around gun ownership and building social structures to leverage that identity into reliably motivated activists and voters. Harlon Carter's Institute for Legislative Action added the third: cultivating relationships with Republican elites. To put it bluntly, the NRA trades votes for policy positions. Just like the teetotaling ASL before it, the organization credibly tells political leaders what positions to take. If they agree, they're blessed with the support of a large bloc of reliable voters. If they disagree, they're threatened with that bloc's ire. The politics around guns in the United States would never be the same.

None of this is some highly guarded industry secret like the Facebook algorithm or the recipe for Coca-Cola. NRA leaders have basically said it's what they were trying to do. In fact, the historian Daniel Okrent argues that the NRA simply "copied to the letter" the tactics of the ASL. Over the years, other groups—from the Tea Party to the Sunrise Movement—have gone on to take pages from the NRA's playbook.

The Sunrise Movement, for example, was inspired by a widely circulated "postmortem" assessment of the failed attempt to pass the 2009 Waxman-Markey cap-and-trade bill. That document attributed the failure to the absence of a social movement pushing the bill through. Without organized outside pressure, Waxman-Markey never made it out of the Senate. Contrast this with the subsequent success in 2022 of the IRA. The IRA's journey to becoming law was long and tortured, but the core of its climate-related policies—which are by far the most significant climate laws the US has ever passed—remained intact through that journey. Sunrise and other groups like it were central to its passage.

All Politics Is Identity Politics

Whereas the NRA targeted its identity building on conservative rural white Christian men, Sunrise grows support by organizing across identity lines.

One pillar of its approach ties the fight for climate justice to the fight for economic justice: "to stop climate change and create millions of good jobs in the process." Another pillar ties the fight to antiracism: "to become the generation that turns the tide against racism and the institutions built upon it." For Sunrise as for the NRA, effective politics is identity politics.

Of course, Harlon Carter and friends would scoff at the idea that they were involved in "identity politics." But they'd be wrong. The term "identity politics" is associated with the left, but Carter and the NRA built their movement by building a community. They cultivated ways for people to feel a sense of comradery and belonging, signal their membership in the group, and relish every opportunity to "dunk" on all the anti-gunners outside it. The structures they built were the conditions that allowed an identity-based group to grow into a political juggernaut.

It's not only NRA members who dislike the term "identity politics." Across the political spectrum, people worry that it can seem exclusionary; creating an "us" also produces a "them." This appears to put identity politics at odds with messages like "we're all in it together" that have widespread appeal.

And of course, groupishness has a dark side too. After all, many of history's worst atrocities were perpetuated by groups exalting their own particular ethnic or religious identity while denigrating others. The Holocaust was one particularly horrifying installment in humankind's long, awful history of identity-based genocide and war. It spurred scientific interest in the psychology of identity, leading scholars to look into why people sort themselves so easily into opposing groups that end up hating and murdering each other.

One of the most alarming things scientists discovered was how ludicrously easy it is to coax people into an "us" versus "them" mentality. Research using what is called the "minimal group paradigm" shows that people start treating in-group members better than out-group members as soon as they have ways to tell the two groups apart. In one experiment, participants were told that a coin flip would put them on team A or B. Then they were given some money and told they could share it with other people in the experiment on either team. Participants were reliably more generous to people on their own team even though they knew the teams were assigned completely at random. Across studies, psychologists have had trouble finding anything that *can't* serve as a basis for groupishness, from coin flips to T-shirt colors.

Put together, it's not surprising that people have doubts about identity politics. We're a little too susceptible to embracing arbitrary and irrational alliances, and those susceptibilities are a little too easy to exploit. If identities highlight our differences and make them exploitable, maybe they're something we should aspire to overcome. Wouldn't it be better if we set aside our differences and focused on common ground?

Not so fast. As we explored in chapter 6, the ability to coordinate and cooperate is one of our species' superpowers. As both the NRA and Sunrise make clear, that superpower is inextricably bound up in the psychology of groupishness, especially our gregariousness and craving for belonging. As much as people might want to "move beyond" it, the truth is that all politics is identity politics. The movements that succeed in making real change in the real world are anchored in a rich sense of who "we" are and what we stand for. Our groupishness remains a powerful pathway to making social change, for better or worse. Rather than lament it, we should continue exploring how to use it for good.

Still, it's one thing to understand that social identities are inseparable from community and belonging. It's another to figure out what leads people who identify with a group to participate in collective action. For every climate activist out in the streets, there's two more people proud to proclaim their staunch environmentalism . . . from the couch.

Fighting the Battle You Expect to Lose

What moves people from identity to action? An answer is beginning to take shape. One piece is perceiving—and feeling outraged by—injustice. Another is believing that you can do something about it.

It's one thing to feel affiliated with a group but it's another to witness something unfair happening to it. Recognizing and being affronted by injustice is key to activating group identity. It's a big step to getting off the couch. A striking example is what often happens when politicians enact voting restrictions: they can fail to have their intended impact. While they may succeed in making it more difficult for some people to vote, they outrage and galvanize others. The effect on turnout can end up a wash.

It also helps when people really think that they can make a difference. A person's sense of efficacy need not take the form of a grandiose belief that they, personally, can save the world. It can be motivating just to believe in their group's collective power. But what about those who don't believe their group can win? Pessimism often seems pretty reasonable and clear-eyed. When it comes to systemic change, the odds of success are long. Whether it's turning back the climate crisis or ending racial segregation, change is slow and piecemeal. If the motivation to work for change depends on the belief that one's group will win but winning seems desperately unlikely, what then? Does the will to fight require a delusion?

Maybe not. Consider Hong Kong's Umbrella Revolutionaries, who took action in the face of extreme risk and long odds. In 1997, when Great Britain's ninety-nine-year lease to govern Hong Kong was up, the area became a "special administrative region" of the People's Republic of China. Part of China's deal with Britain in the negotiations running up to the 1997 handover was that Hong Kong would be given a "high degree of autonomy" until at least 2047. The idea was "one country, two systems."

It didn't take long for China to blur the line. By 2003, Beijing began flouting the terms of the agreement, in both spirit and letter. It tried to pass an anti-subversion law to criminalize speaking out in support of Hong Kong's secession. It stocked the election committee whose job was to choose the region's chief executive with loyalists to the mainland. In 2014, when Beijing nominally followed through on a promise to grant universal suffrage in Hong Kong, it added a last-minute proviso that candidates for office had to be picked by a nominating committee . . . controlled by China.

This sparked the Umbrella Revolution, so-called because pro-democracy protestors in Hong Kong used umbrellas to protect themselves from the police's use of tear gas, pepper spray, batons, and physical force. The protests kicked into a higher gear a few years later, in part due to the proposal of a new extradition law that would subject Hong Kong to China's criminal justice system, which authorized the arbitrary arrest of anyone who displeased the government.

A million people protested peacefully on June 9, 2019, followed by two million on June 12. In August of that year, there was a citywide strike, with protestors occupying the Hong Kong airport. The extradition bill was withdrawn in September, but the protests continued. The demographics of the protestors skewed young, pointing to a generational divide, but local elections in November 2019 vindicated the protestors' claims of widespread support. Record voter turnout flipped all but one of Hong Kong's eighteen district councils, granting overwhelming majority control to pro-democracy candidates.

Protestors in Hong Kong fought despite slim chances of victory, as did others protesting repression around the same time in Russia, Iran, and the countries of the Arab Spring. This is how it often goes for those challenging the status quo and seeking change, whether it's the NRA and the Federalist Society fighting their decades-long battle to reshape the American judiciary or Martin Luther King Jr. acknowledging that he might not reach the mountaintop. King's too-short life is an ominous reminder that the long, uncertain path toward progress is one few see to the end.

To better understand what motivates changemakers to persist in their efforts, social psychologist Arin Ayanian and colleagues surveyed large groups of people who had been active in protests in the 2010s in Russia, Ukraine, Hong Kong, and Turkey. These were places where it was manifestly risky to speak up and organize. The possibility of violent crackdowns was very real.

One thing Ayanian's team confirmed is that outrage is a clear spark to action. In Egypt, for example, the more outraged people felt over how protestors were being treated in the postcoup period after the fall of the Mubarak regime—and the more they perceived themselves to be at risk—the more likely they were to get involved. This is likely why some authoritarian regimes like Hungary's turn to subtle and insidious forms of repression. They don't want to trigger outrage.

A similar dynamic, from repression to outrage to action, has shaped all kinds of nonviolent protest movements, from those in anti-apartheid South Africa to the Civil Rights Movement in the US. By responding to state violence with nonviolence—by turning the other cheek—activists in these movements gain the sympathy of those watching from the sidelines. Bystanders become outraged and join the fray.

A more surprising finding in Ayanian's research reveals how activists think of their own individual role in bringing about change in these high-risk contexts. They don't tend to think, "I, personally, have the power to make change." They don't even necessarily believe their group will prevail in the end. People who get involved in these movements are not usually self-deceived about the chances of success. They don't need to trick themselves into having unrealistic confidence in order to join the fight. Instead, Ayanian found that while activists were often doubtful that they or their movement would achieve all its aims, they felt they could make contributions *to the group*. As one Egyptian activist put it, "I do share part of my life, part of my thinking, part of my ideology with the people around me. . . . I wanted to redress the injustice that was inflicted on us in this country. . . . We were all in this together . . . getting beaten in the same way . . . it was likely for any of us to lose his life for the sake of my goal, which is also his goal and all the protesters' goal. It kind of gives that sense of obligation. I didn't mind then to sacrifice my life for the sake of this goal. . . . It's kind of a shared thing between us."

This activist perspective upends a common way of thinking about what it means to make a difference. When high-risk activists are less sanguine about the prospects for achieving their highest aspirations—ending corruption or protecting human rights or winning the revolution—they remain optimistic about other things: sowing the seeds for future change by broadening national and international support, showing solidarity and love for the fellow activists they protest with, and, above all, building the group together. Although they don't think their movement can make all the difference, they think they can make a difference to the movement.

Voting and Its Paradoxes

When Chris Field, who directs the Woods Institute for the Environment at Stanford, was interviewed about the most impactful things individuals can do for the environment, he didn't dwell on what people recycle or how much they fly. "The most important thing anybody can do," he said, "is to vote for a climate-friendly government agenda." For Field and so many other citizens of democracies, voting is the first thing that comes to mind when they think about their individual power to make a difference.

It's ironic that some people's sense of efficacy is so closely connected to their electoral power because voting is the standard example many philosophers and social scientists use to illustrate individual powerlessness. Given how unlikely one person's vote is to swing an election, it's puzzling why anyone goes through the trouble of voting at all.

Individual votes *can* make a difference. In 1994, Wyoming Governor Mike Sullivan pulled a ping pong ball out of his own battered cowboy hat to determine the next member of the state House of Representatives. The ball read "Randall Luthi," who then proclaimed, "It is democracy at its best." Luthi had tied Independent Larry Call with 1,941 votes each. In the case of a tie, Wyoming state law mandates the drawing of lots. Had any one of those 3,882 total voters made a different pick, or had a single nonvoter cast a ballot: no ping pong balls required.

Ties and one-vote wins do happen in US elections, but hoo boy are they rare. Of course, the odds of any one person casting a pivotal vote in an election go down as the number of voters goes up.

So, we should expect that as elections get larger and the chances that any single vote will swing the outcome shrink, citizens' participation will decline. The bigger the election, the less rational it appears for a person to pay the cost of voting, to bother with the hassle. People still turn out, though, giving rise to what has become known as the Paradox of Voting.

In fact, the elections most Americans turn out for are the presidential ones, and these are *very* large. More than 154 million Americans voted in the 2020 presidential election. The costs of voting in major elections can also be higher than usual, with some people having to navigate past serious obstacles to cast a ballot: restrictive laws, long lines, underfunded elections commissions, and intimidating fascists hovering around polling places. But even voters in the most frictionless system have to invest some effort or money to cast a ballot. When that ballot is just one out of tens of millions cast in an election, what's the point in pushing through such inconveniences, indignities, and injustices?

Despite all the complaints about low turnout and the exhortations people give each other to get to the polls, the Paradox of Voting is not about why such a small percentage of eligible voters actually vote. Rather, it's about why *anyone*, given the dramatically long odds of making a difference, votes at all.

This is even more puzzling in light of how people routinely respond to odds in other parts of their lives. For the average American, the odds of getting in a car accident are 1 in 366 for every thousand miles driven. That's a much higher chance than casting the pivotal vote in an election. Seventy-seven percent of drivers get into at least one accident, and the lifetime odds of dying in these crashes are 1 in 107. These odds go way up whenever drivers speed, text, drink alcohol, feel a little drowsy, or even just toggle the radio dial. The chances of something bad—potentially fatal!— happening in a car are alarmingly high. But those numbers still aren't high enough to change most people's behavior. Everybody keeps getting behind the wheel anyway.

Compare that to voting. A person is much, much less likely to cast a pivotal vote than to get in a car accident. But when it comes to voting, people are willing to change their behavior, disrupt their routines, and take on the costs and inconveniences of getting to the polls. Why do these lower odds have a greater power over what people do?

Whatever motivates people, it's not just odds and outcomes. What else gets people to the voting booth? Social identity. Maybe you vote because you're a Democrat, and voting gives you the feeling of belonging and contributing to the group. Or you do it because you're an American, and you believe voting is part of what it is to be a good American. Maybe you vote because you're a citizen and want to live up to all the democratic privileges and duties that citizenship entails. You vote, in other words, because *you're a voter.*

Research indeed finds that activating people's social identities can mobilize action and boost turnout—even if the identity is something as minimal as "voter." One of the most effective nudges for getting people to vote is simply asking them, "Are you going to vote?" right before an election. This primes people to make their actions consistent with their words, to live up to their sense of themselves as the kind of person who votes.

Recall that the single best predictor of when people quit smoking is when their family and friends start quitting, and the best predictor of when people get solar panels is when their neighbors do. Voting works the same way. We vote when our friends do. We also vote to keep up our reputation. One study emailed people to tell them that lists of eligible voters who stayed home in an election would be printed by the local newspaper. The threat of public shame increased voter turnout.

And here again, we're not just susceptible to social influence but also purveyors of it. It's easy to think of casting a vote solely in terms of its direct impact on the final tally; every vote is just one more ballot in the box. It's the same mistake that's so easy to make about recycling, thinking that any one person's impact is measured only by the number of jars and cans they toss in the blue bin. But as we've seen, individual actions, like recycling and putting solar panels on your house—and voting!—have social consequences, too.

Even in the seemingly solitary act of voting, we're all part of each other's situations, creating the context and shaping the norms that influence each other's decisions. By voting, and making it known that we did—it's what that "I Voted!" sticker is for, after all—we can normalize civic participation, multiply the impact of our actions, affect our friends' choices, and, from there, their friend's choices. There's more to the casting of a vote than its direct impact on the tally. The Paradox of Voting arises from the theoretical difficulty of understanding why anybody votes at all. Social identity and social influence are a big part of the answer. Record numbers of Americans voted in the 2020 presidential election, representing 67 percent of eligible voters.

But that still leaves a whopping 80 million who could have voted and didn't. What motivates *them*? Many reported not being interested in politics, not feeling well-enough informed, not liking any of the available candidates, and—maybe you guessed it—not feeling like their vote will matter. Fifty percent of nonvoters believed that "I'm only one person, so my vote doesn't make a difference." (Only 17 percent of voters felt the same.)

People can have lots of good reasons for not voting. We've already noted how many would-be voters face obstacles like intimidation, confusing ballots, and long lines in the cold November rain. But despite the prevalence of these voter suppression tactics, and even though the 2020 election occurred in the midst of an unprecedented global pandemic, the overwhelming majority of nonvoters did *not* cite the difficulty of voting or concerns about COVID-19 in their decision. A full 75 percent of them said voting was easy. The reason they didn't bother to vote was because it seemed futile.

When do nonvoters become voters? Perhaps when they see the choice to vote in terms of their identities, tied to their need to belong and their commitment to support their communities. For some people, the most motivating ties may be to their friends and family, while for others, they may be to the community at large and the norms of civic engagement that sustain it. Nonvoters might find that voting just makes them feel good too. For Michael, the community vibe in the local elementary school is never better than on Election Day. He never feels closer to the stern old church ladies who check the precinct rolls.

Once the ball gets rolling, people might find that strengthening their connections to community, and doing things like voting as a result, spills over into further changemaking choices down the line. They might even come to be suspicious—as the three of us have—of the whole misleading, incomplete, overly individualist way of thinking about actions as isolated and independent and only adding up in discrete little increments. Maybe they could use some stern old church ladies in their lives.

Oxygen and Kindling: The Structural Background for Effective Collective Action

People crave belonging. It's a craving only satisfied by collective identity. But people can't have a collective identity all by their lonesome. It requires others too, a whole group of people connecting and being there for each other. These are more of the structural conditions that facilitate social movements and change. The craving, the community, the connection, the collective identity—these are the oxygen and kindling, the fuel that feeds the fire as it burns.

The big social movements and small personal choices we've explored in this chapter all take place against a huge array of structural background conditions. The NRA's rise and resilience took more than ginning up identity-based thinking in *American Rifleman* and offering its members life insurance. Its persuasive appeal can only be understood in cultural context. The motto "the only thing that stops a bad guy with a gun is a good guy with a gun" is blatantly false, but it is also an infuriatingly effective appeal to people awash in films, news, religions, and video games championing self-reliance and personal responsibility.

It's much the same background culture of individualism that made "people can stop pollution" and "we fear the jaywalker" and Candace Lightner's campaign against reckless drunk drivers so effective. Nowhere in the US is gun ownership and gun-owner identity as pervasive as in the South, where ideals of self-reliance are especially strong. Alongside these is the idea that violence is an acceptable way to settle conflicts. ("Violence as an acceptable means of settling conflicts"; see Harlon Carter.)

Beyond cultural factors, the NRA's success has been supported by explicit procedural features of the federal government. Gun control legislation is difficult to get through a US Senate that still honors the filibuster. With the filibuster, major legislative bills require 60 out of 100 Senators to support them. Without the filibuster, simple congressional majorities could send gun regulations straight to the president's desk. The US government is replete with these kinds of "veto points." Their effect is to make it much easier to stifle change than to carry it through. Changing the status quo is far from a fair fight.

As a result, ushering in progressive social change is never going to be as simple as xeroxing the NRA's playbook. They've blocked gun regulations by microtargeting and activating a comparatively small group of highly motivated voters. Publicizing how vastly they're outnumbered will help the efforts to push past them. While all politics is identity politics, the more identities in the mix the better.

11 Building the Blaze: Coalitional Politics for Interdependent Individuals

Coalitions and Compromises

The spark is lit. You're outraged, think somebody should do something, and ready for that somebody to be you. Long as the odds may be, you're invested in transformative change and want to do the work. But you and what army?

The groups you're in—your friends, your tenant association, your fellow climate activists, even your political party—can't do it alone. More people need to get involved. That's true whether you're organizing to end the carceral state or persuading your company to divest from fossil fuels. No matter your ambition, you need buy-in. And it's virtually unavoidable that many of those stakeholders will have deep disagreements. If you're working on fossil fuel divestment, you've got to deal with the fact that some of your much-needed allies couldn't care less about rising sea levels, wildfires, and the extinction of polar bears. But they like a good return on their 401(k). Can you get them on board?

Changing structures requires coalitions of diverse people acting *somewhat* cooperatively. The New Deal of the 1930s brought about massive structural changes that radically reshaped American government and culture, so much so that historians sometimes refer to it as the "third American revolution." This third revolution was particularly remarkable because unlike the first two—the American Revolution and the Civil War—it didn't involve military conflict. But it certainly involved struggle.

Among other things, passing the package of laws and reforms that made up the New Deal required historically antagonistic factions on the left to form uneasy alliances. For example, in the US at the beginning of the 1930s, the Communist Party and the Congress of Industrial Organizations (the

CIO, a leading federation of unions) were virtually at war. Their tentative and very short-lived willingness to work together in support of President Roosevelt's agenda helped secure its passage. It also broadened Roosevelt's mandate, leading to the passage of the National Labor Relations, Social Security, and Fair Labor Standards acts. These became known as the "Second New Deal." Meanwhile, both the Communist Party and the CIO grew in membership and influence.

American Communists wanted far "deeper" structural changes than did the CIO and most other rank-and-file Democrats. The former's hesitation to join the union coalition reflected a reluctance to compromise on their more revolutionary agenda, which was basically to burn the system down rather than reform it from within. The groups ended up putting aside their differences temporarily, but the tension between mainstream and more radical flanks of the American left never disappeared.

Progressives and socialists' visions of change conflict in profound ways with those of moderates and "popularists." The latter emphasize that politics is "the art of the possible" and worry that more radical sides of the coalition are an electoral liability. Predictably, these disagreements are often framed in individual versus structural terms: a supposed competition between narrower reforms, which are portrayed as making modest improvements to individuals' lives, versus more sweeping, structural transformations.

During debates about marriage equality in the 1990s and 2000s, advocates wanted to extend the individual rights and privileges of marriage to LGBTQ people. Others rejected the focus on individual rights and wanted to challenge the entire institution of state-sponsored marriage. Likewise, during debates over Obamacare, supporters pointed to the millions of individual people who would become newly eligible for health insurance because of the ACA. Progressive critics worried that the bill would merely prop up a failing employer-based corporatized healthcare system. Again, they wanted to rebuild a new system from the ground up.

These debates seem to force an unhappy choice: someone interested in progressive change can either compromise and end up a centrist normie or refuse to compromise and become a hopeless revolutionary, shouting into the wind. Elements of this conflict may be unavoidable in some cases, but just as the alliance between the Communists and the CIO benefited both organizations, coalitional politics can create synergies between groups, too.

DREAMing of Multiethnic Democracy

In the early 2010s, in California, a group of college-aged kids who had been brought to the US as children decided to push back against the stigma of being "undocumented immigrants." They were part of the group that came to be known as DREAMers. Sociologist Veronica Terriquez documented one of their efforts, around what they called the "Coming out of the Shadows" initiative. Terriquez tells how these California DREAMers "publicly declared their undocumented status in order to combat the stigma associated with their precarious legal situation and humanize their experiences in the eyes of broader audiences."

They were inspired by the realization that many of them belonged to several different marginalized groups at once. Some DREAMers were dark-skinned; others were queer. This realization drove them to take a closer look at their intersecting and overlapping identities. Despite the obstacles to coming out—whether as undocumented or queer or both—many DREAMers did anyway. One student put it to Terriquez this way:

> It wasn't always okay to say that you were undocumented, but I guess when I first started college it was taboo, completely. I think now it's okay to say, "I'm undocumented . . ." For me, I first got comfortable saying that I'm undocumented before I started saying "I'm queer" or "I'm gay" or "I'm LGBTQ." I guess once you go through saying you're undocumented, it's easy to accept a queer identity and be able to talk about it with other people. Maybe it's because you already have this sense of self-empowerment based on your undocumented status, that you can use that for your queer identity.

Terriquez refers to this as a kind of reverberating *social movement spillover*. It's a positive feedback loop: "strategies originated by movement A are borrowed by movement B in pursuit of separate goals; yet in employing that strategy, movement B ends up furthering the aims of movement A." In this case, activists for undocumented migrants borrowed ideas originating in queer activism. Then, the empowerment that queer DREAMers achieved by coming out as undocumented in turn strengthened their resolve to come out as queer.

This positive feedback loop between migrant and queer social movements didn't just occur at the level of ideas and messaging. And it wasn't just about helping individuals come out while leaving the structural status quo in place. Instead, activists built social movement spillover into the structural DNA of their organizations.

LGBTQ organizations created Queer Dream Summer, which set up internships for undocumented queer youth in LGBTQ organizations. Meanwhile, immigration groups created the Queer Undocumented Immigrant Project, whose policies aimed at promoting LGBTQ leadership within their ranks. Immigration groups also organized local workshops, on campuses and in local communities, to introduce straight movement members to the experiences of their queer-identified peers.

It's tempting to assume that building a coalition requires setting differences aside. In that case, one would expect all this attention to the diverging experiences of people within larger movements to divide activists. But it didn't. It had the opposite effect, creating a positive feedback loop of mutually reinforcing empowerment and connection. According to Terriquez's research, more and more people began seeing commonalities between "living in the shadows and living in the closet." And examples of social movement spillover like the queer DREAMers'—and there are many more— suggest that coalition builders can be ambitious. They can lend and borrow ideas and strategies, like the empowering coming-out narrative. They can seek out ways to build intergroup collaboration into the basic nuts and bolts of their organizations. In the best of cases, seemingly separate social movements can push each other past a threshold and become bigger and bolder than they were before.

Race-Class Academy

Even when groups come together, others get cut out. The justly celebrated New Deal was the fruit not just of leftist coalitions but also of notorious exclusions. Roosevelt needed the support of white Southern Democrats to pass legislation, and he and the New Deal coalition made Faustian bargains to get it.

Black Americans were systematically excluded from receiving the benefits of many New Deal programs. For example, agricultural and domestic workers—who "coincidentally" tended to be Black and concentrated in the South—were excluded from the Social Security Act, meaning the federal government would not provide these workers with pensions in their old age. Legislative compromises like this pitted the Black and white working class against each other. Roosevelt even refused to consider federal anti-lynching legislation, fearing it would endanger his coalition. The third American revolution, among the broadest progressive restructurings in US history, was achieved on the backs of Black people.

Where does this leave present-day coalitional politics? If the left emphasizes "kitchen table" issues like providing good middle-class jobs, does it have to stay quiet about hot button social issues like racism and transphobia? Are the coalition-building tactics of the New Deal—which bridge divides between some marginalized groups only to exclude others—the only way forward?

We don't think so. Just as Terriquez's DREAMers found ways to form powerful coalitions between migrants and LGBTQ youth, there are ways to forge ties between the movement against racism and the movement against the evisceration of American workers. A promising path toward forging these ties goes through what law professor Ian Haney-Lopez calls the "race-class narrative." For our money, it's some of the best political both/and thinking around. And it holds general lessons for building coalitions and positive social movement spillover.

Haney-Lopez worked for many years as the cochair of the Advisory Council on Racial and Economic Justice at the AFL-CIO. (That's the same CIO involved in the New Deal; since 1955, it's been a huge part of the largest federation of unions in the US.) While there, Haney-Lopez conducted thousands of interviews, focus groups, and surveys with the aim of figuring out how people and politicians think and talk about race, class, and their intersection. He separated out three common approaches, studying how each one appealed—or didn't—to different groups of voters. He also sought to devise a fourth messaging strategy that combined the strengths of the other three while avoiding their weaknesses.

First is what Haney-Lopez called "dog whistle" politics. Blowing into a dog whistle makes a sound that dogs can hear but humans cannot. Similarly, politicians often hint at race in oblique ways. They use nonracial terms that can seem innocuous and even appealing to outsiders but carry a coded meaning understood by those in the know. A politician might use the expression "people on welfare" as a thinly veiled way to criticize Black people. When then candidate Donald Trump accused Hillary Clinton of "meet[ing] in secret with international banks to plot the destruction of US Sovereignty," he was dog whistling to antisemitic people. Dog whistling gives politicians and others a flimsy kind of deniability, allowing them to point to the literal meaning of their words so that they don't have to stand behind the message they're actually conveying.

Second is the "call them bigots" approach, more popular among many liberals and leftists. The idea is to raise alarms about racism explicitly, whenever and wherever it's found. It's not hard to imagine why this approach is appealing. When someone like Trump launches into yet another racist rant, how could one *not* call it out?

The problem is that calling people bigots often plays right into the dog whistlers' hands. When they're charged with being racist, dog whistlers point to the literal meaning of their superficially nonracist words to "counterpunch." They deny that racism had anything to do with it and then accuse their accusers: "I'm not racist. You're racist for calling me—and my supporters—racist!" It's basically elevated "I'm rubber and you're glue" into one of the most consistently impactful political tactics since the midtwentieth century.

Neither we nor Haney-Lopez think calling out racism is always counterproductive. But it's risky. It sets up the "who me? racist?" counterpunch, and it can also set off spirals of accusations. "When people are called bigots for beliefs that they view as common sense, they react badly," says Haney-Lopez, "insisting they are not racist, and then expressing outrage that anyone would suggest otherwise."

On top of all this, calling people out seems sometimes more about making yourself feel good than about building transformative social change. No doubt it can be satisfying to chew someone out, and occasionally it might help bolster solidarity. But it can alienate potential allies.

The third approach Haney-Lopez studies takes the opposite tack: pretend race doesn't exist. Be "colorblind." Transcend our differences. This is among the most popular messages in politics, both in the US and most everywhere else, as versions of it appeal to voters from lots of different backgrounds. It seems like a straightforward way to get beyond racism. Forget about skin color and other arbitrary ways of putting people into boxes. Stop fixating on differences. Unite!

Reacting to the pitfalls of the "call them bigots" approach, defenders of this "ignore race" approach argue that honest conversations about racism are just too difficult and risky. Depressing as it may be, these conversations can be off-putting, they say, especially for white people. Their idea is to talk up issues that affect everyone instead, like good jobs and affordable healthcare. This crowd advocates prioritizing class over race.

Haney-Lopez found that this approach resonates more strongly with lots of people than "call them bigots." Many voters prefer political candidates and messages who appeal to universalistic values and policies, without mentioning race at all. But here's the big catch: Haney-Lopez found that the "avoid race" approach resonates *less* with voters than dog whistling, especially when it comes to drumming up support from moderate and conservative white people. Pretending racism is not the issue is a less effective political strategy than exploiting racist tropes.

The core takeaway from Haney-Lopez's "Race-Class Academy" is to reorient discussions of racism so that they focus on how "politicians promote racial conflict as a strategy to divide and distract people so they can get and hold onto power." This strategy doesn't shy away from talking about racism. But it holds that we should be talking about *strategic racism* rather than what one might think of as "personal" racism. Politicians, whatever their personal views about race, often use racism for their own political ends, strategically stoking division to gain power and block progressive change. That's what we should be talking about, Haney-Lopez argues.

The race-class narrative has three steps: "distrust powerful elites stoking division," "join together across racial lines," and then "demand government for all." Here's what that looks like in practice, broken down into key elements, with explanations from Haney-Lopez's team in italics:

No matter where we come from or what our color, most of us work hard for our families. *The aim here is to discuss racism explicitly and to make clear that it affects everyone.*

But today, certain politicians and their greedy lobbyists hurt everyone by handing kickbacks to the rich, defunding our schools, and threatening our seniors with cuts to Medicare and Social Security. Then they turn around and point the finger for our hard times at poor families, Black people, and new immigrants. *This message depicts racial scapegoating as something that harms all kinds of people economically.*

We need to join together with people from all walks of life to fight for our future, just like we won better wages, safer workplaces, and civil rights in our past. *The message evokes a sense of collective fate and previously successful cross-racial movements.*

By joining together, we can elect new leaders who work for all of us, not just the wealthy few. *Finally, the message focuses on what people need to do.*

To the extent that Haney-Lopez's approach recommends openly confronting racism (step 1) and building an interracial coalition to overcome it (step 2), it bears little resemblance to approaches that ignore race and focus on kitchen table economic concerns alone. But the last step of the race-class narrative—demanding government for all—is just as important. The narrative shares the end goal of making structural changes that benefit everyone: universal healthcare, pre-K, clean air, and so on.

Building coalitions greater than the sum of their parts means going through race and identity, not bypassing them. This requires both acknowledging differences and finding ways to harmonize them. Consider the fight against climate change. It doesn't affect us all equally—it hits communities marginalized by poverty and prejudice the worst—but it does affect us all.

There aren't any magic solutions in politics, of course. Nobody knows just how effective and broadly appealing Haney-Lopez's approach can be. But more and more political actors are following his lead. The proposed Green New Deal, and its descendants the Build Back Better plan and the IRA, are testaments to this approach's potential. They achieved a critical mass of grassroots and legislative backing by yoking the fight against the climate crisis to the fights for economic and racial justice. More and more researchers are studying similar tactics.

One series of studies, for example, found that when African and Asian Americans reflect on the history of laws prohibiting interracial marriage, they become more supportive of gay marriage. As John Lewis, a 1960s civil rights leader turned US Representative, explained in 2014, "I fought too hard and too long against discrimination based on race and color not to stand up—and speak up—against discrimination against our gay and lesbian brothers and sisters. I see the right to marry as a civil rights issue." Framing gay marriage as a matter of civil rights, continuous with antiracist struggles, highlights the joint importance of our distinctive identities and shared fates. This, in short, is how one social movement spills over into another.

Building Up an Intersectional Mindset

The race-class narrative provides a template for talking about the distinctive struggles that members of oppressed groups face and the role that racism, sexism, and other forms of prejudice and discrimination play in their oppression—while at the same time seeking out points of common ground around which coalitions can be built.

But Haney-Lopez wasn't the first person on the both/and beat. Black American feminists like Anna Julia Cooper, Sojourner Truth, and Maria Stewart, together with oppressed women of color the world over, have been pushing back against zero-sum, either/or thinking since at least the 1800s. Feminists of color have roundly criticized the idea that advancing one important political aim (like racial justice) must come at the expense of advancing others (like gender, class, or environmental justice). In bell hooks's words, "Whenever we love justice and stand on the side of justice we refuse simplistic binaries. We refuse to allow either/or thinking to cloud our judgment. We embrace the logic of both/and. We acknowledge the limits of what we know."

hooks and others sought to see and interact with the world *intersectionally*. The intersectional approach involves a certain way of engaging with the social world and building coalitions to change it. It's an approach exemplified by Terriquez's California DREAMers and queer activists. Without denying the differences in their struggles, they saw opportunities for connection.

The term "intersectionality" dates to 1989, when Kimberlé Crenshaw—building on decades of work by feminists of color like hooks—used it to show how social identities overlap and "intersect" to produce unique kinds of oppression. Black women, readers will be shocked to learn, are both Black people and women. They face many forms of prejudice and discrimination, some of which are shared with other women and people of color. But they face distinctive obstacles, too.

For example, recall a 2023 finding on racial disparities in maternal and infant health, which we first cited in chapter 3. Rich Black women and their children have worse outcomes than poor white women and their children, even in a wealthy, well-funded, liberal state like California: "For every 100,000 births, 173 of the babies born to the richest white mothers die before their first birthday. 350 babies born to the poorest white mothers die. 437 babies born to the richest Black mothers die. 653 babies born to the poorest Black mothers die." For poor Black infants to be nearly four times more likely to die than rich white infants is simply unconscionable. Economist Maya Rossin-Slater concludes that the problems Black children and child bearers face are "much more structural" than just addressing poverty, healthcare, racism, or sexism in isolation.

Despite this, "intersectionality" is among the most controversial of buzz-words. It's criticized as divisive by the colorblind universalists who urge "avoiding race." It's cast by right-wing ideologues as a "conspiracy theory of victimization" and a "new caste system" that places non-white, nonheterosexual people at the top.

These criticisms badly misrepresent the intersectional tradition. As Deborah King explains,

> in addressing the National Association for the Advancement of Colored People (NAACP) Legal Defense Fund in 1971, Fannie Lou Hamer, the daughter of share-croppers and a civil rights activist in Mississippi, commented on the special plight and role of black women over 350 years: "You know I work for the liberation of all people because when I liberate myself, I'm liberating other people . . . her [the white woman's] freedom is shackled in chains to mine, and she realizes for the first time that she is not free until I am free." *The necessity of addressing all oppressions is one of the hallmarks of black feminist thought.*

Addressing all oppressions isn't easy. Black feminists have, since at least the 1800s, decried how feminist groups neglect race, how antiracist groups neglect gender, and how both neglect class. And the same labor groups that made ideas like "class solidarity" salient in American minds were notorious for excluding women and non-white workers. Robin Zheng describes an interview the labor organizer Jane McAlevey gave alongside the organizer of the first national Women's March after the election of Donald Trump:

> [McAlevey] pointed out that numerically the largest organizations of women in the country are trade unions, and that unions are the primary defenders of working-class women's workplace rights. When asked whether the Women's March would demand a mass expansion of trade unions, however, the organizer replied: "That's actually not my topic." McAlevey goes on to declare: "The idea that it's 'not my issue' is what is wrong with the so-called progressive movement in this country."

This "not my issue" approach is exactly what intersectionality opposes. It threatens to feed right into a self-undermining, either/or, zero-sum mentality that fosters division, as each group is liable to see others' gains as their own losses.

Crenshaw pushes back against this mistake when she says that intersectionality is "basically a lens, a prism, for seeing the way in which various forms of inequality often operate together and exacerbate each other." It's more a mindset than a method. Part of the goal is to take seemingly separate movements and find ways to say, "We have our movement, and we support yours."

Adopting an intersectional mindset requires keeping two thoughts in mind: people's social identities and experiences make them different from one another in important ways, *and yet* in virtue of living in unjustly stratified societies, people's identities are also a rich source of connection and coalition. It involves remaining aware of all the different social categories, all the different boxes people put each other in, while appreciating how all the boxes are interrelated.

Researchers who study what they call "intersectional awareness" find that it's intimately tied to other structure-facing skills, traits, and habits of attention. People with an intersectional mindset are more open to new experiences and more willing to adopt others' perspectives. They're more likely to see big-picture political problems as personally relevant to their lives. They value diversity, are less prejudiced toward other groups, and are not afraid to interrupt discrimination when they find it. They're more likely to recognize that the status quo is unjust, and they're more motivated to change it. The more people think in intersectional ways, the more eager they are to engage in collective action.

Intersectional awareness is "a way of thinking about the world that anyone can practice," even white men like the authors of this book. We can learn to better appreciate the ways that our experiences of whiteness are shaped by our experiences of being men, and vice versa. Pretty much everyone has reason to adopt an intersectional mindset, whether they're privileged or oppressed. Doing so helps each of us, regardless of our social identities, better understand the structural injustices that shape our lives, so as to end them.

12 Facing the Fire: Understanding the Social World in a Both/And Way

Strivers

To build winning coalitions, we need to learn to see the structural obstacles holding people back. One person who's done wonders helping others see hidden structures is the philosopher Jennifer Morton, whose focus is on obstacles in higher education. Morton taught for years at the City College of New York, working with hundreds of first-generation college students whom she calls "strivers." These are students from working-class backgrounds, often children of immigrants. They're in college to achieve the American Dream. When people describe education as the engine of upward mobility, strivers are often who they have in mind.

Morton herself was a striver but one with an unusual opportunity to peek over the fence and see what wealth and opportunity looked like. As she explains in an interview, "I grew up in Lima, Peru. My mom got pregnant with me when she was 17. Peru in the '80s was beset by terrorism, high inflation, political instability. I mostly grew up with my grandmother, but I also had a wealthy aunt . . . I grew up . . . having a working-class family life and then going to school with extremely wealthy people, some of whom were the children of the prime minister or owners of big companies in our country. And so it was very strange. I grew up straddling these two worlds."

Teachers, administrators, policymakers, voters, and sometimes strivers themselves think that what these students most need to succeed is individual grit and gumption. The message they get is that the path out of poverty is really difficult, but if you give it your all, then you can push through. In economic terms alone, this message is basically right. College graduates tend to make about $1.2 million more over their lifetime than people who only hold a high school diploma.

But one problem with this message is that strivers rarely have a full picture of the obstacles that make the path out of poverty so difficult. It's not just that they have to study hard and avoid distractions. Many also have to balance schoolwork and a long commute to campus with full-time employment, often at multiple jobs. Professors can be oblivious or indifferent, and bosses can be inflexible. On top of all that, their families might expect them to be available to take care of siblings or elders. Lots of strivers have kids of their own too. They're straddling separate worlds.

Strivers also have the burden of needing to learn new norms at school. From music to clothes to food, college can be an exhausting, alien world. And even once they've learned its unfamiliar ways, they're torn about following them. It can feel like selling out, betraying their past, and losing their authentic selves. Their high school friends won't hesitate to get on their case about putting on airs and forgetting where they came from.

So, one problem Morton points out is that strivers and their families rarely get the whole story about what college demands. The three of us also work at large public universities committed to serving strivers, and we've watched many struggle. The success-through-relentless-grit narrative leaves out a big part of what the experience is really like. Too many students are under the impression that it's on them as individuals to juggle it all by themselves: school, work, commuting, caretaking, homemaking, learning new norms, and holding onto old ones. When strivers are unable to thrive on all these fronts simultaneously, they often think they're the problem. Those who stick with it resolve to just suck it up, work harder, sleep less.

Yet the message that strivers just need to work harder obscures what Morton describes as a genuine ethical dilemma. The economic benefit of a college degree is undeniable, but there's more to life than money. Morton remembers what it was like leaving Lima to carve out her own path in the US: "I was extremely close to [my grandmother] growing up. I mean, for me, she was the world. And now to not be able to be as close to her, it's a very painful cost." Moving up, she realized, meant moving *out*. She wasn't just straddling different worlds but also had to choose between them. To go to college in the US, she had to leave behind relationships, her hometown, her whole familiar sense of self. That's not an easy choice. And it's a choice that students from privileged backgrounds don't usually have to make.

One option for strivers facing this dilemma is to throw themselves headlong into college even if it means being less available to family and old friends. The appeal of this option is real. College can launch strivers into satisfying careers, giving them opportunities to pursue a calling rather than just some job that pays the bills.

The other option is to quit school. Many take it—first-generation students are less likely to finish college—and then have to deal with the stigma of being dropouts. Morton reframes the option, though, showing that many of those who decide to leave college are making a rational, caring, ethical choice. Feeling forced to choose, they choose friends, family, and community.

Striving for Better Options

Both gritting it out in college and returning home incur real costs for strivers. But maybe those aren't the only two options. Once strivers, and the rest of us, get a better view of the structural constraints they're operating within, we can start to ask whether those barriers can be torn down. Maybe it's time to reject this unfair either/or choice and demand better.

There's a lot that individuals and schools can do to ease strivers' dilemma. Professors can be more aware of and sympathetic to their students' situations and acknowledge and discuss their predicaments. For example, Alex assigns a podcast interview with Jen Morton at the beginning of his classes. Professors can also build flexibility into the structure of their courses so that students aren't penalized when they have to cope with unexpected family demands.

Meanwhile, if family members better understand strivers' challenges, they might start putting less unfair pressure on them. Maybe there are tweaks that schools can implement to help family members reframe their perspectives on strivers' situations. Just as there's a student orientation process for onboarding the incoming class, there could be a family orientation process to go along with it.

But it can't just be up to teachers and families to change their expectations, as if in a vacuum. One reason strivers get called home to babysit is the dearth of affordable childcare. One reason they work long hours is that college is too expensive. They keep full-time jobs because they (and their families) need the income. The larger goal has to be creating a fair playing field via further-reaching structural reforms: free tuition, affordable childcare, elder care for students and their families, smaller class sizes to help teachers stay attuned to individual students' needs, and so on.

We shouldn't treat the unjust structures that define higher education as fixed, nonnegotiable facts. They aren't immutable conditions that strivers just have to accept. Black feminist bell hooks argues for coming to see the unjust structures as changeable:

> Often, African Americans are among those students I teach from poor and working-class backgrounds who are most vocal about issues of class. They express frustration, anger, and sadness about the tensions and stress they experience trying to conform to acceptable white, middle-class behaviors in university settings while retaining the ability to "deal" at home. Sharing strategies for coping from my own experience, I encourage students to reject the notion that they must choose between experiences. They must believe they can inhabit comfortably two different worlds, but they must make each space one of comfort. They must creatively invent ways to cross borders. They must believe in their capacity to alter the bourgeois settings they enter. All too often, students from nonmaterially privileged backgrounds assume a position of passivity . . . as though they can only be acted upon against their will. Ultimately, they end up feeling they can only reject or accept the norms imposed upon them. This either/or often sets them up for disappointment and failure.

hooks urges students to reject the choice between fitting in or leaving. Instead, she admires those who realize that the status quo is unjust and who respond by trying to upend it. She encourages students to think of themselves as agents of change, actively reshaping the structures they inhabit rather than passively accepting them.

Many do. There's no shortage of examples of students turning this attitude into organized action. But what's less obvious is how they come to adopt this changemaking mindset in the first place. People often begin thinking of themselves as agents of change when they come to see the world as changeable. But how does that happen?

(Some of) the Kids Are All Right

Kids begin noticing the importance of status at a remarkably young age, but they don't all end up thinking about it the same way. Some come to think of the advantages that certain groups have over others as the natural way of things, while some come to see those advantages as unfair and changeable.

By the time they're seven years old, American kids know that Black people typically have less money than white people and women often have lower-status jobs than men. Similar effects have been found in other countries. In Iran, seven- to twelve-year-old children perceive Iranian kids to be of lower status than their American counterparts. Kids all over the world have a surprising ability to soak up information about group-based inequalities. They also tend to place a lot of weight on language and accents. In India, kids ages five to ten think Indian-English speakers make for "worse leaders" than British-English speakers. In the US, ten-year-olds identify speakers with Southern accents as less "in charge" than those with Northern accents.

These are all examples of kids' "knowledge of social structures." When Iranian children tell researchers that American kids are of higher status than Iranian kids, they're communicating an awareness of how their social world works. Most (but as we'll see, not all) kids also assume that where a group sits in a pecking order reflects something internal to it, like that the group's members are inherently intelligent or assertive (rather than just being lucky inheritors of unearned privileges).

Part of the allure of these intuitive falsehoods about status is that many kids *like* the idea of hierarchy. That might sound ominous. Isn't equality the obvious ideal? But think about how fascinated people get with those at the top of different pecking orders: royalty, celebrities, athletes, billionaires.

That said, enthusiasm for hierarchy isn't universal. Some kids come to see social hierarchies as unfair. Some go on to put their lives on the line to overthrow them. When they do, it's usually a result of what they were taught. Social psychologists repeatedly find that parents' attitudes toward hierarchy make a big difference to their kids. Parents who are structurally alert tend to have kids who are structurally alert too.

In one study, researchers divided preschoolers using the minimal group paradigm we described back in chapter 10. Decades of research show that people play favorites based on group identity even when the groupings are trivial. In this case, preschoolers were arbitrarily sorted into either a red or blue group and then given T-shirts and wristbands with matching colors. Next, they watched a video of a kid from their group (wearing the same shirt) who refused to share a candy bar with a kid from the other group. Later, the preschoolers were asked to give out paper coins to the two kids they saw in the video, the in-group member who refused to share or the out-group kid who got stiffed. How did the preschoolers distribute the coins? Would they give more to the in-group member, overlooking that blatant display of selfishness?

Some kids did show in-group favoritism, but some didn't. The preschoolers' choices were predicted by their *parents'* preferences for social hierarchy. Children with parents who dislike hierarchies penalized the stingy in-group member by giving them fewer coins. Those with parents who like hierarchies didn't penalize the in-group member at all.

It looks like kids whose parents are suspicious of hierarchy have a head start on seeing social systems and grasping how they work. Figuring out how parents pass along these preferences is a work in progress. Some intentionally teach their kids about unfair status differences, but other kids likely absorb their parents' worldview through passive family osmosis. Either way, it's pretty clear that parents who are skeptical about hierarchy have children who share their skepticism.

Dreaming of Structures That Never Were and Asking Why Not

Another thing that stifles people's ability to see and understand social structures is that they're abstract and complex. This also makes imagining alternatives—including other, better ways the world could be structured—incredibly difficult. Social scientists call the general ability to do this "counterfactual reasoning." It's the capacity to consider possibilities that might have been or may be in the future. How would a scenario have played out if earlier conditions had been different from—*counter* to—how they actually—in *fact*—were?

Sometimes history can help us think about how things might have unfolded differently. Writing about enslaved Americans and their descendants, Isabel Wilkerson explains, "On those cotton fields were opera singers, jazz musicians, playwrights, novelists, surgeons, attorneys, accountants, professors, journalists. . . . We know that because that is what they and their children and now their grandchildren and even great-grandchildren have often chosen to become once they had the chance to choose for themselves."

Other times, the only way to use counterfactual reasoning is through imagination. Would Superman still love "truth, justice, and the American way" if his spaceship had landed in Moscow, Russia, instead of Smallville, Kansas? If you think Superman's inner Kryptonian essence would make him inherently good no matter where he landed, you'll expect the story to go one way. But if you think the social systems he grew up with exert a strong influence, you might expect it to unfold differently. How you think about these imaginary scenarios reveals your underlying understanding of what caused what in the story.

Counterfactual reasoning is something we do all the time, but people differ in which kinds of possibilities come most readily to mind. Some people are liable to focus on others' inner characteristics and how they could be different. Maybe if that striver had had more grit, she wouldn't have dropped out of school. Others are liable to imagine leaving individuals as they are while considering how features of their situation could be different. Maybe that striver wouldn't have dropped out if tuition had been more affordable.

The ability to entertain situational counterfactuals—to consider all the different ways that social structures could have been—is a distinctive kind of skill. Like other skills, it can be improved with practice. Imagine that someone named Jamal, who is Black, shows up late for work. His white coworkers don't know why. Maybe it was his fault (he absentmindedly forgot to set the alarm), or maybe there were factors beyond his control (bad traffic due to an accident). Because of cultural stereotypes about Black people, many coworkers leap to the conclusion that Jamal's laziness is to blame. But some of them lack that impulse to stereotype. They're in the habit of considering "situational" explanations first rather than individualist ones.

Some studies have people practice coming up with different kinds of explanations in scenarios like these. Instead of myopically fixating on what that one individual could have done differently to change his fate, participants can build up the skill of looking at how structures shape behavior. As they become less likely to blame people for the things that happen *to* them, they also start to show reduced racial bias. So just as Trish Devine said about prejudice, the individualist impulse to ignore social structures is a habit that can be broken.

Some structural conditions are more or less conducive to breaking these individualist habits. For white American kids to understand racial inequality, for example, they need information about it. But in too many ways, they're prevented from seeing what the lives of non-white people are actually like. They don't have daily interactions with non-white kids because they live in different neighborhoods and attend segregated schools. As they grow up, their media is shaped by cultural segregation, so they're likely to watch different TV shows while being fed different parts of the internet by social media algorithms. "Colorblind" parents who refuse to talk to their kids about race don't help either. Children who grow up in these types of conditions often enter professions marked by occupational segregation, working in spaces with few non-white people.

The upshot is that too often kids and the adults they become don't have enough real-world experience with people from other groups to understand how they end up where they do or what it's like to be there. This makes thinking about alternative explanations for why some groups stay stuck in disadvantaged circumstances that much harder.

There are both individual and structural improvements that can help us do better counterfactual thinking about injustice. Segregation makes it harder for people to notice and understand all the structural factors propping up racial inequity. It's yet one more reason segregation needs to go. But dismantling it is going to require changing attitudes toward segregation. And doing *that*, in turn, is going to involve people becoming more structure facing: learning about how segregation prevents us from noticing and understanding structural racism. Seeing structures as changeable, we'll be freed up to dream of antiracist worlds that never were and ask why not.

All in the Family of Structure-Facing Skills

Learning to reason counterfactually about how social structures affect us is one example of a broader family of structure-facing skills that are both useful and learnable. Here are a handful of others.

Resisting Status Quo Bias and System Justification

There is a powerful tendency to stand pat with "the devil that you know"; it's allegedly better than the devil you don't. But in an unjust world, this "status quo bias" is a weapon for blocking progressive change. Some of its forms are pretty intuitive. If you're wealthy and privileged, it's easy to assume that the world is a relatively just place because things are going well . . . for you.

But what's really striking about status quo bias is that people getting the short end of the stick exhibit it too. Those suffering the worst injustices of hierarchical social systems regularly get duped into thinking the system is acceptable, even just. One reason is they're soaking up the same message that strivers get: rising up the ladder is just a matter of striving hard enough. Many people find comfort in thinking they have personal control over the shape of their own lives, whether they actually climb the ladder or not. It may be safer to think things aren't going well for you because you haven't tried hard enough than it is to think that things aren't going well for you because the system is unfair. At least in the first case, the outcome is up to you. But if you think that, then you're also likely to think that successful people got to where they are because they're naturally gifted or hustled their way to the top. They must deserve their status. Researchers call all this "system justification"—endorsing an unjust social status quo even when people are disadvantaged by it.

Being able to imagine alternative scenarios helps us to break free from status quo bias and system justification. Considering a wide range of different ways the world might operate can dislodge the impulse to roll with the default option. But much as we learned in previous chapters about lighting the spark, coming to realize that the status quo is unjust is just one step. Getting motivated to actually do something about it comes next.

Feeling Engaged Versus Being Engaged

Lots of people who get riled up about racial and environmental injustices never quite make it off the couch. They treat politics like a hobby. Political hobbyism, as political scientist Eitan Hersh calls it, is the tendency to consume, discuss, and emote about politics with like-minded peers, often online. He argues that this is a problem because hobbyists' engagement with politics and social change ends there. All that energy devoted to reading, arguing, or being outraged could be better spent doing things like attending community meetings, participating in political party committees, and recruiting and volunteering on behalf of state legislative candidates.

Hobbyism is a real problem in the United States, particularly for progressives. In survey research from 2018, Hersh finds that a third of respondents reported spending at least two hours a day consuming news and thinking about politics. Of these, virtually none reported spending even a trivial amount of time working or volunteering for any political organization. This disparity between hobbyist activities and time spent engaging in collective action was especially pronounced among well-educated white liberals.

Hersh's view is that hobbyism is a problem for well-educated white liberals because they don't personally have much at stake in the issues they're upset about. They're materially comfortable with the way things are even if they feel strongly about justice and politics. Hobbyism is another mark of status quo bias, in other words. And if Hersh's diagnosis is right, then it's not enough to just start paying attention to and getting upset by existing structural injustices. Structure-facing skill is about seeing all the problems out there, acknowledging the concrete ways you might be benefiting from them, and finding the pathways that *you*, an individual, can take to do something about them.

Humility and Flexibility

Humility, and the desire to be better, is a crucial element of structure-facing skill and both/and thinking. Again, the relationships between individuals and social structures are incredibly complex. Understanding how they contribute to social problems like racism and climate change and poverty is no easy task, nor is figuring out solutions. Predicting the effects of our efforts to tackle these kinds of problems is its own hornet's nest (see chapter 9).

On top of all this—the inherent complexity of social structures and systems and the difficulty of knowing how to change them—we're all constantly bombarded with messages from motivated actors purporting to boil problems down to simple solutions. "It's all because of Fox News!" "The solution is education!" "Real change comes from within." It's never that simple, of course, and a general sense of humility can help inoculate against the worst excesses of oversimplification, overconfidence, and hype.

It's more than a matter of personal humility. There's also room for cultural humility, which is closely tied to the intersectional mindset we explored in the last chapter. The culturally humble tend to be interested in and accepting of how groups other than their own do things. They tend to seek out, rather than be uncomfortable with, unfamiliar people and places. Like other forms of humility, this cultural version is rooted in a learning-oriented mentality. It turns on the idea that one's understanding of others is incomplete.

Think again about segregation and how it obstructs structural change by obstructing our ability to notice oppressive structures. Resisting segregation—of one kind or another—is part of the solution, but individuals vary a lot in how interested, comfortable, and willing they are to spend time with and learn from people unlike themselves. Research from Italy has shown how cultural humility shapes people's willingness to try to overcome this barrier. The more culturally humble a research group of Italians was, the more they thought of contact with Muslim migrants as a positive thing.

Overconfidence leads people to hold on tight to what they think they already know. The antidote is "cognitive flexibility." People who are cognitively flexible are good at seeing things from multiple perspectives and imagining alternative possibilities. They uncover novel links between what they're learning and what they've already learned. Their minds change when the evidence changes, and they generate creative ways to solve problems. Cognitive flexibility looks like it gets better with practice as well.

Cognitively flexible people are also less likely to get suckered in by bullshit—specifically "pseudo-profound bullshit," to use psychologists' technical term. Examples of pseudo-profundity include "guidance is the nature of grace, and of us," "the goal of morphic resonance is to plant the seeds of ecstasy rather than stagnation," and "moisture is the essence of wetness." (For all your own pseudo-profound bullshit needs, visit the generator at http://sebpearce.com/bullshit/.) Lots of people are easily duped into thinking nonsense like this is meaningful, deep, and true. But researchers find that those who enjoy the kind of careful and open-ended thinking required for cognitive flexibility are more suspicious of pseudo-profundity. They're also less susceptible to bogus paranormal and conspiratorial theories, COVID-19 misperceptions, fake science, and political misinformation. They're less confident about predicting the future and less likely to claim to know more than they do.

Whereas cognitively rigid thinkers might try to pin problems like racism and the climate crisis on a handful of bad-acting villains, the cognitively flexible are ready to see how vexed these "everything problems" are. These problems can't be boiled down to a short list of faces and names. Their causes are distributed and dispersed, and their influence over our lives is subtle, statistically diffuse, and ubiquitous.

Seeing Where You Stand

Research suggests that acknowledging one's own racial privilege encourages people to engage in collective action. In one study, researchers showed people videos of highly publicized racialized incidents: one from Yale University, in which a police officer demands to see a Black student's ID, saying "we need to make sure you belong here," and another from a Philadelphia

Starbucks, in which the cops were called on a Black man who was doing nothing but waiting for his friends to arrive before ordering coffee.

Before showing them the videos, the researchers asked participants to fill out a scale measuring their awareness of racial privilege. They were asked to agree or disagree with statements like "White people have privileges that Black people do not have in the United States" and "White people are at an advantage because they hold most of the positions of power in American society." There was a marked difference in how people responded to the videos, depending on how they responded to the "awareness of racial privilege" scale. After seeing the videos, it was the people who acknowledged their own privilege who were more interested in engaging in collective action to fight for racial justice. An awareness of the background structures of racial advantage and disadvantage is key to noticing and mobilizing against the concrete racial injustices right there in front of you, in the foreground.

From Sparking to Building to Seeing to Sustaining the Fire

Structure-facing skills push us to face the fire and sharpen our abilities to pay attention to social structures and understand how they work. Learning them is a both/and endeavor since it involves individual people coming to see how they're connected to the systems that shape their world. Structure-facing skills are tools for directing our passions in the right way, especially once they've been ignited by group identities and enlarged through collaboration and coalition building.

And yet, all of this is still not enough. The goal isn't just to make change. It's to make *lasting* change.

13 Keeping the Fire Going: The Gloriously Unsexy Work of Implementing and Sustaining Change

Implementation: Where Good Ideas Go to Die

Starting social change is tough enough, but implementing and sustaining it might be even tougher. The work often takes place in what political scientist Leah Stokes calls the "fog of enactment." It's the nebulous gap between passing some big, new, complex policy and putting that policy into practice. The fog of enactment is where good ideas too often go to die once the light of public attention and activists' interest falters. This chapter is about learning to navigate through the fog.

Even popular ideas get lost in the fog of enactment. In the 1980s, crime in American cities was bad and trust in the police was low. Reformers were dissatisfied with the emphasis at the time on responding to 911 calls one by one rather than addressing the root problems that led to them. One response came to be known as "community policing."

The idea was to restore a connection between law enforcement and the communities they're supposed to serve. In some ways, community policing was a throwback to the days when officers walked their beats and made house calls. It's an amorphous idea but has a few core tenets. First is decentralization. Police officers are assigned to specific neighborhoods to foster communication and trust between them and the community. Solutions grounded in the local community's concrete needs are prioritized over top-down decisions.

A second tenet is community engagement. Departments are encouraged to share information with communities about the problems they see and what they're doing about them. Officers are encouraged to take a less adversarial stance toward citizens, participating in organized meetings where they can listen to members of the community and come to understand their concerns.

This is closely tied to a third tenet: problem-solving. Rather than preparing for splashy but low frequency events like high-speed car chases after fleeing bank robbers, community policing teaches departments to focus on the day-to-day problems affecting people's lives. Over time, this broadens the scope of police responsibility. If the community is fed up with rats, loud parties, and derelict buildings, community-engaged police can't say "not our problem." Rats, noise, and falling-down buildings become police problems.

Together, these innovations comprised the most important developments in policing in the last quarter of the twentieth century. By 2015, nearly every US city with more than 250,000 people named community policing as a policy priority.

It's no surprise, then, that political scientists, criminologists, and public policymakers wanted to know whether community policing works. Sometimes it seems to. Notable successes, like Chicago's Alternative Policing Strategy, were associated with improved relations between police and residents, more involvement of residents in decision-making, and stronger approval of law enforcement. But larger scientific reviews of community policing have been mixed. Some found that community policing reduced crime, while others found null results.

In 2021, a team of twenty-six researchers—mostly political scientists—published a paper in the journal *Science* reporting their attempts to get a better view of whether, when, and how community policing works. Their project took "robust methodology" to a whole new level. The team ran a randomized control trial of community policing in six different countries: Brazil, Colombia, Liberia, the Philippines, Uganda, and Pakistan. Some "treatment areas" were rural, like in Uganda, while others were urban, like in Medellín, Colombia. The program was administered by the local police in a total of 707 neighborhoods, districts, and villages, covering roughly nine million people.

Four elements of community policing were implemented: foot patrols, town halls, community meetings, and problem-oriented policing. The effects of these programs were compared to carefully matched control areas, where existing policing practices were left in place. In total, 18,382 citizens were interviewed, along with 874 police officers, and crime data from the treatment areas was analyzed.

Here's how Graeme Blair and his twenty-five colleagues summarize their mega-study's findings: "Increases in locally appropriate community policing practices led to no improvements in citizen-police trust, no greater citizen cooperation with the police, and no reduction in crime in any of the six sites. . . . Although citizens reported more frequent and robust exposure to the police in places where community policing was implemented, we have limited evidence of police action in response to citizen reports."

If you listen closely, you can almost hear all twenty-six researchers cursing in unison.

What went wrong? The problem wasn't that citizens refused to cooperate with the police. Or that crime was displaced to other areas. Or that officers resented the new ideas and refused to comply. Interviews, questionnaires, and transcripts from community meetings showed a different pattern, a consistent problem about as unsexy as you can imagine: implementation. Even with everyone on board, and the program funded and approved, putting it into practice—getting it to "take"—turned out to be a nightmare.

There were several big roadblocks. First, the police departments obviously had a lot on their agendas. Despite their best intentions, when push came to shove, they struggled to prioritize community policing reforms even though these specific departments had been selected for the study precisely because of their enthusiasm for the program.

For some locations, the roadblock was cultural. In the Philippines, officers got mixed messages from their superiors. Higher-ups endorsed the program but also told them to continue prioritizing the investigation of major crimes instead of the day-to-day problems raised in community meetings. In other locations, the roadblock was institutional. In Pakistan, police were not allowed by law to respond to "noncognizable" crimes (i.e., those requiring a warrant) like domestic abuse, harassment, and financial misconduct. This diminished their ability to address the concerns of the community.

Shifting to community policing may or may not be the best way to improve law enforcement. But if making that change—and making other structural changes like it—is going to be viable, the boring, pedestrian details of implementation will need close attention.

Sustaining Change: Tree Planting Versus Tree Growing

Tree planting seems innocuous. Who could be against it? But it's actually much maligned by activists and researchers. Part of the reason is that planting trees is a go-to cause for corporations seeking to "greenwash" their reputations. It helps companies look like they're on the right side of history without actually having to do much. By August 2020, Salesforce and Mastercard each committed to planting 100 million trees, Timberland 50 million, and Clif Bar 750,000. They all signed on to the "Trillion Tree Initiative," based on the idea that trees suck carbon pollution out of the air. The initiative was spearheaded by billionaire Marc Benioff, who announced it at the Word Economic Forum in Davos, Switzerland. Then President Donald Trump quickly signed on, undoubtedly convincing the world over that he's "a very big believer in the environment."

With supporters like these, critics hardly had to point out the terrible track record of tree-planting campaigns. As of 2024, Benioff's Trillion Tree Initiative has planted 2.6 billion trees—just about 997 billion shy of its goal. Getting trees in the ground isn't all there is to it either. In the course of planting 11 million trees in 2019, Turkey was recognized by the Guinness Book of World Records for planting the most saplings in one hour and one place (303,150). Within three months, after public attention had moved on to the next thing, 90 percent of those trees were dead. There hadn't been enough rainfall, and (relatedly) the saplings had been planted during the wrong season. As one *Vice* headline explained, "Tree-Planting Schemes Are Just Creating Tree Cemeteries." Another example: India has invested huge sums in large-scale tree planting for decades, but the proportion of forest canopy hasn't budged. All that the investments have done is shift the composition of the forest away from the broadleaf variety of trees preferred by local people.

All else equal, planting trees isn't a bad idea. Fully grown trees pull a lot of carbon pollution out of the air. Even if they didn't, there are good reasons to reforest wild places and get more trees in urban spaces. Still, gathering support, raising money, enacting legislation, and popping a bunch of saplings into the ground isn't enough. Reaping all those wonderful benefits of trees requires follow-through. As climate scientist Lalisa Duguma put it, "we should just stop thinking about only tree *planting*, it has to be tree *growing*."

When tree-growing initiatives are done right, they can have big effects. In southern Brazil, rural residents (predominantly women) have collaborated for over three decades with the nonprofit Institute for Ecological Research to both plant and grow nearly 3 million native trees. These trees provide wood and fruit that local people consume and sell. They also serve as a habitat for threatened species. Replicating this project won't be easy, but its success makes clear that sustaining change over time is just as important as starting it.

Moments of Liberation and Practices of Freedom

We've already hinted at one reason why implementing and sustaining change is difficult: it's boring. Imagine the thrill of finally winning approval to revamp a major city's policing practices or landing millions of dollars of funding for a reforestation initiative. Inking the law or getting the first sapling in the ground would be thrilling. Cutting the ribbon can feel like crossing the finish line—but it's not.

The vital work of implementing and sustaining change feels like a slog by comparison. Working out the minutiae of the officer rotation schedule with fifteen different precinct captains doesn't have the same allure as reimagining the relationships between the community and the police.

One way to protect against this kind of letdown is by thinking about change differently. Developing concepts for change that help us persist through its many stages can contribute to a commitment to seeing things through.

The writer Maggie Nelson draws inspiration from Michel Foucault's distinction between "moments of liberation" and "practices of freedom." Moments of liberation are flashbulb events, like when an oppressed people rises up in revolution against colonial rulers. Statues are toppled, the people gather in the city's central square. These dramatic episodes are often what come to mind when we think of social change. But focusing too much on moments of liberation can make it seem like big social change comes all at once, in a single, revolutionary moment. As essential as these moments are, Nelson argues, they're no replacement for practices of freedom, the persistent struggles for justice that need to follow in their wake.

Daily practices of freedom take different forms for different people—a point we'll explore in the next chapter. But it's not just a matter of foisting more responsibility onto people to think differently and sustain change. Practices of freedom are best understood from a both/and perspective. There are also structural conditions that enable and sustain them.

"Keep Your Government Hands Off My Medicare!"

One reason people can fail to support and sustain beneficial changes is that they don't know about them in the first place. If people aren't aware of how existing structural reforms benefit them and promote a fairer world, why would they show up morning after morning to keep those reforms going?

Before Obama's presidency, Congress passed the Energy Policy Act of 2005, which included a loan program for clean energy technologies. As of 2014, the program loaned a total of $34.2 billion to various businesses. While it wasn't intended to make money, it ended up being profitable for the federal government. Companies defaulted on $780 million, but the program recouped $810 million in interest payments. Far more importantly, it helped kickstart the solar panel industry, driving down prices of panels faster than virtually anyone predicted.

But if anyone heard of this loan program during the 2010s, the overwhelming likelihood is that they associated it with one thing: Solyndra, a solar company that defaulted on its loan. This isn't an accident. Negative TV ads trumpeted Solyndra's default. The FBI raided their headquarters. Republican House Representative Steve Scalise said the Solyndra loan was "disgusting," and so-called moderate Republican Senator Lisa Murkowski called it "a colossal failure." Lost in all this criticism was the fact that the broader loan program both made money and drove the cost of solar down dramatically. It contributed to renewable sources of energy like solar power becoming the cheapest in the world—cheaper than oil, gas, and coal—by the early 2020s.

Critics also failed to mention a similar loan program—Advanced Technology Vehicles Manufacturing—that gave $465 million to a niche, bespoke car company promising to make sexy electric cars. Tesla was launched with nearly a half billion dollars' worth of government help. Lost to the fog of enactment was that the company repaid the $465 million nine years ahead of schedule because it was doing—as the comedian Larry David would say—pretty, pretty, pretty good.

Widespread ignorance about successful government programs like these is not a simple result of people failing to pay attention. Opponents of the programs spread all kinds of nonsense about them, and key to their strategy is playing on people's distrust of government. In this case they were able to connect Solyndra to an older, larger narrative that casts government spending as wasteful and bureaucrats as cutting sweetheart deals for their buddies. Commentators at Fox News and the Wall Street Journal continue to drudge up Solyndra years later to stoke skepticism about federal efforts to promote renewable energy and stem the climate crisis.

The hidden successes surrounding Solyndra's failure represent but a few examples of what political scientist Suzanne Mettler calls the "submerged state." In 2008, she polled 1,400 Americans to ask if they ever used a government social program; 57 percent said they had not. Then she listed twenty-one federal programs, such as Social Security, unemployment insurance, and student loans, and asked the same people whether they had ever used any of them. Ninety-four percent who declared they had never used a government social program had used one of these twenty-one programs. The average person in the poll had used four!

For these people and many others, the role of the government in shaping their lives is submerged. They fail to realize how they benefit from government programs or even that they're using government programs at all. Those programs and their effects are nearly invisible.

It was in 2009, during the Obamacare debates, when a man angrily yelled during a town hall, "keep your government hands off my Medicare!" The deluge of snarky internet memes mocking him was predictable and immediate. *Slate* set up a meme tracker. Conservative intellectuals leapt to his defense with spurious arguments that Medicare somehow isn't a government social program. (It is. Medicare is a state-run insurance program available to all Americans over sixty-five and some younger people with disabilities and chronic illnesses.)

Mettler's response, however, was both charitable and incisive. She pointed out that one in four people who received Medicare benefits that year accessed them through a private insurance company. Maybe the man wasn't so much in denial about receiving government benefits as he was unaware of the fact that even privately administered health benefits are often a government social program.

This ignorance of government's role is a big problem, and it's not specific to Medicare. Many US hospitals are tax-exempt, for starters. The hospitals themselves were built with federal funding, starting with the 1946 Hill-Burton Act signed by Harry Truman. A big portion of American doctors, nurses, and medical technicians got through their training on federal scholarships. Medical research is often underwritten by the federal government through grants and agencies like the National Institutes of Health, the Federal Drug Administration, and the Centers for Disease Control.

Contrast the American health insurance system, or US investments in clean energy, with influential New Deal programs, like Social Security, or with the GI Bill, and it becomes clear why government programs have become so invisible. People knew all those older programs were helping them, and they knew the government was running them. In the American imagination, these big federal efforts are relics of the past. But Mettler makes a convincing case that the US government has remained active in supporting health, education, and poverty reduction. Federal spending on social goods is roughly on par with similar nations.

And the effects of federal social programs can be very real. In 1964, the US child poverty rate was 23 percent, while in 2021, it was 11.6 percent. Many people find this shocking. A major reason why people don't know about this drastic reduction lies in the way it's been achieved. Much of the federal effort has been done through low-profile subsidies and tweaks to the tax code. Instead of handing people money, the government cuts their taxes.

Using tax breaks to share American wealth is the result of an understandable but perhaps ill-advised grand political compromise. Progressive policymakers who have sought to use the state to improve people's lives have had to contend with conservatives pushing for lower taxes and fewer government services. These calls for "smaller government" have been common in American public discourse at least since Republican Ronald Reagan was president in the 1980s, when he famously claimed, "The nine most terrifying words in the English language are: I'm from the Government, and I'm here to help." For our part, we don't find those nine words so scary, at least not compared to conservative activist Grover Norquist, who in 2001 dreamed of shrinking the government "to the size where I can drag it into the bathroom and drown it in the bathtub." But Democrats whose job it is to get bills passed have been forced to acknowledge how appealing the Reagan/Norquist ethos is to many voters. Even Democratic President Bill Clinton declared in 1996 that "the era of big government is over."

All this hostility to big government led Democrats to conclude that the only way to enact problem-solving policies was through the tax code and other dry technocratic venues. If their programs were too visible, they'd get hammered as "big [wasteful, incompetent] government." So—the thinking goes—Democrats have settled for submerged policies.

It's no surprise that the less people see government working for them, the less reason they've got to want more of it. Who would expect them to work their asses off to implement and sustain something, let alone pay more taxes to support it, if they don't even know it's there?

Surfacing the State

The question, then, is how the state and its best social programs can be made more visible. How do we bring these background social structures into the light so that people remain motivated and keep doing the work of sustaining them?

One thing Mettler focuses on is branding. Information about policies that affect the structural conditions of people's lives could be packaged better. For example, Mettler suggests that the federal "government should also provide 'receipts' that inform people of the size of each benefit they get through the tax code." Donald Trump had a similar idea when he insisted that his signature appear on the checks issued to citizens that were funded by the first stimulus bill of his first term, though it seemed like he wanted everyone to think the money was coming from his personal checking account rather than the government.

There's evidence that when the benefits of public programs are direct and visible, not only do people recognize the value of the programs themselves but they also become more involved citizens. For example, research suggests that recipients of Social Security and the GI Bill participated in politics more than they would have otherwise. After seeing what their country could do for them, they did more for their country.

Of course, a big challenge for surfacing the state is that the information environment works a tad bit differently today than it used to. Two-thirds to three-quarters of all American households tuned in to President Roosevelt's "Fireside Chats" in the 1930s and '40s, when he laid out all the advantages of his New Deal programs on all the major radio networks. Yet fewer than one-third of American households saw Obama's State of the Union addresses. And anything he said in them was instantaneously absorbed by predigested media commentary.

Skeptical that just giving people information like this can make a difference? Mettler's own experiments offer some grounds for optimism. She's tested the effects of making people aware of basic information about policies like the Home Mortgage Interest Tax Deduction and the Earned Income Tax Credit—including information about who benefits the most from such programs. The mortgage deduction takes a sizable chunk out of people's taxes while they're paying off their home. The earned income credit offers a tax break to lower-income working people, especially if they have kids, and lifts millions of people out of poverty. Once people see how active government policies like these relate to their material interests, they become more committed to sustaining them.

The mandate to surface the submerged applies to another arena rife with ignorance and confusion: climate change. The lack of awareness here isn't just about policies, programs, and the state. Most people don't know that most people care about the climate crisis. This is a case of "pluralistic ignorance," when there are widely shared misperceptions about public opinion. Americans suffer from it badly.

A 2022 paper finds that pluralistic ignorance about climate change is so widespread that we're living in a "false social reality." For example, 66–80 percent of Americans support major climate change mitigation policies, depending on which policies they are asked about. But when asked how popular they think such programs are—that is, when people are asked to guess what percentage of other Americans support these policies—the average answer is 37–43 percent. Put another way, supporters of major climate policies outnumber opponents two to one, but when Americans are asked what their fellow citizens think, they get it exactly backward. They think opponents outnumber supporters two to one.

You don't have to be a political scientist or a marketing whiz to help surface the state and fight American ignorance. Simply learning and talking about the benefits of government programs like Medicare and energy policy is a step in the right direction.

Working the System

There's more to do than talk. One of the most promising cases of successful social change in recent years was due to good customer service. Where the fog of enactment is about the nebulous space between policy passage and policy implementation, the *fog of uptake* is about the space between well-meaning actors implementing a new policy and the intended beneficiaries making actual use of it.

There's a long-standing debate about why people who live in impoverished neighborhoods tend to stay there. One view is that people stay put because they want to. They have good reasons: remaining close to their families and communities, valuing their neighborhood's culture and diversity, and appreciating the businesses and places of worship tailored to their needs. If they work in those neighborhoods, then their commute is shorter. When Jennifer Morton's strivers feel caught between two different worlds, these are some of the factors keeping them anchored to where they come from. As we said, moving up the socioeconomic ladder too often means moving out of close-knit, supportive communities. When people want to stay put, their preferences should be respected.

Another view is that some people, at least, want to move to different neighborhoods, where there might be better schools and opportunities, but they can't overcome the barriers standing in the way. They might lack information about where to go or how to make it happen. They might lack access to the credit and liquidity needed to rent homes in wealthier neighborhoods. Landlords in those neighborhoods might discriminate against them.

The stakes of this debate are high. Where people live has a huge effect on their lives. Race and class segregation tracks economic opportunities, school quality, healthcare options, and crime. We saw the significance of geography, real estate, and zoning laws to racism back in chapter 2. Part of the perniciousness of segregation is that it cuts people off from economic and social capital (which is about who you know and how connected you are to opportunities). One analysis found that younger children whose families moved to wealthier neighborhoods had an annual income 31 percent higher by their mid-twenties than matched kids who didn't move to wealthier neighborhoods.

For all these reasons, people who want to move out of impoverished neighborhoods should be free and able to. There are publicly financed programs aiming to help them do it, providing families thousands of dollars to move. The waitlists for these housing subsidies are long, suggesting demand is strong. Yet the track record of people using them to move to better neighborhoods has been mixed. The two views we described above point toward competing explanations for why subsidies don't deliver reliable results. On the one hand, maybe people say they want to move, but when push comes to shove, they really don't. On the other hand, maybe there's still something standing in their way, even with the generous subsidies.

There's good evidence now, gathered by a team of social scientists led by Peter Bergman and Raj Chetty, that there are still barriers. The team focused on neighborhoods in Seattle, where local housing authorities have had programs for years providing vouchers to low-income families to encourage them to move to higher-opportunity neighborhoods. As in other places, the uptake of these vouchers for moving to better neighborhoods has been low. The research team tested two different hypotheses about why. They compared a *preferences* model—people don't use vouchers because they don't want to—to a *friction* model—people don't use vouchers because structural barriers get in their way.

In one experiment, they studied 430 families that had applied for and been awarded Housing Choice Vouchers worth on average $1,540/month in rental assistance. Not chump change! Every family had at least one kid below the age of fifteen, and their median income was $19,000 per year. Importantly, the vouchers were scaled to the average neighborhood rent, so their value was proportionate in more and less expensive neighborhoods.

The 430 families were divided into two groups. The control group received the standard information, delivered in the standard way, about how to use the vouchers. Families in the treatment group were enrolled in a program called Creating Moves to Opportunity (CMTO), which connected them to a group of "navigators" dedicated to making voucher use easier.

Navigators did three things. First, they provided assistance in searching for apartments, including preparing rental documents, addressing credit issues, and identifying available units in high-opportunity neighborhoods. Second, they acted as liaisons to landlords, encouraging them to rent to CMTO families. Finally, they provided additional financial assistance for things like security deposits and applications fees. In short, CMTO sought to reduce the friction in moving to a better neighborhood. They acted like good customer service for the families in the program.

To people familiar with the difficulty of creating large impacts in social science experiments, the effect sizes here were breathtaking. Fifteen percent of families in the control group moved to a higher-opportunity neighborhood, whereas 53 percent of those in the CMTO program did. "This is the largest effect I've ever seen in a social science intervention," Chetty said. The benefits of CMTO were consistent across groups within the program regardless of race, immigration status, and income.

The program affected not only whether people moved but also where they moved. In both the treatment and control groups, approximately 87 percent of families used the vouchers to move. But the CMTO families overwhelmingly moved to higher-opportunity neighborhoods, while other families overwhelmingly didn't. After moving, CMTO families were much more likely to stay put over time and be "very satisfied" with the new neighborhood.

If residential segregation is the granddaddy of structural barriers to social justice, what this study shows is that a great deal of the most important work in challenging those barriers resides in the nitty gritty business of implementing and sustaining—and not just starting—change. Housing voucher programs exist in many places, and often they're well-funded, like in Seattle. But all that still isn't enough for them to get uptake. The CMTO program is nothing if not a way of making the implementation of a long-standing idea—housing vouchers—work better. Taking up the role of navigator is one way to practice freedom, in this case freedom for those seeking better opportunities. And it's making a tangible difference in people's lives.

Navigating Toward Your Role in Creating Change

Why not work as a navigator for a program like CMTO? It's instrumental in making meaningful change, and it doesn't require wealth, fame, political connections, or a PhD. It *does* require local knowledge, people skills, and patience. If those are in your wheelhouse, maybe it's a role for you.

There are different roles that other people might be better suited to step into as well, depending on what they've got to offer. Some might donate cold hard cash to a project like CMTO. Others might vote for it if it comes up on the ballot. Others might try to craft a viral video about it or even just tell friends about its importance. Seeing a role for yourself is an essential ingredient of making change and making it stick. This is the subject of the next and final chapter: finding our roles for initiating, implementing, and sustaining change.

14 Fighting from Where You Stand: Finding Your Role in Social Change

My Way of Changing the System Is . . .

A duck glides placidly across the surface of a lake—but underwater its legs are paddling furiously, unseen. You click "Buy Now" on Amazon, and a day or two later a package magically appears at your door—but pulling back the curtain on that "magic" reveals the activity of a whole byzantine empire whose heavy lifting is done by a great many overworked, underpaid, mostly nonunionized laborers. It's easy to forget all the different roles people fill to keep vast systems like Amazon humming along. The furious underwater paddling is mostly out of sight.

A lot can also remain out of sight as systems change. One day you notice how many office buildings have been vacated and find yourself reflecting on how it all happened so fast, wondering what the seemingly overnight rise of remote work portends for the future. The transition was decades in the making, though, made possible by the development and falling cost of high-speed internet and home delivery services. Then it was accelerated by unaffordable office rents and the COVID-19 pandemic. There were people pushing for it too, like programmers and entrepreneurs at businesses like Skype and Zoom.

The list of roles people can play in the fight for a better world is dizzyingly long. For anyone looking for a place to join the ranks, some personal questions can help narrow it down. Which of all the pressing issues out there do I care about the most? What talents and skills do I have to offer, or am I interested in developing? Which projects are important enough to me that I'll be willing to stick around through the fogs of enactment and uptake? What are the concrete opportunities I've got right in front of me?

What are the main forms of friction holding me back? In other words, what roles am I best positioned to play?

Maybe the best place to start is this: What roles am I playing already? Many struggles are well underway, and even if we don't realize it, most of us are already in a position to make immediate contributions. "Sometimes we are blessed with being able to choose the time, and the arena, and the manner of our revolution," Audre Lorde once explained, "but more usually we must do battle where we are standing."

Where each of us stands is within a big cluster of social roles: employee, employer, friend, family member, voter, renter, student, teacher, consumer, commuter, pedestrian, surfer, dog walker, cat person, bad art friend, and so on. Each of these roles comes with norms and guidelines—stuff we're told to do explicitly by higher-ups and stuff we implicitly pick up from imitating others in similar roles. But each role, as the philosopher Robin Zheng points out, also comes with a whole lot of leeway. With that leeway comes distinctive opportunities that anyone occupying the role can take advantage of to make change. This last chapter will look at agents of change who have made the most of their opportunities by leveraging the roles they've occupied.

The Lioness of Lisabi

Fela Aníkúlápó Kuti became an international musical sensation in the 1970s. He pioneered Afrobeat, a genre blending West African songs with jazz and funk. But his mother, though less remembered now, was a bigger deal in her time.

Funmilayo Ransome-Kuti came to be known as the "Lioness of Lisabi" for her anti-colonial feminist activism in Nigeria. She was intersectional before it was cool, weaving together analyses of class, gender, local tribal identity, and Pan-Africanism. But much of her early community work wasn't explicitly political. She kicked into gear in 1942, when she founded the Abeokuta Ladies Club, which taught individual women strategies for "self-improvement"—mostly through sewing, catering, and etiquette.

But Ransome-Kuti's interactions with the diverse ladies of Abeokuta changed her perspective. First a friend who couldn't read asked her for literacy lessons. Ransome-Kuti obliged and soon after opened her lessons to "market women," who got by selling food and wares in the city market. Before long, Ransome-Kuti came to see it wasn't a lack of etiquette or marketable skills holding the market women back. Misogynistic men and sexist structures stood in their way.

Market women were being treated despicably by the Nigerian colonial government. They were extorted, abused, and compelled to pay excessive taxes. Policemen would strip girls naked (and worse) to decide whether they were old enough to pay. Government representatives coerced women into selling goods below market rate only to turn around and resell them to the British for profit.

In 1944, Ransome-Kuti organized a campaign to stop the government's theft and abuse. Two year later, the Ladies Club became the Abeokuta Women's Union (AWU). The goal was no longer just to change conditions for individual women; it was to change the system. The AWU demanded genuine political representation. They contacted newspapers, held long vigils, and circulated petitions demanding "no taxation without representation."

Sensing the seriousness of the threat, the colonial government issued a ban on AWU protests. Ransome-Kuti renamed them "picnics" and "festivals." Eventually, 20,000 women joined the AWU, at a time when the entire population of Abeokuta numbered less than 100,000. In February 1948, thousands blockaded the government palace, leading to the local ruler's temporary abdication in 1949. The taxes were finally suspended a few months later. Ransome-Kuti and the AWU had become structure facing. They were people changing systems that change people.

Ransome-Kuti's influence began to be felt nationally and then internationally. She organized a new political party—the Nigerian Women's Union—as well as the Federation of Nigerian Women's Societies. They sought universal suffrage for Nigerian adults, voting accommodations for people who couldn't read, and quotas allocating positions of power to women. Ransome-Kuti's work was wide-ranging and decidedly both/and. In the 1960s, she demanded greater healthcare for Nigerians, urging doctors to advise women about maintaining a nutritious diet based on locally grown fruits and vegetables. At the same time, she urged women to appeal to the government to provide structural support for cooperative farming (to make it easier to grow and eat locally). She found time to start schools across the country (dubbing literacy the "weapon of liberty") and to travel internationally to receive awards and honorary doctorates. She was given "The Lenin" in 1970.

She also made enemies. In 1977, her son Fela released his hit album *Zombie*, which portrayed Nigerian soldiers as submissive, unthinking drones.

Soon after, a thousand soldiers stormed the Ransome-Kuti compound and threw Funmilayo out of a second-floor window. She survived the fall but sustained injuries that took her life a year later. Funmilayo lived to be seventy-seven years old, not quite long enough to see universal suffrage come to Nigeria in 1979.

Funmilayo Ransome-Kuti didn't abandon her interest in "self-improvement." She redirected and broadened it. Unlike the Ladies Club, membership in the AWU was not about learning how to "move up" as an isolated individual in an otherwise unchanged system. It was about developing a critical awareness of the intertwining structures holding Nigerian women and workers back and then drawing on that critical awareness to see what to do to transform the system. Ransome-Kuti learned how to leverage her concrete social roles—her elite position, educated status, and social connections—to adopt new roles, resist the patriarchy, and hasten Nigeria's exit from the colonial system.

Obviously, not everyone can be a Lioness of Lisabi. Fighting for change requires work and sacrifice, but not everyone will put their lives on the line, decade after decade, in the pursuit of justice and the practice of freedom. Still, there are all kinds of roles people can play in the fight for a better world.

YIMBY

One of the most underappreciated scourges of structural change is the *NIMBY*. This person supports progressive policies in general (or professes to), but in practice, their support stops short when change affects them personally. They want change somewhere but *Not In My BackYard*. In big blue California, NIMBY resistance has repeatedly blocked plans for building more homes, perpetuating a full-blown humanitarian housing crisis. While writing this book, Alex has lived in a liberal SoCal town that is doing its best to block an affordable development for low-income, unhoused people. NIMBYs are concerned about "drug dealing and other crimes." (Research consistently shows that subsidized housing doesn't harm neighborhoods or suppress home values. Sometimes it increases them.) NIMBYs in California have also obstructed other important projects, like high-speed rail lines connecting Los Angeles to San Francisco and Las Vegas.

Not to be outdone by their West Coast counterparts, East Coast elite NIMBYs have organized to block offshore wind power developments (even when they're ten to fifteen miles offshore and nearly invisible from land), residential rooftop solar installations (claiming they don't "fit" in historic districts), and more.

Against the NIMBYs have risen up the YIMBYs, people who say *Yes In My BackYard*. More and more, they've been racking up wins, even in belly-of-the-beast NIMBY California, where single-unit zoning was banned in 2021. Four states—Vermont, Montana, Rhode Island, and Washington—passed sweeping housing reform legislation in 2023. State legislatures considered 200 other housing supply laws in the same year, from removing restrictions on multifamily apartment buildings to allowing faith-based and educational institutions to build affordable housing on their land. A person can be a YIMBY and support structural change by literally doing nothing and just staying out of change's way. But a YIMBY can also be a vocal advocate for changes like these, talking up their benefits and touting the advantages of rezoning or sustainable ways of living. Being this kind of YIMBY sends social signals, normalizing YIMBY choices and acting as a role model for others to emulate. When a person embraces YIMBYism, it can spill over into their other personal choices too. Adopting the identity can lead them to seek out opportunities to say yes to other kinds of social change.

The overall effectiveness of the IRA, the US's signature climate legislation, will be determined not just by what's written in the law but also by how it gets implemented at local levels—and how it gets stymied by opponents. Exactly how consequential it turns out to be will depend—at least in part—on the struggle between NIMBYs and YIMBYs. If you want to join the fray, there are lots of roles that need filling on team YIMBY. Maybe you can help say yes to a solar farm in your town, recognizing its potential for bringing down energy costs, improving local air quality, and reducing reliance on the larger, less predictable grid. Maybe you can show up at the zoning board meeting to debate changes to the building code. Meetings like these are underattended and famously dominated by NIMBYs. They're low-hanging fruit for agents of social change.

Single-Issue Crusader

Saying yes to more housing often means saying no to something else—for instance, places to park cars. There are two billion parking spots in the United States; seven for every car. Parking covers more acres in the country than any other single thing. The culprits, from one point of view, are car companies, urban planners, and aspiring politicians who worked together throughout the twentieth century. One of the most significant things they did was institute minimum parking requirements for new housing and commercial developments across the country. These force developers to provide specific numbers of parking spaces per apartment unit and per square footage of commercial space. Parking spot mandates made it possible to live in one place, work in another, and shop in a third. They were instrumental in creating the physical layout of the US's deeply WEIRD suburban world.

Now the tide is turning against minimum parking requirements. They're increasingly seen as impediments to reducing congestion, cleaning the air, building affordable housing, and combating climate change. Hundreds of American cities have overhauled or repealed these laws in recent years, from Buffalo, New York, to San Jose, California, to Anchorage, Alaska. Some developers are providing incentives to would-be customers with allowances for mass transit and car-sharing agreements. Progressive federal legislators have even tried to get in on the act. Their proposed Yes in My Backyard Act would mandate that awardees of federal community development grants show what steps they're taking to promote affordable housing. One way they can do it is by eliminating parking requirements.

If you want to do research, and you want to do research that affects people's lives, unsexy subjects like parking may give you a better chance than hot button ones like artificial intelligence. You can be a bit of a bigger fish in a smaller pond. In fact, one single person's research is widely credited with helping turn the tide against minimum parking requirements. On Donald Shoup's website, you can read scholarly articles going back to 1968 about zoning and parking rules. His 2005 book *The High Cost of Free Parking* is now considered a classic. His acolytes call themselves Shoupistas.

Shoup didn't turn the tide against parking requirements himself, of course. But he's an example of someone who plugged away for decades in relative obscurity on a single issue that many people would find totally boring. Right up until everyone cared about it and his work made a big impact.

Teacher

Lots of people still want lots of parking near where they live and work. But some things pretty much nobody wants near their backyards, like factory farms. They spread reeking odors and pollutants into neighbors' air, soil, and water. They cause asthma, heart attacks, and acid rain. They're also often located next to marginalized racial and indigenous communities. But factory farms, which furnish 90 percent of the world's meat, aren't just bad for the smells and toxins they pump into the air. They're a big source of carbon pollution. And it probably goes without saying that they subject both animals and employees to atrocious conditions. As a result, more and more people are committing to cutting back on food produced on factory farms. Some become vegetarian or vegan; others become "reducetarians."

Principled plant eaters are often haunted by a familiar thought, though: that their individual eating choices are just a drop in the bucket. Opting out of eating meat might clear their conscience but fail to make a dent on the factory farm industry. But what if they can scale up the consequences of their role by convincing others to join in? Sounds nice: after all, everyone loves being lectured about the virtues of veganism!

Under the right conditions, however, persuasion seems possible. An ethics class with a unit on the evils of factory farming might be just the place, or so several studies suggest. In one, students in two large classes read an influential essay about animal suffering on factory farms. Their responses were compared to students in other classes who read about a different issue (the ethics of charity). All the students (1,143 in total) discussed the essays in smaller-sized, fifty-minute meetings with their teaching assistants. Then they filled out questionnaires about their likelihood of donating money to charity and eating meat. The students were also sent vouchers they could use for on-campus dining. The results? Modest but meaningful.

Their stated values changed significantly. Forty-three percent of students who learned about animal suffering agreed that "eating the meat of factory farmed animals is unethical," while only 29 percent of those who got the lesson about charitable giving did. Before the intervention, in both groups, about 30 percent of the students' purchases at the campus cafeterias contained meat. Afterward, that percentage fell to 23 for students in the animal ethics class but stayed steady for students in the charitable giving class. The effects lasted at least a couple months.

For teachers, parents, coaches, and would-be role models, evidence for even modest effects like these is terrific news. It's a welcome balm for the creeping cynicism that has become an occupational hazard for so many of us. Maybe we don't always come off as Charlie Brown's parents

wah-woo-wah-ing on the trombone. Maybe sometimes the message actually gets through.

Eating less meat may have modest impact by itself, but as we learned in
chapter 7 "*my* choices are *your* situation," and so no single person's choices
are really just their own. Who knows what that lone student who takes the
animal rights lesson to heart might go on to do? Eating less meat also helps
shape the situations in which you make your own future choices. Who
knows what you might go on to do?!

It's unclear what's driving the effects in the ethics class, but we suspect
one factor is the teachers' effectiveness. Recall what an impassioned leader
like Devine can do in a classroom, encouraging a mindset of growth and
empowerment in their students, and compare that to some backbencher
who's just phoning it in.

Sponsor

One role model of ours is Jennifer Nagel, who occupies the role of philosopher at the University of Toronto. Now, philosophers are somewhat
notorious for talking the talk without walking the walk. Nagel wonderfully
subverts this stereotype. During the Syrian refugee crisis of 2015, like many
others, she was appalled by the image of a drowned three-year-old who had
washed up on the shore in Turkey, trying to flee from the war in his home-
land. "As a Canadian," she wrote, "there was something more I could do."

She decided to take advantage of a Canadian immigration policy that
allows private citizens to sponsor refugee families. Nagel posted about it
on Facebook, organized the fifteen friends who responded, and filled out
the simple two-page form. After she passed a background check, she soon
found herself organizing the arrival of a family—a widow and five of her
children who had been living in a refugee camp in Lebanon. The sponsorship lasted a year and involved considerable work, from finding a doctor
and school for the family to helping them shop for groceries. But the family
became self-sufficient and changed Nagel's perspective in the process.

She tells us she reflects on the experience with a real sense of appreciation for how much people from very different places can learn from each
other, stressing that the learning went both ways:

> This family didn't have much, materially, but they really knew how to live. I'd go
> over to their apartment to get them to sign some kind of school form, hoping to

be in and out in ten minutes, and it would always take two hours, because we'd have to have coffee, which would be prepared very slowly, and served on a tray. Then we would look at pictures on people's phones, and talk about everything that had happened since we saw each other, and about all our mutual acquaintances, with Google Translate barely enabling us to converse.

It was exasperating at first, but I realized over time that I had been making a mistake in my life, always being in a rush to get things done, and they were getting it right. I learned a lot from them, about everything from their religion to the hidden workings of my city, and we're still in touch.

Canada's history of refugee sponsorship is grounded in a commitment to upholding international rights, which was itself spurred by Canadian churches and neighborhood groups moved by the plights of people fleeing persecution. But evidence also suggests that—while the work of hosting is intensive and expensive—Canada's privately sponsored refugees end up better integrated and employed than refugees admitted solely with government assistance. And reams of data clarify how migration, including from refugees, benefits host countries. More immigration leads to stronger economies and innovation in culture and business.

But immigration has costs too, especially in the short term. Newcomers suffer a dip in well-being after moving, in part because immigration is arduous, in part because they suffer discrimination. NIMBYs and housing shortages don't help either. There are political costs too, at least from a progressive perspective. Sharp spikes in immigration can lead to commensurate spikes in support for radical right-wing parties. Sweden shocked the world in September 2022 when, after decades of dominance by progressive and center-left politics, recent waves of immigration were followed by the election of a far-right coalition. This result came to seem less shocking by 2025, as far-right parties gained electoral ground the world over.

Backlash like this doesn't affect all white people the same. People who feel strongly identified with their white ethnicity are more likely to react this way. In contrast, white people who feel less attached to their racial identity are readier to be sponsors in the vein of Jennifer Nagel. (The power of racial identification to either drive or dull white backlash is another reminder: all politics is identity politics.)

The downsides of spikes in immigration tend to be short-lived. For those who migrate, well-being eventually improves. For the countries that take them in, initial boosts in support for populist right-wing parties also fade over time. What drives both these positive longer-term trends is intergroup contact. Students get immersed in their new culture at school; adults get to know one another; trust slowly builds.

But as we found in chapter 5, not every form of intergroup contact does the trick. It's important that people be on equal footing and have opportunities to pursue goals together. College campuses offer a great example. For students attending diverse colleges, stereotypes about out-groups diminish. The effect is especially pronounced for students randomly assigned to interracial roommates.

Learning-oriented mindsets matter here too. When philosophy professors from Toronto host refugees from Syria, help them to enroll their children in school, and celebrate seasonal feasts together, they're ready to learn and work as equals toward shared goals.

The seeds sown from one role can bear fruit that grows into another. Many of today's refugee sponsors were themselves sponsored in the past. In 2016, almost forty years after coming to Canada from Vietnam at the age of five, Nhung Tran-Davies sponsored a Syrian refugee family. Like the doubly empowered DREAMers we met in chapter 11, many former refugees become politically engaged leaders.

As with housing vouchers in Seattle, Canada's private sponsorship program for refugees was already on the books. But securing uptake for these programs takes people stepping into "sustainer roles" like housing navigators and migration sponsors.

Happy Warrior

This book has profiled a wide range of people who took their roles to a whole other level, demonstrating degrees of commitment, ingenuity, and sacrifice few will match. But everyone's life provides all sorts of smaller windows for doing good, making a difference, and catalyzing change.

Random acts of kindness are a great example. In one experiment, participants offered free hot chocolate to someone at a public skating rink. This small kindness delivered big jolts of joy to recipients and givers alike, a result replicated in numerous similar studies. Yet many people remain unlikely to do little good deeds like this, for an all-too-familiar reason: they consistently underestimate the personal and social consequences of their actions. Again and again, people forget how much impact their actions have, on others and themselves. That's partly because they forget how much impact others have had on them.

Some people do manage to remember. One study interviewed hospital cleaning staff, finding that some saw their jobs as dreary and low skilled, while others saw their work as meaningful and high skilled. The difference, explains psychologist Amy Wrzesniewski, was driven by proactive engagement with doctors, nurses, and patients. Some staff members described the importance of paying attention to the cleanliness of the hospital room ceilings since they could imagine patients having to stare at the ceiling all day. Others said to themselves: "this could be my father or my mother or my brother or sister, and how would I care for them?"

These hospital staff members are using their leeway to do what Wrzesniewski calls "job crafting," (re)defining their roles in ways that focus on meaning and change. And it's not just jobs that can be crafted like this. When we show up for someone, just to be there for them, we're crafting a relationship. We can also use our leeway to perform random acts of kindness. It's another way to be a happy warrior, helping ourselves and those around us have a better time while we're fighting for a better world.

Conclusion
Time Doesn't Tell; We Tell Time

"Drys"—as teetotalers and temperance advocates were known—must have been devastated looking back on the ruins of their cause. After nearly a century of activism, they revised the Constitution of the United States, only to see their work backfire. In the fight for social change, what looks like victory can dissolve into failure.

On the other hand, what looks like defeat can turn into success. The League of Nations seemed like one of the most colossal failures in modern history. Established in the aftermath of World War I, it was the first transnational organization whose mission was to prevent war and promote world peace. The founding agreement, infused with postwar zeal, promised a fundamental departure from the international system of the nineteenth century. US President Woodrow Wilson won the Nobel Peace Prize for spearheading its creation. Then the United States refused to join. The organization dedicated to ensuring world peace succumbed to the world's worst war in less than twenty years.

Facing such setbacks, Robert Cecil, an architect of the League and another Nobel Peace Prize winner, took a longer view. On August 18, 1946, at its final meeting, he proclaimed, "The League is dead. Long live the United Nations." As the forerunner to the United Nations, the League's legacy has been overwhelmingly positive. It began the process of institutionalizing the rule of law, sparked interest in and theorizing about collective security, and gave smaller nations a bigger voice than ever before. It turned global attention to shared problems like epidemics, slavery, child labor, and refugee crises.

Without the benefit of hindsight, it's hard to tell the successes from the failures. And no one can predict the future. Stories of the past provide guidance, though. They shape the paths we chart into the future. Before World War II, people called World War I the "Great War." It was only after the horrors of Auschwitz, Pearl Harbor, Hiroshima, and Dresden that world wars were assigned numbers like movie sequels. This numbering has consequences. Ever since World War II, people have wondered, "What might World War III be like?" Thinking of World War I and II as a sequence makes us brace for more to come.

It's true that only time will tell what happens next. But it's also true that time is ours to tell. History is remembered, and told, by people. How we remember directs what we look for and find. Our stories become lessons that shape the events that we spin new stories about.

We've told many stories in this book. We started with one about how large corporations conspired to dupe us into futile forms of individualism, saddling us with responsibility for the carbon we emit and the hate we give. Those stories push us to consume better and recycle more. When it comes to fighting racism and sexism, they imply that our main job is to root out our internal biases, to master our own minds.

This propaganda has been effective, leaving many of us believing individualist fairytales that "real change comes from within" and social change starts with each of us on our own.

These stories retain incredible power, often propping up the status quo. It's a testament to their power that activists, politicians, and citizens intent on making change fall so easily under their sway. That includes us and our environment-themed bar mitzvahs. (Well, really, just one environment-themed bar mitzvah. And it was a long time ago!)

It can be tempting to completely reverse course, to swing all the way in the other direction. Abandon not just the idea that individual change "comes first" but that personal choices matter *at all*. Champion the view that we need to change the system directly.

But these responses to rampant individualism just substitute one monolithic, oversimplified, either/or view for another. The stories in this book all try to show how policies and people, institutions and ideas are thoroughly intertwined and mutually reinforcing. Both need to change, and there's no real sense to be made of the question of which to change first or which is more important. As the people who change systems that change people, we can work on both simultaneously. Considering who we are and how we're situated within social networks, we can see how being pressured by our peers shows that we're capable of pressuring them in return. The roles we occupy, whether we inherit or adopt them, give us real options. We can be housing navigators, antibias innovators, coalition-building DREAMers, or even just happy warriors.

As Tamin Ansary put it, the ceaseless task is to "keep correcting our narrative." One kind of story misses the structural duck by focusing too much on the individualist rabbit. Another turns its back on the individualist rabbit, mistaking it as nothing but corporate propaganda. The world needs big structural change. Filling it with the right kinds of stories can help it get there. Perhaps you'll go on to change some systems yourself and contribute a duck-rabbit story of your own. As the powerful play goes on, maybe you will contribute a verse.

Acknowledgments

We are deeply grateful for the extensive feedback that we received on drafts of this book. Our two book scrub workshops were incredibly useful. Our thanks go out to the Purdue Book Scrubbers: Sarah Constantino, Barry Lam, Noah Nathan, Heidi Vuletich, and Robin Zheng. And to the CUNY Scrubbers: Hans Bernier, Michael Coren, John Jost, Keith Payne, Ana Gantman, and Vanessa Wills. Funding for these workshops was provided by Purdue University, John Jay College, the CUNY Graduate Center, and the American Council for Learned Societies.

Friends and colleagues read enormous and unwieldy drafts too. Our heartfelt thanks to Rima Basu, Erin Beeghly, Carolina Flores, Katie Gasdaglis, Reine Hewitt, Reema Hijazi, Carla Loecke, Stephen Madva, Thomas Schminke, Marmar Tavasol, and Deborah Zateeny. Thanks also to Lindsey Alexander for helping us edit the enormous draft down to something readable.

We presented ideas that appear in the book to many audiences. Thanks for questions and feedback from participants at the following workshops and conferences. In 2021: the Philosophy and the Climate Crisis Conference, CUNY's Workshop on Individual and Structural Change, Purdue's Building Sustainable Communities Open Monthly Gathering, and the Cal Poly Pomona Colloquium. In 2022: the Southern Society of Philosophy and Psychology Conference, the Midwest Philosophy Colloquium at the University of Minnesota, and the online workshop on Moral Psychology and the Goals of Moral Education. In 2023: the workshop on The Ethical Dimensions of Self-Control at the University of Konstanz; the Princeton University Cognitive Science Colloquium; the Workshop on Public Philosophy and Social Change at Utrecht University; the University of California, Santa Cruz Colloquium; the Cognitive Science Speaker Series at the

Graduate Center, CUNY; the Center for the Experimental-Philosophical Study of Discrimination's minicourse at Aarhus University; the Group for Empirical Approaches to Morality and Society; and the Climate Change Working Group at Columbia University.

Special thanks for our YurtFriends: Zed Adams, Lacey Davidson, Jason D'Cruz, Katie Elliot, Peter Epstein, Ellen Fridland, Dan Harris, Gabrielle Johnson, Sari Kivilesky, Eric Mandelbaum, Mathew Mandelkern, Michaela McSweeney, Jessica Moss, Colin O'Neil, Jonathan Phillips, Kate Ritchie, Umrao Sethi, Susanna Siegel, and Natalia Washington, as well as those mentioned above.

For technical support at various stages, as well as substantive feedback, thanks to our research assistants, Dan Linford, Jake Sweet, and Petro Rosu (to whom we're also grateful for assembling the index). For fact-checking specific stories, thanks to Jennifer Nagel, Jennifer Morton, and Olúfẹ́mi O. Táíwò.

Many thanks also to three anonymous reviewers for MIT Press, one of whom revealed his identity to us as Joshua May, and to Phillip Laughlin for excellent advice and feedback.

In addition to our collective thanks, there are those we'd like to individually thank as well.

Alex is grateful to the students who have taken his Philosophy and Science of Implicit Bias course at Cal Poly Pomona going back to 2016, some of whom also completed independent studies and outstanding senior theses on topics related to this book, including Josh Ebiner, Bernard Granados, Derick Hughes, Valerie Marquez, Karina Ortiz Villa, and Jay Ramzy. Alex also benefited tremendously from his time thinking, debating, and writing about discrimination and social change in the summer 2023 as a visiting scholar at the Center for the Experimental-Philosophical Study of Discrimination in Aarhus. He is also grateful for ongoing discussions with Sean Norton and with past and present colleagues in the Cal Poly Pomona philosophy department, including David Adams, Michael Cholbi, Itzel Garcia, Megs Gendreau, Brian Kim, Peter Ross, Dale Turner, and Christine Wieseler. He eagerly awaits Cory Aragon's devastating rejoinder to this book: "A Plea for Anti-Anti-Anti-Individualism."

Dan would like to thank the participants in his Moral Psychology and Climate Change class who read and discussed a draft of the manuscript in the fall of 2022: James Blomgren, Henry Castro, Joshua Christian, Spenser

Davis, Tucker Ensmenger, Payton Ginestra, Ethan Guardado, William Heagerty, Kyle Howard, Yalan Huo, Amellia Klute, Lillian Millspaugh, Caleb Neal, Colin Newman, Eddie Null, Samantha Seybold, Brandon Stahl, Jonathan Sumita, Kermote Yao, and Kaitlyn Ying. Casual but ongoing discussions with Melissa Will and Milind and Monique Kilkarni about the book as it emerged from nonexistence were always fun and invigorating.

The collegial environment at Purdue's philosophy department has been an invigorating place to philosophize through the years, and Dan is thankful for the consistent support of the university, including the grant to fund our first book scrub. Purdue's interdisciplinary climate and sustainability community has and continues to be a great source of inspiration; thanks especially to Leigh Raymond, Laura Zanotti, and the other members of the Building Sustainable Communities team. The Center for Advanced Study in the Behavioral Sciences at Stanford is a fantastic place to think and talk about ideas. During Dan's year there, he was lucky enough to learn about the dimensions of social change from terrific researchers from around the globe and across the disciplinary spectrum. Thanks to all his fellow fellows from the 2018–2019 class (and he still thinks it should have been "Abolish Global Capitalism").

Michael would like to thank the students in his 2023 seminar, Individuals, Systems, and Social Change: Emma Arvedon, Noah Davis, Eleanor Jerome, Georgina Malone, Itsue Nakayama, Esther Neff, Maximiliana Rifkin, Petru Rosu, Lara Schadde, Maya Von Ziegesar, and Sean Apparicio. Thanks also to students from the 2021 seminar, Climate Change and Social Change, who weren't subjected to this book but helped spark relevant discussion. Friends who helped him think more clearly along the way include all his classmates from the Center for Advanced Study in the Behavioral Sciences and especially Michael Albertus, Jefferson Cowie, Guy Grossman, Mai Hassan, Michael Hiscox, and Robert Jackson. For discussion and advice, thanks also to Mahzarin Banaji, David Broockman, Eugene Chislenko, Miranda Fricker, Robert Keohane, Ewan Kingston, Benedek Kurdi, Tania Lombrozo, Rebecca Marwege, David Roberts, and Gregg Sparkman. Finally, he'd like to apologize to all the sea turtles for the bar mitzvah balloons and for adding insult to injury by joking about them. The rest of the jokes in this book will surely offend nobody, and if they do, blame Alex and Dan.

Notes

Introduction

Page 1 *"We are living in a motor age"*: Norton (2007). All the quotations from people about car culture are drawn from here as well. See also Norton (2008) for larger context as well as McKibben (2022b).

Page 2 *"Guns don't kill people"*: See Selinger (2012) for discussion. Browder's quote is found in Friedman et al. (2015).

Page 3 *"distract from the systemic changes"*: As of January 2024, Michael Mann's (2019) personal tweet linking to the article had over 750 retweets and nearly 1,400 likes. The original article was written by Mann and Jonathan Brockopp (2019). In other moments, Mann seems to share some of our worries around how the "urgency" of the climate crisis gets described (Carrington 2023).

Page 4 *"What is my role in changing the system?"*: Zheng (2018b).

Page 4 *"the most important thing"*: Ardagh, Wheal, and McKibben (2021).

Page 4 *climate change is an "everything problem"*: As design theorists Horst Rittel and Melvin Webber (1973) would say, it is a "wicked problem." See also Levin et al. (2012) as well as Brennan and Lo (2021) and Gardiner (2013) on the "perfect moral storm."

Page 5 *An average American refrigerator*: McDonough (2022). Data on historic US and EU emissions is from Ritchie (2019).

Page 5 *below where they were in 1913*: Data on per capita carbon pollution in the US in 2022 compared to 1913 is from Our World in Data (2024). On the furiously growing clean energy economy, see Office of Energy Efficiency and Renewable Energy (n.d.).

Page 6 *Segregation is an essential throughline*: For reconsiderations of and revisions to the history told by, for example, Rothstein (2017), see Blumgart (2021), Fishback et al. (2022), and Hynsjö and Perdoni (2023). See also chapter 2. On mortgage banking, see, for example, Coates (2014). On white parents and school choice, see, for example, Brinkman et al. (2023) and *Nice White Parents* by Joffe-Walt et al. (2020).

Page 6 ***becoming a full-time revolutionary***: Sometimes becoming a full-time revolutionary is the thing to do. We'll discuss examples in this book.

Page 7 ***an idea found across contemporary social science***: There are many, many forerunners and fellow travelers who adopt versions of the both/and approach we advocate, including Alcoff (2005); Alexander (2020); Allen (2004); Antonoplis (2024); Anzaldúa (2012); Aragon and Jaggar (2018); Atkin (2021); Ayala-López and Beeghly (2020); Bourdieu (1977, 1990); Broockman and Kalla (2016); Carroll et al. (2023); Charlesworth and Banaji (2023); Christman (2012); Code (1987); Collins (1999); Cooley, Brown-Iannuzzi, and Boudreau (2019); Coren (2022); Corner (2020); Cortland et al. (2017); Cox (2023); Davidson and Gruver (2020); Dillon (2012); Ferkany and Whyte (2012); Fleeson (2004); Freire (2018); Fricker (2012); Haslanger (2021); hooks (1994); Hourdequin (2010); Jost et al. (2017); Koggel, Harbin, and Llewellyn (2022); Kurtis, Salter, and Adams (2015); Lewin (1936, 1946); Markus and Kitayama (2010); Medina (2013); Nielsen et al. (2021); Norlock (2010); Pettigrew (2018), Reed-Sandoval (2020); Sarkissian (2010); Saul (2018); Skinner-Dorkenoo et al. (2023); Stewart et al. (2022); Ture and Hamilton (1992); van Zomeren, Kutlaca, and Turner-Zwinkels (2018), Vasil [Vasilyeva] and Ayala-López (2019); Vial et al. (2021); Wills (2024); and Young (2011). We'll cite many more in the pages to follow.

Page 7 ***Our focus will be on climate change and racism***: The debate takes subtly but importantly different forms in the two cases. Critics of individualist approaches to climate change focus on how corporations brainwashed us into thinking the solution is for each of us as individuals to change our behavior, specifically taking personal responsibility to reduce our carbon footprint. See chapter 1. There's a further dimension to criticisms of individualist approaches to race, which also give a prominent place to personal responsibility: Is there too much emphasis on rooting out our inner prejudices and stereotypes? Racism is (so the concern goes) mistakenly thought to be primarily located in hearts and minds rather than embedded in larger structures. See chapter 2. In both cases, though, people say that the upshot is to stop thinking about individuals and start changing systems.

Chapter 1

Page 11 ***He was reputedly***: Aleiss (1996) and Yamada (2014).

Page 11 ***He played the "Crying Indian"***: Wax-Thibodeaux (2013).

Page 12 ***It won multiple awards***: Crockett (2014). On more recent ratings of the PSA, see Metrix (2014).

Page 12 ***collective acknowledgment of the genocide***: See, for example, Dunbar-Ortiz (2015), Hinton, Woolford, and Benvenutol (2014), and Peck (2021). Collective acknowledgment of the genocide and its legacy and political implications is far from fully achieved (e.g., Foxworth and Boulding 2022). Growing awareness has not just passively "happened" to Americans; it reflects the tireless efforts of organized activists from the American Indian Movement (e.g., Hersher 2017).

Page 12 *the message is catastrophically misleading*: On how misleading and invalid this argument is, see this book's appendix at https://www.somebody-book.com.

Page 13 *Keep America Beautiful*: Keep America Beautiful (n.d.). On Keep America Beautiful's founders, see Strand (2008).

Page 13 *The Crying Indian ad was their masterstroke*: For discussions of "responsibilization" and the related notion of "individualization," see Giesler and Veresiu (2014), Maniates (2001), and Shamir (2008). See also Chater and Loewenstein (2023), along with the replies, including ours (Madva, Brownstein, and Kelly 2023).

Page 13 *"friends don't let friends drive drunk"*: Strand (2008). On the origin of "litterbug," see Dannhausen Jr. (2020).

Page 13 *a 1994 message about water pollution*: Strand (2008). See also Abdelfatah (2019).

Page 14 *threaten anyone's bottom line*: See Táíwò (2022) on ways that vested interests "capture" those who might resist them.

Page 14 *BP popularized the term*: Apparently, BP coopted the carbon footprint idea from Mathis Wackernagel and William Rees's (1996) "ecological footprint."

Page 14 *disastrous consequences to the environment*: For pioneering work here, see Supran and Oreskes (2021).

Page 16 *Exxon's own scientists*: Supran, Rahmstorf, and Oreskes (2023).

Page 16 *told consumers to "drink responsibly"*: Smith, Cukier, and Jernigan (2014).

Page 16 *Coca-Cola fought back*: O'Connor (2015). On food industry lobbying, see Brownell and Warner (2009).

Page 16 *Dr. Dean Schillinger explained*: Rabin (2022). The recent advent of medications like Ozempic, while surely not powerful enough to counter the effects of poverty and so forth, may be important "game changers" for people suffering from type 2 diabetes and certain causes of obesity (Lenharo 2023).

Page 16 *enormous amounts of money*: Lewandowsky and van der Linden (2022): "The annual budget (2003–2010) of think tanks that are known to be involved in creating and disseminating climate disinformation was around $900 million (Brulle 2014). Moreover, between 2000 and 2016, more than $2 billion was spent by Congressional lobbyists to oppose climate legislation."

Page 18 *the film offers concrete suggestions*: Guggenheim (2006).

Page 18 **The four most impactful options**: Wynes and Nicholas (2017). Blog posts like "9 Things You Can Do to Save the Environment" are ubiquitous, and books like Greenberg's (2021) *The Climate Diet: 50 Simple Ways to Trim Your Carbon Footprint* offer a similar angle. This thought-provoking book starts with lifestyle and consumer choices but then transitions to suggestions about political and—as we discuss later—"structural change." For more on examples like "9 Things You Can Do to Save the Environment," see Brownstein, Kelly, and Madva (2022). Another fascinating way that the impulse to make a difference gets channeled into consumption habits is through mechanisms that allow people to make nominal donations to good causes (Whalen 2023).

Page 19 **more knowledgeable and more concerned**: Nolan (2010). This study could be more methodologically robust, so we take caution in inferring too much from it. Although *An Inconvenient Truth* evidently failed to move the needle in the short term, it might have sewn seeds of social change that blossomed later. See chapter 8.

Page 19 **changes to their personal behavior**: Lots of earnest academics, journalists, and activists think that focusing on personal behavior change is a distraction from the real political work of holding fossil fuel companies to account (e.g., Hale 2022; Illing 2021; Kingston and Sinnott-Armstrong 2018; Santos 2024; Sinnott-Armstrong 2005; Yglesias 2018; Klebl and Jetten 2023; Buse et al. 2022). In one speech, Gore (2008) himself stressed the importance of changing "not just light bulbs, but laws." One study with nearly two thousand participants found that flat-footed recommendations to consume better (eat less meat, use less hot water) undermined how willing people were to reduce their footprint and vote for climate-concerned candidates. What's more, it reduced people's beliefs in the reality of human-caused climate change as well as their trust in the science (Palm, Bolsen, and Kingsland 2020).

Page 19 **"I Don't Care if You Recycle"**: Heglar (2019). For the Sunrise Movement's aims, see Sunrise Movement (n.d.b.). See also Selig and Guskin (2023).

Page 20 **"if you want the beef, get the beef"**: Marantz (2022).

Page 20 **standing athwart, yelling stop**: Buckley (1955) rolls over in his grave.

Chapter 2

Page 21 **The Accumulation of (Dis)advantage**: See Valian (1999) and Merton (1968) on the Matthew Effect. Stewart and Valian (2018) is our go-to recommendation for anyone looking for a book on how to resist the accumulation of (dis)advantage for academic faculty.

Page 21 **Imagine 100 people have**: We're focused here on structural inequities for urban Black versus white people. Some but not all of the studies we cite here found that Hispanic and Asian Americans were also treated inequitably in comparison to white people. See also Gasdaglis and Madva (2020) and Madva (2016b).

Page 21 ***Black Americans suffer more power outages***: In February 2021, a brutal winter storm hit Texas and knocked out many people's power for days, but predominantly minority communities endured *four times* more blackouts than predominantly white communities. See Carvallo et al. (2021) and Flores et al. (2023).

Page 21 ***half of service sector workers***: This estimate is taken specifically from Bellew, Schneider, and Harknett's (2022, 3) policy brief comparing fast-food and other service workers in California. However, see their Shift website for a range of additional policy briefs and publications, including Storer, Schneider, and Harknett's (2020) piece on racial and ethnic inequalities in the service sector across the US. For racial and ethnic data on labor force participation, including the service sector, see US Bureau of Labor Statistics (2023). We'll say more about the terrible either/or options that oppressed people face, especially college students from disadvantaged backgrounds who are the first in their family to go to college, in chapter 12.

Page 22 ***Black Americans have less access***: Latham et al. (2021) and Hollett and Frankenberg (2022a, 2022b). On Black kids' ER wait times, see Zhang et al. (2019), which controls for socioeconomic status and other factors, as do many of the other studies we cite in this chapter. On racial health disparities, see related research on the "weathering hypothesis," which is the suggestion that long-term exposure to social and economic disparities contributes to racial disparities in people's heath. See, for example, Forde et al. (2019) and Williams et al. (1997).

Page 22 ***Research finds that government officials***: See Giulietti, Tonin, and Vlassopoulos (2019), Wolfers (2017), and Butler and Broockman (2011).

Page 22 ***18 percent of Black households are carless***: On car ownership, see National Equity Atlas (n.d.). The racial wealth and pay gaps in the United States are staggering. As the Federal Reserve explained in 2021, "in the United States, the average Black and Hispanic or Latino households earn about half as much as the average White household and own only about 15 to 20 percent as much net wealth" (Aladangady and Forde 2021). A great deal of people's wealth is tied up in their homes, but Black-owned homes increase in value far more slowly than white homes: "owner-occupied homes in Black neighborhoods are undervalued by $48,000 per home on average, amounting to $156 billion in cumulative losses" (Perry, Rothwell, and Harshbarger 2018). Of course, with less inherited wealth and lower average pay, Black people are more likely to rent. And even just focusing on renters, there are further inequities. Black renters have to put down larger security deposits on their apartments, and then their rent eats up more of their monthly paychecks (Zillow MediaRoom 2022). As a National Association of Realtors (2022) analysis found, "in terms of renter households, half of Black Americans spend more than 30% of their monthly income on rent. Almost three out of 10 Black renter households (28%) and one in five White renter households (20%) are severely cost-burdened—defined as spending more than 50% of monthly income on rent."

Page 22 *used car salespeople offer*: Ayres and Siegelman (1995). For a more recent review of field experiments on discrimination like this, see, for example, Bertrand and Duflo (2017). Another example is Edelman, Luca, and Svirsky (2017), wherein experimenters created Airbnb guest accounts that differed only by name and found that those with African American–sounding names had a 16 percent smaller chance of booking a spot. On "driving while Black," see Pierson et al. (2020). In a Lyft study, drivers of color were, if anything, slightly *less* likely to speed than white drivers, but the difference was not statistically significant (Aggarwal 2022). See Charlesworth and Banaji (2023) for a review of evidence of regional implicit bias correlating with a range of practices and outcomes, including police pulling drivers over.

Page 22 *a one-hour increase*: Hoffman and Strezhnev (2023).

Page 23 *two times more likely*: Mujcic and Frijters (2021).

Page 23 *one species of structural injustice*: As the philosopher Tommie Shelby (2008, 81) explains, "the question we should be asking . . . is whether the denizens of the ghetto are entitled to a better set of options, and if so, whose responsibility it is to provide them."

Many structural factors make things *easier* versus *harder* for members of certain groups rather than create explicit permissions and prohibitions based on social groups. A scene in the film *Hidden Figures* vividly illustrates this, when the women's bathroom is in an entirely different building from where the newly hired women mathematicians work (Melfi 2016; for discussion, see Holroyd and Puddifoot 2020). This easier/harder contrast has also been analogized to the difference between playing the same video game on easy versus hard settings. The science fiction author John Scalzi (2012) argues that being a white man in the US is like playing a video game on the easiest setting. The analogy of structural injustice to video games is apt, though there are lots of ways in which men are not doing well in countries like the US (Reeves 2022).

Page 23 *to the grades they receive*: See Walker (2022). Note also that the structures that organize our lives are not just abstract things like rules, district boundaries, and economies but also the concrete artifacts and built environment with which we interact. See, for example, Hu (2019), Liao and Huebner (2021), Timms and Spurrett (2023), and Coninx (2023).

Page 23 *beliefs, goals, and personality traits*: Though several theorists have explored the ways in which the boundary between the two is vague and porous (e.g., Davidson and Kelly 2020). See chapter 7. Theorists including Bourdieu (1990), Zheng (2018a), and Martín (2020) also argue that much of what's "inside" people should be conceived as "internalized social structures." See also appendix section 2a on Strong Structuralism.

Page 24 *racially restrictive covenants*: Seattle Civil Rights and Labor History Project (n.d.).

Page 24 *Eighty percent of American cities*: Menendian, Gambhir, and Gailes (2021). See also Semuels (2021).

Page 24 *racial segregation is the "linchpin"*: For arguments about segregation being the "linchpin" of contemporary racial inequality, see Anderson (2010, 25; 2012, 71). The quote from Malcolm X is from his 1963 speech at UC-Berkeley (see BlackPast 2013). See Sugrue (2014, xl) for discussion of his claim that "geography is destiny." See Nelson et al. (2023) for a vivid, interactive analysis of redlining.

Page 24 *"Zoning" is the term*: Kenton (2022b).

Page 25 *Milpitas quickly moved*: Rothstein (2017, 19–20).

Page 25 *Redlining systematically shut people out*: From these origins, redlining now refers to any discriminatory practice denying services to neighborhoods based on the race or ethnicity of its residents (Legal Information Institute 2022).

Page 25 *Home Owners' Loan Corporation*: There is some controversy about exactly how much the Home Owners' Loan Corporation and the infamous colored maps per se contributed to discriminatory mortgage practices. However, the disputants agree that the federal government's lending practices were discriminatory contributors to segregation (Fishback et al. 2022; Blumgart 2021; Hynsjo and Perdoni 2023).

Page 25 *are like time machines*: Griffith (2021).

Page 25 *non-white applicants received*: Fulwood III (2016). This is according to the "testimony of George Lipsitz of the University of California-Santa Barbara before the National Commission on Fair Housing and Equal Opportunity."

Page 26 *$3 to $4 billion*: Coates (2014) and George et al. (2019).

Page 26 *Southern congressmen insisted*: For example, Social Security was not made available to agricultural or domestic workers, meaning that the jobs Black people were much more likely to have were not going to get retirement pensions (Johnson 2020; Delmont 2022). See chapter 11.

Page 26 *residential segregation declined*: Intrator, Tannen, and Massey (2016).

Page 26 *four out of five students*: Nowicki (2022).

Page 26 *poorer areas will have poorer schools*: For more on the complexities of local, state, and federal school funding in the US, see Chingos and Blagg (2017) and Kenyon, Paquin, and Munteanu (2022). On Black neighborhoods' exposure to environmental toxins, see Bravo et al. (2022).

Page 27 *"spatial mismatch"*: Wilson (2012) and Anderson (2010). On payday lenders, see Small et al. (2021). On the "time tax," see Lowrey (2021). Speaking of difficult commutes, how about people in rural communities, who often live long distances from necessary services like healthcare (including reproductive care) and jobs? As we mentioned in a previous note, although our focus here is on structural injustices in urban Black communities, there are complex, racialized, and intersectional injustices facing other communities as well (Gasdaglis and Madva 2020), including white ones. That said, lots of rural people aren't white, and some of the worst-off Black rural communities are still scarred from the legacy of slavery (Payne, Vuletich, and Brown-Iannuzzi 2019; Acharya, Blackwell, and Sen 2018).

Page 27 *"segregation along lines of"*: Anderson (2012, 71). See also Shelby (2016) and Madva (2020b). For an accessible, interactive introduction to Schelling's (1969) model of segregation and rational choice, see Hart and Case (2014).

Page 27 *people contributing to segregation*: See appendix section 2a on Strong Structuralism, especially the footnote on *the patterned nature of oppression*.

Page 27 *Many companies today*: See Dobbin and Kalev (2022) and Choi et al. (2023). The Supreme Court has, for decades and especially in 2023, also made it harder for organizations, like universities, to try to push back against all these racist trends through "affirmative" practices that account for people's race when deciding whom to admit to the school or hire for the job (Montague 2023; Students for Fair Admissions Inc. v. President & Fellows of Harvard College 2023).

Page 28 *twice as good to get half as much*: White (2015).

Page 28 *between 15 and 26 million people*: Buchanan, Bui, and Patel (2020). The murder of George Floyd was a relatively rare instance where the officers were subsequently both charged and convicted (e.g., Ray 2020; Archbold 2021), though the rate of officers being charged has increased since 2020 (Burch and Manley 2024).

Page 29 *tripled their hiring*: Norwood (2021) attributes this finding to Russell Reynolds Associates, which also found that DEI hiring had increased in the preceding three years (Paikeday 2019). On DEI hiring overall, see Stansell and Zhao (2020). On DEI spending, see Newkirk (2019) and Mehta (2019). On projected growth in the DEI industry, see Research and Markets LTD (2021). On the other hand, evidence suggests that the fervor for diversity has cooled (Elias 2023) and is being reversed at many corporations and universities (e.g., Confessore and Friess 2024). For discussion of how the demand for DEI services retracted, focusing on the specific case study of a white woman and Black woman who worked together before falling out, see Kaleem (2023).

Page 29 *J. C. Pan wrote*: Pan (2020). Leading social theorists like Ibram X. Kendi draw similar conclusions, criticizing efforts like these for being too individualist (focused on "racist minds") and insufficiently attentive to social structures of power. "The problem of race has always been at its core the problem of power, not the problem of immorality or ignorance," he writes (Kendi 2019, 213), which entails that efforts to remove people's ignorance through diversity trainings is a waste of time. See also Haslanger (2015, 10). We'll rethink these criticisms of diversity training in chapter 5.

Page 29 *"Head Off Potential Lawsuits"*: Leaders' Choice Insurance (2019).

Page 30 *Pan gets at the economic sense of this*: Pan (2020). Sunkara's statement about inclusivity seminars is found in Sunkara (2020). See also Táíwò (2022).

Chapter 3

Page 31 *Big Structural Change*: Warren (2019).

Page 31 *2020 Democratic primary*: Gross (2019). During the primary, Senator Cory Booker accused Biden of promoting mass incarceration and coming late to the structural change party (Corasaniti, Glueck, and Stevens 2019). For Sanders' proposals, see Sanders (n.d.). For more on Senator Booker's proposed "baby bonds" legislation, cosponsored with Representative Ayanna Pressley, see Cineas (2021).

Page 32 *free breakfast to children*: According to Hassberg (2020, 87), "The Black Panther Party and its survival programs were born from a desire to meet the basic needs of Black urban communities that had long been neglected by the state (Abron 1998). The party developed dozens of free programs, including armed 'cop watches' to monitor and curb racially motivated police brutality, health clinics and sickle cell anemia testing services, community schools, ambulatory services, legal aid, a commissary for incarcerated people, escort services for senior citizens, and food programs for poor families and children." See also Blakemore (2021). By our lights, these are all examples of nonstate-based structural changes for Black communities.

Page 32 *"indoctrinating children with Panther propaganda"*: Bloom and Martin (2016, 186). Many of the examples we'll discuss in this book are structural changes that work through the state, so thanks to Hans Bernier for bringing our attention to this example that does not (or did not start that way, at least). For more on the Black Panther Party's vision of structural change, see BlackPast (2018). We say more about state-based hostility toward the Black Panthers in chapter 10.

Page 32 *feudal kingdoms to capitalist democracies*: Most of the examples of social change that we discuss in this book are less profound than the shift from feudalism to capitalism. But we maintain that even for such world-historical transformations, *no matter how "fundamental" and urgent one thinks they are*, there will be a story to tell about the individual changes in beliefs, values, habits, and so on needed to cause those "deeper" structural transformations, alongside the story about the effects of those deep structural transformations on individual beliefs, values, and habits.

Page 32 *humanity's "Great Escape"*: Deaton (2015).

Page 32 *human life has doubled*: DeLong (2022); see also Matthews (2022). For people who made it past infancy, though, the average lifespan was more like fifty-five years (Roser 2023). For the comparison between 1820 and 2020, if the world consisted of one hundred people, see Roser (2024). Another astounding, and little-known feat is that worldwide child mortality has declined *over 62 percent* from 1990 to 2022. According to the United Nations, 4.9 million children under the age of 5 died worldwide in 2022. That number was 13 million in 1990 (see Scott 2024).

Page 33 *"Distracted Boyfriend" memes*: Know Your Meme (2017). On the relationship between the Great Fire of London and city planning, see Hebbert (2020). See the appendix for more discussion of the mix of factors that drives historical change. Actually, pretty much everything except perhaps a massive meteor crashing into the Earth should probably be explained in terms of a complex mix of luck, structural preconditions, and individual agency. And now that human beings have the power to nuke incoming asteroids, even events like this will, in the future, have to be explained partly in terms of human agency (i.e., perhaps people failing to dedicate enough resources to prevent such an event). Even many so-called natural disasters are influenced by human agency, such as climate change intensifying hurricanes and fracking causing earthquakes (Reuters 2022; National Geographic 2023), and there are better and worse ways to prepare, respond, and so forth.

Page 33 *for every 100,000 births*: Kliff, Miller, and Buchanan (2023). See also ProPublica's "Lost Mothers" series (ProPublica 2017).

Page 34 *fair, safe, and democratic*: Dilemmas like these are what environmental justice is all about (e.g., Riofrancos 2020; Abdelfatah et al. 2023). See also chapters 7 and 9.

Page 34 *Payne and Heidi Vuletich insist*: Payne and Vuletich (2018, 49) and Payne and Hannay (2021, 933). Payne and Vuletich at times endorse a more both/and view (Vuletich, Sommet, and Payne 2023, 9). See the appendix. Similarly, psychologist Glenn Adams calls for a shift "from the task of changing individual hearts and minds to changing the sociocultural worlds in which those hearts and minds are immersed" (Nordell 2017). Adams's claim here is striking in that elsewhere he has spearheaded important research on the power of race education to take a both/and approach, which teaches both how structures shape biases and biases shape structures (Adams et al. 2008; Kurtis, Salter, and Adams 2015).

Page 34 *"I became a college professor"*: Kendi (2019, 234–235). The subsequent passage is from Kendi (2016, 9).

Page 35 *a by-product, not a cause*: Payne and Hannay (2021, 928): "Implicit bias is a byproduct of a mind that draws inferences based on statistical regularities, when that mind is immersed in an environment of systemic racism." Forscher et al. (2019, 544) construe implicit biases as residual "scars" of concepts, and Henry (2025) writes "A better metaphor in my mind is that people are 'Geiger counters,' akin to devices that report radiation in the environment but do not spread it. It is more parsimonious to consider the IAT [the Implicit Association Test, a measure of people's implicit biases] similarly, a report on the associations people are exposed to in their environment and not a vehicle for their spread." See also Mallon (2017). Madva (2016a) discusses several further theorists who construe biases as "mirror-like reflections" of social realities.

Page 35 *"rules of the road"*: Effective institutions, according to North, align private and social interests. They create structures that incentivize people to act in ways that produce socially desirable outcomes, even if people act in narrowly self-interested ways, as rational egoists in the classical economic sense. In the context of race and racism, North might say that good institutions are those that create incentives for otherwise racist politicians to govern in antiracist ways. North might also contrast this with the idea that the way to produce racially egalitarian outcomes is to elect politicians who personally reject racism (North and Thomas 1973; North 1990). Thanks to Noah Nathan for discussion. We're all for creating good institutions in North's sense. See chapter 5 on how pretty much everything is "two degrees" from race. However, people often fail to support institutions that align public and private interests because they see those institutions as helping people unlike themselves.

Page 35 **Without persuading anyone**: For example, in presenting the ideas in this book, we have been asked a version of this question many times: "Isn't the climate crisis so terrible and urgent that we must address its causes *directly* through large-scale structural change, rather than through persuasion or one by one individual change?" Compare, for example, the conclusions of Kinney and Bright (2023) and Bright et al. (in press). We agree about the urgency but firmly believe there's no circumventing the need to change hearts and minds. If previous ways of persuading people to take action haven't worked—via appeals to "follow the science" or "love Mother Earth"—then motivated individuals, working in collaboration, need to find *other ways* to motivate and organize people. See, for example, chapter 5 on the Return of the Allegedly Irrelevant. To the extent that efficiency and urgency are key, the upshot is just that we should pursue the more rather than less efficient ways of coaxing or cajoling enough individuals to start, sustain, and accept structural change.

Page 35 **carbon pollution rebounded**: Meyer (2021). Meyer is a terrific climate journalist who in all other respects appreciates the complex, both/and nature of problems like climate change (Meyer 2022). Our point here is that his systems-over-individuals logic shares an either/or framework with the messaging of Keep America Beautiful.

Page 36 **Political scientist Matto Mildenberger**: Mildenberger (2019); emphasis added. For similar statements, see chapter 1's note on *"changes to their personal behavior,"* such as Illing (2021).

Page 36 **I guess we're done here**: In personal correspondence, the *Washington Post's* "climate coach" Michael Coren reports that most of the people who contact him feel precisely this kind of hopelessness. See also the growing body of science and media commentary on "climate anxiety" (e.g., Clayton and Karazsia 2020; Piper 2022a; Doherty et al. 2022).

Page 36 **Civil rights activist Bayard Rustin**: Abdelfatah (2021).

Page 37 **a subtler form of either/or thinking**: In the appendix, we have more to say about those we call individual *prioritizers*, who recognize that the goal isn't just to change the minds of random people but rather to change enough people's minds and choices so that fundamental parts of social life ultimately change. What they often think is that system change *starts* with individuals.

Page 37 **outside corporate contexts, within alternative structures**: The Black Panthers' free breakfast program was launched, for example, in a church. That church, that physical building, had to be there for the Black Panther Party to start feeding kids—and changing their hearts and minds at the same time. In fact, Hoover wasn't wrong to worry that the Black Panther Party was using its free breakfast program to change hearts and minds (he was arguably wrong to call it "indoctrination" rather than "education"). As Hassberg (2020, 88) explains, "For the Panthers, food was a medium to politicize Black communities about the limits and failures of capitalism and the merit and praxis of revolution. Their survival programs provided tangible resources, cultivated racial pride and self-determination, and functionally challenged power structures that exploit, dominate, and control Black bodies. . . . It was common knowledge that the state did not deliver basic protections to Black people but the Panthers did."

Page 37 **structural change is more important**: Some really do follow pessimism about "people power" to its extremes. See section 2a of the appendix.

Page 37 **"What 'Structural Racism' Really Means"**: Bouie (2021), citing Cox (1948). For further work on racial capitalism, see Robinson (2005).

Page 38 **they take priority**: On race, see also Banks and Ford (2008, 2011), Haslanger (2015), Dixon and Levine (2012), Dixon et al. (2012), Wright and Baray (2012, 236), and Ross (2023). Note that many of those who say structural change "takes priority" over individual change in some moments nevertheless say much more both/ and things in other contexts, for example, Haslanger (2021). On climate, see also, for example, Sobel (2021) and Karpf, Lacombe, and Flum (2023). We discuss other prioritizers elsewhere (Madva 2016a, 2017; Davidson and Kelly 2020; Madva 2020a; Brownstein, Kelly, and Madva 2022; Madva, Brownstein, and Kelly 2023; Madva, Kelly, and Brownstein 2024). See also Flores (2022a) and Soon (2020, 2021a, 2021b).

Page 38 **lead instead to system-changing action?**: Bouie elsewhere makes a range of variously general and concrete proposals for structural change, for example, in Rodia (2022) and Bouie (2022).

Page 39 **"Power concedes nothing without a demand"**: BlackPast (2007).

Chapter 4

Page 43 **Fliegende Blätter *in 1892***: See McManus et al. (2010) for further history. We considered the duck-rabbit as an analogy in Brownstein, Kelly, and Madva (2022). We also introduced versions of the e-scooter, phone banking, and COVID-19 examples that appear below.

Page 43 *zoo-going Zürchers saw a bird*: Brugger and Brugger (1993). One way to make sense of these findings is that people's individual mindsets determine what they see in the duck-rabbit. If you're thinking about birds because you're *en route* to the zoo, you're liable to see a duck. If you're thinking about Easter, hello bunny. Victory to individualists?! Not so fast. What explains our mindsets? In this case, it's that zoos house birds or that the calendar says it's Easter. These features of the world—contexts and background structures—shape our thoughts. Victory to structuralists?! Not so fast, since some people hate the zoo and wouldn't be caught dead there, some people obsessed with their pet rabbits might see bunnies everywhere they go, and Zürich's Jews and Muslims might not be primed to think about bunnies around the spring equinox anyway. These are all individual differences in how people's minds interact with the outer world. But where did those individual differences come from? Round and round we go.

Page 44 *Reduced global carbon pollution*: Tollefson (2021). For seeing this slowdown as vindicating the power of individual action, see, for example, Grunwald (2020). Taking a wider perspective on this example, it can also be framed as vindicating structuralism because, as we noted in the previous chapter, even with this massive reduction in emissions due to behavior change, and even if we continued reducing emissions by 6 percent every year, we would not have been on pace to meet our climate goals (Meyer 2021). As it turned out, carbon emissions completely rebounded the following year.

In fact, these social events can be interpreted and explained in *all sorts* of ways. Although in the main text we talk about seeing the "whole picture," we are just interested in seeing *enough* of the picture to understand and effect social change. See Anderson (2016), Gadamer (2004), Malpas (2022), and Madva (2019a) for more on the idea that there's always a range of plausible interpretations and explanations. Sometimes explanations can be adequate even though they only to appeal to individuals or to structures, without mentioning both. What people want from explanations depends on background assumptions, current goals, and context-specific questions. See the appendix. For debate, see Haslanger (2015), Saul (2018), and Ayala-López and Beeghly (2020).

Page 44 *Why not both?*: Know Your Meme (2011).

Page 46 *she started MADD*: See Lightner's (n.d.) description of these events in her own words (see also Galloway 1985; Wire Services 1985; Yune 2023; History, n.d.).

Page 46 *alcohol-related traffic deaths*: Fell and Voas (2006), which is also the source for the Gallup poll. See also Responsibility.org (2022).

Page 46 *effectively reduced drunk driving*: Carpenter and Dobkin (2011).

Page 46 *driving drunk is shameful*: Norms and attitudes were quite different not so long ago (EllieVisionOG 2023).

Page 47 *"the only thing that ever has"*: For a history of similar quotations, and an attempt to trace exactly when (if ever) Mead said this, see Quote Investigator (2017). For empirical work on related ideas, see Xie et al. (2011).

Page 47 *"Mothers Against Drunk* **Drivers***"*: Lightner (n.d.; emphasis added) is the source for the quotations in this paragraph and the next. See chapter 1 for discussion of "responsibilization" (foisting responsibility onto individuals).

Page 48 *the background of American minds*: There were lots of other background structures enabling Lightner's success, including air for her to breathe, solid ground to stand on (rather than lava or a Biblical flood), the physical laws of the universe and the Big Bang—not to mention an American democratic system that allows people to vote, lobby, campaign, and so on—and a history of American activism replete with social movements. Lightner is light-skinned, from a middle-class family that gave her enough wealth and free time to commit to activism rather than working all day for minimum wage, and already had a history of activist work and community engagement.

Page 48 *cleanest air in the world*: Grunwald (2020). One could argue that all these changes are net negatives since they arguably helped keep single-use container companies and car manufacturers in business. We worry that this critique could be levied against any instance of incremental progress. Chipping away at a big problem can easily be seen as keeping the basic structures intact, whether it's imposing ethical standards on animal agriculture (and thus keeping agribusiness afloat) or passing Obamacare (and thus keeping the United States's private health system running). We discuss anti-incrementalism biases in chapter 8.

Page 48 *downtown Copenhagen, in 2018*: richmond33 (2018); see also Cortright (2019).

Page 48 *Copenhageners are happy with it*: See Copenhagen's tourism website (Thoem n.d.).

Page 48 *Amsterdam in 1971 and 2020*: Taylor (2022).

Page 50 *raze the Vesterbro neighborhood*: Cathcart-Keays and Warin (2016).

Page 50 *Shopkeepers pushed back*: Greenfield (2022).

Page 50 *used to be a parking lot*: Lee (2019).

Page 50 *twelve official public titles*: Caro (1975).

Page 51 *influence, ego, and racism*: Campanella (2017). Caro's memory of Moses is found in Robbins (2018).

Page 51 *"people will read no further"*: New York Preservation Archive Project (n.d.).

Page 52 *extensive public transportation networks*: To be fair to Stockholm, which is an incredible city, average driving levels there are not overwhelmingly higher than in

Copenhagen. Stockholm commuters are less likely to bike than Copenhagen commuters but *more* likely to ride the metro. Additionally, Stockholm's air pollution levels are comparably low to Copenhagen's and dramatically lower than Los Angeles's. See Numbeo (n.d.a., n.d.b.).

Page 52 *highest levels of social trust*: Ortiz-Ospina and Roser (2016) and Tinggaard (2020). Nordic populations of countries are also relatively ethnically homogenous, which may influence rates of happiness and trust (Åkerströmp 2023; but see Martela et al. 2020).

Page 53 *a "category mistake"*: Magidor (2022).

Page 53 *consider the many pros and cons*: Although we are talking about comparing consequences in these cases, we aren't making assumptions about what kinds of consequences to consider, and we are definitely not making the utilitarian assumption that all of our actions ought to maximize happiness. Someone might compare the potential consequences of their individual choices on their mental health, or they might consider which of two structural changes does the least injustice. People might also choose to do things regardless of their estimated consequences. The point is about what to do *when* you've chosen to do something in order to make change in the world. See chapter 14.

Page 54 *Schools can start "bike buses"*: Surico (2023).

Page 55 *to create feedback loops*: See chapter 8.

Page 55 *to show up for court*: See chapter 2. Even *with* a PhD in neuroscience, their predictions about how to boost attendance wouldn't outperform commonsense. Scientists are, on average, not much (if any) better at prediction than laypeople (Grossmann et al. 2023; Krugman 2023; Economist 2023), though there are exciting developments happening in prediction science (Tetlock and Gardner 2016).

Page 56 *treating Black bodies as exotic*: See, for example, the story of Sara Baartman (Parkinson 2016): "Brought to Europe seemingly on false pretences by a British doctor, stage-named the 'Hottentot Venus,' she was paraded around 'freak shows' in London and Paris. . . . Her brain, skeleton and sexual organs remained on display in a Paris museum until 1974. Her remains weren't repatriated and buried until 2002."

Chapter 5

Page 57 *Obama was taking another risk*: We are not claiming that American politics was *never* more polarized; the Civil War leaps immediately to mind. But even during periods of great upheaval and division, like the Civil Rights Movement, neither one's political party nor one's race were such consistently strong predictors of all of one's political views (Klein 2020). On Obama's bet for the success of healthcare reform: he had always known that he would have to navigate American attitudes about race. What he specifically didn't expect was that polarized and ideological opposition to his policies would be driven by racism per se (Obama 2020).

Page 58 *ballooned by 20 percentage points*: The huge-to-huger racial split over support for healthcare reform during this time period is stunning: "Averaging across the four pooled 1993–94 and 2009–10 samples in the display, 69% of African Americans favored Bill Clinton's health care plan compared to 43% of whites. That 26-point racial division in 1993–94 expanded into a 45-point gulf in 2009–10, with 83% of blacks supporting President Obama's health care proposals and only 38% of whites doing the same" (Tesler 2012, 701).

Page 58 *Tesler had a hunch*: Desmond-Harris (2015). Obama's acknowledgment about the role of race in American's attitudes toward the ACA is quoted from Gregory and Obama (2009), and his quote that the debate is not about race is from Tesler (2012). While the difference between Black and white Americans' attitudes toward healthcare could be explained by many different things, the different things are largely interrelated. Partisan polarization likely explains some of the racial differences toward Obamacare. But racial attitudes partly explain partisan polarization, and another axis of growing political polarization, between urban and rural communities. Nelsen and Petsko (2021, 1205) furnish evidence that "while white rural consciousness may not be reducible to racism, racism certainly plays a central role." Brown and Mettler (2023, 9–11, 17–18) find that until 2008, urban and rural communities had similar views about whether "the government in Washington should help improve the economic and social conditions of Black people." By 2020, however, a majority of people in urban communities agreed with this idea, while rural communities continued to oppose it, with many instead reporting that "Blacks should help themselves." These racial attitudes predict increased votes for Republicans.

Page 58 *The most racially resentful white voters*: Tesler (2012); see also Kinder and Sanders (1996). Tesler and others measure racial resentment by assessing participants' agreement with statements including "Irish, Italian, Jewish, and many other minorities overcame prejudice and worked their way up. Blacks should do the same without any special favors," and "It's really a matter of some people just not trying hard enough: if Blacks would only try harder they could be just as well off as whites." Kam and Burge (2018, 314) argue that the racial resentment scale, which is often thought to measure more modern forms of antiblack racism (in contrast to "old-fashioned" bigotry), "should be recast as Structural versus Individual Attributions for Black Americans' Economic and Social Status." They think the scale measures how much people either (a) *individualize* and *responsibilize* Black disadvantage—by blaming Black people's decisions, effort, and culture for their oppression and putting the onus on them to dig themselves out of it—or (b) interpret Black people's disadvantages as flowing from unjust structural causes, putting the onus on everyone to treat Black people fairly.

Page 58 *The racialization of American politics*: See Enders and Scott (2019, 285–286) for examples. It's honestly hard to wrap one's head around how dramatically the correlations between racial resentment and a range of other political factors grew from 1988 to 2016, from negligibly small to overpoweringly large. Similar findings using other measures of racial and ethnic bias abound (Payne et al. 2010; Lundberg and Payne 2014; Lundberg et al. 2017; Bartels 2020).

Pervasive racial stereotypes about violence and hard work have contributed to opposition to the ACA: Many white people have not wanted to extend health benefits to poor people because they are picturing Black people who want handouts, not realizing that most of the beneficiaries of Medicaid expansion would be white people (Cooley, Brown-Iannuzzi, and Boudreau 2019; Brown-Iannuzzi et al. 2019; Snowden and Graaf 2019; Franz, Milner, and Brown 2021).

For data on racial attitudes affecting people's beliefs about Social Security, tax policy, and the Iraq War, see Tesler (2012). The quote about race eclipsing class is from Alexander (2020, 59); see also Kuziemko and Washington (2018). We of course don't deny the significance of class or capitalism but insist they must be understood in relation to race and racism and vice versa (Arablouei et al. 2022). That's part of what's involved in thinking of these as "everything problems."

Page 59 *84 percent of white Republicans*: Benegal (2018, 747–748; see also Chanin 2018; Uenal, Sidanius, and van der Linden 2021). We expect there to be similar interrelations between other dimensions of politics and axes of oppression, such as sexism (Wayne, Valentino, and Oceno 2016; Valentino, Wayne, and Oceno 2018).

Page 59 *"total and complete shutdown"*: Taylor (2015). For insightful philosophical analysis of the rhetorical "fig leaves" that Trump cloaked over otherwise nakedly racist statements, see Saul (2017, 2024).

Page 59 *presidential hopeful Bernie Sanders said*: Roberts (2015).

Page 60 *In 2017, 86 percent of pro-Trump white millennials*: Fowler, Medenica, and Cohen (2017). A good synthesis of studies on Trump and racial resentment up to 2017 can be found in Lopez (2017). See also Mutz (2018) and Major, Blodorn, and Major Blascovich (2018) and Abramowitz and McCoy (2019). Although our focus is on the US, these patterns replicate in Europe, Latin America, and beyond (Van Assche, Dhont, and Pettigrew 2019; Etchezahar, Ungaretti, and Marchiano 2022).

Page 60 *"policy change over mental change"*: Kendi (2019, 230).

Page 60 *through, not around, biased minds*: To the persnickety segment of our readership: it doesn't follow as a matter of logic from the fact that racial biases are a source of resistance to system change that we *must* combat racial biases to promote system change. We claim that this is empirically true, not logically true. See also Johnson's (2021, 2022) insightful analysis of how the entanglement of race with social life influences and is influenced by biases in machine-learning algorithms. Give nearly any example of some ostensibly nonracial thing that you think needs to change, and it's very likely there is a world of ways that thing is actually tangled up with race (Madva 2020b). Note that this also goes for ostensibly nonracial *psychological* or *individual* factors, such as right-wing authoritarianism, social dominance orientation, and a range of perceptual, cognitive, and personality dispositions (Tagar et al. 2017; Federico and Aguilera 2019; Lin and Alvarez 2020; Guidetti, Carraro, and Castelli 2021; Zmigrod et al. 2021).

Page 61 *"prejudice is a habit that can be broken"*: Nordell (2017). If you only read one academic article on this habit-breaking approach to prejudice reduction, read Cox (2023).

Page 61 *"Biased responses become the default"*: Cox and Devine (2019).

Page 62 *"cognitive dissonance"*: On cognitive dissonance, see Festinger (1957). Several studies use cognitive dissonance and consistency principles (or related ideas about the perception of norms and the "construction" of emotions) to explain the connections between racial resentment (also called "symbolic racism" or "modern racism") and the kinds of implicit biases and racialized gut feelings and habits explored in DEI trainings (Gawronski et al. 2008; Cooley et al. 2015; Lee, Lindquist, and Payne 2023). See also work on the "psychological immune system" (Gilbert et al. 1998; Mandelbaum 2019; Flores 2022a).

Page 62 *"don't think about a white bear"*: Wegner et al. (1987).

Page 62 *"Devine intervention"*: For a relatively comprehensive list of the research team's results, including works in progress, see Cox (2023; see also Devine et al. 2012). The data is mixed on the extent to which these trainings durably reduce people's biases (Madva 2017).

Page 62 *Yes, stereotypes are bad*: Actually, the "goodness" versus "badness" of stereotypes is a richly complicated issue (Antony 1993; Valian 1999; Beeghly 2015; Basu 2020; Greene 2020; Beeghly 2025). How do you distinguish the good, true, rational, and moral generalizations (like "Black Americans are treated badly") from the pernicious generalizations (like "Black Americans don't want to work")?

Page 63 *secret sauce to the Devine intervention*: On DEI efforts coming up short, see Paluck et al. (2021). Earlier we noted that Devine's training has three components: belief, desire, and know-how. Cox (2023) makes a compelling case that the reason so many other bias interventions fail is because they are locked into an "information deficit model" rather than a model based on empowering people to be agents of change (Freire 2018; hooks 1994). We agree.

Page 63 *distinguish good from bad workshops*: To leap to the conclusion that all forms of antibias education are a waste of time is to commit the *fallacy of hasty generalization*. This is the mistake of making big generalizations based on small samples. Another example would be concluding that climate change is a hoax after two big back-to-back snowstorms in March. See Purdue University Global Academic Success

Center (2024). Kabengele et al. (2023) provide empirical evidence about the tendency to "jump to conclusions" and its relation to delusional ideation and especially conspiracy thinking.

Once we appreciate that there can be good and bad workshops, however, it's not as simple as saying "so just copy what Devine does." It could be that some of the factors that might make Devine's training successful—such as the instructor's knowledge and charisma—are difficult to scale up (although in several of their studies, such as Devine et al. (2012), participants did the training on a computer). There might be other "hidden" features driving her program's success that we don't even know to look for, let alone measure. Furthermore, what happens more than a year or two out? We discuss scaling, policy implementation, and the need for intellectual humility and a relentlessly experimental mindset in the final five chapters. Ultimately, our claim is not that we already know everything there is to know about the constituents of effective antibias education but that these are the important questions we need to be asking and testing, in both the labs of academic psychology and the labs of lived experience.

Page 64 *another form of victim blaming*: Chater and Loewenstein (2023; see also Adams et al. 2019; Greene 2020; Tulshyan and Burey 2021; Brownstein, Kelly, and Madva 2022; Madva, Brownstein, and Kelly 2023; Madva, Kelly, and Brownstein 2024). Similar points arise in structuralist and both/and criticisms of positive psychology (a field dedicated to exploring strategies for promoting well-being, self-control, character strengths, and flourishing) as too individualist and insufficiently attentive to the systems and environments that shape happiness (Becker and Marecek 2008a, 2008b; Miller et al. 2015; Brownstein 2018a). For skeptical readers who expect growth-mindset interventions to have negligibly small effects, see Yeager et al. (2022) for thinking through effect size expectations. For a meta-analysis of growth mindset literature, see Macnamara and Burgoyne (2023). For the idea of growth "taking root," Kathryn Kroeper and colleagues (2022, 373) appeal to this seed-and-soil metaphor.

Page 64 *teachers' mindsets matter*: A next generation of exciting research is exploring effective strategies for cultivating growth mindsets among teachers (Hecht, Bryan, and Yeager 2023; Hecht et al. 2023; Heyder, Steinmayr, and Cimpian 2023). Researchers are focused on *efficient* methods that don't burden exploited and burned-out teachers more than they already are. Cox (2023, 15) also cites work in progress by Saad et al. that the achievement gap between Hispanic and white high school students "disappears" when students have several teachers who have undergone the Devine intervention.

Page 64 *Racism is a caste system*: See, for example, Cox (1948), Robinson (2005), Alexander (2020), and Wilkerson (2020).

Page 64 *rootedness in social structures*: Sociologist Pierre Bourdieu (1977, 1990; see also Leboeuf 2020) has contributed influential ideas for thinking about these types of phenomena.

Page 65 *restaurants normalized it*: For information on the relationship between poverty and cigarette smoking, see, for example, CDCTobaccoFree (2023): people whose formal education ended at high school are likely to smoke for more than twice as long as those with bachelor's degrees.

Page 65 *It's creating more smokers*: Frank (2020, 115–118). See also May and Kumar (2023). On social networks driving decisions to quit smoking, see Christakis and Fowler (2008).

Page 65 *more likely to work for social change*: Forscher (2017). On friends reducing prejudice, see Hildebrand, Monteith, and Arriaga (2024).

Page 65 *essential ingredients of individual change*: This emphasis on doing things under the right conditions at the right time in the right way is a hallmark of virtue ethics, especially for Aristotle (Aristotle 2009, book 4, chapter 5). We say more about virtue in chapters 7 and 12 (and in Kelly, Faucher, and Machery 2010; Brownstein 2014, 2016, 2018a, 2018b, 2020; Madva 2019b; Madva, Kelly, and Brownstein 2024).

Page 66 *"a tool far more useful than unconscious bias trainings"*: Sunkara (2020) has fellow travelers. Pan (2020)—whom we quoted in chapter 2—contrasts the fight to support unions as an alternative to antibias workshops, asking "so what actually works to reduce interpersonal racism in the workplace?"

Page 66 *prohibiting unions from requiring*: A moment's reflection reveals how unjust these laws are. It's one thing if you want to prohibit unions from requiring that nonmembers pay dues, but then unions shouldn't have to represent or negotiate on behalf of these free riders. Alternatively, if you want to require unions to negotiate on behalf of nonmembers, it's only fair that the unions should require the nonmembers to pay dues. It's hard to even *make sense* of these laws unless you assume their purpose is to weaken unions. For history, references, and summaries of arguments for and against right-to-work laws, see Kenton (2022a). King's quote about "right-to-work" laws is from Economic Policy Institute (2011).

Page 67 *prejudices tend to lessen*: On prejudice reduction and intergroup contact, see Pettigrew (1998, 2018). For research on first-year college roommates, see Shook and Fazio (2008; see also Albuja et al. 2024; Gaither and Sommers 2013; Niu and Brown 2023). For Mormon missionaries, see Berinsky et al. (2023).

Page 67 *like the ones Alex and Michael lead*: Alex's own antibias workshops for university faculty and administrators highlight the debiasing power of unions along with other opportunities for intergroup cooperation. Some employers won't want to hire antibias trainers who encourage unionization. Employer-sponsored workshops may have inherent limitations. Unions are, of course, not the only way people can organize. And, in our personal experience as antibias trainers, there's lots of room to communicate the structure-changing message. We say more about antiracist education oriented toward structural change and introduce the term "structure facing" in

Madva (2019b, 2020c); Madva, Kelly, and Brownstein (2024), and chapter 12. (As far as we know, researchers have not tested the power of Devine-style trainings to promote unions per se. Nevertheless, her team's research confirms that there's nothing inherently individualist about prejudice-reduction workshops. What matters is what they teach, and how.)

Strikingly, when Payne and Hannay (2021, 933) discuss how to revise educational efforts, they write only that "training efforts should focus not on changing individuals' attitudes, but on learning how policies and procedures can decrease bias." We agree with the latter suggestion, of course, but conspicuously absent from their recommendations is training people *how* to change policies, not just on how policies affect bias once they're already in place.

Page 68 ***growth mindsets about institutions***: Johnson and Fujita (2012) and Stewart et al. (2010).

Page 68 ***forces standing against clean energy***: Mildenberger (2020). On sexism and racism in unions, see, for example, Cassedy (1997) and Fraser (1994). For nuanced reflection on police unions, see Levin (2020).

Page 68 ***what seems to make the difference***: Frymer and Grumbach (2021).

Page 68 ***Unions thrive when***: For an example of how labor activists helpfully discuss race as a tool for dividing the working class, see Action Network (n.d.). Also see chapter 11. On the near undoing of Obamacare, see Ramzy (2017).

Chapter 6

Page 71 ***traditions from around the world***: For example, see Whyte and Cuomo (2017), Wildcat and Voth (2023), White (1999), and many of the selections in Waters (2003), especially Cordova's "Ethics: The We and the I." We will discuss similar strands of thought in Confucian and feminist traditions in coming chapters. In a similar vein, Hartman (2021) explores ideas in the Christian ethical tradition to develop an account of the virtue of cooperativeness, and Koehrsen (2021) surveys ideas about "interconnectedness" in "Islamic environmentalism." Further, Rabbi Nina Beth Cardin (2024) anchors a commandment connecting "self and earth" along with "self and other" that "would highlight the value of caring for the world as a sacred organizing principle and urge us to integrate its pursuit into all we do."

Page 71 ***most individualist culture of all time***: On distinctively American individualism, see Freakonomics's (2021) compelling series, including how the US is "the most individualistic country on earth." For an up-close look at *Ragged Dick*, see Alger (2009).

Page 72 ***"rugged individualism" was coined***: Digital History (2021). The Emerson quote is from (Emerson 2017), and similar sentiments are clearly evident in, say, the conclusion of *Captain America: Civil War* (Russo and Russo 2016).

Page 72 **Western, Educated, Industrialized, Rich, and Democratic**: WEIRD cultures rarely fit each descriptor perfectly; see Broesch et al. (2020). The US is WEIRD but not especially industrial anymore.

Part of the purpose of the acronym "WEIRD" is to draw attention to features of human psychology that researchers used to think of as universal that are, in fact, culturally variable. See Henrich et al. (2010) and Kelly and De Block (2022). On the motto of the Enlightenment, see Kant (1996). For Hobbes's quote, see Hobbes (2017).

Page 72 **The "nuclear family" is a good example**: One feature of this picture is a marriage of loving soulmates; see Finkel (2017). On jobs becoming the all-consuming center of our lives, see Thompson (2019). For more on contemporary manifestations of individualism, see Putnam (2000). See also Elliott (2003) on medicine and self-enhancement, Hyde (2010) on creativity and intellectual property rights, Crawford (2015) on distraction and personal fulfillment, Storr (2018) on selfies and narcissism, and Burton (2023) on identity self-creation in individualist societies. On the widespread desire to live in the suburbs, see Lerner (2021) and Green (2023).

Page 73 **already *equipped to be agents of social change***: Our claims here about what "all" human beings are like and how we're "all" equipped have to be qualified and clarified to reflect the enormous range of neurodiversity that human beings display, including the different kinds of minds people have (Manalili et al. 2023). You might think that some people with some disorders, such as intense social anxiety, are not "social animals" after all. While it's needless to say that some people are more social (more groupish, more gregarious, more outgoing, more extraverted) than others, this duck of neurodiversity still only occurs against a rabbit background of underlying sociality. The very fact that someone with social anxiety could learn how to speak and use tools and then say, "I've decided to build a cabin in the woods and become a hermit and spend the rest of my days alone" shows that the decision to be alone is itself only possible on the basis of being a social animal. And the overwhelming majority of hermits do in fact depend on other people (for reasons that should become clear in the remainder of this chapter). Moreover, social-scientific work into what "normie" human beings are like has been valuable for making strides in teaching neurodiverse children: developing strategies for explicit instruction and targeted practice of certain social skills that some children learn informally, such as following other people's gaze to figure out what they're talking about. See, for example, Taylor and Vestergaard (2022) on dyslexia. On being "outside-in," see Setman and Kelly (2021) and Westra and Kelly (2025).

Page 74 **"Who would you bet on"**: Henrich (2015, 2).

Page 75 **"collective brains *of our communities*"**: Henrich (2015, 5; see also Kelly and Hoburg 2017; Kelly and De Block 2022; Griffiths and Linquist 2022; Samet and Zaitchik 2022).

Page 75 *"Any adult chimp can readily overpower us"*: There are some exceptions. Human beings "are oddly good at long-distance running and fast, accurate throwing" (Henrich 2015, 16).

Page 75 *The Cultural Evolution of Human Nature*: This section takes its title from Stanford (2020).

Page 75 *the Scottish philosopher David Hume*: Hume (1734, book 2, section 11).

Page 76 *the work of feminists*: We'll have more to say about both/and intersectional work by feminists of color in the coming chapters (see also Gasdaglis and Madva 2020; Madva, Gasdaglis, and Doberneck 2023). There are too many relevant feminist scholars to count, but a brief history of more mainstream academic feminist relational theory can be found in Koggel, Harbin, and Llewellyn (2022). We have also been influenced by Witt (2011) and Lindemann (2013).

Page 76 *"I am because my little dog knows me"*: Stein's claim was brought to our attention by Linda Martín Alcoff's (2005) synthesis of research on the social, relational, embodied, historical, racialized-and-gendered self. On *ubuntu*, see Paulson (2020) and Birhane (2017). Nelson Mandela's quote is found in R. Thompson (2020).

Page 76 *human beings are equipped with sophisticated capacities*: Morton (2014). We'll say more about people's skills for navigating overlapping social worlds in chapter 12.

Page 77 *more useful ideas and behaviors are adopted*: Again, we are not saying that *all* that gets transmitted is useful. Cultural information is not inherently good. There are random traits and mutations that just hitch along for the ride, and there are bad cultural ideas that get passed along as well. Later we'll talk about how although people buy guns for protection, gun owners are more likely to die from gun violence than non-gun owners due to things like accidents, suicides, domestic violence, and the ease of killing when tempers flare. Gun-toting ideology is cultural, but it's bad for people. *Lots* of what gets transmitted is useful but not all of it (Richerson and Boyd 2005, chapter 5). And cultural inheritance need not just keep improving indefinitely; for example, when conditions in the environment change, formerly well-adapted traits can become problematic.

Page 77 *Evolutionary geneticists have traced this trait*: Arjamaa and Vuorisalo (2017). For an accessible narrative tour through the history of research on lactase persistence and deficiency, and extensive references (and withering criticism of the view that milk is a "superfood"), see Mendelson (2023).

Page 78 *"apes on a plane"*: Hrdy (2009, 1–3).

Page 78 *unparalleled capacity for cooperation*: Though see Powell (2023).

Page 79 *distinctively human social emotions*: See, for example, Kelly (2011), Kurth (2018), and Munch-Jurisic (2022).

Page 80 *(and it is)*: Purnell (2013).

Page 80 *even in the Bushmen of Africa's Kalahari Desert*: Nielsen and Tomaselli (2010).

Page 80 *comparing 4-year-olds to chimpanzees*: Horner and Whiten (2005). Nielsen's quote is found in Telis (2010). See Allen and Andrews (2024) on the methodology in these experiments.

Page 81 *creates "bone coal"*: Gansum (2004) and Davis (2019).

Chapter 7

Page 83 *"I don't care if you recycle"*: Heglar (2019; see also Selig and Guskin 2023).

Page 83 *"Our personal actions do matter"*: Marchese (2022).

Page 84 *Microplastics are found*: Lerner (2019). On emissions from plastic production, see Altman (2022) and Karali, Khanna, and Shah (2024).

Page 84 *68 percent of paper gets recycled*: Enck and Dell (2022), which also provides information about the difficulties of plastic recycling. On how much US plastic gets recycled, see Cho (2020). This figure is as of 2017.

Page 84 *house the overwhelming majority of plastic incinerators*: GAIA (2019). The environmental justice movement focuses on how racism, colonialism, and other forms of social oppression intersect with the unjust distribution of benefits and harms flowing from climate change, resource extraction, and environmental degradation, as the National Association for the Advancement of Colored People (2023) explains.

Page 85 *in the ocean, the sky, our food, your lungs*: Lerner (2019; see also Allen et al. 2019).

Page 85 *to feel like you're doing your part*: One example comes from the *New York Times* (Choi-Schagrin and Tabuchi 2022). Another occurred in an April 22, 2022, episode of *Science Friday* (Flatow and Victor 2022; emphasis added): "IRA FLATOW: Do you see that people view this as a problem that, they cannot take action themselves, individually? Are there things that people can do to *make them feel like they're having an impact*? DAVID VICTOR: There's a lot that people can do to make themselves feel that they're having an impact, but I think it's also important that we be realistic about how much is in our individual control and how much of this is a larger societal problem and therefore really requires society-wide policies." The very phrasing of Flatow's question suggests that we're in the business of *emotion management*—learning how to feel like we're having an impact, to avoid despair, rather than actually making an impact. And then Victor doubles down on "don't bother" structuralist messaging.

Page 85 *Maine, Oregon, and California*: Choi-Schagrin (2022). Several other states including New York, Indiana, and Massachusetts have considered similar laws (Kimmelman and Doherty 2021).

Page 86 *at worst pernicious scams*: There are interesting reasons why they are such popular diversions (Conaboy 2023; Burton 2020). On Myers-Briggs: its unscientific status hasn't stopped it from being incredibly influential. According to one report, 89 of the *Fortune 100* companies in the US use some version of it (Essig 2014). This wastes time and resources. The relationship between your supposed personality type on these measures and how you act in the world is zero. Myers-Briggs's own FAQ page (Myers-Briggs Company n.d.) states that the test is not appropriate for selecting or hiring applicants: "there have . . . been no meaningful studies evaluating the MBTI's ability to predict job performance." Its FAQ links to its own unpublished scientific review paper, which claims that "the MBTI assessment is designed to be descriptive, not predictive." Instead, Myers-Briggs claims that the test is valuable "in the context of individual development"—whatever that means (Kerwin 2018). For a summary of criticisms and further references, see Stromberg and Caswell (2014). For empirical overviews, see Gardner and Martinko (1996) and Pittenger (1993).

Page 87 *personality is both real but also highly situation dependent*: Fleeson (2004). In fact, "interactionist" views have been around much longer, across different scientific and cultural traditions. Within psychology, for example, Kurt Lewin (1936, 12) wrote "Every psychological event depends upon the state of the person and at the same time on the environment, although their relative importance is different in different cases." See also Lewin (1946, 794). Lewin's approach to the necessity and interdependence of person and environment in shaping behavior is so famous that it got named after him: Lewin's Equation (Shoda 2004, 119).

There's also a big third variable in addition to innate or early developing features of people and features of the situation: sheer randomness, both in terms of how people's traits form and change and how people act in any given situation. Also, personality is both stable and malleable; it can change over the lifespan. Someone who prefers to stay home and just tweet their support for social causes (also called "slactivism") can gradually grow to become the sort of person who enjoys protesting in the streets. These gradual changes can be influenced by the sorts of factors we focus on throughout this chapter; see Bleidorn et al. (2019) and Bonner (2020).

Page 87 *to predict whether someone will become a smoker*: Really, as per the current science, it's by looking at how self-disciplined someone is in *interaction* with how much time they spend around other smokers.

Page 88 *"we also shape our situations"*: Sarkissian (2010, 2; see also 2018).

Page 88 *The Analects of Confucius is packed*: Confucius (2022). According to Dickie and Pye (n.d.), red was appropriate for women only.

Page 88 *a vital part of moral charisma*: In Confucianism, the "ability to control situational contexts and influence others through noncoercive means was associated," Sarkissian (2010, 9) writes, "with a potent source of moral power or moral charisma, often associated with the virtue of *de* (德)." Regarding black and dark attire being more common in the US, it is also more common in China now (Rahmanan 2023).

Page 88 *unstated rules about "what we do"*: Norms are quintessentially duck-rabbitable (Davidson and Kelly 2020). They're psychological things "in the heads" of individual people, like ordinary beliefs, expectations, and so on. They're also part of the structures of the world, features of cultures and groups. They shape minds as much as inhabit them. Norms might be thought of as "soft structures" (in contrast to the "hard" structures of our laws and built environments) since norms exist in this both/ and in-between space. They glue us to our groups, providing a key conduit by which individuals can shape structures and structures can shape individuals. For what a polite person would or would not say in Victorian England, see Chilton (2020). For avoiding looking like "dead fish," see Vartanian (n.d.).

Page 89 *they're powerful*: See Kelly, Westra, and Setman (2025) and references therein for specific applications and debates.

Page 90 *norm enforcement in action*: See Davidson and Kelly (2020) on informal versus formal institutions and explicit versus implicit rules (see also Reiland 2023). On enforcement, see House et al. (2020), Molho et al. (2020), and Claessens, Atkinson, and Raihani (2024).

Page 90 *who try kicking their blicketts*: For real examples, see, for instance, Roberts, Gelman, and Ho (2017) and Schmidt et al. (2016). Following and enforcing norms becomes something like an end in itself (Kelly and Davis 2018; Kelly 2020).

Page 90 *Live In A Society*: Cherones (1991).

Page 90 *"and he is us"*: Grunwald (2020).

Page 90 *to scale up the potency of personal choices*: Recall also that the Devine intervention explored in chapter 5 leverages social influence in this way.

Page 91 *comparing our choices to others' choices*: One meta-analysis of meta-analyses based on 430 field-based interventions found that "social comparisons"—comparing other people's choices with one's own—were one of the two most effective tools for promoting pro-environmental behavior change (the other: financial incentives). Social comparisons were more effective than appeals to values and responsibility, goal setting and public commitments, education using energy labels and statistics, and household feedback (Bergquist et al. 2023). On sacrificing personal gains to conform to norms, see Stürmer et al. (2003).

Page 91 *"I was onto that before it was cool"*: Of course, the motivation to be early on a trend grips individual people to varying degrees and in different ways for different topics. There can be a prideful joy in sticking to the old practice rather than hopping on the passing fad. On individual differences, ideology, and politics, see Furnham and Home (2022). For *The Hill*'s article on vegetarianism, see Visé (2022). On telling people that "more and more" people are reducing their meat consumption, see Sparkman and Walton (2017).

Page 91 *many cases of tipping points and "norm cascades"*: Nyborg et al. (2016), Milko-reit et al. (2018), and Otto et al. (2020).

Page 92 *applaud others for adopting them*: See, for example, Paluck et al. (2016). Praise is especially pertinent in diverse settings, where members of underrepresented groups are often ignored and undervalued. When people can see that they're valued, the group becomes more cohesive and effective. People feel valued when high-standing group members express appreciation for their perspectives and contributions (Begeny et al. 2022 and the references therein; for complementary perspectives, see Renger et al. 2020).

Page 92 *Belgian King Leopold II won acclaim*: Hochschild (1999). The International Stalin Prize for Strengthening Peace Among Peoples was renamed The Lenin Peace Prize—often referred to as "The Lenin"—in 1956 by Nikita Khrushchev, in the wake of his denunciation of Stalin. Notable winners of the prize include W. E. B. Du Bois, Fidel Castro, Angela Davis, Pablo Picasso, and Nelson Mandela (Wikipedia 2023c). Jelani Cobb's quote is from Cobb (2017). Cases like these are often thought of as examples of "moral licensing," or thinking that the good things you do cancel out the bad. It's also possible that these malevolent actors didn't care about canceling out their evil deeds and just wanted good PR. This phenomenon is closely related to what's called the "problem of clean hands"—that doing some good thing "washes your hands" of some bad thing you've done. Part of the drive here is that many of us want to think of ourselves as good people, though this varies across cultures and genders (Mesoudi, Magid, and Hussain 2016).

Page 93 *to get away with a peccadillo or two*: This example was inspired by empirical research like Burger, Schuler, and Eberling (2022).

Page 93 *people who weatherize their homes*: Hirst, White, and Goeltz (1985). The decrease in savings and increase in pollution is relative to what would have happened had they not weatherized in the first place. Recognized all the way back in the 1860s, the Jevons Paradox arises when technological developments that improve efficiency lead people to consume more. For example, if aviation improvements lead to cheaper airline tickets, people might fly more and end up spending more money on them than when they were expensive (York and McGee 2016).

Page 93 *"turns environmentalism into an individual choice"*: Heglar (2019). For another example, see Selig and Guskin (2023). Well "below the fold" in this article (i.e., well past a point that the overwhelming majority of readers will get to), the authors cite Chris Field, who argues that the *truly impactful* individual action is not about consumption at all: "The most important thing anybody can do is to vote for a climate-friendly government agenda." Claims like these are very common and intuitive, and we'll address them later. For Michael and Alex, who live in extremely reliably Democratic electoral districts, counties, and states, *are* our climate-friendly votes the most important things we can do as individuals? If one of us were to skip voting one year, would anything turn out differently?

Page 94 *save more energy and water*: Sintov et al. (2019). On reusing towels, see Baca-Motes et al. (2013).

Page 94 *more supportive of wind power projects*: Thøgersen and Noblet (2012). Though this study reveals yet another way in which we create each other's situations, it isn't the most earth-shattering of findings. It was a survey, not an experiment. It asked people about their support for wind power, which is important, but it didn't measure anything they actually did to support wind power.

Page 95 *more likely to vote for the Green Party*: Comin and Rode (2023).

Page 95 *helps people see themselves as good*: Willis and Schor (2012), Truelove et al. (2014), and Sparkman, Attari, and Weber (2021); see also Ainslie (2021). On predicting positive spillover and finding zilch, see Maki et al. (2019).

Chapter 8

Page 98 *origins in countless smaller acts*: For more on this idea, see Johnson (2021).

Page 98 *about 40 years*: Dattani et al. (2023). On declining life expectancy, see Johnson (2021). On milk traveling long distances to cities, see Suozzo (2015).

Page 98 *"bluish, white compound"*: New York Times (1858). On dairies adding pureed calf brains to milk, see Blum (2018). On 1890 US child mortality rates, see O'Neill (2022). On the claim that two-thirds of kids' deaths could be attributed to drinking impure milk, see Fernandez (2018). We can't vouch for this reporter's numerical estimate.

Page 98 *about one in four American kids*: O'Neill (2022).

Page 99 *saved the French wine and beer industries*: Gregersen (2023).

Page 99 *Infant mortality plunged to 7 percent*: Wikipedia (2023e).

Page 99 *Pasteurization didn't become standard practice*: Johnson (2021). On the first state-wide pasteurization requirement, see Centers for Disease Control (2023). On the "sour milk cure," see Suozzo (2015) and Goop (2017). On the American Pediatric Society warning against pasteurization, see Blum (2018).

Page 100 *Served 1,135,731 penny meals*: On Nathan Straus's biography, see New York Times (1931), Wikisource (2013), and Wikipedia (2023e). On the point that there's no telling what fraction of credit Straus deserves for popularizing pasteurization: One could offer a completely different kind of account of declining infant mortality in the early twentieth-century US. Grant Miller (2008), for example, shows how structural changes to seemingly unrelated political institutions—in this case, through the gradual granting of women's suffrage—shifted incentives in such a way as to have major impacts on infant mortality. On Alice Evans's work, see Hunt (2023).

Page 100 **welcoming gay congregants**: In December 2023, Pope Francis began allowing priests to bless same-sex couples (but not to provide a marriage sacrament) (Horowitz 2023).

Page 100 **that percentage rose to 61**: The relationship between the opinions that people report on surveys and their genuine attitudes remains unclear, though (Tankard and Paluck 2017; Brownstein, Madva, and Gawronski 2019, 2020; Gawronski, Brownstein, and Madva 2022). But see Charlesworth and Banaji (2022) for both direct and indirect measures of the stunningly rapid changes in attitudes toward sexuality, across all American social groups.

Page 100 **and Native Americans**: For many indigenous American communities, evolving views about sexuality are arguably more a return to a precolonial history rather than a completely newfound acceptance (Davis-Young 2019; Vinyeta, Whyte, and Lynn 2015). The list of groups for whom attitudes toward same-sex marriage have changed is from Kumar and Campbell (2022). We emphasize that the change has been fast compared to other social movements. From the perspective of gay Americans suffering lifetimes of discrimination, these changes have not come nearly fast nor far enough.

Page 101 **"come out" to the wider world**: See Terriquez (2015), Puddifoot (2021), and Rüsch and Kösters (2021). Our telling here doesn't highlight the role of activists. We have much more to say about activism in subsequent chapters.

Page 101 **Nathan Straus and Will & Grace**: *Will & Grace* was a sitcom that prominently portrayed gay characters, and evidence suggests that it reduced viewers' homophobia (Schiappa, Gregg, and Hewes 2006).

Page 101 **"Make a fortune"**: See chapter 14 for brief discussion of effective altruism. For attempts to work out the messy details of social tipping points, see Abson et al. (2017), Centola et al. (2018), and Milkoreit et al. (2018).

Page 102 **using feedback intentionally**: Odstel (2013).

Page 102 **terrifying courses that climate change could take**: Michael first discussed this case in Brownstein and Levy (2021, 538–539; citing Steffen et al. 2018 and Shepherd et al. 2020). On permafrost sequestering carbon, see National Geographic (n.d.).

Page 103 **bigger and better ways to blow up the world**: As long as there's been armed conflict, there's been a positive feedback loop to make more devastating weapons and sturdier systems of defense. It continues to this day, with spy technology, drones, and the like. Forces restraining these tendencies have so far prevented total nuclear holocaust but failed to prevent tens of thousands of deaths from the atomic bombings of Hiroshima and Nagasaki in 1945. Also, there have been lots of awful test blasts, with radioactive fallout from, for example, the Manhattan Project's bomb test spreading from New Mexico to forty-six other states and Canada in ten days (Blume 2023; see also Philippe et al. 2023).

Page 104 *saved the world*: So said Thomas S. Blanton, director of the US National Security Archive, in 2002 (Savranskaya 2005).

Page 104 *experience as "climate anxiety"*: see the references in the note to chapter 3, page 36, *I guess we're done here*.

Page 104 *may not be that far off*: See Kuran (1991) on behavioral cascades—unanticipated even by the revolutionaries—that led to the East European Revolution of 1989 and the fall of the USSR.

Page 105 *two years and two months later*: Clymer (2000) and Brown (2021).

Page 105 *change in complex social systems*: Though see Otto et al. (2020) and Roberts (2020).

Page 105 *the storied butterfly*: The butterfly effect is a name for an illustration of chaos theory (Vernon 2017). But the idea that certain small acts can, in the right structural conditions, add up to big effects is embodied in folklore dating back centuries, such as the "For want of a nail" (Wikipedia 2023b) proverb endorsed by George Herbert and Benjamin Franklin: "For want of a nail the shoe was lost. For want of a shoe the horse was lost. For want of a horse the rider was lost. For want of a rider the message was lost. For want of a message the battle was lost. For want of a battle the kingdom was lost. And all for the want of a horseshoe nail."

Page 106 **the cobra effect**: Siebert (2002) and Dubner (2023). The story's veracity is unknown to us but there are lots of verified examples.

Page 106 *in hopes of cooling the overheated Earth*: see Nolen and Gormalova (2023) and McKibben (2022a).

Page 106 *honest about what they don't know*: A big source of uncertainty revolves around scaling: It's nearly impossible to know when some specific intervention—no matter how promising the evidence for it—will successfully "scale up" to have widespread impact. One reason for this is just that complex systems intrinsically behave in counterintuitive and hard-to-predict ways. Another has to do with the challenges of implementation we'll discuss in chapter 13. Ideal-sounding policies are often sunk by their opponents *after* they've been approved by voters, when no one's paying attention anymore. On scaling challenges, see, for example, Duflo (2017). Philosophers have argued that even interventions passing randomized control trials should not lead us to increase our confidence that the intervention will scale (Deaton and Cartwright 2018). We offer no distinctive solution for scaling challenges, but we submit that individuals must understand and pay attention to them (chapter 12), can be humble and experimental about their preferred strategies for overcoming them (chapter 12), and can look for unique roles to play in the process (chapter 14). Above all, we think interventions are more likely to scale successfully if they're guided by a both/and perspective on how people change systems that change people. For related discussion on "implementation science," see Bauer and Kirchner (2020) and Dubner (2020, 2022).

Page 106 *an experimental mindset*: For more on the experimental mindset, see Madva (2020a, 2020b) and the pragmatist philosophical tradition (Legg and Hookway 2021), including, at some points in his career, W. E. B. Du Bois (1987, 426, 431).

Page 107 *200 million cane toads*: Turvey (2013). On the (conservative) idea attributed to G. K. Chesterton that we shouldn't change something until we know why it exists in the first place (aka Chesterton's Fence), see Turner (2022).

Page 108 *susceptible to giving up*: O'Brien (2022). Some researchers, clinicians, and counselors who work on dieting, such as Levitt (2011), describe a similar "oh fuck it" syndrome.

Page 109 *declining since its peak*: US Environmental Protection Agency (2015, 2016). On Black incarceration rates, see Mitchell and Tetlock (2023) for a catalog of ways that people across the political spectrum believe there's regress where there's progress. The Black incarceration rate has declined faster than the white (15 percent) and Hispanic (25 percent) rates. See chapter 13 for further discussion of the importance of talking up successful change, when it happens.

Page 109 *inspiring a fifteen-year-old Swedish girl*: Watts (2019).

Chapter 9

Page 113 *nothing short of a major social movement*: Alexander (2020, 323, 22). Alexander's anti-incrementalism stands in stark contrast to, say, James Forman Jr. (Ford and Forman Jr. 2017; see also Forman Jr. 2017), who says that mass incarceration "was built with all these tiny little legislative pieces and in the private arena. We're going to have to unwind it the same way. Some of them are going to look very small by themselves, but collectively they'll be powerful. And yes, it's going to also have to be all of us in our personal spheres of influence." Despite their rhetorical disagreements about the role of "tinkering" in social change, both are excellent exemplars of both/and thinking who recognize the need to both restructure the system and change hearts and minds. Alexander (2020, 22–23), for example, maintains that a massive social movement is necessary but not sufficient for ending American mass incarceration and other racial caste systems. See also Moody-Adams (2022).

Page 113 *social movements can be powerful*: Utilitarianism started out as an extreme social movement advocating for what at the time seemed like outlandish ends. It is difficult today to appreciate how radical it was at its inception exactly because it was so successful, and versions of its core ideas—that the business of morality was to minimize suffering and promote (something like) happiness, that everyone's suffering and happiness mattered equally, that customs and institutions can and should be evaluated by utilitarian criteria, and so on—have become entrenched and commonplace. See Millgram (2019). We say more about a contemporary movement descended from utilitarianism, effective altruism, in the second note in chapter 14, on *what roles am I best positioned to play?*

Page 113 *Taking the* **right** *small steps*: Sally Haslanger (2015, 10–11) urges that we replace the question "What should I do?" with the question "What should we do?" We feel the force of this, but it's too oppositional. The two questions are like figure and ground. As we explain in chapter 10, the activists most likely to continue standing up to oppressive regimes when everything is on the line are not necessarily those with grand delusions about their power to bring about lasting change. But they are, it seems, more likely to have a strong sense of what they as individuals can bring to their movement. They understand what they as individuals should do in terms of what their group is trying to accomplish, and they understand their group as part of who they are.

Erica Chenoweth—an influential theorist of social movements—and colleagues emphasize the people-driven side of social movements and the dependency of state power on the voluntary cooperation and obedience of others (Chenoweth and Stephan 2011; Beck et al. 2022). Chenoweth's claims about state power translate to systems and structures. Often, their power extends as far as our consent to them goes. Appreciating this is key to building power. See Marantz (2020) for discussion and philosopher Robin Zheng (2023) on "solidarity from below."

Page 114 *shocking and successful unionization movements*: Wikipedia (2023a) and Alter (2022).

Page 115 *The average fatality rate*: C. Thompson (2020).

Page 116 *dressing "Black"*: Cherelus (2022). Zapolsky's quote is from Wong (2020). On Amazon's infamous union busting, see Streitfeld (2021). Thanks to Reema Hijazi (personal communication)—the long-time labor organizer—for insight into Smalls's and company's unusual tactics. Palmer's quote is from Leon (2022), as is Smalls's quote thanking Jeff Bezos for going to space. Maldonado's quote is from Maldonado (2022).

Page 117 *"failing forward"*: Streitfeld (2021).

Page 117 *schools for cross-racial cooperation*: Frymer and Grumbach (2021).

Page 117 *"half-and-half"*: Arnesen (1991).

Page 117 *standing in the way*: Mildenberger (2020). On police unions, see Greenhouse (2020) and Scheiber, Stockman, and Goodman (2020). On unions and intergroup harmony, see Frymer and Grumbach (2021) and Day (2020). On Americans' attitudes toward unions, see Molla (2022) citing a Gallup poll.

Page 118 *successful movement across Latin America*: Osborn (2022). Decriminalization of abortion in Mexico began in 2021 (Romero and Mega 2023).

Page 118 *Green Tide movement*: See Evans (2020). It still has a long way to go. Abortion remains completely banned in several Latin American countries.

Page 119 *women's freedom to work was severely restricted*: Note that restrictions on women's (and men's) freedom to work in Latin America is not a pure result of factors internal to those countries, like macho culture. The US has actively destabilized the region in countless ways for decades (Borger 2018).

Page 119 *rise along with the number of working women*: Evans (2020).

Page 119 *requiring gender parity*: Freidenberg and Gilas (2023), citing their (2022) Spanish-language collected volume. See also Piscopo (2020).

Page 120 *performing the coordinated dance*: Videos surfaced from Santiago, Mexico City, Bogotá, and other cities. For analysis, see Serafini (2020).

Page 120 *Social movements come up short*: On how social movements fail, see Davenport (2014).

Page 120 *1.7 million tweets*: Frank (2020).

Page 120 *"Me Too" workshops*: Burke's quotes about healing are found in Me Too (2024). The rest are found in Burke (2021).

Page 121 *rates of sexual harassment and assault*: Statista (2023). On the discrepancy between reports of sexual assault and accountability for perpetrators, see North (2019). On retaliation, see Dobbin and Kalev (2020), Aegis Law (2023), and Golshan (2017).

Page 122 **fallen** *to 42 percent*: Pepin and Cotter (2017). On whether millennials consider themselves feminists, see Kawashima-Ginsberg (2017). On young voters increased support for Trump, see Cohn (2024) and Moore (2024).

Page 123 **Lean In**: Sandberg (2013).

Page 123 *Pop feminism's Achilles' heel*: Faludi (2022). The 2016 poll of millennial women is also reported there.

Page 123 *Faludi's both/and diagnosis*: Faludi (2022). Another lesson illustrated by #MeToo is that virality on its own is not a solution to structural problems. Rapid and widespread circulation of an idea or message might be tremendously helpful, even necessary when it comes to organizing in the twenty-first century. But it's not sufficient to achieve a movement's aims (Jackson, Bailey, and Welles 2020). For a more positive assessment of #MeToo's impact, as "moving the culture beneath the law of sexual abuse," see MacKinnon (2019).

Page 124 *field study done in Milwaukee*: Pager (2003). The follow-up field studies are found in Pager, Western, and Bonikowski (2009) and Pager, Western, and Sugie (2009). This section draws from Madva (2020a).

Page 124 *37 states and over 150 cities*: Avery and Lu (2021).

Page 124 **less** *likely to be employed*: Doleac and Hansen (2020), which is also the source (on p. 329) for the quote about well-intentioned policies doing harm. See also Doleac (2019). Alexander's quote is from her (2020, 191).

Page 125 *not structural enough*: Alexander agrees that individual-level prejudice and indifference are profound obstacles to racial justice, and so also sees the need for widespread individual-level changes in "compassionate race consciousness" (2020, 304). See also the powerful conclusion of Wills (2018).

Page 126 **a lot** *of alcohol*: Braul (2011).

Page 126 *from whose snouts visitors drank water*: New York Times (1894).

Page 126 *sharply declined during Prohibition*: Tracy and Acker (2004). On declining rates of death from liver cirrhosis during Prohibition, see Dills and Miron (2004). On public support for the Eighteenth Amendment, see Okrent (2011) and Lopez (2015).

Page 127 *"we will elect you"*: Blake (2015). See chapter 10 where we unpack this idea in more detail through an examination of the NRA and the gun rights movement in the US.

Page 127 *reinterpret clearly written amendments*: See, for example, the Fourth Amendment's unambiguous protections against warrantless search and seizure, which were nevertheless dismantled by a series of twentieth-century Supreme Court decisions (Alexander 2020).

Chapter 10

Page 129 *convicted of murder*: Two years later, the Texas Court of Appeals overturned the ruling, deciding that the judge in the initial case had given the jury incorrect instructions about "self-defense" (Davidson 1998). Naturally, Carter's testimony differed from the two surviving boys', but they basically agreed about the facts as we've described them.

Page 129 *Harlon B. Carter Legislative Achievement Award*: Past winners include the former darling of the Republican Party and governor of Wisconsin Scott Walker; Zell Miller, for his efforts while serving as the Democratic governor of Georgia; and Republican Senator Larry Craig, an aggressive opponent of gay rights who later came to national prominence when he was arrested for soliciting sex in a men's bathroom in the Minneapolis–St. Paul International Airport, and famously defended his innocence on the grounds of his "wide stance" on the toilet. For video of Craig using the "wide stance" defense, see Bash and Yellin (2007). On Craig's heterosexist political career, see, for example, Saletan (2007).

Page 129 *He spearheaded the transformation of the NRA*: Carter wasn't alone, of course. The *New York Times* uncovered the powerful role that Democratic Congressman John D. Dingell Jr. and other lawmakers played in guiding the NRA's lobbying efforts and political actions (McIntire 2023; Barbaro et al. 2023).

Page 130 *"Operation Wetback"*: Most of the people targeted by the operation had entered the country legally on joint-work programs, and many turned out to be American citizens (though the government's militarized approach would have been racist, xenophobic, and unjust regardless of their targets' national and immigration status). See Gonzales (2019) and Blakemore (2023).

Page 130 *A 1968 federal report*: Winkler (2011).

Page 130 *"Black people have begged"*: Winkler (2011), which is also the source for Reagan's quote.

Page 131 *its budget and influence skyrocketed*: Lambert (1991) and Davidson (1998).

Page 131 *Americans want more gun control*: Schaeffer (2019). For data on public attitudes toward background checks and safety courses, see Lupkin (2013), Parker et al. (2017), and Lacombe (2021a, 2021b).

Page 132 *predates its political spending*: Lacombe (2021a, 2021b). On the horrific shooting at Sandy Hook Elementary School, see Ray (2023). On gun owners being likelier to die from gun violence than non-gun owners, see Studdert et al. (2020) and Studdert et al. (2022). On gun ownership and domestic partner violence, see Davidson (1998).

Page 133 *publicizing a specific social identity*: Lacombe (2019, 1342).

Page 134 *voting for a pro-gun candidate*: Aronow and Miller (2016). Political scientists deem this "salience." The more salient an issue is for a person, the more she will cognitively and behaviorally engage with it.

Page 134 *trades votes for policy positions*: See Han and Barnett-Loro (2018). On the NRA's description of their use of this political strategy, Lacombe quotes David Keene, a former NRA president, explaining, "'The difference between the NRA and other groups is that we've developed a community [and] when they see Second Amendment rights threatened they vote. They do whatever they need to do'" (Lacombe 2021a, 1353). On the NRA learning from the ASL, see Lopez (2015). See Meyer (2020) on leveraging coal and fracking communities' close ties for votes. On the Sunrise Movement's similar strategy, see Skocpol (2013) and Roberts (2013).

Page 134 *All Politics Is Identity Politics*: Yglesias (2015). See also Klein (2020) and Alcoff (2005).

Page 135 *pillar of its approach*: Sunrise Movement (n.d.a.).

Page 135 *associated with the left*: The term "identity politics" was coined by the Combahee River Collective (BlackPast 2012), though the term has taken on a life of its own since they defined it. The Collective articulated a groundbreaking both/and political approach to identity, and Alex has discussed their work elsewhere (Gasdaglis and Madva 2020). We'll say more about work inspired by them in the next chapter.

Page 135 *from coin flips to T-shirt colors*: See, for example, Tajfel and Turner (2000; see also Jetten et al. 2021). Famously, Tajfel intended the coin-flip experiment to establish a neutral baseline. That is, he expected it would not create meaningful group boundaries. Then he'd go on to do more experiments, which would involve dividing people up in more meaningful ways—perhaps based on their political views or class—to explore the minimal conditions that would lead to in-group favoritism. However, Tajfel's plan ran into an unexpected but deeply illuminating problem. Everything he tried made people groupish! He couldn't find *any* conditions minimal or arbitrary enough that they didn't activate in-group favoritism. No matter how arbitrarily he divided people up, they would start to invest value and emotional significance in their groups, favoring them at the expense of others.

Page 136 *The movements that succeed*: See van Zomeren, Kutlaca, and Turner-Zwinkels (2018).

Page 136 *activating group identity*: See Folger and Martin (1986) and Runciman (1966) for historical precursors. See Walker and Smith (2002) and Smith et al. (2012) for more recent developments. Studies on the effects of voter restrictions find mixed results related to "backlash" effects (Waldman 2020; Cantoni and Pons 2021; Ferreri 2021; Abramowitz 2022; MIT Election Data & Science Lab 2021). Note that because everything is two degrees from race, the group that these laws often *do* effectively deter from voting—outrageously—is Black people.

Page 136 *think that they can make a difference*: Psychologists refer to this with the soul-stirring term "efficacy beliefs." See Bandura (1978, 1997). On believing in the collective power to make a difference, see Mummendey (1999, 232) and van Zomeren, Kutlaca, and Turner-Zwinkels (2018).

Page 137 *flouting the terms of the agreement*: Ayanian et al. (2021) and Al Jazeera (2022). In 2003, close to five hundred thousand people protested the anti-subversion law. Beijing made concessions, but passed a very similar law in 2020.

Page 137 *flipped all but one*: As impressive as this is, things cooled off after these initial victories. The COVID-19 pandemic put a chill on pro-democracy organizing, while Beijing quietly arrested the leaders who hadn't already fled Hong Kong; see Kirby (2019).

Page 138 *perceived themselves to be at risk*: Ayanian and Tausch (2016).

Page 138 *from repression to outrage to action*: See Chenoweth and Stephan (2011) and Chenoweth (2021). Ayanian et al. (2021) discuss both the traditional "economic model" of protest, which predicts that people will be disincentivized to protest as the risks for doing so increase (e.g., Olson 1971; Hardin 1982), and alternatives to that model that stress various collective processes, for example, that repression stokes group-based anger and protest (Gurr 1970).

Page 138 *trick themselves into having unrealistic confidence*: We're thinking here of William James's (2009) idea of the "will to believe." If you go mountain climbing and need to jump over a wide chasm to get home safely, James thought, you better will yourself to believe you can jump over the chasm. James applied this idea to believing in God, which he thought would be good to do even if you have to trick yourself into it, against all the evidence.

On activists who get involved because they feel they can make contributions to the group, see Ayanian et al. (2021). Relatedly, Ginzburg and Guerra (2021) find that people who have participated in collective action show more altruism and trust in general than people who haven't. The quote from the Egyptian activist is in Ayanian and Tausch (2016).

Page 139 *make a difference to the movement*: See Ayanian et al. (2021) and McAdam (1986). This line of thinking is also reflected in Patricia Hill Collins's work (1999, xiii).

Page 139 *"the most important thing anybody can do"*: We support the suggestion to get involved with politics, but there are lots of other political actions besides voting. Unfortunately, as we've discussed, people often propose voting or other forms of political action as alternatives to "making personal choices," which they say are ineffectual. In addition to the many problems with this that we've covered, there is also the problem of what might be called *universal solvents*: the ostensible reasons against the potential for individuals to make a difference through one channel (e.g., reducing their carbon footprint) also work against the proposed arguments for individuals to make a difference through another channel (e.g., political action). As we discuss in this section, while Field isn't wrong to implore people to vote for pro-climate political candidates, voting can feel like a drop in the bucket just as much as biking to work or buying an EV. For examples of the problematic logic of universal solvents, see chapter 1 (see also Sinnott-Armstrong 2005; Yglesias 2018; Mann and Brockopp 2019; Zurcher 2021; Hale 2022; Santos 2024). Others have rightly objected to this politics-instead-of-consumption argument (e.g., Hourdequin 2010; Hiller 2011; Jamieson 2014; Berkey 2018a, 2018b). For an attempt to reply to these objections, see Kingston and Sinnott-Armstrong (2018, n. 22). See also Cripps (2013, 2020) for in-depth discussion.

Page 139 *democracy at its best*: Associated Press (1994).

Page 140 *Ties and one-vote wins do happen*: Mulligan and Hunter (2003). The truth is that it's extremely hard to know just how many elections come down to precisely one vote or a tie, because as election counts get closer and closer, everything gets real squirrely: There are recounts, controversial choices about how to count or throw out votes, and strategic political choices by those in power that steer the outcome. See examples at Wikipedia (2023d).

Page 140 *the Paradox of Voting*: For a summary and further references on the paradox, see Wikipedia (2023f). This observation of the paradox helped make Marquis de Condorcet famous in the eighteenth century. He also came to be known for a different problem, confusingly known as the "Voting Paradox," which has to do with situations in which collective preferences and individual preferences are at odds.

Page 140 *154 million Americans*: US Census Bureau (2022). On having to invest effort or money to vote, and further discussion of the costs of participation in elections, see Aytaç and Stokes (2019). Think of it like placing a bet. All bets cost something. A good bet is one where your chance of winning multiplied by how much you'll win is greater than the cost of the bet. From this perspective, voting is usually a bad bet. The chances of your vote throwing the election to one candidate over another are so vanishingly small, practically speaking, that no matter how much you prefer candidate A to B, the bet costs too much, even if it's just the cost of a stamp. When you look at this this way, only in small elections or elections with life and death stakes does it make obvious sense to vote. (Framing elections in terms of life and death stakes makes good sense for candidates for this reason.)

That said, casting the deciding vote in a presidential election, however unlikely, would sway human history. Some thus argue that the "value" of voting approaches a constant rather than zero because a) as elections get smaller, your chances of casting the deciding vote go up, but the overall impact of that decisive vote goes down (it's just a local election), whereas b) as elections get bigger, your chances of being decisive go down, but the overall impact of the decisive vote goes up (human history hangs in the balance). See Kaplan and Gelman (2008) and Edlin, Gelman, and Kaplan (2007). Some philosophers agree that voting is rational by the good-old fashioned standards of expected utility, though debate continues. See, for example, Kagan (2011), Parfit (1984), and Nefsky (2017).

Page 140 *votes at all*: Many academics treat voting as the quintessential example of individual futility and use it to model other cases, like carbon pollution. Trying to reduce your footprint can look like a waste of time. Burning a gallon of gas in a car creates about 20 pounds of CO_2 equivalent. In 2019, the United States produced 6.558 million metric tons of CO_2 equivalent. That's a ratio of about 1 to 723 million, a teeny tiny drop in one big ass bucket (US Environmental Protection Agency 2016).

Page 140 *lifetime odds of dying*: Injury Facts (2023).

Page 141 *lower odds have a greater power*: Oh, hi there, are you the reader who really worries about driving risks and never glimpses at your phone until you pull over? We salute you, truly. But we bet there are lots of other risks you're ignoring, like the three of us do. As David Leonhardt (2024) points out, "Car drivers and passengers would be safer if they wore helmets, for instance, but who wears a helmet in a car? . . . society regularly decides that some amount of additional safety isn't worth it."

Page 141 *"Are you going to vote?"* American Psychological Association (2020). There are other important factors driving voting behavior, of course, like having a plan for voting day and negative partisanship (Harder and Krosnick 2008). Other researchers find that those people most likely to vote are moved by sympathy for the worst off, the kind of people willing to go a little bit out of their way to help others. They think of the potential payoff of their vote on other people, not just themselves; see Jankowski (2002).

Page 141 *We vote when our friends do*: Bond et al. (2012). See Panagopoulos (2010) on printing lists of eligible nonvoters in the local newspaper.

Page 142 *80 million who could have voted*: Montanaro (2020). See Newall and Machi (2020) on people explaining staying home on Election Day because they feel their vote won't make a difference.

Page 142 *did not cite the difficulty of voting*: People likely underestimate the various ways that structural friction prevents them from voting (Mazar et al. 2022), just as they fail to realize how living just a little bit farther away from their gym makes them less likely to go (Bachman 2017; see also Reed and Phillips 2005; Ani and Zheng 2014; Guo et al. 2015). On the power of structural friction, see chapter 2.

Page 143 *violence is an acceptable way*: Vidal, Páez, and Shields (2021).

Page 143 *Without the filibuster*: Of course, in a filibuster-free world, simple Republican majorities could then undo any of these changes, as could the Supreme Court. We discuss questions about the durability of hard-fought structural change in chapter 13, but one conviction we have is that America's leading political parties would have less unreasonable policies in their platforms if they expected they'd have the chance to actually implement them. Republicans' decades-long pursuit of overturning *Roe v. Wade* is one example. As an electoral matter, anti-choice signaling was more valuable to Republicans as an unfulfilled promise than as a policy voters would reward them for. On "veto points" in the US government, see Fukuyama (cited in Klein 2016), who calls the US a "vetocracy."

Chapter 11

Page 145 *the "third American revolution"*: Degler (1983). The National Labor Relations Act established the National Labor Relations Board, which organizes elections for union recognition. The Social Security Act established not only pensions for elderly people but also unemployment insurance. The Fair Labor Standards Act established a national minimum wage and overtime pay (Post 2016; Cowie 2017). It's important to note that the alliance between the CIO and Communist Party wasn't all flowers and roses. Each may have thought they were using the other. When asked about allying with communists, for example, the CIO's John Lewis said, "who gets the bird, the hunter or the dog?" (Cowie, personal communication). Lewis thought the communists were acting like an obedient dog for the labor movement.

Page 146 *moderates and "popularists"*: Piper (2022b).

Page 147 *"Coming out of the Shadows"*: Terriquez (2015, 344). Our discussion here is adapted from Gasdaglis and Madva (2020). The students' quotes are from Terriquez (2015, 352–354). Her quote about movements A and B reciprocally influencing each other is from Terriquez (2015, 347).

Page 148 *"living in the shadows"*: Terriquez (2015, 355). These "coming out" narratives and activist practices have been taken up by other communities, such as in mental health activism (Rüsch and Kösters 2021; Puddifoot 2021).

Page 148 *there are many more*: Meyer and Whittier (1994). For a more "realist" perspective on the prospects of coalitions, particularly between Black and white people, see Bell (1980) and Hoag (2020).

Page 148 *excluded from the Social Security Act*: see the note on *Southern congressmen insisted* in chapter 2, section 3, "The Cycle Is the Story."

Page 149 *achieved on the backs of Black people*: On the other hand, New Deal programs *did* benefit Black Americans, in meaningful and durable ways, especially over time. See Cowie (2017).

Page 149 *the "race-class narrative"*: An engaging and accessible series of videos and worksheets introducing his (2019) research program can be found at Race-Class Academy (2022).

Page 150 *a flimsy kind of deniability*: See also Saul (2017, 2024). On Trump's antisemitic dog whistle about Clinton, see Olasov (2016). Note that a key component of the devastating effectiveness of dog whistling as a political strategy, among many white and even some non-white people, consists in how it interacts with the next approach that Haney-Lopez studied.

Page 150 *"When people are called bigots"*: Haney-Lopez (2020).

Page 150 *can alienate potential allies*: Findings in the burgeoning literature on prejudice confrontation are rich and complex (e.g., Czopp, Monteith, and Mark 2006; Chaney, Young, and Sanchez 2015; Karmali, Kawakami, and Page-Gould 2017; Burns and Granz 2021).

Page 151 *explanations from Haney-Lopez's team*: Race-Class Academy (2022) and Haney-López (2019, 176).

Page 152 *how effective and broadly appealing*: For related research indirectly substantiating Haney-Lopez's approach, see Broockman and Kalla (2025) and McRaney (2022).

Page 152 *become more supportive of gay marriage*: Cortland et al. (2017). John Lewis's quote is found in Bates (2015), and Patricia Hill Collins's quote is found in Collins (1999, 43).

Page 153 *Black American feminists*: In 1892, for example, Anna Julia Cooper wrote, "The colored woman of to-day occupies, one may say, a unique position in this country. In a period of itself transitional and unsettled, her status seems one of the least ascertainable and definitive of all the forces which make for our civilization. She is confronted by both a woman question and a race problem, and is as yet an unknown or an unacknowledged factor in both" (Cooper 2017, 76/134). For historical overviews of women of color feminisms, see, for example, Brah and Phoenix (2013), Collins and Bilge (2016, chapter 3), and Hancock (2016). These and other writers explore precursors to intersectionality in nineteenth- and early twentieth-century black feminists including Cooper, Sojourner Truth, Maria Stewart, and Mary Church Terrell. bell hooks's quote is from hooks (2003, 10). See Gasdaglis and Madva (2020) for a survey of different interpretations of intersectionality and a defense of the idea that intersectionality is at its core about methodology, how to do feminism, and social science. Notably, some scholars argue that intersectionality is fundamentally a call to center the experiences and oppression of Black women or women of color, and downplay the coalitional dimensions of the intersectional tradition (e.g., Alexander-Floyd 2012).

Page 153 *For every 100,000 births*: Kliff, Miller, and Buchanan (2023), which is also the source for Maya Rossin-Slater's quote.

Page 154 *"conspiracy theory of victimization"*: Mohamed (2019) and Bloch (2019). Portraying Black feminist and other intersectional traditions as seeking out a "new caste system" has, evidently, been a canny political strategy for stabilizing existing hierarchies and preserving the status quo. It has basically no bearing on what these movements aim to do. Nevertheless, this strategy has arguably helped prevent many progressive political actors from absorbing longstanding intersectional lessons.

Page 154 *"hallmarks of black feminist thought"*: Deborah King (1988, 43; emphasis added). See also Collins (1999, 43). You could tell a similar story about the roots of "identity politics" in the Combahee River Collective (BlackPast 2012), as a movement that aimed to both address the specificity of the oppressions faced by the collective's members (predominantly queer Black women) and end oppression for everyone.

Page 154 *"not my issue"*: Zheng (2023, 913).

Page 154 *"a lens, a prism"*: Crenshaw's quote is found in Steinmetz (2020).

Page 155 **People with an intersectional mindset**: Curtin et al. (2015; see also Buchanan, Rios, and Case 2020; Greenwood 2008; Greenwood and Christian 2008).

Chapter 12

Page 157 **students whom she calls "strivers"**: Morton (2019; see also 2014). Quotations from Morton are drawn from Vedantam (2020). For more on the American Dream, see chapter 6, section 2, on "WEIRD Culture."

Page 157 **$1.2 million more**: Association of Public and Land-Grant Universities (n.d.).

Page 158 **college can be an exhausting, alien world**: Strivers face many other struggles as well. For example, some have undocumented migrant family members who lack the same opportunities for good-paying jobs that citizens have, putting more pressure on strivers to support their families. See also Hochschild (1983) and Grandey (2000) on emotional labor, and on double binds, see Frye (1983) and Hirji (2021). See Brownstein (2018a) for discussion of research (such as Miller et al. 2015) on negative health effects for strivers. Strivers face the threat of feeling like a sellout (Morton 2019, 68–69, 77–88). Even the seemingly straightforward "study hard and avoid distractions" piece of advice papers over a more complicated situation. Many strivers have to do a lot of catching up in college since they often come to college from high schools that didn't prepare them as well as the private and better-funded schools that their college classmates attended.

Page 158 **The three of us also work at large public universities**: Indiana's Purdue University, where Dan works, has frozen tuition at 2012 levels, while the City University of New York (CUNY)—the system in which Michael teaches and where Morton formerly taught—and the California State University (CSU) systems—where Alex teaches—have the most consistently successful track records in the US for moving people up the socioeconomic ladder (Morning Edition 2022). Seven of the top ten universities for social mobility (and nineteen of the top twenty-five) are CUNY or CSU schools, with Cal Poly Pomona and John Jay coming in at number three and fifteen, respectively (CollegeNET 2023).

Page 159 **less likely to finish college**: Bowen and McPherson (2016; see also Education Advisory Board 2024).

Page 159 **family orientation process**: See, for example, Indiana State University's approach to "family orientation" (Indiana State University n.d.). In the spring 2021 *APA Newsletter on Feminism and Philosophy*, a range of commentators on Morton's book—themselves former strivers—describe specific steps instructors and administrators can take to support students, including Basevich (2021) and Peterson (2021).

Page 159 **further-reaching structural reforms:** This list could be much, much longer. Most of Alex's and Michael's students commute, so making it easy for them to get to campus is also huge: better bike lanes, public transportation, and parking. To the extent that strivers have inflexible bosses, better collective bargaining and unions might force bosses to let strivers work at times that fit better with their class schedules.

Page 160 **bell hooks argues:** hooks (hooks 1994, 182–183; see also Freire 2018; Mansbridge and Morris 2001; Haslanger 2021; Proios 2021; Herrmann et al. 2022). We first worked out some of the ideas presented here in Madva, Kelly, and Brownstein (2024). In chapter 5, we discussed how growth mindsets can be directed toward social systems. We can come to perceive systems as changeable rather than immutable. Of course, the idea that we can cultivate the skill of seeing structures as changeable isn't a cure-all. Strivers do face many unavoidable dilemmas, as Morton details. Do you take your mom to the doctor's office or show up for your chemistry exam? But the existence of unavoidable dilemmas takes nothing away from the importance of one's attitude toward the possibility of changing the situation that gives rise to those dilemmas. As we described in chapter 4, section 5, "The Real Remaining Trade-Offs," calling for a both/and approach does not entail denying the ubiquity of difficult dilemmas, and we are not saying that strivers or anyone else can literally do everything or "have it all." We are instead calling for assessing the difficult dilemmas *clearly and accurately.* This includes questioning the way the dilemma is framed and seeking out third options when we're told there are only two (especially when, for example, the two options we're given both take existing social structures for granted, as immutable). Where there are better third options, these will not be costless, but their costs may be fewer or at least easier to bear. See, for example, Proios's (2021) case, grounded in his own experiences, that strivers ought to cultivate an "oppositional consciousness."

Page 160 **students turning this attitude into organized action:** See Astor (2018) for seven examples of student-led change.

Page 160 **By the time they're seven years old:** We learned of the studies we cite here through an excellent piece by Amemiya et al. (2023), citing Iranian attitudes in Yazdi, Barner, and Heyman (2020); Indian attitudes in Santhanagopalan et al. (2021; these kids also ranked British-English speakers of Tamil and Hindi speakers), and anti-Southern US attitudes in Kinzler and DeJesus (2013; on essentialism, see also Neufeld 2022 and Noyes et al. 2023).

Page 161 **where a group sits in a pecking order:** The cool kids call this "social dominance orientation" (SDO). It's one of the leading survey constructs for measuring preferences for authoritarianism or inequality. Statements used to measure SDO include "To get ahead in life, it is sometimes necessary to step on other groups" and "In getting what your group wants, it is sometimes necessary to use force against other groups" (Pratto et al. 1994; Sidanius and Pratto 1999).

Page 161 *a result of what they were taught*: See Heck, Shutts, and Kinzler (2022, 601). Heck and colleagues don't rule out a cultural explanation for this apparent default tendency to explain outcomes in terms of internal causes. See also Vasil [Vasilyeva] et al. (2018) and Vasil et al. (2024). (If Heck is right, then South Pacific had it backward (Hammerstein et al. 1949). Kids "have to be carefully taught" to think structurally. They pick up racism, and preferences for explanations that focus on features internal to individuals and groups, without much explicit instruction.) Research suggests parents who think structurally have more structurally alert kids (Kluegel 1990; Mistry et al. 2016; Godfrey et al. 2019; Diemer et al. 2019; Amemiya et al. 2023; Barreiro and Wainryb 2023).

The study using the minimal group paradigm is Tagar et al. (2017). Brinkman and colleagues (2023) found that parents' explicit and implicit biases predicted whether they wanted their kids to be in racially diverse classrooms. Studies like this pose difficulties for certain structuralist defenders of integrationist strategies who argue "let's not worry about changing people's biases; people's biases will change once we make structural changes to get them into diverse settings" (see chapter 2 for examples). In this case, parents' biases are *preventing* their kids from entering diverse settings. This is the Return of the Allegedly Irrelevant. Racial biases end up being key obstacles to structural reform.

Page 162 *Isabel Wilkerson explains*: Pangambam (2018), transcribing Wilkerson (2017).

Page 162 *Moscow, Russia, instead of Smallville, Kansas*: Millar (2014).

Page 163 *their situation could be different*: There are also cultural differences. For example, people in less WEIRD cultures are more likely to think of situational explanations (Kuhn and McPartland 1954; see also Henrich 2020, chapter 1).

Page 163 *Some studies have people practice*: See Stewart et al. (2022). See Madva (2017) on similar debiasing techniques.

Page 163 *media is shaped by cultural segregation*: When it comes to content consumption, there are two problems. First, kids are exposed to much less content about other groups. *Everybody* gets less exposed to groups other than white people and men (e.g., Scharrer and Ramasubramanian 2015; Scharrer, Ramasubramanian, and Banjo 2022). Second, portrayals of other groups are likely to be biased, perpetuating stereotypes and legitimizing discrimination (e.g., Weisbuch, Pauker, and Ambady 2009; Lamer et al. 2022; Meyers et al. 2022). According to one estimate, "nearly half of Middle Eastern characters on entertainment television are portrayed as supporting terrorism," and exposure to these characters predicts hostility to immigration and naturalization (Hawkins et al. 2024). Under conditions of physical and social segregation, biased media is liable to swamp whatever else they might learn about other social groups (Anderson 2010; Madva 2016a). See also Flores (2022b) on the importance of establishing integrated social structures to pave the way for belief change.

The power of segregation to shape our understanding of the world is one reason it's crucial to account for people's *epistemic standpoints* when trying to gain knowledge (Harding 2003; Collins 2003; Anderson 2020; Toole 2022). It also follows from the fact that people's knowledge and perspectives vary so widely that some may be better positioned to develop structure-facing skills than others. For example, it may be easier for the oppressed than the privileged to notice and accept the power of social structures to influence their lives.

Page 164 *structure-facing skills*: We discuss the concept of structure-facing virtue in more depth in Madva, Kelly, and Brownstein (2024). Our account draws inspiration from many theorists, including those we cite in the note to chapter 1, *an idea found across contemporary social science* (e.g., Young 2011), and an earlier note in this chapter, *bell hooks argues*. Curious about the connections between structure-facing skills and both/and thinking? See the appendix.

Page 164 *duped into thinking the system is acceptable*: See especially Jost and colleagues' work on system justification, synthesized in Jost (2020). Numerous thinkers and researchers have focused on the outlooks of the disadvantaged (e.g., Frank 2004; Azevedo et al. 2019; Wills 2021; Pichardo, Jost, and Benet-Martínez 2022).

Page 165 *treat politics like a hobby*: Hersh (2020). It's possible that hobbyism (sometimes) creates positive spillover, leading people from online chatter to more meaningful action. But, so far as we know, no one has found evidence of positive spillover of this kind. This paragraph is adapted from Madva, Kelly, and Brownstein (2024) and Brownstein and Levy (2021).

Page 166 *room for cultural humility*: On cultural humility, see Rullo et al. (2022), which is the research from Italy we describe below and had some complex findings worth exploring further. But see also Hook et al. (2013) and Foronda et al. (2016). For connections between cultural humility and an intersectional mindset, see Buchanan et al. (2020; see also Curtin, Stewart, and Cole 2015; Greenwood and Christian 2008).

Page 167 *Overconfidence leads people*: See, for example, Tetlock and Gardner (2016) on superforecasters. Overconfidence is presumably part of the explanation of why experts are often so mediocre at making predictions (Grossmann et al. 2023). See note *to show up for court* near the end of chapter 4.

Page 167 *Cognitive flexibility looks like it gets better*: Zmigrod et al. (2019) and Zmigrod, Rentfrow, and Robbins (2020). For a promising pilot study suggesting that cognitive flexibility is learnable, at least in the context of romantic relationships, see Silverman, Fu, and Teachman (2023; see also Schwarz 2023).

Page 167 *"pseudo-profound bullshit"*: Salvi et al. (2023), building on Pennycook et al. (2015). On open-ended thinking, analytic reasoning, and cognitive flexibility, see Pennycook and Rand (2019) and Pennycook (2023). Some of the research we describe in this paragraph mostly focuses on analytic reasoning, the kind of slow thinking it takes to solve "37 x 41" (rather than the quick thinking we use to solve "2 + 2"). But analytic reasoning and cognitive flexibility are closely correlated. An exciting area for future research is how much of the effects are driven by the sheer pleasure involved in difficult thinking versus just having a knack for it, and how much of that knack is a matter of native talent versus a skill learnable with practice.

Page 167 *acknowledging one's own racial privilege*: Uluğ and Tropp (2021).

Chapter 13

Page 169 *fog of enactment*: Stokes (2020). Stokes's focus is the political battlegrounds that develop after new policies are written and signed into law. Interest groups and politicians—by their own admission, Stokes shows—are often unsure of what the effects of public policies will be. Because people pay less attention to implementation than horse trading and political intrigue, interest groups often operate successfully in the fog. They steer policy details in their favor or work to repeal parts of them before they become entrenched and supportive constituencies can be created.

Page 169 *"community policing"*: What follows about community policing is drawn from Skogan (2003).

Page 170 *nearly every US city*: Reaves (2015).

Page 170 *found null results*: Null results were more likely when it came to the effects of community meetings and other "community-presence" interventions (Blair et al. 2021).

Page 170 *six different countries*: The authors note that most previous studies on community policing have focused on the United States, the UK, and Australia, hence their focus on countries in the Global South.

Page 170 *summarize their mega-study's findings*: Blair et al. (2021, 1). Blair and his colleagues didn't find evidence from any of their six sites that community policing affected the main outcomes they were most interested in: "crime victimization, perceptions of insecurity, citizen perceptions of police, police abuse, or citizen cooperation with the police." They did find some outliers, though. In Liberia and Pakistan, there were sizable shifts in citizens' perceptions of police intentions.

Page 171 *improve law enforcement*: For a promising exploratory study to build bridges between police and community members in Santa Barbara, California, see Nuño et al. (2023).

Page 171 *boring, pedestrian details of implementation*: These details include the shifting and misaligned incentives that individual face. The things people actually get paid and rewarded and penalized for are often out of sync with the goals of the program and the new reform (Makowsky, Stratmann, and Tabarrok 2019; Goldstein, Sances, and You 2020; Reisenwitz 2023). For striking illustration, see *The Wire* (Simon 2002), a fictionalized version of the Baltimore Police Department, which was incentivized to tally up arrests above everything else rather than promote the needs of the community. Measurement here is also an issue. The stuff that scientists can measure is not necessarily the stuff you're really trying to promote. This is the point of the old joke about a person looking for his lost keys under a streetlamp at night, and when asked if this is where he lost them, he replies, "no, but this is where the light is good."

Page 171 *"greenwash" their reputations*: Another problem with tree planting as a solution to climate change is that—because of climate change itself—many forests are catching fire and becoming sources of carbon pollution rather than "sinks" for it. See, for example, Cecco (2023). For corporate commitments to plant trees, see Peters (2020). The "Trillion Tree Initiative" drew inspiration from a (controversial) scientific paper (Bastin et al. 2019). For Benioff's announcement, see Schleifer (2020). For Trump's endorsement of the initiative, see Samuels (2020). For the Trillion Tree Initiative's "progress" as of 2024, see Alexander (2024). For Turkey's record-breaking and failed tree planting, see Jones (2021) and Kent (2020). The *Vice* headline is from Galer (2022). On India's tree planting, see Coleman et al. (2021).

Page 172 *more trees in urban spaces*: Branas et al. (2018), Venter et al. (2022), and Shepley et al. (2019). For discussion and further references on reforesting, see Early (2021).

Page 172 *"tree growing"*: Duguma (2019; original emphasis). See Nakate (2021) for an excellent discussion of how to integrate tree planting into childhood education.

Page 172 *rural residents (predominantly women)*: Kimbrough (2021), also discussed in Jones (2021).

Page 173 *Moments of liberation*: Nelson (2021, 7).

Page 174 *Energy Policy Act of 2005*: Brady (2014). On the loan to Tesla, see Overly (2021). On Tesla making EVs cool (changing normative perceptions), see Long et al. (2019). Yet Tesla CEO Elon Musk has been far from forthcoming about the role of government support behind Tesla and his other endeavors, like SpaceX. He has spoken out against government subsidies and taxes on billionaires like himself (Lal-ljee 2021). As CEO of X (formerly Twitter), he put a "government-funded media" label on the account of National Public Radio (NPR). Some suggested that he should have also put the same label on his own companies (Al-Sibai 2023).

Page 174 *Opponents of the programs*: Aka Republicans. See, for example, the *Wall Street Journal*'s flagship podcast (Linebaugh 2023) and pieces on Fox News (Diaz 2019; Richard 2023), running headlines like "Biden Revives Obama-Era Loan Program That Funded Solyndra and Cost US Taxpayers More Than $500 Million" (Associated Press 2022).

Page 175 *polled 1,400 Americans*: See Mettler (2011b, chapter 2).

Page 175 *a meme tracker*: Noah (2009). On conservatives' spurious arguments that Medicare isn't a government social program, see Lind (2021).

Page 175 *not specific to Medicare*: Mettler (2011b, chapter 1; see also Cubanski, Biniek, and Neuman 2023).

Page 176 *on par with similar nations*: The US spends considerably more on healthcare than on the military (Congressional Budget Office 2023), but it's also complicated (Frakt and Carroll 2018; Howard 2023). Nevertheless, a pivotal feature of Mettler's argument is that the American federal government *has remained* active in creating programs trying to redress economic inequality, stagnating rates of educational attainment, and health insecurity. "As a percentage of GDP," she writes, "US government obligations to social welfare have kept pace with those of comparable nations. What is distinct in the United States is the extent to which those commitments are channeled through the submerged state, rather than through visible governance, and in a manner that is upwardly redistributive" (Mettler 2011b, 121). By "upwardly redistributive," Mettler means that some of the government spending goes toward more wealthy people, such as Medicare and Social Security spending going to already-wealthy older adults, or generous mortgage tax benefits going to already-wealthy homeowners. While much American social spending has been upwardly redistributive, and has all kinds of other shortcomings, it is important to recognize and learn from successes.

Page 176 *US child poverty rate*: US Census Bureau (2023). A relevant datum here is that child poverty increased after COVID-19 spending decreased due to the expiration of the expanded Child Tax Credit.

Page 176 *"The nine most terrifying words"*: Ronald Reagan Presidential Foundation and Institute (n.d.). Grover Norquist's quote is found in Nelson (2019). President Clinton's quote is from his State of the Union Address (Clinton 1996).

Page 176 *dry technocratic venues*: Mettler (2011b, 108).

Page 176 *settled for submerged policies*: Research suggests, for example, that de-emphasizing the role of government closes the partisan gap between Democrats and Republicans in their support of the ACA (Lerman, Sadin, and Trachtman 2017). The tide, however, may be turning. President Biden's Presidential term was rife with discussion of the return of "industrial policy," where the government takes a more active and visible role in shaping economic priorities and incentivizing the market to promote those priorities. The 2021 Infrastructure Investment and Jobs Act and the 2022 IRA are some examples. In many ways, both still operate through the tax code, as they were passed using budget reconciliation, but both are structured to show what big government can do for people. Still, late 2023 polling suggests that most Americans are not aware of Biden's efforts to "unsubmerge" the state (Glasser 2023).

Page 176 *to want more of it*: As Mettler (2011b, 113) explains, "The question is, can reform be considered successful if it goes unnoticed? In a system of representative government, the answer is no."

Page 177 *"provide 'receipts'"*: Mettler (2011a; see also 2011b, 120).

Page 177 *Donald Trump had a similar idea*: Long and Miller (2020), writing for the Associated Press, described the insertion of Trump's signature onto the stimulus checks as an "unprecedented move" because "a president is not an authorized signer for money sent by the US Treasury." Trump himself was initially cagey about the reasons for the move, though he inevitably said the quiet part out loud: "I'm sure people will be very happy to get a big, fat, beautiful check and my name is on it" (Long and Miller 2020).

Page 177 *participated in politics*: Campbell (2003) and Mettler (2005). On Roosevelt's and Obama's audiences, see Mettler (2011b, 111).

Page 178 *out of poverty*: On the Home Mortgage Interest Tax Deduction, see Matthews (2015). On the Earned Income Tax Credit, see Cohen (2022). Albeit flawed, each program counters economic inequality. On seeing how government policies like these benefit people, see Guardino and Mettler (2020). Sharing more information about climate change mitigation policies could pay dividends (Dechezleprêtre et al. 2022).

Page 178 *"pluralistic ignorance"*: Miller (2023). Pluralistic ignorance is weaponized by autocrats. If you're living in an authoritarian state that controls the news, not only do you not know what's happening, but you also don't know what other people think is happening. If you don't know whether your neighbors will join you in the streets because you don't know what they know, it's also likely terrifying enough to keep you home. The 2022 paper on pluralistic ignorance and climate change is Sparkman, Geiger, and Weber (2022). Notably, there's a widespread perception that non-white groups care less about climate change than white Americans, but the reverse is true (Pearson et al. 2018).

Page 178 *long-standing debate*: These two views are described in Bergman et al. (2024; see also Madva 2020b, 2020d).

Page 179 *annual income 31 percent higher*: Chetty, Hendren, and Katz (2016). If children were under thirteen when their families moved, they had better outcomes (including health and well-being). The same was not true for older kids.

Page 179 *a team of social scientists*: Bergman et al. (2024).

Page 180 *scaled to the average neighborhood rent*: This scaling has long been the case, not just in this experiment.

Page 180 *good customer service*: We take the "customer service" description of the program from Matthews (2023). Chetty's quote about the large effect is from Matthews (2019).

Page 180 *"very satisfied"*: San Diego represents another exciting case study (Kaur 2022). Chetty acknowledges that the CMTO program's approach helps people move out of high-poverty neighborhoods rather than trying to improve the neighborhoods they started in. CMTO can't move everyone and shouldn't try. Chetty's both/and view is that cities must dedicate resources to poor neighborhoods *and* help people who want to move (Vedantam 2018).

Chapter 14

Page 184 ***what roles am I best positioned to play?***: Organizations like 80,000 Hours (80,000 Hours n.d.), affiliated with the Centre for Effective Altruism, purport to help make decisions like this. We support efforts to help people figure out the most effective roles they can play to make change. While we sympathize with some aspects of effective altruism more broadly, the very things that make implementing and sustaining change so difficult may also apply to it. "Earning to give" can become derailed in implementation, as Sam Bankman-Fried demonstrates. Becoming wealthy can change, and distort, people's intentions. For like-minded worries about effective altruism, see Srinivasan (2015) and Setiya (2022). For both/and defenses of some aspects of effective altruism, and the importance of individuals taking responsibility to address everything problems, see Berkey (2018a, 2018b).

We can't neglect how new roles can change us. See, for example, Olúfẹ́mi O. Táíwò's (2022) important work on "elite capture." Historically, progressive thinkers pinned hopes for change on the promotion of members of marginalized groups to elite positions. These hopes overlook the extent to which the elite may have been selected precisely for their willingness to preserve the status quo—or these new elites may be changed by the process of promotion. See also Alexander (2020, chapter 6) and Madva (2016a, sec. 2).

Page 184 ***"do battle where we are standing"***: Lorde (2017). See also Lorde (2020, 133).

Page 184 ***wasn't explicitly political***: Ransome-Kuti hadn't been entirely apolitical at the start but became much more politically engaged over time. Thanks to Olúfẹ́mi O. Táíwò for constructive feedback and discussion here. Facts about Ransome-Kuti are primarily from Johnson-Odim (1992), who also emphasizes Ransome-Kuti's intersectional outlook (1992, 144). Some details here are also drawn from Agunbiade (2020) and Wikipedia (2024). We first learned about her through Adamson (2023).

Page 185 ***given "The Lenin"***: See chapter 7.

Page 186 ***universal suffrage***: Women obtained the right to vote in Ransome-Kuti's part of Nigeria much earlier, in 1954, but women's suffrage took much longer to reach Nigeria's northern regions.

Page 186 **NIMBY**: NIMBYism is a global problem. UK young adults stay living with their parents because NIMBY resistance blocks new housing (Hinsliff 2023).

Infrastructure development in urban China has been canceled or relocated after NIMBY protests (Gu 2016). See also Maiorino (2012).

Page 186 *"drug dealing and other crimes"*: Felschundneff (2023). Yet California has threatened to sue the city for failing to provide adequate affordable housing (Li and Carney 2022). On subsidized housing and home prices, see Voith et al. (2022). On NIMBYism and high-speed rail, see Rosenberg (2009).

Page 187 *racking up wins*: On YIMBY successes, see Yglesias (2023). On California's ban on single-unit zoning, see Healy and Ballinger (2021). On state legislative action, see Kahn and Furth (2023). On faith-based and educational institutions, see Senator Scott Wiener (2023).

Page 187 *show up at the zoning board*: See also Klein (2022a, 2022b). On French YIM-BYism, see Ortiz (2021).

Page 187 *seven for every car*: Margolies (2023). On parking acreage, see Seaside Institute (2022). On minimum parking requirements, see Ben-Joseph (2020). On Shoup's influence, see Steuteville (2023) and Thurber (2020).

Page 188 *factory farms*: Flesher (2020).

Page 189 *"reducetarians"*: See Kateman (2017) and May and Kumar (2023).

Page 189 *An ethics class*: Schwitzgebel, Cokelet, and Singer (2020, 2023).

Page 189 *lasted at least a couple months*: The effects on meat purchases that we report are from a preregistered replication of the original study (Schwitzgebel, Cokelet, and Singer 2023) and were a bit larger than in the original study. The 2020 study found that meat purchases go from 28 to 25 percent in the animal rights class and from 28 to 29 percent in the other class. In the replication, looking only at food purchases over $4.99 (when students were likely sitting down for a full meal rather than just grabbing a snack on the go), the percentage containing meat dropped from 51 to 42. This replication included an eleven-minute video advocating vegetarianism. Similar effects on college students' purchases were observed by a separate team, after teaching about the effects of meat consumption on climate change and personal health (Jalil, Tasoff, and Bustamante 2020).

Page 190 *"there was something more I could do"*: Nagel (2015). See also Margolis (2015). Her quote about the learning going both ways is from personal communication (September 8, 2023).

Page 191 *Canada's history of refugee sponsorship*: Pfrimmer (2019). Thanks to Jen Nagel for pointing us to this history. On outcomes for Canada's privately sponsored refugees, see Kaida, Hou, and Stick (2020). Many refugees are so-called low-skilled migrants, who may contribute less economically to host countries than migrants with advanced degrees. Yet a large number of studies found either positive or nonsignificant (i.e., nonnegative!) results on "household well-being, prices, employment, and wages" in host countries (Verme and Schuettler 2021; Verme 2023). See Lim (2023) on the philosophical and political implications of pernicious stereotypes and misperceptions surrounding low-skilled migration. On migration and the US economy, see, for example, Rouse et al. (2021). A large literature explores immigration's political ramifications (e.g., Mehic 2019; Shehaj, Shin, and Inglehart 2021; Ramos, Schumann, and Hewstone 2022; Erlanger and Anderson 2022).

Page 191 *less attached to their racial identity*: Major, Blodorn, and Blascovich (2018). Studies like Major et al.'s take for granted that strongly identifying as white is effectively equivalent to identifying as a white *supremacist*. But it's also possible to accept one's *white privilege* as important to one's identity (Alcoff 2005, chap. 9; 2015; Plaut 2010; Goren and Plaut 2012; Knowles et al. 2014; Shuman et al. 2022)—a noncolorblind, structure-facing, both/and perspective on one's own whiteness.

Page 191 *well-being eventually improves*: Li et al. (2021), who also show that intergroup contact drives these effects. Intergroup contact is among the most extensively studied phenomena in social science (Pettigrew 1998, 2018; Van Assche et al. 2023; Turner, Hodson, and Dhont 2020; Vezzali et al. 2023; but for contrasting perspectives, see, for example, Sengupta et al. 2023; Kotzur and Wagner 2021; Dixon and Levine 2012). For research on college campuses and interracial roommates providing venues for intergroup contact, see Bai, Ramos, and Fiske (2020). See also Shook and Fazio (2008), Gaither and Sommers (2013), Niu and Brown (2023), and Albuja et al. (2024).

Page 192 *forty years after coming to Canada*: Stewart (2016). Nagel's quote is from Nagel (2015). Her then member of Parliament, Arif Virani, became minister of justice and attorney general of Canada (Moosapeta 2023). After leaving politics in 2021, Maryam Monsef launched a consulting firm to support women leaders (Hassan 2022).

Page 193 *how much impact others have had on them*: Kumar and Epley (2023). Studies show that kids as young as eight underestimate the impact of small acts of kindness (Echelbarger and Epley 2023). On hospital staff, see Vedantam (2016). See also Berg et al. (2023).

Page 193 *happy warrior*: Goddard (2023). We're not saying you need to be happy to fight for social change or should feel guilty if you're unhappy. But self-care and care for others is a genuine part of the struggle, and it's too easily overlooked.

Conclusion

Page 195 *to see their work backfire*: See chapter 9, section 4, "Failed Successes."

Page 195 *the League's legacy*: As the historian David Kennedy (2004) argues. See also Ostrower (1979).

Page 195 *tell the successes from the failures*: And even then, it depends on how much hindsight you have. This point is made vivid by the fable of the old man who lost his horse, who wisely reserves judgment about whether he is lucky or unlucky as he undergoes a series of changing fortunes. First, he loses his horse, and others bemoan his bad luck. Then the horse returns with more strong horses, and they celebrate his good luck. Then his son falls off one of the horses and breaks his leg. Then there's a military draft, and all the drafted soldiers are killed—but his son stays home with the broken leg, and so forth (Wikipedia 2023g).

Page 196 *History is remembered, and told, by people*: And not just by history's "victors," though many have said so (Phelan 2019). Of course, many of today's victors become tomorrow's losers. Despite being outmatched by the most powerful military force in history, the Taliban waited out the US occupation of Afghanistan for twenty years and regained control before the final US airplane had left. Part of what sustained their cause was a narrative sense of their identity and the stories they told about who they were and what they were willing to endure. As one captured Taliban fighter purportedly said during the US occupation of Afghanistan: "You have the watches. We have the time" (Yousafzai 2011). The power of narrative also helps to understand the activists we profiled in chapter 10, who persisted despite exceedingly long odds of victory.

Page 196 *the hate we give*: We are alluding to the novel *The Hate U Give* (Thomas 2017).

Page 197 *"keep correcting our narrative"*: Caine et al. (2022).

References

80,000 Hours. n.d. "You Have 80,000 Hours in Your Career." Accessed January 16, 2024. https://80000hours.org/.

Abdelfatah, Rund, host. 2021. *Throughline*. "Remembering Bayard Rustin: The Man Behind the March on Washington." Podcast, February 25. https://www.npr.org/2021/02/22/970292302/remembering-bayard-rustin-the-man-behind-the-march-on-washington.

Abdelfatah, Rund, Ramtin Arablouei, Devin Katayama, Julie Caine, Casey Miner, Lawrence Wu, Anya Steinberg, Cristina Kim, and Yolanda Sangweni. 2023. *Throughline*. "The Ghost in Your Phone." Podcast, June 1. https://www.npr.org/2023/05/31/1179117816/the-ghost-in-your-phone.

Abdelfatah, Rund, host. 2019. *Throughline*. "The Litter Myth." Podcast, September 5. https://www.npr.org/2019/09/04/757539617/the-litter-myth.

Abramowitz, Alan I. 2022. "Why Voter Suppression Probably Won't Work." Center for Politics, February 3. https://centerforpolitics.org/crystalball/articles/why-voter-suppression-probably-wont-work/.

Abramowitz, Alan, and Jennifer McCoy. 2019 "United States: Racial Resentment, Negative Partisanship, and Polarization in Trump's America." *Annals of the American Academy of Political and Social Science* 681 (1): 137–156. https://doi.org/10.1177/0002716218811309.

Abron, JoNina. 1998. "'Serving the People': The Survival Programs of the Black Panther Party." In *The Black Panther Party [Reconsidered]*, edited by Charles Earl Jones. Black Classic Press.

Abson, David J., Joern Fischer, Julia Leventon, et al. 2017. "Leverage Points for Sustainability Transformation." *Ambio* 46 (1): 30–39. https://doi.org/10.1007/s13280-016-0800-y.

Acharya, Avidit, Matthew Blackwell, and Maya Sen. 2018. *Deep Roots: How Slavery Still Shapes Southern Politics*. Princeton University Press.

Action Network. n.d. "US Labor Against Racism and War." Accessed October 28, 2023. https://actionnetwork.org/groups/laboragainstracismandwar.

Adams, Glenn, Vanessa Edkins, Dominika Lacka, Kate M. Pickett, and Sapna Cheryan. 2008. "Teaching about Racism: Pernicious Implications of Standard Portrayal." *Basic and Applied Social Psychology* 30 (4): 349–361. https://doi.org/10.1080/01973530802502309.

Adams, Glenn, Sara Estrada-Villalta, Daniel Sullivan, and Hazel R. Markus. 2019. "The Psychology of Neoliberalism and the Neoliberalism of Psychology." *Journal of Social Issues* 75 (1): 189–216. https://doi.org/10.1111/josi.12305.

Adamson, Peter, host. 2023. *History of Philosophy Without Any Gaps*. "121. No Agreement: Fela Kuti and Wole Soyinka." Podcast, April 2. https://historyofphilosophy.net/fela-kuti-wole-soyinka.

Aegis Law. 2023. "Workplace Sexual Harassment Statistics." Posted May 9, 2023. https://www.aegislawfirm.com/blog/2023/05/workplace-sexual-harassment-statistics/.

Aggarwal, Pradhi. 2022. "Using Rideshare Data to Evaluate Racial Bias in the Issuance of Speeding Citations." Medium, December 21. https://eng.lyft.com/using-rideshare-data-to-evaluate-racial-bias-in-the-issuance-of-speeding-citations-9997af34488e.

Agunbiade, Tayo. 2020. "Remembering Funmilayo Ransome-Kuti: Nigeria's 'Lioness of Lisabi.'" *Al Jazeera*, October 1. https://www.aljazeera.com/features/2020/10/1/the-lioness-of-lisabi-who-ended-unfair-taxes-for-nigerian-women.

Ainslie, George. 2021. "Willpower With and Without Effort." *Behavioral and Brain Sciences* 44 (January): e30. https://doi.org/10.1017/S0140525X20000357.

Åkerströmp, Lola A. 2023. "'Sweden Is One of the "Happiest" Countries in the World—But as a Black Woman I Don't Always Agree.'" *Cosmopolitan*, October 26. https://www.cosmopolitan.com/uk/reports/a45614652/nordic-countries-happiness-race/.

Aladangady, Aditya, and Akila Forde. 2021. "Wealth Inequality and the Racial Wealth Gap." *FEDS Notes* (2861). https://doi.org/10.17016/2380-7172.2861.

Albuja, A.F., Gaither, S.E., Sanchez, D.T., Nixon, J., 2024. "Testing Intergroup Contact Theory Through a Natural Experiment of Randomized College Roommate Assignments in the United States." *Journal of Personality and Social Psychology* 127: 277–290. https://doi.org/10.1037/pspa0000393.

Alcoff, Linda Martín. 2005. *Visible Identities: Race, Gender, and the Self*. Oxford University Press.

Alcoff, Linda Martín. 2015. *The Future of Whiteness*. Polity.

Aleiss, Angela. 1996. "Native Son." *Times-Picayune*, May 26. https://www.academia.edu/11282618/Native_Son_Italian_American_Identity_of_Iron_Eyes_Cody_.

Alexander, Michelle. 2020. *The New Jim Crow: Mass Incarceration in the Age of Color-blindness*. 10th anniversary ed. The New Press.

Alexander, Sophie. 2024. "A Billionaire Wanted to Save 1 Trillion Trees by 2030. It's Not Going Great." *Bloomberg.Com*, May 3. https://www.bloomberg.com/graphics/2024-benioff-save-trillion-trees/.

Alexander-Floyd, Nikol G. 2012. "Disappearing Acts: Reclaiming Intersectionality in the Social Sciences in a Post-Black Feminist Era." *Feminist Formations* 24 (1): 1–25.

Alger, Horatio. 2009. *Ragged Dick*. CreateSpace Independent Publishing Platform.

Al Jazeera. 2022. "Hong Kong: 25 Years Under Chinese Rule." June 30. https://www.aljazeera.com/news/2022/6/30/hong-kong-timeline-1997-to-2022.

Allen, Danielle. 2004. *Talking to Strangers: Anxieties of Citizenship Since Brown v. Board of Education*. University of Chicago Press.

Allen, Jedediah, and Kristin Andrews. 2024. "How Not to Find Over-Imitation in Animals." *Human Development* 68 (2).

Allen, Steve, Deonie Allen, Vernon R. Phoenix, Gaël Le Roux, Pilar Durántez Jiménez, Anaëlle Simonneau, Stéphane Binet, and Didier Galop. 2019. "Atmospheric Transport and Deposition of Microplastics in a Remote Mountain Catchment." *Nature Geoscience* 12 (5): 339–344. https://doi.org/10.1038/s41561-019-0335-5.

Al-Sibai, Noor. 2023. "SpaceX and Tesla Get Way More Government Money Than NPR." The Byte, April 15. https://futurism.com/the-byte/spacex-tesla-government-money-npr.

Alter, Charlotte. 2022. "Is Chris Smalls the Future of Labor?" *Time*, April 25. https://time.com/6169185/chris-smalls-amazon-labor-union/.

Altman, Rebecca. 2022. "How Bad Are Plastics, Really?" *Atlantic*, January 3. https://www.theatlantic.com/science/archive/2022/01/plastic-history-climate-change/621033/.

Amemiya, Jamie, Elizabeth Mortenson, Gail D. Heyman, and Caren M. Walker. 2023. "Thinking Structurally: A Cognitive Framework for Understanding How People Attribute Inequality to Structural Causes." *Perspectives on Psychological Science* 18 (2): 259–274. https://doi.org/10.1177/17456916221093593.

American Psychological Association. 2020. "What Drives Voter Behavior? With Jon Krosnick, PhD." Posted October 7, 2020. YouTube, 50:00. https://www.youtube.com/watch?v=DwjOVEUD0-E.

Anderson, Elizabeth. 2010. *The Imperative of Integration*. Princeton University Press. https://doi.org/10.1515/9781400836826.

Anderson, Elizabeth. 2012. "Epistemic Justice as a Virtue of Social Institutions." *Social Epistemology* 26 (2): 163–173. https://doi.org/10.1080/02691728.2011.652211.

Anderson, Elizabeth. 2020. "Feminist Epistemology and Philosophy of Science." *Stanford Encyclopedia of Philosophy*. https://plato.stanford.edu/archives/spr2020/entries/feminism-epistemology/.

Anderson, Robert. 2016. "The Rashomon Effect and Communication." *Canadian Journal of Communication* 41 (2): 249–270. https://doi.org/10.22230/cjc.2016v41n2a 3068.

Ani, Ruopeng, and Jiakun Zheng. 2014. "Proximity to an Exercise Facility and Physical Activity in China." *Southeast Asian Journal of Tropical Medicine and Public Health* 45 (6): 1483–1491.

Antonoplis, Stephen. 2024. "Studying Personality and Social Structure." *Social and Personality Psychology Compass* 18 (1): e12932. https://doi.org/10.1111/spc3.12932.

Antony, Louise. 1993. "Quine as Feminist: The Radical Import of Naturalized Epistemology." In *A Mind of One's Own: Feminist Essays on Reason and Objectivity*, edited by Louise Antony and Charlotte Witt. Westview Press.

Anzaldúa, Gloria. 2012. *Borderlands/La Frontera: The New Mestiza*. 4th ed. Aunt Lute Books.

Arablouei, Ramtin, Rund Abdelfatah, Julie Caine, Lawrence Wu, Laine Kaplan-Levenson, Schuyler Swenson, Kumari Devarajan, Victor Yvellez, and Mansee Khurana. 2022. *Throughline*. "There Are No Utopias." Podcast, February 24. https://www.npr.org/2022/02/20/1082030426/there-are-no-utopias.

Aragon, Corwin, and Alison M. Jaggar. 2018. "Agency, Complicity, and the Responsibility to Resist Structural Injustice." *Journal of Social Philosophy* 49 (3): 439–460. https://doi.org/10.1111/josp.12251.

Archbold, Carol A. 2021. "Police Accountability in the USA: Gaining Traction or Spinning Wheels?" *Policing: A Journal of Policy and Practice* 15 (3): 1665–1683. https://doi.org/10.1093/police/paab033.

Ardagh, Abhi, Jamie Wheal, and Bill McKibben. 2021. "Individuals Must Join Together for Climate Change—An Interview with Bill McKibben." Neurohacker Collective, July 14. https://neurohacker.com/individuals-must-join-together-for-climate-change-an-interview-with-bill-mckibben.

Aristotle. 2009. *The Nicomachean Ethics*. New edition. Oxford University Press.

Arjamaa, Olli, and Timo Vuorisalo. 2017. "Gene-Culture Coevolution and Human Diet." *American Scientist*, February 6. https://www.americanscientist.org/article/gene-culture-coevolution-and-human-diet.

Arnesen, Eric. 1991. *Waterfront Workers of New Orleans: Race, Class, and Politics, 1863–1923*. Oxford University Press.

Aronow, Peter M., and Benjamin T. Miller. 2016. "Policy Misperceptions and Support for Gun Control Legislation." *The Lancet* 387 (10015): 223. https://doi.org/10.1016/S0140-6736(16)00042-8.

Associated Press. 1994. "Drawing from a Hat Decides Wyoming Race." *Los Angeles Times*, November 17, sec. World & Nation. https://www.latimes.com/archives/la-xpm-1994-11-17-mn-63661-story.html.

Associated Press. 2022. "Biden Revives Obama-Era Loan Program That Funded Solyndra and Cost US Taxpayers More Than $500 Million." Fox News, January 26. https://www.foxnews.com/us/biden-revives-obama-era-program-loan-program-millions-solyndra.

Association of Public and Land-Grant Universities. n.d. "How Does a College Degree Improve Graduates' Employment and Earnings Potential?" Accessed November 14, 2023. https://www.aplu.org/our-work/4-policy-and-advocacy/publicuvalues/employment-earnings/.

Astor, Maggie. 2018. "7 Times in History When Students Turned to Activism." *New York Times*, March 5, sec. US. https://www.nytimes.com/2018/03/05/us/student-protest-movements.html.

Atkin, Emily. 2021. "'What Can I Do?' Anything." Heated, July 12. https://heated.world/p/what-can-i-do-anything.

Avery, Beth, and Han Lu. 2021. "Ban the Box: US Cities, Counties, and States Adopt Fair Hiring Policies." National Employment Law Project, October 1. https://www.nelp.org/publication/ban-the-box-fair-chance-hiring-state-and-local-guide/.

Ayala-López, Saray, and Erin Beeghly. 2020. "Explaining Injustice: Structural Analysis, Bias, and Individuals." In *An Introduction to Implicit Bias: Knowledge, Justice, and the Social Mind*, edited by Erin Beeghly and Alex Madva. Routledge. https://doi.org/10.4324/9781315107615-11.

Ayanian, Arin H., and Nicole Tausch. 2016. "How Risk Perception Shapes Collective Action Intentions in Repressive Contexts: A Study of Egyptian Activists During the 2013 Post-Coup Uprising." *British Journal of Social Psychology* 55 (4): 700–721. https://doi.org/10.1111/bjso.12164.

Ayanian, Arin H., Nicole Tausch, Yasemin Gülsüm Acar, Maria Chayinska, Wing-Yee Cheung, and Yulia Lukyanova. 2021. "Resistance in Repressive Contexts: A Comprehensive Test of Psychological Predictors." *Journal of Personality and Social Psychology* 120 (4): 912–939. https://doi.org/10.1037/pspi0000285.

Ayres, Ian, and Peter Siegelman. 1995. "Race and Gender Discrimination in Bargaining for a New Car." *American Economic Review* 85 (3): 304–321.

Aytaç, S. Erdem, and Susan C. Stokes. 2019. *Why Bother? Rethinking Participation in Elections and Protests*. Cambridge University Press.

Azevedo, Flavio, John T. Jost, Tobias Rothmund, and Joanna Sterling. 2019. "Neoliberal Ideology and the Justification of Inequality in Capitalist Societies: Why Social and Economic Dimensions of Ideology Are Intertwined." *Journal of Social Issues* 75 (1): 49–88. https://doi.org/10.1111/josi.12310.

Baca-Motes, Katie, Amber Brown, Ayelet Gneezy, Elizabeth A. Keenan, and Leif D. Nelson. 2013. "Commitment and Behavior Change: Evidence from the Field." *Journal of Consumer Research* 39 (5): 1070–1084. https://doi.org/10.1086/667226.

Bachman, Rachel. 2017. "How Close Do You Need to Be to Your Gym?" *Wall Street Journal*, March 21, sec. Life. https://www.wsj.com/articles/how-close-do-you-need-to-be-to-your-gym-1490111186.

Bai, Xuechunzi, Miguel R. Ramos, and Susan T. Fiske. 2020. "As Diversity Increases, People Paradoxically Perceive Social Groups as More Similar." *Proceedings of the National Academy of Sciences* 117 (23): 12741–12749. https://doi.org/10.1073/pnas.2000333117.

Bandura, Albert. 1978. "Self-Efficacy: Toward a Unifying Theory of Behavioral Change." *Advances in Behaviour Research and Therapy* 1 (4): 139–161. https://doi.org/10.1016/0146-6402(78)90002-4.

Bandura, Albert. 1997. *Self-Efficacy: The Exercise of Control.* Worth Publishers.

Banks, Ralph R., and Richard T. Ford. 2008. "(How) Does Unconscious Bias Matter: Law, Politics, and Racial Inequality." *Emory Law Journal* 58: 1053.

Banks, Ralph R., and Richard T. Ford. 2011. "Does Unconscious Bias Matter?" *Poverty & Race* 20 (5): 1–2.

Barbaro, Michael, Shannon Lin, Lynsea Garrison, et al. 2023. "The Secret History of Gun Rights." *New York Times*, August 1, sec. Podcasts. https://www.nytimes.com/2023/08/01/podcasts/the-daily/nra-gun-rights.html?showTranscript=1.

Barreiro, Alicia, and Cecilia Wainryb. 2023. "Adolescents Thinking on Economic Inequality: Expanding the Discussion Beyond the Global North." *New Ideas in Psychology* 71 (December): 101045. https://doi.org/10.1016/j.newideapsych.2023.101045.

Bartels, Larry M. 2020. "Ethnic Antagonism Erodes Republicans' Commitment to Democracy." *Proceedings of the National Academy of Sciences* 117 (37): 22752–22759. https://doi.org/10.1073/pnas.2007747117.

Basevich, Elvira. 2021. "What It's Like to Grow Up Poor, but Fall in Love with Philosophy: A Notice to the Profession in Case It Forgot." *APA Newsletter on Feminism and Philosophy* 20 (3): 15–19.

Bash, Dana, and Jessica Yellin. 2007. "Craig: I Did Nothing 'Inappropriate' in Airport Bathroom." CNN Politics, August 28. https://edition.cnn.com/2007/POLITICS/08/28/craig.arrest/.

Bastin, Jean-Francois, Yelena Finegold, Claude Garcia, et al. 2019. "The Global Tree Restoration Potential." *Science* 365 (6448): 76–79. https://doi.org/10.1126/science .aax0848.

Basu, Rima. 2020. "The Specter of Normative Conflict: Does Fairness Require Inaccuracy?" In *An Introduction to Implicit Bias: Knowledge, Justice, and the Social Mind*, edited by Erin Beeghly and Alex Madva. Routledge. https://doi.org/10.4324/97813 15107615-10.

Bates, Karen Grigsby. 2015. "African-Americans Question Comparing Gay Rights Movement to Civil Rights." NPR, July 2, sec. Race. https://www.npr.org/2015/07/02 /419554758/african-americans-question-comparing-gay-rights-movement-to-civil -rights.

Bauer, Mark S., and JoAnn Kirchner. 2020. "Implementation Science: What Is It and Why Should I Care?" *Psychiatry Research* 283 (January): 112376. https://doi.org /10.1016/j.psychres.2019.04.025.

Beck, Colin J., Mlada Bukovansky, Erica Chenoweth, George Lawson, Sharon Erickson Nepstad, and Daniel P. Ritter. 2022. *On Revolutions: Unruly Politics in the Contemporary World*. Oxford University Press.

Becker, Dana, and Jeanne M. 2008a. "Dreaming the American Dream: Individualism and Positive Psychology." *Social and Personality Psychology Compass* 2 (5): 1767–1780. https://doi.org/10.1111/j.1751-9004.2008.00139.x.

Becker, Dana, and Jeanne M. 2008b. "Positive Psychology: History in the Remaking?" *Theory & Psychology* 18 (5): 591–604. https://doi.org/10.1177/0959354308093397.

Beeghly, Erin. 2015. "What Is a Stereotype?" *Hypatia* 30 (4): 675–691. https://doi .org/10.1111/hypa.12170.

Beeghly, Erin. 2025. *What's Wrong with Stereotyping?* Oxford University Press.

Begeny, Christopher T., Jolien van Breen, Colin Wayne Leach, Martijn van Zomeren, and Aarti Iyer. 2022. "The Power of the Ingroup for Promoting Collective Action: How Distinctive Treatment from Fellow Minority Members Motivates Collective Action." *Journal of Experimental Social Psychology* 101 (July): 104346. https:// doi.org/10.1016/j.jesp.2022.104346.

Bell, Derrick A. 1980. "Brown v. Board of Education and the Interest-Convergence Dilemma." *Harvard Law Review* 93 (3): 518–533. https://doi.org/10.2307/1340546.

Bellew, Evelyn, Kristen Harknett, and Daniel Schneider. 2022. "Low Pay, Less Predictability: Fast Food Jobs in California." Malcolm Wiener Center for Social Policy, Harvard Kennedy School. https://shift.hks.harvard.edu/wp-content/uploads/2022/07 /CA_Fast_Food_DRAFT.pdf.

Benegal, Salil D. 2018. "The Spillover of Race and Racial Attitudes into Public Opinion About Climate Change." *Environmental Politics* 27 (4): 733–756. https://doi.org/10.1080/09644016.2018.1457287.

Ben-Joseph, Eran. 2020. "From Chaos to Order: A Brief Cultural History of the Parking Lot." The MIT Press Reader, September 3. https://thereader.mitpress.mit.edu/brief-cultural-history-of-the-parking-lot/.

Berg, Justin M., Amy Wrzesniewski, Adam M. Grant, Jennifer Kurkoski, and Brian Welle. 2023. "Getting Unstuck: The Effects of Growth Mindsets about the Self and Job on Happiness at Work." *Journal of Applied Psychology* 108 (1): 152–166. https://doi.org/10.1037/apl0001021.

Bergman, Peter, Raj Chetty, Stefanie DeLuca, Nathaniel Hendren, Lawrence F. Katz, and Christopher Palmer. 2024. "Creating Moves to Opportunity: Experimental Evidence on Barriers to Neighborhood Choice." *American Economic Review* 114 (5): 1281–1337.

Bergquist, Magnus, Maximilian Thiel, Matthew H. Goldberg, and Sander van der Linden. 2023. "Field Interventions for Climate Change Mitigation Behaviors: A Second-Order Meta-Analysis." *Proceedings of the National Academy of Sciences* 120 (13): e2214851120. https://doi.org/10.1073/pnas.2214851120.

Berinsky, Adam J., Christopher F. Karpowitz, Zeyu Chris Peng, Jonathan A. Rodden, and Cara J. Wong. 2023. "How Social Context Affects Immigration Attitudes." *Journal of Politics* 85 (2): 372–388. https://doi.org/10.1086/722339.

Berkey, Brian. 2018a. "Obligations of Productive Justice: Individual or Institutional?" *Critical Review of International Social and Political Philosophy* 21 (6): 726–753. https://doi.org/10.1080/13698230.2016.1262315.

Berkey, Brian. 2018b. "The Institutional Critique of Effective Altruism." *Utilitas* 30 (2): 143–171. https://doi.org/10.1017/S0953820817000176.

Bertrand, Marianne, and Esther Duflo. 2017. "Field Experiments on Discrimination." In *Handbook of Economic Field Experiments*, edited by Abhijit Vinayak Banerjee and Esther Duflo. North-Holland. https://doi.org/10.1016/bs.hefe.2016.08.004.

Birhane, Abeba. 2017. "Descartes Was Wrong: 'A Person Is a Person Through Other Persons.'" *Aeon*, April 7. https://aeon.co/ideas/descartes-was-wrong-a-person-is-a-person-through-other-persons.

Blair, Graeme, Jeremy M. Weinstein, Fotini Christia, et al. 2021. "Community Policing Does Not Build Citizen Trust in Police or Reduce Crime in the Global South." *Science* 374 (6571): eabd3446. https://doi.org/10.1126/science.abd3446.

BlackPast. 2007. "(1857) Frederick Douglass, 'If There Is No Struggle, There Is No Progress,' West India Emancipation." https://www.blackpast.org/african-american-history/1857-frederick-douglass-if-there-no-struggle-there-no-progress/.

BlackPast. 2018. "(1966) The Black Panther Party Ten-Point Program." https://www
.blackpast.org/african-american-history/primary-documents-african-american-history
/black-panther-party-ten-point-program-1966/.

BlackPast. 2012. "(1977) The Combahee River Collective Statement." https://www
.blackpast.org/african-american-history/combahee-river-collective-statement-1977/.

BlackPast. 2013. "(1963) Malcolm X, "Racial Separation.'" https://www.blackpast.org
/african-american-history/speeches-african-american-history/1963-malcolm-x-racial
-separation/.

Blake, John. 2015. "This Is How the NRA Loses." CNN Politics, October 16. https://
www.cnn.com/2015/10/15/politics/defy-gun-lobby/index.html.

Blakemore, Erin. 2021. "How the Black Panthers' Breakfast Program Both Inspired
and Threatened the Government." History, January 29. https://www.history.com
/news/free-school-breakfast-black-panther-party.

Blakemore, Erin. 2023. "The Largest Mass Deportation in American History." History, October 4. https://www.history.com/news/operation-wetback-eisenhower-1954
-deportation.

Bleidorn, Wiebke, Patrick L. Hill, Mitja D. Back, et al. 2019. "The Policy Relevance of
Personality Traits." *American Psychologist* 74 (9): 1056–1067. https://doi.org/10.1037
/amp0000503.

Bloch, Karen Lehrman. 2019. "Intersectionality: The New Caste System." *Jewish Journal*, February 27. https://jewishjournal.com/commentary/columnist/294500/inter
sectionality-the-new-caste-system/.

Bloom, Joshua, and Waldo E. Martin, Jr. 2016. *Black Against Empire: The History and
Politics of the Black Panther Party.* University of California Press.

Blum, Deborah. 2018. "The 19th-Century Fight Against Bacteria-Ridden Milk
Preserved with Embalming Fluid." *Smithsonian Magazine*, October 5. https://www
.smithsonianmag.com/science-nature/19th-century-fight-bacteria-ridden-milk
-embalming-fluid-180970473/.

Blume, Lesley M. M. 2023. "Trinity Nuclear Test's Fallout Reached 46 States, Canada
and Mexico, Study Finds." *New York Times,* July 21, sec. Science. https://www.nytimes
.com/2023/07/20/science/trinity-nuclear-test-atomic-bomb-oppenheimer.html.

Blumgart, Jake. 2021. "Redlining Didn't Happen Quite the Way We Thought It
Did." Governing, September 21. https://www.governing.com/context/redlining-didnt
-happen-quite-the-way-we-thought-it-did.

Bond, Robert M., Christopher J. Fariss, Jason J. Jones, Adam D. I. Kramer, Cameron
Marlow, Jaime E. Settle, and James H. Fowler. 2012. "A 61-Million-Person Experiment in Social Influence and Political Mobilization." *Nature* 489 (7415): 295–298.
https://doi.org/10.1038/nature11421.

Bonner, Marla, host. 2020. *APA Journals Dialogue.* "How Personality Traits Change Over Time." Podcast, January 2. https://www.apa.org/pubs/highlights/podcasts /episode-30.

Borger, Julian. 2018. "Fleeing a Hell the US Helped Create: Why Central Americans Journey North." *The Guardian,* December 19, sec. US news. https://www.theguardian .com/us-news/2018/dec/19/central-america-migrants-us-foreign-policy.

Bouie, Jamelle. 2021. "What 'Structural Racism' Really Means." *New York Times,* November 9, sec. Opinion. https://www.nytimes.com/2021/11/09/opinion/structural -racism.html.

Bouie, Jamelle. 2022. "What if We Let Majoritarian Democracy Take Root?" *New York Times,* October 21, sec. Opinion. https://www.nytimes.com/2022/10/21/opinion /minority-rule-majoritarian-democracy.html.

Bourdieu, Pierre. 1977. *Outline of a Theory of Practice.* Translated by Richard Nice. Cambridge University Press.

Bourdieu, Pierre. 1990. *In Other Words: Essays Towards a Reflexive Sociology.* Stanford University Press.

Bowen, William G., and Michael McPherson. 2016. *Lesson Plan: An Agenda for Change in American Higher Education.* Princeton University Press.

Brady, Jeff. 2014. "After Solyndra Loss, US Energy Loan Program Turning A Profit." *NPR,* November 13, sec. National. https://www.npr.org/2014/11/13/363572151/after -solyndra-loss-u-s-energy-loan-program-turning-a-profit.

Brah, Avtar, and Ann Phoenix. 2013. "Ain't I a Woman? Revisiting Intersectionality." *Journal of International Women's Studies* 5 (3): 75–86.

Branas, Charles C., Eugenia South, Michelle C. Kondo, et al. 2018. "Citywide Cluster Randomized Trial to Restore Blighted Vacant Land and Its Effects on Violence, Crime, and Fear." *Proceedings of the National Academy of Sciences* 115 (12): 2946–2951. https://doi.org/10.1073/pnas.1718503115.

Braul, Peter. 2011. "We'll Never Be That Drunk Again." Maisonneuve, January 20. http://maisonneuve.org/post/2011/01/20/well-never-be-drunk-again/.

Bravo, Mercedes A., Dominique Zephyr, Daniel Kowal, Katherine Ensor, and Marie Lynn Miranda. 2022. "Racial Residential Segregation Shapes the Relationship Between Early Childhood Lead Exposure and Fourth-Grade Standardized Test Scores." *Proceedings of the National Academy of Sciences* 119 (34): e2117868119. https://doi.org/10 .1073/pnas.2117868119.

Brennan, Andrew, and Norva Y. S. Lo. 2022. "Environmental Ethics." *Stanford Encyclopedia of Philosophy.* https://plato.stanford.edu/archives/sum2022/entries/ethics -environmental/.

Bright, Liam K., Nathan Gabriel, Cailin O'Connor, and Olufemi Taiwo. In press. "On the Stability of Racial Capitalism." *Ergo, An Open Access Journal of Philosophy.* https:// doi.org/10.31235/osf.io/syk4m.

Brinkman, Craig S., Shira Gabriel, Shelley M. Kimelberg, Michael J. Poulin, Jennifer Valenti, and Kurt Hugenberg. 2023. "The Psychological Determinants of Classroom Preferences: Implicit and Explicit Racial Attitudes and Racial Composition of Classrooms." *Journal of Community & Applied Social Psychology* 33 (4): 914–928. https://doi .org/10.1002/casp.2680.

Broesch, Tanya, Alyssa N. Crittenden, Bret A. Beheim, et al. 2020. "Navigating Cross-Cultural Research: Methodological and Ethical Considerations." *Proceedings of the Royal Society B: Biological Sciences* 287 (1935): 20201245. https://doi.org/10.1098 /rspb.2020.1245.

Broockman, David, and Joshua Kalla. 2016. "Durably Reducing Transphobia: A Field Experiment on Door-to-Door Canvassing." *Science* 352 (6282): 220–224. https://doi .org/10.1126/science.aad9713.

Broockman, David E., and Joshua L. Kalla. 2025. "Consuming Cross-Cutting Media Causes Learning and Moderates Attitudes: A Field Experiment with Fox News Viewers." *Journal of Politics* 87 (1): 246–261. https://doi.org/10.1086/730725.

Brown, DeNeen L. 2021. "'The Post' and the Forgotten Security Guard Who Discovered the Watergate Break-In." *Washington Post*, October 28. https://www.washing tonpost.com/news/retropolis/wp/2017/12/22/the-post-and-the-forgotten-security -guard-who-discovered-the-watergate-break-in/.

Brown, Trevor E., and Suzanne Mettler. 2023. "Sequential Polarization: The Development of the Rural-Urban Political Divide, 1976–2020." *Perspectives on Politics*, December, 1–29. https://doi.org/10.1017/S1537592723002918.

Brownell, Kelly D., and Kenneth E. Warner. 2009. "The Perils of Ignoring History: Big Tobacco Played Dirty and Millions Died. How Similar Is Big Food?" *Milbank Quarterly* 87 (1): 259–294. https://doi.org/10.1111/j.1468-0009.2009.00555.x.

Brown-Iannuzzi, Jazmin L., Erin Cooley, Stephanie E. McKee, and Charly Hyden. 2019. "Wealthy Whites and Poor Blacks: Implicit Associations Between Racial Groups and Wealth Predict Explicit Opposition Toward Helping the Poor." *Journal of Experimental Social Psychology* 82 (May): 26–34. https://doi.org/10.1016/j.jesp.2018 .11.006.

Brownstein, Michael. 2014. "Rationalizing Flow: Agency in Skilled Unreflective Action." *Philosophical Studies* 168 (2): 545–568. https://doi.org/10.1007/s11098-013-0143-5.

Brownstein, Michael. 2016. "Context and the Ethics of Implicit Bias." In *Implicit Bias and Philosophy*, volume 2, edited by Michael Brownstein and Jennifer Saul. Oxford University Press. https://doi.org/10.1093/acprof:oso/9780198766179.003.0010.

Brownstein, Michael. 2018a. "Self-Control and Overcontrol: Conceptual, Ethical, and Ideological Issues in Positive Psychology." *Review of Philosophy and Psychology* 9, March. https://doi.org/10.1007/s13164-018-0390-7.

Brownstein, Michael. 2018b. *The Implicit Mind: Cognitive Architecture, the Self, and Ethics.* Oxford University Press.

Brownstein, Michael. 2020. "De-Biasing, Skill, and Intergroup Virtue." In *The Routledge Handbook of Philosophy of Skill and Expertise*, edited by Ellen Fridland and Carlotta Pavese. Routledge. https://www.taylorfrancis.com/chapters/edit/10.4324/97813 15180809-47/de-biasing-skill-intergroup-virtue-michael-brownstein.

Brownstein, Michael, Daniel Kelly, and Alex Madva. 2022. "Individualism, Structuralism, and Climate Change." *Environmental Communication* 16 (2): 269–288. https://doi.org/10.1080/17524032.2021.1982745.

Brownstein, Michael, and Neil Levy. 2021. "Philosophy's Other Climate Problem." *Journal of Social Philosophy* 52 (4): 536–553. https://doi.org/10.1111/josp.12396.

Brownstein, Michael, Alex Madva, and Bertram Gawronski. 2019. "What Do Implicit Measures Measure?" *WIREs Cognitive Science* 10 (5): 1–13. https://doi.org/10.1002/wcs.1501.

Brownstein, Michael, Alex Madva, and Bertram Gawronski. 2020. "Understanding Implicit Bias: Putting the Criticism into Perspective." *Pacific Philosophical Quarterly* 101 (2): 276–307. https://doi.org/10.1111/papq.12302.

Brugger, Peter, and Susanne Brugger. 1993. "The Easter Bunny in October: Is It Disguised as a Duck?" *Perceptual and Motor Skills* 76 (2): 577–578. https://doi.org/10.2466/pms.1993.76.2.577.

Brulle, Robert J. 2014. "Institutionalizing Delay: Foundation Funding and the Creation of US Climate Change Counter-Movement Organizations." *Climatic Change* 122 (4): 681–694. https://doi.org/10.1007/s10584-013-1018-7.

Buchanan, Larry, Quoctrung Bui, and Jugal K. Patel. 2020. "Black Lives Matter May Be the Largest Movement in US History." *New York Times*, July 3, sec. US. https://www.nytimes.com/interactive/2020/07/03/us/george-floyd-protests-crowd-size.html.

Buchanan, NiCole T., Desdamona Rios, and Kim A. Case. 2020. "Intersectional Cultural Humility: Aligning Critical Inquiry with Critical Praxis in Psychology." *Women & Therapy* 43 (3–4): 235–243. https://doi.org/10.1080/02703149.2020.1729469.

Buckley, William F. 1955. "Our Mission Statement." *National Review*, November 19. https://www.nationalreview.com/1955/11/our-mission-statement-william-f-buckley-jr/.

Burch, Audra D. S., and Kelley Manley. 2024. "Police Officers Are Charged with Crimes, but Are Juries Convicting?" *New York Times*, January 1, sec. US. https://

www.nytimes.com/2024/01/01/us/george-floyd-elijah-mcclain-police-brutality-black
-lives-matter-trials-civil-rights.html.

Burger, Axel M., Johannes Schuler, and Elisabeth Eberling. 2022. "Guilty Pleasures:
Moral Licensing in Climate-Related Behavior." *Global Environmental Change* 72
(January): 102415. https://doi.org/10.1016/j.gloenvcha.2021.102415.

Burke, Tarana. 2021. "Watching #MeToo Go Viral in 2017." *Time*, September 14.
https://time.com/6097392/tarana-burke-me-too-unbound-excerpt/.

Burns, Mason D., and Erica L. Granz. 2021. "Confronting Sexism: Promoting Confrontation Acceptance and Reducing Stereotyping Through Stereotype Framing." *Sex
Roles* 84 (9): 503–521. https://doi.org/10.1007/s11199-020-01183-5.

Burton, Tara I. 2020. *Strange Rites: New Religions for a Godless World*. PublicAffairs.

Burton, Tara I. 2023. *Self-Made: Creating Our Identities from Da Vinci to the Kardashi-
ans*. PublicAffairs.

Buse, Kent, Soumyadeep Bhaumik, J. Jaime Miranda, Chelsea Hunnisett, Claudia
Selin Batz, and Emma Feeny. 2022. "Individual Responsibility: A Red Herring That
Lets the Fossil Fuel Industry Off the Climate Catastrophe Hook." *BMJ* 378 (July):
o1656. https://doi.org/10.1136/bmj.o1656.

Butler, Daniel M., and David E. Broockman. 2011. "Do Politicians Racially Discriminate Against Constituents? A Field Experiment on State Legislators." *American Journal
of Political Science* 55 (3): 463–477. https://doi.org/10.1111/j.1540-5907.2011.00515.x.

Caine, Julie, Lawrence Wu, Rund Abdelfatah, Ramtin Arablouei, Camila Beiner,
Mansee Khurana, Laine Kaplan-Levenson, Schuyler Swenson, and Victor Yvellez.
2022. "A Story of Us?" NPR, February 3. https://www.npr.org/2022/02/02/1077733601
/a-story-of-us.

Campanella, Thomas. 2017. "The True Measure of Robert Moses (and His Racist
Bridges)." *Bloomberg.Com*, July 9. https://www.bloomberg.com/news/articles/2017
-07-09/robert-moses-and-his-racist-parkway-explained.

Campbell, Andrea L. 2003. *How Policies Make Citizens: Senior Political Activism and
the American Welfare State*. Princeton University Press. https://press.princeton.edu
/books/paperback/9780691122502/how-policies-make-citizens.

Cantoni, Enrico, and Vincent Pons. 2021. "Strict ID Laws Don't Stop Voters: Evidence from a US Nationwide Panel, 2008–2018." *Quarterly Journal of Economics* 136
(4): 2615–2660. https://doi.org/10.1093/qje/qjab019.

Cardin, Nina Beth. 2024. "Understanding the Jewish Call to Sustainability." Exploring Judaism, January 3. https://www.exploringjudaism.org/living/climate-and-envi
ronment/sustainability/understanding-the-jewish-call-to-sustainability/.

Caro, Robert A. 1975. *The Power Broker: Robert Moses and the Fall of New York*. Vintage.

Carpenter, Christopher, and Carlos Dobkin. 2011. "The Minimum Legal Drinking Age and Public Health." *Journal of Economic Perspectives* 25 (2): 133–156.

Carrington, Damian. 2023. "'We're Not Doomed Yet': Climate Scientist Michael Mann on Our Last Chance to Save Human Civilisation." *The Guardian*, September 30, sec. Environment. https://www.theguardian.com/environment/2023/sep/30/human -civilisation-climate-scientist-prof-michael-mann.

Carroll, Jamie M., David S. Yeager, Jenny Buontempo, Cameron Hecht, Andrei Cimpian, Pratik Mhatre, Chandra Muller, and Robert Crosnoe. 2023. "Mindset × Context: Schools, Classrooms, and the Unequal Translation of Expectations into Math Achievement." *Monographs of the Society for Research in Child Development* 88 (2): 7–109. https://doi.org/10.1111/mono.12471.

Carvallo, J. P., Feng Chi Hsu, Zeal Shah, and Jay Taneja. 2021. "Frozen Out in Texas: Blackouts and Inequity." Rockefeller Foundation. https://www.rockefellerfounda tion.org/insights/grantee-impact-story/frozen-out-in-texas-blackouts-and-inequity/.

Cassedy, James G. 1997. "African Americans and the American Labor Movement." *Prologue* 29 (2).

Cathcart-Keays, Athlyn, and Tim Warin. 2016. "Story of Cities #36: How Copenha-gen Rejected 1960s Modernist 'Utopia.'" *The Guardian*, May 5, sec. Cities. https:// www.theguardian.com/cities/2016/may/05/story-cities-copenhagen-denmark-mod ernist-utopia.

CDCTobaccoFree. 2023. "Burden of Tobacco Use in the US." Centers for Disease Con-trol and Prevention, May 4. https://www.cdc.gov/tobacco/campaign/tips/resources /data/cigarette-smoking-in-united-states.html.

Cecco, Leyland. 2023. "Wildfires Turn Canada's Vast Forests from Carbon Sink into Super-Emitter." *The Guardian*, September 22, sec. World news. https://www.the guardian.com/world/2023/sep/22/canada-wildfires-forests-carbon-emissions.

Centers for Disease Control. 2023. "Raw Milk: A Research Anthology of Legal and Public Health Resources." https://www.cdc.gov/phlp/publications/topic/anthologies /anthologies-rawmilk.html.

Centola, Damon, Joshua Becker, Devon Brackbill, and Andrea Baronchelli. 2018. "Experimental Evidence for Tipping Points in Social Convention." *Science* 360 (6393): 1116–1119. https://doi.org/10.1126/science.aas8827.

Chaney, Kimberly E., Danielle M. Young, and Diana T. Sanchez. 2015. "Confronta-tion's Health Outcomes and Promotion of Egalitarianism (C-HOPE) Framework." *Translational Issues in Psychological Science* 1 (4): 363–371. https://doi.org/10.1037 /tps0000042.

Chanin, Jesse. 2018. "The Effect of Symbolic Racism on Environmental Concern and Environmental Action." *Environmental Sociology* 4 (4): 457–469. https://doi.org/10.10 80/23251042.2018.1449340.

Charlesworth, Tessa E. S., and Mahzarin R. Banaji. 2022. "Patterns of Implicit and Explicit Attitudes: IV. Change and Stability from 2007 to 2020." *Psychological Science* 33 (9): 1347–1371. https://doi.org/10.1177/09567976221084257.

Charlesworth, Tessa E. S., and Mahzarin R. Banaji. 2023. "Evidence of Covariation Between Regional Implicit Bias and Socially Significant Outcomes in Healthcare, Education, and Law Enforcement." In *Handbook on Economics of Discrimination and Affirmative Action*, edited by Ashwini Deshpande. Springer Nature. https://doi.org /10.1007/978-981-19-4166-5_7.

Chater, Nick, and George Loewenstein. 2023. "The I-Frame and the S-Frame: How Focusing on Individual-Level Solutions Has Led Behavioral Public Policy Astray." *Behavioral and Brain Sciences* 46 (January): 1–84. https://doi.org/10.1017/S0140525 X22002023.

Chenoweth, Erica. 2021. *Civil Resistance: What Everyone Needs to Know*. Oxford University Press.

Chenoweth, Erica, and Maria Stephan. 2011. *Why Civil Resistance Works: The Strategic Logic of Nonviolent Conflict*. Columbia University Press.

Cherelus, Gina. 2022. "Christian Smalls Is Leading a Labor Movement in Sweats and Sneakers." *New York Times*, April 6, sec. Style. https://www.nytimes.com/2022/04/06 /style/christian-smalls-style-amazon-union.html.

Cherones, Tom, dir. 1991. "The Chinese Restaurant." *Seinfeld*.

Chetty, Raj, Nathaniel Hendren, and Lawrence F. Katz. 2016. "The Effects of Exposure to Better Neighborhoods on Children: New Evidence from the Moving to Opportunity Experiment." *American Economic Review* 106 (4): 855–902. https://doi.org /10.1257/aer.20150572.

Chilton, Charlotte. 2020. "The Weirdest Etiquette Advice from the Past 100 Years." *Good Housekeeping*, March 31. https://www.goodhousekeeping.com/life/g30809332 /weird-etiquette-advice-from-the-past-100-years/.

Chingos, Matthew, and Kristin Blagg. 2017. "Do Poor Kids Get Their Fair Share of School Funding?" Urban Institute. https://www.urban.org/research/publication/do -poor-kids-get-their-fair-share-school-funding.

Cho, Renee. 2020. "Recycling in the US Is Broken. How Do We Fix It?" State of the Planet, March 13. https://news.climate.columbia.edu/2020/03/13/fix-recycling -america/.

Choi, Jung Ho, Joseph Pacelli, Kristina M. Rennekamp, and Sorabh Tomar. 2023. "Do Jobseekers Value Diversity Information? Evidence from a Field Experiment and Human Capital Disclosures." *Journal of Accounting Research* 61 (3): 695–735. https://doi.org/10.2139/ssrn.4025383.

Choi-Schagrin, Winston. 2022. "California Requires Plastics Makers to Foot the Bill for Recycling." *New York Times*, July 1, sec. Climate. https://www.nytimes.com/2022/07/01/climate/california-plastics-recycling-law.html.

Choi-Schagrin, Winston, and Hiroko Tabuchi. 2022. "Trash or Recycling? Why Plastic Keeps Us Guessing." *New York Times*, April 21, sec. Climate. https://www.nytimes.com/interactive/2022/04/21/climate/plastics-recycling-trash-environment.html.

Christakis, Nicholas A., and James H. Fowler. 2008. "The Collective Dynamics of Smoking in a Large Social Network." *New England Journal of Medicine* 358 (21): 2249–2258. https://doi.org/10.1056/NEJMsa0706154.

Christman, John. 2012. "Comments on Elizabeth Anderson, 'Epistemic Justice as a Virtue of Social Institutions.'" *Social Epistemology Review and Reply Collective* 1 (7): 15–16.

Cineas, Fabiola. 2021. "Baby Bonds Could Shrink the Black-White Wealth Gap." *Vox*, February 17. https://www.vox.com/22268500/baby-bonds-black-white-wealth-gap-booker-pressley.

Claessens, Scott, Quentin Atkinson, and Nichola Raihani. 2024. "Why Do People Punish? Evidence for a Range of Strategic Concerns." https://doi.org/10.31234/osf.io/ys6rm.

Clayton, Susan, and Bryan T. Karazsia. 2020. "Development and Validation of a Measure of Climate Change Anxiety." *Journal of Environmental Psychology* 69 (June): 101434. https://doi.org/10.1016/j.jenvp.2020.101434.

Clinton, William J. 1996. "State of the Union Address." US Capitol, January 23. https://clintonwhitehouse4.archives.gov/WH/New/other/sotu.html#.

Clymer, Adam. 2000. "Frank Wills, 52; Watchman Foiled Watergate Break-In." *New York Times*, September 29, sec. US. https://www.nytimes.com/2000/09/29/us/frank-wills-52-watchman-foiled-watergate-break-in.html.

Coates, Ta-Nehisi. 2014. "The Case for Reparations." *Atlantic*, May 22. https://www.theatlantic.com/magazine/archive/2014/06/the-case-for-reparations/361631/.

Cobb, Jelani. 2017. "Harvey Weinstein, Bill Cosby, and the Cloak of Charity." *New Yorker*, October 14. https://www.newyorker.com/news/daily-comment/harvey-weinstein-bill-cosby-and-the-cloak-of-charity.

Code, Lorraine. 1987. *Epistemic Responsibility*. University Press of New England.

Cohen, Rachel M. 2022. "The Expanded Child Tax Credit Kept 4 Million Kids Out of Poverty. Can It Come Back?" *Vox*, August 30. https://www.vox.com/policy-and -politics/2022/8/30/23317834/child-tax-credit-ctc-ira.

Cohn, Nate. 2024. "Why Is Trump Gaining with Black and Hispanic Voters?" *New York Times*, October 13, sec. The Upshot. https://www.nytimes.com/2024/10/13/upshot /trump-black-hispanic-voters-harris.html.

Coleman, Eric A., Bill Schultz, Vijay Ramprasad, et al. 2021. "Limited Effects of Tree Planting on Forest Canopy Cover and Rural Livelihoods in Northern India." *Nature Sustainability* 4 (11): 997–1004. https://doi.org/10.1038/s41893-021-00761-z.

CollegeNET. 2023. "Social Mobility Index College Rankings by CollegeNET." http:// www.socialmobilityindex.org.

Collins, Patricia Hill. 1999. *Black Feminist Thought: Knowledge, Consciousness, and the Politics of Empowerment*. Revised, 10th anniv., 2nd ed. Routledge.

Collins, Patricia Hill. 2003. "Some Group Matters: Intersectionality, Situated Standpoints, and Black Feminist Thought." In *A Companion to African-American Philosophy*, edited by Tommy L. Lott and John P. Pittman. Blackwell Publishing. https://doi.org /10.1002/9780470751640.ch12.

Collins, Patricia Hill, and Sirma Bilge. 2016. *Intersectionality*. John Wiley & Sons.

Comin, Diego A., and Johannes Rode. 2023. "Do Green Users Become Green Voters?" Working Paper No. 31324. National Bureau of Economic Research. https:// doi.org/10.3386/w31324.

Conaboy, Kelly. 2023. "What Your Favorite Personality Test Says About You." *Atlantic*, April 18. https://www.theatlantic.com/family/archive/2023/04/personality-test-quiz -myers-briggs-astrology-big-five/673541/.

Confessore, N., Friess, S., 2024. "University of Michigan Ends Required Diversity Statements." *New York Times*, December 5. https://www.nytimes.com/2024/12/05/us /university-of-michigan-dei-diversity-statemements.html.

Confucius. 2022. *The Analects of Confucius*. Translated by James Legge. Independently published.

Congressional Budget Office. 2023. "The Federal Budget in Fiscal Year 2022: An Infographic." https://www.cbo.gov/publication/58888.

Coninx, Sabrina. 2023. "The Dark Side of Niche Construction." *Philosophical Studies* 180 (10): 3003–3030. https://doi.org/10.1007/s11098-023-02024-3.

Cooley, Erin, Jazmin L. Brown-Iannuzzi, and Caroline Boudreau. 2019. "Shifting Stereotypes of Welfare Recipients Can Reverse Racial Biases in Support for Wealth

Redistribution." *Social Psychological and Personality Science* 10 (8): 1065–1074. https:// doi.org/10.1177/1948550619829062.

Cooley, Erin, B. Keith Payne, Chris Loersch, and Ryan Lei. 2015. "Who Owns Implicit Attitudes? Testing a Metacognitive Perspective." *Personality and Social Psychology Bulletin* 41 (1): 103–115. https://doi.org/10.1177/0146167214559712.

Cooper, Anna J. 2017. "The Status of Woman in America." In *A Voice from the South*. University of North Carolina Press. https://www.jstor.org/stable/10.5149/978 1469633329_cooper.6.

Corasaniti, Nick, Katie Glueck, and Matt Stevens. 2019. "Booker Joins Harris in Clashing with Biden Over Race." *New York Times*, July 25, sec. US. https://www.nytimes .com/2019/07/25/us/politics/biden-booker-black-voters.html.

Coren, Michael. 2022. "Why The Washington Post Is Starting a Climate Advice Column." *The Washington Post*, November 28, sec. Green Living. https://www.wash ingtonpost.com/climate-environment/2022/11/28/why-washington-post-is-start ing-climate-advice-column/.

Corner, Adam. 2020. "System Change vs Behaviour Change Is a False Choice— Covid-19 Shows How They're Connected." Climate Outreach, May 27. https:// climateoutreach.org/system-change-vs-behaviour-change-is-a-false-choice-covid-19 -shows-how-theyre-connected/.

Cortland, Clarissa I., Maureen A. Craig, Jenessa R. Shapiro, Jennifer A. Richeson, Rebecca Neel, and Noah J. Goldstein. 2017. "Solidarity Through Shared Disadvantage: Highlighting Shared Experiences of Discrimination Improves Relations between Stigmatized Groups." *Journal of Personality and Social Psychology* 113 (4): 547–567. https://doi.org/10.1037/pspi0000100.

Cortright, Joe. 2019. "Copenhagen: More Than Bike Lanes." Strong Towns, August 16. https://www.strongtowns.org/journal/2019/8/16/copenhagen-more-than-bike-lanes.

Cowie, Jefferson. 2017. *The Great Exception: The New Deal and the Limits of American Politics*. Reprint ed. Princeton University Press.

Cox, Oliver Cromwell. 1948. *Caste, Class, and Race: A Study in Social Dynamics*. Monthly Review Press.

Cox, William T. L. 2023. "Developing Scientifically Validated Bias and Diversity Trainings That Work: Empowering Agents of Change to Reduce Bias, Create Inclusion, and Promote Equity." *Management Decision* 61 (4): 1038–1061. https://doi.org /10.1108/MD-06-2021-0839.

Cox, William T. L., and Patricia G. Devine. 2019. "The Prejudice Habit-Breaking Intervention: An Empowerment-Based Confrontation Approach." In *Confronting Prejudice and Discrimination*, edited by Robyn K. Mallett and Margo J. Monteith. Academic Press. https://doi.org/10.1016/B978-0-12-814715-3.00015-1.

Crawford, Matthew B. 2015. *The World Beyond Your Head: How to Flourish in an Age of Distraction*. Penguin.

Cripps, Elizabeth. 2013. *Climate Change and the Moral Agent: Individual Duties in an Interdependent World*. Oxford University Press.

Cripps, Elizabeth. 2020. "Individual Climate Justice Duties: The Cooperative Promotional Model and Its Challenges." In *Climate Justice and Non-State Actors*, edited by Jeremy Moss and Lachlan Umbers. Routledge.

Crockett, Zachary. 2014. "The True Story of 'The Crying Indian.'" *Priceonomics*, September 9. https://priceonomics.com/the-true-story-of-the-crying-indian/.

Cubanski, Juliette, Jeannie Fuglesten Biniek, and Tricia Neuman. 2023. "FAQs on Health Spending, the Federal Budget, and Budget Enforcement Tools." KFF, March 20. https://www.kff.org/medicare/issue-brief/faqs-on-health-spending-the-federal-budget-and-budget-enforcement-tools/.

Curtin, Nicola, Abigail J. Stewart, and Elizabeth R. Cole. 2015. "Challenging the Status Quo: The Role of Intersectional Awareness in Activism for Social Change and Pro-Social Intergroup Attitudes." *Psychology of Women Quarterly* 39 (4): 512–529. https://doi.org/10.1177/0361684315580439.

Czopp, Alexander M., Margo J. Monteith, and Aimee Y. Mark. 2006. "Standing up for a Change: Reducing Bias through Interpersonal Confrontation." *Journal of Personality and Social Psychology* 90 (5): 784–803. https://doi.org/10.1037/0022-3514.90.5.784.

Dannhausen Jr., Miles. 2020. "Changing Habits: Looking Back at Classic Anti-Litter Campaigns." *Door County Pulse*, April 17. https://doorcountypulse.com/changing-habits-classic-anti-litter-campaigns/.

Dattani, Saloni, Lucas Rodés-Guirao, Hannah Ritchie, Esteban Ortiz-Ospina, and Max Roser. 2023. "Life Expectancy." Our World in Data. https://ourworldindata.org/life-expectancy.

Davenport, Christian. 2014. *How Social Movements Die: Repression and Demobilization of the Republic of New Africa*. Cambridge University Press.

Davidson, Lacey J., and Melissa D. Gruver. 2020. "Epistemic Labor and the Power in (Fat) Identity: Three Fat Archetypes as Experienced in the Local Bar, the Streets, and Other Public Places." *Fat Studies* 9 (2): 148–162. https://doi.org/10.1080/21604851.2019.1629806.

Davidson, Lacey J., and Daniel Kelly. 2020. "Minding the Gap: Bias, Soft Structures, and the Double Life of Social Norms." *Journal of Applied Philosophy* 37 (2): 190–210. https://doi.org/10.1111/japp.12351.

Davidson, Osha Gray. 1998. *Under Fire: The NRA and the Battle for Gun Control*. Revised ed. University of Iowa Press.

Davis, Matt. 2019. "Vikings Unwittingly Made Their Swords Stronger by Trying to Imbue Them with Spirits." Big Think, March 22. https://bigthink.com/hard-science /norse-rituals/.

Davis-Young, Katherine. 2019. "For Many Native Americans, Embracing LGBT Members Is a Return to the Past." *Washington Post*, March 29. https://www.washing tonpost.com/national/for-many-native-americans-embracing-lgbt-members-is-a-return -to-the-past/2019/03/29/24d1e6c6-4f2c-11e9-88a1-ed346f0ec94f_story.html.

Day, Meagan. 2020. "Unions Are Essential for Eliminating Racism." *Jacobin*, July 7. https://jacobin.com/2020/07/multiracial-solidarity-unions.

Deaton, Angus. 2015. *The Great Escape: Health, Wealth, and the Origins of Inequality.* Princeton University Press.

Deaton, Angus, and Nancy Cartwright. 2018. "Understanding and Misunderstanding Randomized Controlled Trials." *Social Science & Medicine* 210 (August): 2–21. https://doi.org/10.1016/j.socscimed.2017.12.005.

Dechezleprêtre, Antoine, Adrien Fabre, Tobias Kruse, Bluebery Planterose, Ana Sanchez Chico, and Stefanie Stantcheva. 2022. "Fighting Climate Change: International Attitudes Toward Climate Policies." Working Paper No. 30265. National Bureau of Economic Research. https://doi.org/10.3386/w30265.

Degler, Carl N. 1983. *Out of Our Past: The Forces That Shaped Modern America.* 3rd ed. Harper Perennial.

Delmont, Matthew. 2022. "How a Hostile America Undermined Its Black WWII Veterans." *Mother Jones*, October. https://www.motherjones.com/politics/2022/10 /black-world-war-wwii-veterans-denied-gi-bill-restoration-act-benefits-half-american -matthew-delmont/.

DeLong, Bradford. 2022. *Slouching Towards Utopia: An Economic History of the Twentieth Century.* Basic Books.

Desmond-Harris, Jenée. 2015. "The Irony of Obama's Optimism on Race and Politics." *Vox*, February 10. https://www.vox.com/2015/2/10/7992653/obama-interview -race-politics.

Devine, Patricia G., Patrick S. Forscher, Anthony J. Austin, and William T. L. Cox. 2012. "Long-Term Reduction in Implicit Race Bias: A Prejudice Habit-Breaking Intervention." *Journal of Experimental Social Psychology* 48 (6): 1267–1278. https://doi.org /10.1016/j.jesp.2012.06.003.

Diaz, Alex. 2019. "Remember Solyndra? Loss of Taxpayer Millions Now Seems Forgotten, Expert Says," Fox News, March 20. https://www.foxnews.com/politics/remember -solyndra-loss-of-taxpayer-millions-seems-forgotten-expert-says.

Dickie, James, and E. Michael Pye. n.d. "Religious Dress—Chinese Religions, Rituals, Customs." *Britannica*. Accessed October 30, 2023. https://www.britannica.com/topic /religious-dress/Chinese-religions.

Diemer, Matthew A., Adam M. Voight, Aixa D. Marchand, and Josefina Bañales. 2019. "Political Identification, Political Ideology, and Critical Social Analysis of Inequality among Marginalized Youth." *Developmental Psychology* 55 (3): 538–549. https://doi.org/10.1037/dev0000559.

Digital History. 2021. "Herbert Hoover, 'Rugged Individualism' Campaign Speech." https://www.digitalhistory.uh.edu/disp_textbook.cfm?smtID=3&psid=1334.

Dillon, Robin S. 2012. "Critical Character Theory: Toward a Feminist Perspective on 'Vice' (and 'Virtue')." In *Out from the Shadows: Analytical Feminist Contributions to Traditional Philosophy*, edited by Sharon L. Crasnow and Anita M. Superson. Oxford University Press. https://doi.org/10.1093/acprof:oso/9780199855469.003.0005.

Dills, Angela K., and Jeffrey A. Miron. 2004. "Alcohol Prohibition and Cirrhosis." *American Law and Economics Review* 6 (2): 285–318.

Dixon, John, and Mark Levine, eds. 2012. *Beyond Prejudice: Extending the Social Psychology of Conflict, Inequality and Social Change*. Cambridge University Press.

Dixon, John, Mark Levine, Steve Reicher, and Kevin Durrheim. 2012. "Beyond Prejudice: Are Negative Evaluations the Problem and Is Getting Us to Like One Another More the Solution?" *Behavioral and Brain Sciences* 35 (6): 411–425.

Dobbin, Frank, and Alexandra Kalev. 2020. "Why Sexual Harassment Programs Backfire." *Harvard Business Review*, May. https://hbr.org/2020/05/why-sexual-harassment -programs-backfire.

Dobbin, Frank, and Alexandra Kalev. 2022. *Getting to Diversity: What Works and What Doesn't*. Belknap Press.

Doherty, Thomas J., Amy D. Lykins, Nancy A. Piotrowski, Zoey Rogers, Derrick D. Sebree, and Kristi E. White. 2022. "Clinical Psychology Responses to the Climate Crisis." In *Comprehensive Clinical Psychology (Second Edition)*, edited by Gordon J. G. Asmundson. Elsevier. https://doi.org/10.1016/B978-0-12-818697-8.00236-3.

Doleac, Jennifer L., host. 2019. *Probable Causation*. "Episode 8: Amanda Agan." Podcast, July 23. https://www.probablecausation.com/podcasts/episode-8-amanda -agan.

Doleac, Jennifer L., and Benjamin Hansen. 2020. "The Unintended Consequences of 'Ban the Box': Statistical Discrimination and Employment Outcomes When Criminal Histories Are Hidden." *Journal of Labor Economics* 38 (2): 321–374. https://doi.org /10.1086/705880.

Du Bois, W. E. B. 1987. *W. E. B. Du Bois: Writings: The Suppression of the African Slave-Trade/The Souls of Black Folk/Dusk of Dawn/Essays and Articles*. Library of America.

Dubner, Stephen J., host. 2012. *Freakonomics*. "The Cobra Effect." Podcast, October 11. https://freakonomics.com/podcast/the-cobra-effect-2/.

Dubner, Stephen J., host. 2020. *Freakonomics*. "Policymaking Is Not a Science (Yet)." Podcast, February 12. https://freakonomics.com/podcast/policymaking-is-not-a-science-yet-ep-405/.

Dubner, Stephen J., host. 2022. *Freakonomics*. "Why Do Most Ideas Fail to Scale?" Podcast, February 23. https://freakonomics.com/podcast/why-do-most-ideas-fail-to-scale/.

Duflo, Esther. 2017. "The Economist as Plumber." *American Economic Review* 107 (5): 1–26. https://doi.org/10.1257/aer.p20171153.

Duguma, Lalisa. 2019. "Forget Tree Planting, Start Tree Growing." Interview by Dominique Lyons. Forests News. https://forestsnews.cifor.org/61174/forget-tree-planting-start-tree-growing?fnl=en.

Dunbar-Ortiz, Roxanne. 2015. *An Indigenous Peoples' History of the United States*. Reprint ed. Beacon Press.

Early, Catherine. 2021. "The 'Messy' Alternative to Tree-Planting." *BBC*, May 24. https://www.bbc.com/future/article/20210524-the-reason-wild-forests-beat-plantations.

Echelbarger, Margaret, and Nicholas Epley. 2023. "Undervaluing the Positive Impact of Kindness Starts Early." *Journal of Experimental Psychology: General* 152 (10): 2989–2994. https://doi.org/10.1037/xge0001433.

Economic Policy Institute. 2011. "Martin Luther King on 'Right to Work.'" April 4, 2011. https://www.epi.org/publication/martin_luther_king_on_right_to_work/.

Economist. 2023. "Economists Had a Dreadful 2023." December 20, 2023. https://www.economist.com/leaders/2023/12/20/economists-had-a-dreadful-2023.

Edelman, Benjamin, Michael Luca, and Dan Svirsky. 2017. "Racial Discrimination in the Sharing Economy: Evidence from a Field Experiment." *American Economic Journal: Applied Economics* 9 (2): 1–22.

Edlin, Aaron, Andrew Gelman, and Noah Kaplan. 2007. "Voting as a Rational Choice: Why and How People Vote to Improve the Well-Being of Others." *Rationality and Society* 19 (3): 293–314. https://doi.org/10.1177/1043463107077384.

Education Advisory Board. 2024. "Improve Outcomes for First-Generation Students." https://eab.com/resources/roadmaps/supporting-first-generation-college-students/.

Elias, Jennifer. 2023. "Tech Companies like Google and Meta Made Cuts to DEI Programs in 2023 after Big Promises in Prior Years." *CNBC*, December 22. https://www

.cnbc.com/2023/12/22/google-meta-other-tech-giants-cut-dei-programs-in-2023
.html.

EllieVisionOG (@EllieVisionOG). 2023. "How Americans Reacted to the Drink Driving Ban in the 1980s." Instagram, June 13. https://www.instagram.com/reel/CtdOE
-DIiP_/.

Elliott, Carl. 2003. *Better Than Well: American Medicine Meets the American Dream.*
W. W. Norton.

Emerson, Ralph W. 2017. *Self-Reliance.* CreateSpace Independent Publishing
Platform.

Enck, Judith, and Jan Dell. 2022. "Plastic Recycling Doesn't Work and Will Never
Work." *Atlantic*, May 30. https://www.theatlantic.com/ideas/archive/2022/05/single
-use-plastic-chemical-recycling-disposal/661141/.

Enders, Adam M., and Jamil S. Scott. 2019. "The Increasing Racialization of American Electoral Politics, 1988–2016." *American Politics Research* 47 (2): 275–303. https://
doi.org/10.1177/1532673X18755654.

Erlanger, Steven, and Christina Anderson. 2022. "Rise of Far-Right Party in Sweden
Was Both Expected and Shocking." *New York Times*, September 15, sec. World. https://
www.nytimes.com/2022/09/15/world/europe/sweden-election-far-right.html.

Essig, Todd. 2014. "The Mysterious Popularity Of The Meaningless Myers-Briggs
(MBTI)." Forbes, September 29. https://www.forbes.com/sites/toddessig/2014/09/29
/the-mysterious-popularity-of-the-meaningless-myers-briggs-mbti/.

Etchezahar, Edgardo, Joaquín Ungaretti, and Federico Marchiano. 2022. "'Economic
Support? They Don't Really Need It.' Prejudice Towards Latin American Immigrants
in Argentina." *International Journal of Intercultural Relations* 87 (March): 37–41. https://
doi.org/10.1016/j.ijintrel.2022.01.007.

Evans, Alice. 2020. "Why Is Feminist Activism Thriving in Latin America?" December 30. https://www.draliceevans.com/post/why-is-feminist-activism-thriving-in-latin
-america.

Faludi, Susan. 2022. "Feminism Made a Faustian Bargain with Celebrity Culture. Now
It's Paying the Price." *New York Times*, June 20, sec. Opinion. https://www.nytimes
.com/2022/06/20/opinion/roe-heard-feminism-backlash.html.

Federico, Christopher M., and Rafael Aguilera. 2019. "The Distinct Pattern of Relationships Between the Big Five and Racial Resentment Among White Americans."
Social Psychological and Personality Science 10 (2): 274–284. https://doi.org/10.1177
/1948550617752063.

Fell, James C., and Robert B. Voas. 2006. "The Effectiveness of Reducing Illegal Blood
Alcohol Concentration (BAC) Limits for Driving: Evidence for Lowering the Limit

to .05 BAC." *Journal of Safety Research* 37 (3): 233–243. https://doi.org/10.1016/j.jsr.2005.07.006.

Felschundneff, Steven. 2023. "Larkin Place Application Making Progress." *Claremont Courier*, March 24. https://claremont-courier.com/latest-news/larkin-place-application-making-progress-73020/.

Ferkany, Matt, and Kyle Powys Whyte. 2012. "The Importance of Participatory Virtues in the Future of Environmental Education." *Journal of Agricultural and Environmental Ethics* 25 (3): 419–434. https://doi.org/10.1007/s10806-011-9312-8.

Fernandez, Daniel. 2018. "The Surprisingly Intolerant History of Milk." *Smithsonian Magazine*, May 11. https://www.smithsonianmag.com/history/surprisingly-intolerant-history-milk-180969056/.

Ferreri, Eric. 2021. "New Voting Restrictions May 'Backfire,' Expert Says." *Duke Today*, June 22. https://today.duke.edu/2021/06/new-voting-restrictions-may-backfire-expert-says.

Festinger, Leon. 1957. *A Theory of Cognitive Dissonance*. Stanford University Press.

Fishback, Price, Jonathan Rose, Kenneth A. Snowden, and Thomas Storrs. 2022. "New Evidence on Redlining by Federal Housing Programs in the 1930s." *Journal of Urban Economics* 1, May, 103462. https://doi.org/10.1016/j.jue.2022.103462.

Finkel, Eli J. 2017. *The All-or-Nothing Marriage: How the Best Marriages Work*. Dutton.

Flatow, Ira, and David Victor. 2022. "Can the Latest IPCC Report Pave the Way to Better Climate Policy?" Science Friday, April 22. https://www.sciencefriday.com/segments/ipcc-report-climate-policy/.

Fleeson, William. 2004. "Moving Personality Beyond the Person-Situation Debate: The Challenge and the Opportunity of Within-Person Variability." *Current Directions in Psychological Science* 13 (2): 83–87. https://doi.org/10.1111/j.0963-7214.2004.00280.x.

Flesher, Jon. 2020. "Factory Farms Provide Abundant Food, but Environment Suffers." *PBS NewsHour*, February 6, sec. Economy. https://www.pbs.org/newshour/economy/factory-farms-provide-abundant-food-but-environment-suffers.

Flores, Carolina. 2022a. "Bad Believers: Evidence-Resistance, Rational Persuasion, and Social Change." Working paper. Rutgers University. https://Doi.Org/10.7282/T3-Vy9h-5g28.

Flores, Carolina. 2022b. "Belief Change and Social Change." Working paper. Rutgers University.

Flores, Nina M., Heather McBrien, Vivian Do, Mathew V. Kiang, Jeffrey Schlegelmilch, and Joan A. Casey. 2023. "The 2021 Texas Power Crisis: Distribution,

Duration, and Disparities." *Journal of Exposure Science & Environmental Epidemiology* 33 (1): 21–31. https://doi.org/10.1038/s41370-022-00462-5.

Folger, Robert, and Chris Martin. 1986. "Relative Deprivation and Referent Cognitions: Distributive and Procedural Justice Effects." *Journal of Experimental Social Psychology* 22 (6): 531–546. https://doi.org/10.1016/0022-1031(86)90049-1.

Ford, Matt, and James Forman Jr. 2017. "'Until the Drug Dealer's Teeth Rattle.'" *Atlantic*, April 26. https://www.theatlantic.com/politics/archive/2017/04/james-forman -mass-incarceration/524328/.

Forde, Allana T., Danielle M. Crookes, Shakira F. Suglia, and Ryan T. Demmer. 2019. "The Weathering Hypothesis as an Explanation for Racial Disparities in Health: A Systematic Review." *Annals of Epidemiology* 33 (May): 1–18. https://doi.org/10.1016/j .annepidem.2019.02.011.

Forman Jr., James. 2017. *Locking Up Our Own: Crime and Punishment in Black America*. Farrar, Straus and Giroux.

Foronda, Cynthia, Diana-Lyn Baptiste, Maren M. Reinholdt, and Kevin Ousman. 2016. "Cultural Humility: A Concept Analysis." *Journal of Transcultural Nursing: Official Journal of the Transcultural Nursing Society* 27 (3): 210–217. https://doi.org/10.1177 /1043659615592677.

Forscher, Patrick S. 2017. "The Individually-Targeted Habit-Breaking Intervention and Group-Level Change." PhD diss., University of Wisconsin-Madison. https://doi .org/10.31237/osf.io/4t7fy.

Forscher, Patrick S., Calvin K. Lai, Jordan R. Axt, Charles R. Ebersole, Michelle Herman, Patricia G. Devine, and Brian A. Nosek. 2019. "A Meta-Analysis of Procedures to Change Implicit Measures." *Journal of Personality and Social Psychology* 117 (3): 522–559. https://doi.org/10.1037/pspa0000160.

Fowler, Matthew, Vladimir Medenica, and Cathy Cohen. 2017. "Why 41 Percent of White Millennials Voted for Trump." *Washington Post*, December 15. https://www .washingtonpost.com/news/monkey-cage/wp/2017/12/15/racial-resentment-is -why-41-percent-of-white-millennials-voted-for-trump-in-2016/.

Foxworth, Raymond, and Carew Boulding. 2022. "Discrimination and Resentment: Examining American Attitudes About Native Americans." *Journal of Race, Ethnicity, and Politics* 7 (1): 9–36. https://doi.org/10.1017/rep.2021.23.

Frakt, Austin, and Aaron E. Carroll. 2018. "Why the US Spends So Much More Than Other Nations on Health Care." *New York Times*, January 2, sec. The Upshot. https:// www.nytimes.com/2018/01/02/upshot/us-health-care-expensive-country-compari son.html.

Frank, Robert. 2020. *Under the Influence: Putting Peer Pressure to Work*. Princeton University Press.

Frank, Thomas. 2004. *What's the Matter with Kansas? How Conservatives Won the Heart of America*. Metropolitan Books.

Franz, Berkeley, Adrienne N. Milner, and R. Khari Brown. 2021. "Opposition to the Affordable Care Act Has Little to Do with Health Care." *Race and Social Problems* 13 (2): 161–169. https://doi.org/10.1007/s12552-020-09306-z.

Fraser, Nancy. 1994. "After the Family Wage: Gender Equity and the Welfare State." *Political Theory* 22: 591–618.

Freakonomics. 2021. "The US Is Just Different." https://freakonomics.com/podcast -tag/american-culture-series/.

Freidenberg, Flavia, and Karolina Gilas, eds. 2022. *La Construcción de Democracias Paritarias en América Latina: Regimen electoral de género, actores críticos, y representación descriptiva de las mujeres (1990–2022)*. Universidad Nacional Autonoma de Mexico, https://archivos.juridicas.unam.mx/www/bjv/libros/15/7158/29.pdf.

Freidenberg, Flavia, and Karolina Gilas. 2023. "Strategies for Strengthening Women's Political Participation in Latin America." *LSE Latin America and Caribbean Blog*, March 2. https://blogs.lse.ac.uk/latamcaribbean/2023/03/02/strategies-for-bigger-womens -political-participation-latin-america/.

Freire, Paulo. 2018. *Pedagogy of the Oppressed: 50th Anniversary Edition*. 4th ed. Bloomsbury Academic.

Fricker, Miranda. 2012. "Silence and Institutional Prejudice." In *Out from the Shadows: Analytical Feminist Contributions to Traditional Philosophy*, edited by Sharon L. Crasnow and Anita M. Superson. Oxford University Press. https://doi.org/10.1093 /acprof:oso/9780199855469.001.0001.

Friedman, Lissy C., Andrew Cheyne, Daniel Givelber, Mark A. Gottlieb, and Richard A. Daynard. 2015. "Tobacco Industry Use of Personal Responsibility Rhetoric in Public Relations and Litigation: Disguising Freedom to Blame as Freedom of Choice." *American Journal of Public Health* 105 (2): 250–260. https://doi.org/10.2105 /AJPH.2014.302226.

Frye, Marilyn. 1983. *Politics of Reality: Essays in Feminist Theory*. Clarkson Potter/Ten Speed.

Frymer, Paul, and Jacob M. Grumbach. 2021. "Labor Unions and White Racial Politics." *American Journal of Political Science* 65 (1): 225–240. https://doi.org/10.1111 /ajps.12537.

Fulwood III, Sam. 2016. "The United States' History of Segregated Housing Continues to Limit Affordable Housing." Center for American Progress, December 15. https://www.americanprogress.org/article/the-united-states-history-of-segregated -housing-continues-to-limit-affordable-housing/.

Furnham, Adrian, and George Horne. 2022. "Personality and Demographic Correlates of Political Ideology." *Personality and Individual Differences* 186 (February): 111320. https://doi.org/10.1016/j.paid.2021.111320.

Gadamer, Hans-Georg. 2004. *Truth and Method*. Translated by Joel Weinsheimer and Donald G. Marshall. Bloomsbury Publishing.

GAIA. 2019. "US Municipal Solid Waste Incinerators: An Industry in Decline." https://www.no-burn.org/u-s-municipal-solid-waste-incinerators-an-industry-in -decline/.

Gaither, Sarah E., and Samuel R. Sommers. 2013. "Living with an Other-Race Roommate Shapes Whites' Behavior in Subsequent Diverse Settings." *Journal of Experimental Social Psychology* 49 (2): 272–276. https://doi.org/10.1016/j.jesp.2012.10.020.

Galer, Sophia Smith. 2022. "'Greenwashing': Tree-Planting Schemes Are Just Creating Tree Cemeteries." *Vice*, September 1. https://www.vice.com/en/article/v7v75a /tree-planting-schemes-england.

Galloway, Paul. 1985. "Booze and Death Travel Our Roads, Courts Look the Other Way." *Chicago Tribune*, June 30, sec. TEMPO.

Gansum, Terje. 2004. "Role the Bones—From Iron to Steel." *Norwegian Archaeological Review* 37 (1): 41–57. https://doi.org/10.1080/00293650410001199.

Gardiner, Stephen M. 2013. *A Perfect Moral Storm: The Ethical Tragedy of Climate Change*. Oxford University Press.

Gardner, William L., and Mark J. Martinko. 1996. "Using the Myers-Briggs Type Indicator to Study Managers: A Literature Review and Research Agenda." *Journal of Management* 22 (1): 45–83. https://doi.org/10.1177/014920639602200103.

Gasdaglis, Katherine, and Alex Madva. 2020. "Intersectionality as a Regulative Ideal." *Ergo, an Open Access Journal of Philosophy* 6 (44): 1287–1330. https://doi.org /10.3998/ergo.12405314.0006.044.

Gawronski, Bertram, Michael Brownstein, and Alex Madva. 2022. "How Should We Think about Implicit Measures and Their Empirical 'Anomalies'?" *WIREs Cognitive Science* 13, February, e1590. https://doi.org/10.1002/wcs.1590.

Gawronski, Bertram, Kurt R. Peters, Paula M. Brochu, and Fritz Strack. 2008. "Understanding the Relations Between Different Forms of Racial Prejudice: A Cognitive Consistency Perspective." *Personality and Social Psychology Bulletin* 34 (5): 648–665. https://doi.org/10.1177/0146167207313729.

George, Samuel, Amber Hendley, Jack Macnamara, et al. 2019. "The Plunder of Black Wealth in Chicago: New Findings on the Lasting Toll of Predatory Housing Contracts." Samuel DuBois Cook Center on Social Equity, Duke University. https://

socialequity-staging.oit.duke.edu/cms/wp-content/uploads/2023/08/Plunder-of
-Black-Wealth-in-Chicago.pdf.

Giesler, Markus, and Ela Veresiu. 2014. "Creating the Responsible Consumer: Moralistic Governance Regimes and Consumer Subjectivity." *Journal of Consumer Research*
41 (3): 840–857. https://doi.org/10.1086/677842.

Gilbert, Daniel T., Elizabeth C. Pinel, Timothy D. Wilson, Stephen J. Blumberg, and
Thalia P. Wheatley. 1998. "Immune Neglect: A Source of Durability Bias in Affective
Forecasting." *Journal of Personality and Social Psychology* 75 (3): 617–638. https://doi
.org/10.1037/0022-3514.75.3.617.

Ginzburg, Boris, and José-Alberto Guerra. 2021. "Guns, Pets, and Strikes: An Experiment on Identity and Political Action." Working paper. https://doi.org/10.2139/ssrn
.4007379.

Giulietti, Corrado, Mirco Tonin, and Michael Vlassopoulos. 2019. "Racial Discrimination in Local Public Services: A Field Experiment in the United States." *Journal of the
European Economic Association* 17 (1): 165–204. https://doi.org/10.1093/jeea/jvx045.

Glasser, Susan B. 2023. "Bidenomics Is a Political Bust for Biden." *New Yorker*,
November 30. https://www.newyorker.com/news/letter-from-bidens-washington
/bidenomics-is-a-political-bust-for-biden.

Goddard, Taegan. 2023. "Happy Warrior." Political Dictionary, August 27. https://
politicaldictionary.com/words/happy-warrior/.

Godfrey, Erin B., Esther L. Burson, Tess M. Yanisch, Diane Hughes, and Niobe Way.
2019. "A Bitter Pill to Swallow? Patterns of Critical Consciousness and Socioemo-
tional and Academic Well-Being in Early Adolescence." *Developmental Psychology* 55
(3): 525–537. https://doi.org/10.1037/dev0000558.

Goldstein, Rebecca, Michael W. Sances, and Hye Young You. 2020. "Exploitative
Revenues, Law Enforcement, and the Quality of Government Service." *Urban Affairs
Review* 56 (1): 5–31. https://doi.org/10.1177/1078087418791775.

Golshan, Tara. 2017. "Study Finds 75 Percent of Workplace Harassment Victims
Experienced Retaliation When They Spoke Up." *Vox*, October 15. https://www.vox
.com/identities/2017/10/15/16438750/weinstein-sexual-harassment-facts.

Gonzales, Manuel G. 2019. *Mexicanos, Third Edition: A History of Mexicans in the
United States*. 3rd ed. Indiana University Press.

Goop. 2017. "You Probably Have a Parasite—Here's What to Do About It." Posted
January 5. https://goop.com/wellness/detox/you-probably-have-a-parasite-heres-what
-to-do-about-it/.

Gore, Al. 2008. "We Need A New Start." NPR, July 17, sec. Environment. https://
www.npr.org/2008/07/17/92634635/al-gore-we-need-a-new-start.

Goren, Matt J., and Victoria C. Plaut. 2012. "Identity Form Matters: White Racial Identity and Attitudes Toward Diversity." *Self and Identity* 11 (2): 237–354. https://doi.org/10.1080/15298868.2011.556804.

Grandey, Alicia A. 2000. "Emotional Regulation in the Workplace: A New Way to Conceptualize Emotional Labor." *Journal of Occupational Health Psychology* 5 (1): 95–110. https://doi.org/10.1037/1076-8998.5.1.95.

Green, Ted Van. 2023. "Majority of Americans Prefer a Community with Big Houses, Even if Local Amenities Are Farther Away." Pew Research Center, August 2. https://www.pewresearch.org/short-reads/2023/08/02/majority-of-americans-prefer-a-community-with-big-houses-even-if-local-amenities-are-farther-away/.

Greenberg, Paul. 2021. *The Climate Diet: 50 Simple Ways to Trim Your Carbon Footprint.* Penguin Books.

Greene, Nathifa. 2020. "Stereotype Threat, Identity, and the Disruption of Habit." In *An Introduction to Implicit Bias: Knowledge, Justice, and the Social Mind*, edited by Erin Beeghly and Alex Madva. Routledge. https://doi.org/10.4324/9781315107615-7.

Greenfield, John. 2022. "Denmark Responded to 1973 Oil Crisis by Reducing Car-Dependency. Let's Do That Now." *StreetsBlog Chicago*, March 9. https://chi.streetsblog.org/2022/03/09/denmark-responded-to-1973-oil-crisis-by-reducing-car-dependency-lets-do-that-now.

Greenhouse, Steven. 2020. "How Police Unions Enable and Conceal Abuses of Power." *New Yorker*, June 18. https://www.newyorker.com/news/news-desk/how-police-union-power-helped-increase-abuses.

Greenwood, Ronni M. 2008. "Intersectional Political Consciousness: Appreciation for Intragroup Differences and Solidarity in Diverse Groups." *Psychology of Women Quarterly* 32 (1): 36–47. https://doi.org/10.1111/j.1471-6402.2007.00405.x.

Greenwood, Ronni M., and Aidan Christian. 2008. "What Happens When We Unpack the Invisible Knapsack? Intersectional Political Consciousness and Inter-Group Appraisals." *Sex Roles* 59 (5): 404–417. https://doi.org/10.1007/s11199-008-9439-x.

Gregersen, Erik. 2023. "Louis Pasteur—Microbiology, Germ Theory, Pasteurization." *Britannica.* https://www.britannica.com/biography/Louis-Pasteur/Spontaneous-generation.

Gregory, David, and Barack Obama. 2009. "Interview on NBC News' 'Meet the Press.'" https://www.presidency.ucsb.edu/documents/interview-with-david-gregory-nbc-news-meet-the-press.

Griffith, Saul. 2021. "A Mortgage Is a Time Machine." In *Electrify: An Optimist's Playbook for Our Clean Energy Future.* MIT Press. https://ieeexplore.ieee.org/abstract/document/9603326/.

Griffiths, Paul, and Stefan Linquist. 2024. "The Distinction Between Innate and Acquired Characteristics." *Stanford Encyclopedia of Philosophy.* https://plato.stanford.edu/archives/fall2024/entries/innate-acquired/.

Gross, Neil. 2019. "Why Do the Democrats Keep Saying 'Structural'?" *New York Times,* July 31, sec. Opinion. https://www.nytimes.com/2019/07/31/opinion/2020-democrats-change-structural.html.

Grossmann, Igor, Michael E. W. Varnum, Cendri A. Hutcherson, and David R. Mandel. 2023. "When Expert Predictions Fail." *Trends in Cognitive Sciences* 28 (2): 113–123. https://doi.org/10.1016/j.tics.2023.10.005.

Grunwald, Michael. 2020. "What Covid Is Exposing About the Climate Movement." *Politico,* April 21. https://www.politico.com/news/magazine/2020/04/21/earth-day-individual-climate-impact-198835.

Gu, Hongyan. 2016. "NIMBYism in China: Issues and Prospects of Public Participation in Facility Siting." *Land Use Policy* 52 (C): 527–534.

Guardino, Matt, and Suzanne Mettler. 2020. "Revealing the 'Hidden Welfare State': How Policy Information Influences Public Attitudes about Tax Expenditures." *Journal of Behavioral Public Administration* 3 (1): 1–15. https://doi.org/10.30636/jbpa.31.108.

Guggenheim, Davis, dir. 2016. *An Inconvenient Truth.* Lawrence Bender Productions.

Guidetti, Margherita, Luciana Carraro, and Luigi Castelli. 2021. "Children's Inequality Aversion in Intergroup Contexts: The Role of Parents' Social Dominance Orientation, Right-Wing Authoritarianism and Moral Foundations." *PLoS ONE* 16 (12): e0261603. https://doi.org/10.1371/journal.pone.0261603.

Guo, Xiujin, Jian Dai, Pengcheng Xun, Lynn M. Jamieson, and Ka He. 2015. "Sport Facility Proximity and Physical Activity: Results from the Study of Community Sports in China." *European Journal of Sport Science* 15 (7): 663–669. https://doi.org/10.1080/17461391.2014.982203.

Gurr, Ted R. 1970. *Why Men Rebel.* Princeton University Press.

Hale, Benjamin. 2022. "Indeterminacy and Impotence." *Synthese* 200 (3). https://doi.org/10.1007/s11229-022-03718-7.

Hammerstein, Oscar, Richard Rodgers, James A. Michener, and Joshua Logan. 1949. *South Pacific.* Random House.

Han, Hahrie, and Carina Barnett-Loro. 2018. "To Support a Stronger Climate Movement, Focus Research on Building Collective Power." *Frontiers in Communication* 3: 1–5.

Hancock, Ange-Marie. 2016. *Intersectionality: An Intellectual History.* Oxford University Press.

Haney-López, Ian. 2019. *Merge Left: Fusing Race and Class, Winning Elections, and Saving America*. The New Press.

Haney-López, Ian. 2020. "Discussion Guide: The 'Call Them Bigots' Approach." Race-Class Academy. https://static1.squarespace.com/static/5f242778987a1d1b201 fa593/t/5f594427b6a4e460fbe858b9/1599685672237/Discussion+Guide+2.1+UP DATED.pdf.

Harder, Joshua, and Jon A. Krosnick. 2008. "Why Do People Vote? A Psychological Analysis of the Causes of Voter Turnout." *Journal of Social Issues* 64 (3): 525–649. https://doi.org/10.1111/j.1540-4560.2008.00576.x.

Hardin, Russell. 1982. "Exchange Theory on Strategic Bases." *Social Science Information* 21 (2): 251–272. https://doi.org/10.1177/053901882021002004.

Harding, Sandra, ed. 2003. *The Feminist Standpoint Theory Reader: Intellectual and Political Controversies*. Routledge.

Hart, Vi, and Nicky Case. 2014. "Parable of the Polygons: A Playable Post on the Shape of Society." Parable of the Polygons. http://ncase.me/polygons.

Hartman, Laura M. 2021. "Cooperativeness as a Virtue of Sustainability." In *The Virtues of Sustainability*, edited by Jason Kawall. Oxford University Press. https://doi .org/10.1093/oso/9780190919818.003.0007.

Haslanger, Sally. 2015. "Social Structure, Narrative and Explanation." *Canadian Journal of Philosophy* 45 (1): 1–15. https://doi.org/10.1080/00455091.2015.1019176.

Haslanger, Sally. 2021. "Reproducing Social Hierarchy." *Philosophy of Education* 77 (2): 185–222. https://doi.org/10.47925/77.2.185.

Hassan, Yasmine. 2022. "Former MPs Find New Paths and Purpose after Politics." *CBC News*, October 1. https://www.cbc.ca/news/politics/former-mps-defeated-1.6599177.

Hassberg, Analena H. 2020. "Nurturing the Revolution: The Black Panther Party and the Early Seeds of the Food Justice Movement." In *Black Food Matters: Racial Justice in the Wake of Food Justice*, edited by Hanna Garth and Ashanté M. Reese. University of Minnesota Press. https://doi.org/10.5749/j.ctv182jtk0.6.

Hawkins, Ian, Stewart M. Coles, Muniba Saleem, Jessica D. Moorman, and Haleemah Aqel. 2024. "How Reel Middle Easterners' Portrayals Cultivate Stereotypical Beliefs and Policy Support." *Mass Communication and Society* 27 (1): 1–25. https://doi.org /10.1080/15205436.2022.2062000.

Healy, Jon, and Matthew Ballinger. 2021. "What Just Happened with Single-Family Zoning in California?" *Los Angeles Times*, September 17, sec. Housing & Homelessness. https://www.latimes.com/homeless-housing/story/2021-09-17/what-just-happened -with-single-family-zoning-in-california.

Hebbert, Michael. 2020. "The Long After-Life of Christopher Wren's Short-Lived London Plan of 1666." *Planning Perspectives* 35 (2): 231–252. https://doi.org/10.1080 /02665433.2018.1552837.

Hecht, Cameron A., Christopher J. Bryan, and David S. Yeager. 2023. "A Values-Aligned Intervention Fosters Growth Mindset–Supportive Teaching and Reduces Inequality in Educational Outcomes." *Proceedings of the National Academy of Sciences* 120 (25): e2210704120. https://doi.org/10.1073/pnas.2210704120.

Hecht, Cameron A., Mary Murphy, Carol Dweck, et al. 2023. "Shifting the Mindset Culture to Address Global Educational Disparities." *NPJ Science of Learning*, June.

Heck, Isobel A., Kristin Shutts, and Katherine D. Kinzler. 2022. "Children's Thinking About Group-Based Social Hierarchies." *Trends in Cognitive Sciences* 26 (7): 593–606. https://doi.org/10.1016/j.tics.2022.04.004.

Heglar, Mary Annaïse. 2019. "I Work in the Environmental Movement. I Don't Care if You Recycle." *Vox*, May 28. https://www.vox.com/the-highlight/2019/5/28 /18629833/climate-change-2019-green-new-deal.

Henrich, Joseph. 2015. *The Secret of Our Success: How Culture Is Driving Human Evolution, Domesticating Our Species, and Making Us Smarter*. Reprint ed. Princeton University Press.

Henrich, Joseph. 2020. *The WEIRDest People in the World: How the West Became Psychologically Peculiar and Particularly Prosperous*. Farrar, Straus and Giroux.

Henrich, Joseph, Steven J. Heine, and Ara Norenzayan. 2010. "The Weirdest People in the World?" *Behavioral and Brain Sciences* 33 (2–3): 61–83. https://doi.org/10.1017 /S0140525X0999152X.

Henry, P. J. 2025. "A Survey Researcher's Response to the Implicit Revolution: Listen to What People Say." In *The Cambridge Handbook of Implicit Bias and Racism*, edited by Amanda L. Scott, Jon A. Krosnick, and Tobias H. Stark, 595–615. Cambridge Handbooks in Psychology. Cambridge University Press. https://doi.org/10.1017 /9781108885492.037.

Herrmann, Sarah D., Michael E. W. Varnum, Brenda C. Straka, and Sarah E. Gaither. 2022. "Social Class Identity Integration and Success for First-Generation College Students: Antecedents, Mechanisms, and Generalizability." *Self and Identity* 21 (5): 553–587. https://doi.org/10.1080/15298868.2021.1924251.

Hersh, Eitan. 2020. *Politics Is for Power: How to Move Beyond Political Hobbyism, Take Action, and Make Real Change*. Scribner.

Hersher, Rebecca. 2017. "Key Moments in the Dakota Access Pipeline Fight." *NPR*, February 22, sec. America. https://www.npr.org/sections/thetwo-way/2017/02/22 /514988040/key-moments-in-the-dakota-access-pipeline-fight.

Heyder, Anke, Ricarda Steinmayr, and Andrei Cimpian. 2023. "Reflecting on Their Mission Increases Preservice Teachers' Growth Mindsets." *Learning and Instruction* 86 (August): 101770. https://doi.org/10.1016/j.learninstruc.2023.101770.

Hildebrand, Laura K., Margo J. Monteith, and Ximena B. Arriaga. 2024. "The Role of Trust in Reducing Confrontation-Related Social Costs." *Journal of Personality and Social Psychology* 126 (2): 240–261. https://doi.org/10.1037/pspi0000429.

Hiller, Avram. 2011. "Climate Change and Individual Responsibility." *The Monist* 94 (3): 349–368.

Hinsliff, Gaby. 2023. "Britain's Nimby Homeowners: Do You Really Want Your Children Living with You for Ever?" *The Guardian*, May 12, sec. Opinion. https://www.theguardian.com/commentisfree/2023/may/12/home-ownership-house-building-property-prices.

Hinton, Alexander, Andrew Woolford, and Jeffrey Benvenuto, eds. 2014. *Colonial Genocide in Indigenous North America*. Duke University Press. https://doi.org/10.1515/9780822376149.

Hirji, Sukaina. 2021. "Oppressive Double Binds." *Ethics* 131 (4): 643–669. https://doi.org/10.1086/713943.

Hirst, Eric, Dennis White, and Richard Goeltz. 1985. "Indoor Temperature Changes in Retrofit Homes." *Energy* 10 (7): 861–870. https://doi.org/10.1016/0360-5442(85)90119-7.

History. n.d. "MADD Founder's Daughter Killed by Drunk Driver." Accessed January 4, 2024. https://www.history.com/this-day-in-history/madd-founders-daughter-killed-by-drunk-driver.

Hoag, Alexis. 2020. "Derrick Bell's Interest Convergence and the Permanence of Racism: A Reflection on Resistance." *Harvard Law Review* (blog), August 24. https://harvardlawreview.org/blog/2020/08/derrick-bells-interest-convergence-and-the-permanence-of-racism-a-reflection-on-resistance/.

Hobbes, Thomas. 2017. *Leviathan*. Penguin Classics.

Hochschild, Adam. 1999. *King Leopold's Ghost: A Story of Greed, Terror, and Heroism in Colonial Africa*. HarperCollins.

Hochschild, Arlie R. 1983. *Managed Heart: Commercialization of Human Feeling*. 2nd ed. University of California Press.

Hoffman, David, and Anton Strezhnev. 2023. "Longer Trips to Court Cause Evictions." *Proceedings of the National Academy of Sciences* 120 (2): e2210467120. https://doi.org/10.1073/pnas.2210467120.

Hollett, Karen Babbs, and Erica Frankenberg. 2022a. "A Critical Analysis of Racial Disparities in ECE Subsidy Funding." *Education Policy Analysis Archives* 30 (February). https://doi.org/10.14507/epaa.30.7003.

Hollett, Karen Babbs, and Erica Frankenberg. 2022b. "Racial Disparities in Preschool Access: Differences in Enrollment and Quality Within and Between Two State Programs in Pennsylvania." Penn State Center for Education and Civil Rights. https://cecr.ed.psu.edu/sites/default/files/CECR.ECE.Report_2.14_FINAL.pdf.

Holroyd, Jules, and Katherine Puddifoot. 2020. "Epistemic Injustice and Implicit Bias." In *An Introduction to Implicit Bias: Knowledge, Justice, and the Social Mind*, edited by Erin Beeghly and Alex Madva. Routledge. https://doi.org/10.4324/9781315107615-6.

Hook, Joshua N., Don E. Davis, Jesse Owen, Everett L. Worthington, and Shawn O. Utsey. 2013. "Cultural Humility: Measuring Openness to Culturally Diverse Clients." *Journal of Counseling Psychology* 60 (3): 353–366. https://doi.org/10.1037/a0032595.

hooks, bell. 1994. *Teaching to Transgress: Education as the Practice of Freedom*. Routledge.

hooks, bell. 2003. *Teaching Community: A Pedagogy of Hope*. Routledge. https://doi.org/10.4324/9780203957769.

Horner, Victoria, and Andrew Whiten. 2005. "Causal Knowledge and Imitation/Emulation Switching in Chimpanzees (Pan Troglodytes) and Children (Homo Sapiens)." *Animal Cognition* 8 (3): 164–181. https://doi.org/10.1007/s10071-004-0239-6.

Horowitz, Jason. 2023. "Pope Francis Allows Priests to Bless Same-Sex Couples." *New York Times*, December 18, sec. World. https://www.nytimes.com/2023/12/18/world/europe/pope-gay-lesbian-same-sex-blessing.html.

Hourdequin, Marion. 2010. "Climate, Collective Action and Individual Ethical Obligations." *Environmental Values* 19 (4): 443–464.

House, Bailey R., Patricia Kanngiesser, H. Clark Barrett, Süheyla Yilmaz, Andrew Marcus Smith, Carla Sebastian-Enesco, Alejandro Erut, and Joan B. Silk. 2020. "Social Norms and Cultural Diversity in the Development of Third-Party Punishment." *Proceedings of the Royal Society B: Biological Sciences* 287 (1925): 20192794. https://doi.org/10.1098/rspb.2019.2794.

Howard, Jacqueline. 2023. "US Spends Most on Health Care but Has Worst Health Outcomes Among High-Income Countries, New Report Finds." CNN, January 31. https://www.cnn.com/2023/01/31/health/us-health-care-spending-global-perspective/index.html.

Hrdy, Sarah Blaffer. 2009. *Mothers and Others: The Evolutionary Origins of Mutual Understanding*. Belknap Press of Harvard University Press.

Hu, Winnie. 2019. "'Hostile Architecture': How Public Spaces Keep the Public Out." *New York Times*, November 8, sec. New York. https://www.nytimes.com/2019/11/08/nyregion/hostile-architecture-nyc.html.

Hume, David. 1734. "Of the Love of Fame." DIGIT.EN.S. https://www.digitens.org/en/anthologies/love-fame-1734.html.

Hunt, Geoffrey. 2023. "Alice Evans, A Pioneer for Women in Microbiology." ASM, March 30. https://asm.org:443/Articles/2023/March/Alice-Evans,-A-Pioneer-for-Women-in-Microbiology.

Hyde, Lewis. 2010. *Common as Air: Revolution, Art, and Ownership*. Farrar, Straus and Giroux.

Hynsjo, Disa M., and Luca Perdoni. 2023. "The Effects of Federal 'Redlining' Maps: A New Empirical Strategy." Working paper. University of Edinburgh. https://www.research.ed.ac.uk/en/publications/the-effects-of-federal-redlining-maps-a-new-empirical-strategy.

Illing, Sean, host. 2021. *The Gray Area with Sean Illing*. "Fighting a World on Fire with Fire." Podcast, September 27. https://www.listennotes.com/podcasts/vox-conversations/fighting-a-world-on-fire-0BLfviEmgXh/.

Indiana State University. n.d. "Parent & Family Orientation." Accessed January 21, 2025. https://www.csudh.edu/parent-family-programs/parent-family-orientation/.

Injury Facts. 2023. "Preliminary Semiannual Motor Vehicle Death Estimates." https://injuryfacts.nsc.org/motor-vehicle/overview/preliminary-estimates/.

Intrator, Jake, Jonathan Tannen, and Douglas S. Massey. 2016. "Segregation by Race and Income in the United States 1970–2010." *Social Science Research* 60 (November): 45–60. https://doi.org/10.1016/j.ssresearch.2016.08.003.

Jackson, Sarah J., Moya Bailey, and Brooke Foucault Welles. 2020. *#HashtagActivism: Networks of Race and Gender Justice*. MIT Press.

Jacobs, Jane. 1961. *The Death and Life of Great American Cities*. Vintage.

Jalil, Andrew J., Joshua Tasoff, and Arturo Vargas Bustamante. 2020. "Eating to Save the Planet: Evidence from a Randomized Controlled Trial Using Individual-Level Food Purchase Data." *Food Policy* 95 (August): 101950. https://doi.org/10.1016/j.foodpol.2020.101950.

James, William. 2009. *The Will to Believe*. Project Gutenberg. https://www.gutenberg.org/files/26659/26659-h/26659-h.htm.

Jamieson, Dale. 2014. *Reason in a Dark Time: Why the Struggle Against Climate Change Failed—and What It Means for Our Future*. Oxford University Press.

Jankowski, Richard. 2002. "Buying a Lottery Ticket to Help the Poor: Altruism, Civic Duty, and Self-Interest in the Decision to Vote." *Rationality and Society* 14 (1): 55–77. https://doi.org/10.1177/1043463102014001003.

Jetten, Jolanda, Kim Peters, Belén Álvarez, et al. 2021. "Consequences of Economic Inequality for the Social and Political Vitality of Society: A Social Identity Analysis." *Political Psychology* 42 (S1): 241–266. https://doi.org/10.1111/pops.12800.

Joffe-Walt, Chana, Julie Snyder, Sarah Koenig, Neil Drumming, Ira Glass, Eve L. Ewing, Rachel Lissy, and Stowe Nelson. 2020. "Nice White Parents." *New York Times*, July 23, sec. Podcasts. https://www.nytimes.com/2020/07/23/podcasts/nice-white -parents-serial.html.

Johnson, Derrick. 2020. "Viewing Social Security Through the Civil Rights Lens." NAACP, August 14. https://naacp.org/articles/viewing-social-security-through-civil -rights-lens.

Johnson, Gabbrielle M. 2021. "Algorithmic Bias: On the Implicit Biases of Social Technology." *Synthese* 198 (10): 9941–9961. https://doi.org/10.1007/s11229-020-02696-y.

Johnson, Gabbrielle M. 2022. "Excerpt from Are Algorithms Value-Free? Feminist Theoretical Virtues in Machine Learning." In *Ethics of Data and Analytics*. Auerbach Publications.

Johnson, India R., and Kentaro Fujita. 2012. "Change We Can Believe In: Using Perceptions of Changeability to Promote System-Change Motives Over System-Justification Motives in Information Search." *Psychological Science* 23 (2): 133–140. https://doi.org/10.1177/0956797611423670.

Johnson, Steven. 2021. *Extra Life: A Short History of Living Longer*. Riverhead Books.

Johnson-Odim, Cheryl. 1992. "On Behalf of Women and the Nation: Funmilayo Ransome-Kuti and the Struggles for Nigerian Independence and Women's Equality." In *Expanding the Boundaries of Women's History: Essays on Women in the Third World*, edited by Cheryl Johnson-Odim and Margaret Strobel. Indiana University Press.

Jones, Benji. 2021. "The Surprising Downsides to Planting Trillions of Trees." *Vox*, September 22. https://www.vox.com/down-to-earth/22679378/tree-planting-forest -restoration-climate-solutions.

Jost, John T. 2020. *A Theory of System Justification*. Harvard University Press.

Jost, John T., Julia Becker, Danny Osborne, and Vivienne Badaan. 2017. "Missing in (Collective) Action: Ideology, System Justification, and the Motivational Antecedents of Two Types of Protest Behavior." *Current Directions in Psychological Science* 26 (2): 99–108. https://doi.org/10.1177/0963721417690633.

Kabengele, Marie-Claire, Peter M. Gollwitzer, and Lucas Keller. 2023. "Conspiracy Beliefs and Jumping to Conclusions." Working paper. University of Konstanz. https://doi.org/10.31234/osf.io/63apz.

Kagan, Shelly. 2011. "Do I Make a Difference?" *Philosophy & Public Affairs* 39 (2): 105–141.

Kahn, Eli, and Salim Furth. 2023. "Breaking Ground: An Examination of Effective State Housing Reforms in 2023." Mercatus. https://www.mercatus.org/research /policy-briefs/breaking-ground-examination-effective-state-housing-reforms-2023.

Kaida, Lisa, Feng Hou, and Max Stick. 2020. "The Long-Term Economic Outcomes of Refugee Private Sponsorship." 11F0019M No. 433. Analytical Studies Branch Research Paper Series. https://www150.statcan.gc.ca/n1/pub/11f0019m/11f0019m 2019021-eng.htm.

Kaleem, Jaweed. 2023. "A Black Woman and a White Woman Went Viral Fighting Racism. Then They Stopped Speaking to Each Other." *Los Angeles Times*, May 17, sec. World & Nation. https://www.latimes.com/world-nation/story/2023-05-17 /starbucks-racism-viral-fame-led-to-diversity-dei-project-that-the-founders-canceled.

Kam, Cindy D., and Camille D. Burge. 2018. "Uncovering Reactions to the Racial Resentment Scale Across the Racial Divide." *The Journal of Politics* 80 (1): 314–320. https://doi.org/10.1086/693907.

Kant, Immanuel. 1996. "An Answer to the Question: What Is Enlightenment? (1784)." In *Practical Philosophy*, edited by Mary J. Gregor. Cambridge University Press. https://doi.org/10.1017/CBO9780511813306.005.

Kaplan, Noah, and Andrew Gelman. 2008. "Voting as a Rational Decision." Centre for Economic Policy Research, May 4. https://cepr.org/voxeu/columns/voting-rational -decision.

Karali, Nihan, Nina Khanna, and Nihar Shah. 2024. "Climate Impact of Primary Plastic Production." LBNL-2001585. Lawrence Berkeley National Laboratory. https:// energyanalysis.lbl.gov/publications/climate-impact-primary-plastic.

Karmali, Francine, Kerry Kawakami, and Elizabeth Page-Gould. 2017. "He Said What? Physiological and Cognitive Responses to Imagining and Witnessing Outgroup Racism." *Journal of Experimental Psychology. General* 146 (8): 1073–1085. https://doi .org/10.1037/xge0000304.

Karpf, David, Matthew J. Lacombe, and Michaela Flum. 2023. "Green Distractions? When Did Environmental Politics Become a Matter of Personal Responsibility?" *Interest Groups & Advocacy*, August. https://doi.org/10.1057/s41309-023-00192-5.

Kateman, Brian. 2017. *The Reducetarian Solution: How the Surprisingly Simple Act of Reducing the Amount of Meat in Your Diet Can Transform Your Health and the Planet.* TarcherPerigee.

Kaur, Anumita. 2022. "How San Diego Achieved Surprising Success Housing Homeless People." *Los Angeles Times*, November 4, sec. Housing & Homelessness. https://www .latimes.com/homeless-housing/story/2022-11-04/san-diego-homeless-housing-success.

Kawashima-Ginsberg, Kei. 2017. "How Gender Mattered to Millennials in the 2016 Election and Beyond." Council on Contemporary Families, March 31.

Keep America Beautiful. n.d. "Our History." Accessed October 21, 2023. https://kab
.org/our-history/.

Kelly, Daniel. 2011. *Yuck! The Nature and Moral Significance of Disgust*. MIT Press.

Kelly, Daniel. 2020. "Internalized Norms and Intrinsic Motivations: Are Normative
Motivations Psychologically Primitive?" *Emotion Researcher*, 36–45.

Kelly, Daniel, and Taylor Davis. 2018. "Social Norms and Human Normative Psychology." *Social Philosophy and Policy* 35 (1): 54–76. https://doi.org/10.1017/S02650
52518000122.

Kelly, Daniel, and Andreas De Block. 2022. "Culture and Cognitive Science." *Stanford Encyclopedia of Philosophy*. https://plato.stanford.edu/archives/sum2022/entries
/culture-cogsci/.

Kelly, Daniel, Luc Faucher, and Edouard Machery. 2010. "Getting Rid of Racism:
Assessing Three Proposals in Light of Psychological Evidence." *Journal of Social Philosophy* 41 (3): 293–322. https://doi.org/10.1111/j.1467-9833.2010.01495.x.

Kelly, Daniel, and Patrick Hoburg. 2017. "A Tale of Two Processes: On Joseph
Henrich's the Secret of Our Success: How Culture Is Driving Human Evolution,
Domesticating Our Species, and Making Us Smarter." *Philosophical Psychology* 30 (6):
832–848. https://doi.org/10.1080/09515089.2017.1299857.

Kelly, Daniel, Evan Westra, and Stephen Setman. 2025. "The Psychology of Normative Cognition." *Stanford Encyclopedia of Philosophy*. https://plato.stanford.edu
/archives/spr2021/entries/psychology-normative-cognition/.

Kendi, Ibram X. 2016. *Stamped from the Beginning: The Definitive History of Racist Ideas
in America*. Bold Type Books.

Kendi, Ibram X. 2019. *How to Be an Antiracist*. One World.

Kennedy, David M. 2004. *Over Here: The First World War and American Society*. 25th
anniversary ed. Oxford University Press.

Kent, Sami. 2020. "Most of 11m Trees Planted in Turkish Project 'May Be Dead.'" *The
Guardian*, January 30, sec. World News. https://www.theguardian.com/world/2020
/jan/30/most-of-11m-trees-planted-in-turkish-project-may-be-dead.

Kenton, Will. 2022a. "What Is a Right-to-Work Law, and How Does It Work?"
Investopedia. https://www.investopedia.com/terms/r/righttowork-law.asp.

Kenton, Will. 2022b. "Zoning: What It Is, How It Works, Classification Examples."
Investopedia. https://www.investopedia.com/terms/z/zoning.asp.

Kenyon, Daphne, Bethany Paquin, and Semida Munteanu. 2022. "Public Schools
and the Property Tax: A Comparison of Education Funding Models in Three US
States." *Land Lines*, April 2022.

Kerwin, Patrick L. 2018. "Addressing Misconceptions about the MBTI® Assessment." Myers-Briggs Company. https://www.themyersbriggs.com/-/media/Myers-Briggs/Files /Resources-Hub-Files/Guides/White-Papers/MBTI/White-Paper_Creating-Clarity -Addressing-Micsconceptions-About-the-MBTI-Assessment.pdf.

Kimbrough, Liz. 2021. "How Settlers, Scientists, and a Women-Led Industry Saved Brazil's Rarest Primate." *Mongabay Environmental News*, May 14. https://news.mon gabay.com/2021/05/how-settlers-scientists-and-a-women-led-industry-saved-brazils -rarest-primate/.

Kimmelman, Michael, and Bobby Doherty. 2021. "Recycling in America Is a Mess. A New Bill Could Clean It Up." *New York Times*, January 27, sec. Arts. https://www .nytimes.com/2021/01/27/arts/design/recycling-packaging-new-york.html.

Kinder, Donald R., and Lynn M. Sanders. 1996. *Divided by Color: Racial Politics and Democratic Ideals*. University of Chicago Press.

King, Deborah K. 1988. "Multiple Jeopardy, Multiple Consciousness: The Context of a Black Feminist Ideology." *Signs* 14 (1): 42–72.

Kingston, Ewan, and Walter Sinnott-Armstrong. 2018. "What's Wrong with Joyguzzling?" *Ethical Theory and Moral Practice* 21 (1): 169–186. https://doi.org/10.1007 /s10677-017-9859-1.

Kinney, David, and Liam K. Bright. 2023. "Risk Aversion and Elite-Group Ignorance." *Philosophy and Phenomenological Research* 106 (1): 35–57. https://doi.org/10.1111 /phpr.12837.

Kinzler, Katherine D., and Jasmine M. DeJesus. 2013. "Northern = Smart and Southern = Nice: The Development of Accent Attitudes in the United States." *Quarterly Journal of Experimental Psychology* 66 (6): 1146–1158. https://doi.org/10.1080/17470 218.2012.731695.

Kirby, Jen. 2019. "9 Questions about the Hong Kong Protests You Were Too Embarrassed to Ask." *Vox*, August 22. https://www.vox.com/world/2019/8/22/20804294 /hong-kong-protests-9-questions.

Klebl, Christoph, and Jolanda Jetten. 2023. "Perceived Inequality Increases Support for Structural Solutions to Climate Change." *Social Psychological and Personality Science* 15 (2). https://doi.org/10.1177/19485506231169328.

Klein, Ezra. 2016. "Francis Fukuyama: America Is in 'One of the Most Severe Political Crises I Have Experienced.'" *Vox*, October 26. https://www.vox.com/2016/10/26 /13352946/francis-fukuyama-ezra-klein.

Klein, Ezra. 2020. *Why We're Polarized*. Avid Reader Press/Simon & Schuster.

Klein, Ezra. 2022a. "Now All Biden Has to Do Is Build It." *New York Times*, September 16, sec. Opinion. https://www.nytimes.com/2022/09/16/opinion/ezra-klein-podcast-felicia-wong.html.

Klein, Ezra. 2022b. "The Single Best Guide to Decarbonization I've Heard." *New York Times*, September 20, sec. Opinion. https://www.nytimes.com/2022/09/20/opinion/ezra-klein-podcast-jesse-jenkins.html.

Kliff, Sarah, Claire C. Miller, and Larry Buchanan. 2023. "Childbirth Is Deadlier for Black Families Even When They're Rich, Expansive Study Finds." *New York Times*, February 12, sec. The Upshot. https://www.nytimes.com/interactive/2023/02/12/upshot/child-maternal-mortality-rich-poor.html.

Kluegel, James R. 1990. "Trends in Whites' Explanations of the Black-White Gap in Socioeconomic Status, 1977–1989." *American Sociological Review* 55 (4): 512–525. https://doi.org/10.2307/2095804.

Knowles, Eric D., Brian S. Lowery, Rosalind M. Chow, and Miguel M. Unzueta. 2014. "Deny, Distance, or Dismantle? How White Americans Manage a Privileged Identity." *Perspectives on Psychological Science* 9: 594–609. https://doi.org/10.1177/1745691614554658.

Know Your Meme. 2011. "Why Not Both?/Why Don't We Have Both?" Added August 24. https://knowyourmeme.com/memes/why-not-both-why-dont-we-have-both.

Know Your Meme. 2017. "Distracted Boyfriend." Added August 22. https://knowyourmeme.com/memes/distracted-boyfriend.

Koehrsen, Jens. 2021. "Muslims and Climate Change: How Islam, Muslim Organizations, and Religious Leaders Influence Climate Change Perceptions and Mitigation Activities." *WIREs Climate Change* 12 (3): e702. https://doi.org/10.1002/wcc.702.

Koggel, Christine M., Ami Harbin, and Jennifer J. Llewellyn. 2022. "Feminist Relational Theory." *Journal of Global Ethics* 18 (1): 1–14. https://doi.org/10.1080/17449626.2022.2073702.

Kotzur, Patrick F., and Ulrich Wagner. 2021. "The Dynamic Relationship between Contact Opportunities, Positive and Negative Intergroup Contact, and Prejudice: A Longitudinal Investigation." *Journal of Personality and Social Psychology* 120 (2): 418–442. https://doi.org/10.1037/pspi0000258.

Kroeper, Kathryn M., Audrey C. Fried, and Mary C. Murphy. 2022. "Towards Fostering Growth Mindset Classrooms: Identifying Teaching Behaviors That Signal Instructors' Fixed and Growth Mindsets Beliefs to Students." *Social Psychology of Education* 25: 371–398. https://doi.org/10.1007/s11218-022-09689-4.

Krugman, Paul. 2023. "Why Did So Many Economists Get Disinflation Wrong?" *New York Times*, November 7, sec. Opinion. https://www.nytimes.com/2023/11/07/opinion/economists-disinflation-economy.html.

Kuhn, Manford H., and Thomas S. McPartland. 1954. "An Empirical Investigation of Self-Attitudes." *American Sociological Review* 19 (1): 68–76. https://doi.org/10.2307/2088175.

Kumar, Amit, and Nicholas Epley. 2023. "A Little Good Goes an Unexpectedly Long Way: Underestimating the Positive Impact of Kindness on Recipients." *Journal of Experimental Psychology. General* 152 (1): 236–252. https://doi.org/10.1037/xge0001271.

Kumar, Victor, and Richmond Campbell. 2022. *A Better Ape: The Evolution of the Moral Mind and How It Made Us Human.* Oxford University Press.

Kuran, Timur. 1991. "Now out of Never: The Element of Surprise in the East European Revolution of 1989." *World Politics* 44 (1): 7–48. https://doi.org/10.2307/2010422.

Kurth, Charlie. 2018. *The Anxious Mind: An Investigation into the Varieties and Virtues of Anxiety.* MIT Press.

Kurtis, Tugce, Phia Salter, and Glenn Adams. 2015. "A Sociocultural Approach to Teaching about Racism." *Race and Pedagogy Journal: Teaching and Learning for Justice* 1 (1): 1–30.

Kuziemko, Ilyana, and Ebonya Washington. 2018. "Why Did the Democrats Lose the South? Bringing New Data to an Old Debate." *American Economic Review* 108 (10): 2830–2867. https://doi.org/10.1257/aer.20161413.

Lacombe, Matthew J. 2019. "The Political Weaponization of Gun Owners: The National Rifle Association's Cultivation, Dissemination, and Use of a Group Social Identity." *Journal of Politics* 81 (4): 1342–1356. https://doi.org/10.1086/704329.

Lacombe, Matthew J. 2021a. *Firepower: How the NRA Turned Gun Owners into a Political Force.* Princeton University Press.

Lacombe, Matthew J. 2021b. "The Political Weaponization of Gun Owners: The NRA and Gun Ownership as Social Identity." In *Firepower: How the NRA Turned Gun Owners into a Political Force*, edited by Matthew J. Lacombe. Princeton University Press. https://doi.org/10.23943/princeton/9780691207445.003.0003.

Lalljee, Jason. 2021. "Elon Musk Is Speaking Out Against Government Subsidies. Here's a List of the Billions of Dollars His Businesses Have Received." *Business Insider*, December 15. https://www.businessinsider.com/elon-musk-list-government-subsidies-tesla-billions-spacex-solarcity-2021-12.

Lambert, Bruce. 1991. "Harlon B. Carter, Longtime Head of Rifle Association, Dies at 78." *New York Times*, November 22, sec. US. https://www.nytimes.com/1991/11/22/us/harlon-b-carter-longtime-head-of-rifle-association-dies-at-78.html.

Lamer, Sarah Ariel, Paige Dvorak, Ashley M. Biddle, Kristin Pauker, and Max Weisbuch. 2022. "The Transmission of Gender Stereotypes Through Televised Patterns of Nonverbal Bias." *Journal of Personality and Social Psychology* 123 (6): 1315–1335. https://doi.org/10.1037/pspi0000390.

Latham, Scott, Sean P. Corcoran, Carolyn Sattin-Bajaj, and Jennifer L. Jennings. 2021. "Racial Disparities in Pre-K Quality: Evidence from New York City's Universal Pre-K Program." *Educational Researcher* 50 (9). https://doi.org/10.3102/0013189 X211028214.

Leaders' Choice Insurance. 2019. "Conduct Diversity Training to Head Off Potential Lawsuits." June 20. https://www.leaderschoiceinsurance.com/blog/conduct-diversity -training-to-head-off-potential-lawsuits/.

Leboeuf, Céline. 2020. "The Embodied Biased Mind." In *An Introduction to Implicit Bias*, edited by Alex Madva and Erin Beeghly. Routledge.

Lee, Harry. 2019. "Old Photos of Washington Square: A Journey to the Analog Past." NYU Local, February 8. https://nyulocal.com/old-photos-of-washington-square-a -journey-to-the-analog-past-8cb7fe3bcd06.

Lee, Kent M., Kristen A. Lindquist, and B. Keith Payne. 2023. "Constructing Explicit Prejudice: Evidence from Large Sample Datasets." *Personality and Social Psychology Bulletin* 49 (4): 541–553. https://doi.org/10.1177/01461672221075926.

Legal Information Institute. 2022. "Redlining." Last updated April 2022. https:// www.law.cornell.edu/wex/redlining.

Legg, Catherine, and Christopher Hookway. 2021. "Pragmatism." *Stanford Encyclopedia of Philosophy*. https://plato.stanford.edu/archives/sum2021/entries/pragmatism/.

Lenharo, Mariana. 2023. "Game-Changing Obesity Drugs Go Mainstream: What Scientists Are Learning." *Nature* 618 (7963): 17–18. https://doi.org/10.1038/d41586 -023-01712-8.

Leon, Luis F. 2022. "Amazon Workers on Staten Island Clinch a Historic Victory." Labor Notes, April 1. https://labornotes.org/2022/04/amazon-workers-staten-island -clinch-historic-victory.

Leonhardt, David. "Covid Shots for Children." *New York Times*, February 13, sec. Briefing. https://www.nytimes.com/2024/02/13/briefing/covid-boosters-children-cdc .html.

Lerman, Amy E., Meredith L. Sadin, and Samuel Trachtman. 2017. "Policy Uptake as Political Behavior: Evidence from the Affordable Care Act." *American Political Science Review* 111 (4): 755–770. https://doi.org/10.1017/S0003055417000272.

Lerner, Michele. 2021. "Americans Want Larger Homes, Greater Distance from Others, New Poll Finds." *Washington Post*, September 1. https://www.washingtonpost .com/business/2021/09/14/new-nationwide-poll-says-more-americans-prefer-live -suburbs-instead-cities/.

Lerner, Sharon. 2019. "How the Plastics Industry Is Fighting to Keep Polluting the World." *The Intercept*, July 20. https://theintercept.com/2019/07/20/plastics-industry-plastic-recycling/.

Levin, Benjamin. 2020. "What's Wrong with Police Unions?" *Columbia Law Review* 120 (5): 1333–1402.

Levin, Kelly, Benjamin Cashore, Steven Bernstein, and Graeme Auld. 2012. "Overcoming the Tragedy of Super Wicked Problems: Constraining Our Future Selves to Ameliorate Global Climate Change." *Policy Sciences* 45 (2): 123–152. https://doi.org/10.1007/s11077-012-9151-0.

Levitt, Alice. 2011. "Live Free or Diet." *Seven Days*, January 19. https://www.sevendaysvt.com/food-drink/live-free-or-diet-2142335.

Lewandowsky, Stephan, and Sander van der Linden. 2022. "Interventions Based on Social Norms Could Benefit From Considering Adversarial Information Environments: Comment on Constantino et al. (2022)." *Psychological Science in the Public Interest* 23 (2): 43–49. https://doi.org/10.1177/15291006221114132.

Lewin, Kurt. 1936. *Principles of Topological Psychology*. McGraw-Hill. https://doi.org/10.1037/10019-000.

Lewin, Kurt. 1946. "Behavior and Development as a Function of the Total Situation." In *Manual of Child Psychology*, edited by L. Carmichael. John Wiley & Sons, Inc. https://doi.org/10.1037/10756-016.

Li, Danying, Miguel R. Ramos, Matthew R. Bennett, Douglas S. Massey, and Miles Hewstone. 2021. "Does Increasing Immigration Affect Ethnic Minority Groups?" *Annals of the American Academy of Political and Social Science* 697 (1): 49–65. https://doi.org/10.1177/00027162211051999.

Li, Reia, and Quentin Carney. 2022. "What's Going on with Larkin Place? Legal Troubles Loom for Claremont over Affordable Housing Initiative." The Student Life, October 7. https://tsl.news/larkin-place/.

Liao, Shen-yi, and Bryce Huebner. 2021. "Oppressive Things." *Philosophy and Phenomenological Research* 103 (1): 92–113. https://doi.org/10.1111/phpr.12701.

Lightner, Candace. n.d. "Candace Lightner." Accessed October 25, 2023. https://www.candacelightner.com/.

Lim, Désirée. 2023. *Immigration and Social Equality: The Ethics of Skill-Selective Immigration Policy*. Oxford University Press.

Lin, Chujun, and R. Michael Alvarez. 2020. "Personality Traits Are Directly Associated with Anti-Black Prejudice in the United States." *PLoS ONE* 15 (7): e0235436. https://doi.org/10.1371/journal.pone.0235436.

Lind, Michael. 2021. "The Government Should Keep Its Hands Off Your Medicare." American Compass, October 15. https://americancompass.org/the-government -should-keep-its-hands-off-your-medicare/.

Lindemann, Hilde. 2013. *Holding and Letting Go: The Social Practice of Personal Identities*. Oxford University Press.

Linebaugh, Kate, host. 2023. *The Journal*. "The Government Banker Channeling Billions into Clean Energy." Podcast, June 13. https://www.wsj.com/podcasts/the -journal/the-government-banker-channeling-billions-into-clean-energy/1ad9206c -cfc9-4c45-a308-ca70a857edb8.

Long, Colleen, and Zeke Miller. 2020. "Stimulus Checks to Bear Trump's Name in Unprecedented Move." AP News, April 15. https://apnews.com/article/virus-outbreak -donald-trump-us-news-business-ap-top-news-8eafb90e92a676278a5644a2b72b734c.

Long, Zoe, Jonn Axsen, Inger Miller, and Christine Kormos. 2019. "What Does Tesla Mean to Car Buyers? Exploring the Role of Automotive Brand in Perceptions of Battery Electric Vehicles." *Transportation Research Part A: Policy and Practice* 129 (November): 185–204. https://doi.org/10.1016/j.tra.2019.08.006.

Lopez, German. 2015. "What People Get Wrong About Prohibition." *Vox*, October 19. https://www.vox.com/2015/10/19/9566935/prohibition-myths-misconceptions -facts.

Lopez, German. 2017. "The Past Year of Research Has Made It Very Clear: Trump Won Because of Racial Resentment." *Vox*, December 15. https://www.vox.com /identities/2017/12/15/16781222/trump-racism-economic-anxiety-study.

Lorde, Audre. 2017. *A Burst of Light: And Other Essays*. Ixia Press.

Lorde, Audre. 2020. *Sister Outsider: Essays and Speeches*. Penguin Books.

Lowrey, Annie. 2021. "The Time Tax." *Atlantic*, July 27. https://www.theatlantic.com /politics/archive/2021/07/how-government-learned-waste-your-time-tax/619568/.

Lundberg, Kristjen B., and B. Keith Payne. 2014. "Decisions Among the Undecided: Implicit Attitudes Predict Future Voting Behavior of Undecided Voters." *PLoS ONE* 9 (1): e85680. https://doi.org/10.1371/journal.pone.0085680.

Lundberg, Kristjen B., B. Keith Payne, Josh Pasek, and Jon A. Krosnick. 2017. "Racial Attitudes Predicted Changes in Ostensibly Race-Neutral Political Attitudes Under the Obama Administration." *Political Psychology* 38 (2): 313–330. https://doi.org/10.1111 /pops.12315.

Lupkin, Sydney. 2013. "US Has More Guns—And Gun Deaths—Than Any Other Country, Study Finds." *ABC News*, September 19. http://abcnews.go.com/blogs /health/2013/09/19/u-s-has-more-guns-and-gun-deaths-than-any-other-country-study -finds.

MacKinnon, Catharine A. 2019. "Where #MeToo Came From, and Where It's Going." *Atlantic*, March 24. https://www.theatlantic.com/ideas/archive/2019/03/catharine-mackinnon-what-metoo-has-changed/585313/.

Macnamara, Brooke N., and Alexander P. Burgoyne. 2023. "Do Growth Mindset Interventions Impact Students' Academic Achievement? A Systematic Review and Meta-Analysis with Recommendations for Best Practices." *Psychological Bulletin* 149 (3–4): 133–173. https://doi.org/10.1037/bul0000352.

Madva, Alex. 2016a. "A Plea for Anti-Anti-Individualism: How Oversimple Psychology Misleads Social Policy." *Ergo, an Open Access Journal of Philosophy* 3 (27): 701–728. https://doi.org/10.3998/ergo.12405314.0003.027.

Madva, Alex. 2016b "Implicit Bias and Latina/os in Philosophy." *APA Newsletter on Hispanic/Latino Issues in Philosophy* 16 (1): 8–15.

Madva, Alex. 2017. "Biased Against Debiasing: On the Role of (Institutionally Sponsored) Self-Transformation in the Struggle Against Prejudice." *Ergo, an Open Access Journal of Philosophy* 4 (6): 145–179. http://dx.doi.org/10.3998/ergo.12405314.0004.006.

Madva, Alex. 2019a. "Social Psychology, Phenomenology, and the Indeterminate Content of Unreflective Racial Bias." In *Race as Phenomena: Between Phenomenology and Philosophy of Race*, edited by Emily S. Lee. Rowman & Littlefield International.

Madva, Alex. 2019b. "The Inevitability of Aiming for Virtue." In *Overcoming Epistemic Injustice: Social and Psychological Perspectives*, edited by Benjamin R. Sherman and Goguen Stacey. Rowman & Littlefield International.

Madva, Alex. 2020a. "Individual and Structural Interventions." In *An Introduction to Implicit Bias: Knowledge, Justice, and the Social Mind*, edited by Erin Beeghly and Alex Madva. Routledge. https://doi.org/10.4324/9781315107615-12.

Madva, Alex. 2020b. "Integration, Community, and the Medical Model of Social Injustice." *Journal of Applied Philosophy* 37 (2): 211–232. https://doi.org/10.1111/japp.12356.

Madva, Alex. 2020c. "Resistance Training." *The Philosophers' Magazine* 91 (November): 40–45. https://doi.org/10.5840/tpm20209191.

Madva, Alex. 2020d. "Structural Change, Individual Change, and Four-Story Walkups." Justice Everywhere, May 29. https://justice-everywhere.org/distribution/structural-change-individual-change-and-four-story-walkups/.

Madva, Alex, Michael Brownstein, and Daniel Kelly. 2023. "It's Always Both: Changing Individuals Requires Changing Systems and Changing Systems Requires Changing Individuals." *Behavioral and Brain Sciences* 46 (January): e168. https://doi.org/10.1017/S0140525X23001164.

Madva, Alex, Katherine Gasdaglis, and Shannon Doberneck. 2023. "Duties of Social Identity? Intersectional Objections to Sen's Identity Politics." *Inquiry*, 1–30. https://doi.org/10.1080/0020174X.2023.2270527.

Madva, Alex, Daniel Kelly, and Michael Brownstein. 2024. "Change the People or Change the Policy? On the Moral Education of Antiracists." *Ethical Theory and Moral Practice* 27 (1): 91–110. https://doi.org/10.1007/s10677-023-10363-7.

Magidor, Ofra. 2022. "Category Mistakes." *Stanford Encyclopedia of Philosophy.* https://plato.stanford.edu/archives/fall2022/entries/category-mistakes/.

Maiorino, Al. 2012. "The 12 Months of NIMBY." *Renewable Energy Magazine*, December 5. https://www.renewableenergymagazine.com/Al_Maiorino/the-12-months-of-nimby-20121205.

Major, Brenda, Alison Blodorn, and Gregory Major Blascovich. 2018. "The Threat of Increasing Diversity: Why Many White Americans Support Trump in the 2016 Presidential Election." *Group Processes & Intergroup Relations* 21 (6): 931–940. https://doi.org/10.1177/1368430216677304.

Maki, Alexander, Amanda R. Carrico, Kaitlin T. Raimi, Heather Barnes Truelove, Brandon Araujo, and Kam Leung Yeung. 2019. "Meta-Analysis of Pro-Environmental Behaviour Spillover." *Nature Sustainability* 2 (4): 307–115. https://doi.org/10.1038/s41893-019-0263-9.

Makowsky, Michael D., Thomas Stratmann, and Alex Tabarrok. 2019. "To Serve and Collect: The Fiscal and Racial Determinants of Law Enforcement." *Journal of Legal Studies* 48 (1): 189–216. https://doi.org/10.1086/700589.

Maldonado, Angelika. 2022. Here's How We Beat Amazon Interview by Eric Blanc." *Jacobin*, April 2. https://jacobin.com/2022/04/amazon-labor-union-alu-staten-island-organizing.

Mallon, Ron. 2017. "Psychology, Accumulation Mechanisms, and Race." Johns Hopkins University.

Malpas, Jeff. 2022. "Hans-Georg Gadamer." *Stanford Encyclopedia of Philosophy.* https://plato.stanford.edu/archives/win2022/entries/gadamer/.

Manalili, Marie A. R., Amy Pearson, Justin Sulik, et al. 2023. "From Puzzle to Progress: How Engaging With Neurodiversity Can Improve Cognitive Science." *Cognitive Science* 47 (2): e13255. https://doi.org/10.1111/cogs.13255.

Mandelbaum, Eric. 2019. "Troubles with Bayesianism: An Introduction to the Psychological Immune System." *Mind & Language* 34 (2): 141–157. https://doi.org/10.1111/mila.12205.

Maniates, Michael F. 2001. "Individualization: Plant a Tree, Buy a Bike, Save the World?" *Global Environmental Politics* 1 (3): 31–52. https://doi.org/10.1162/152638001316881395.

Mann, Michael, and Jonathan Brockopp. 2019. "Climate Change Requires Government Action, Not Just Personal Steps." *USA Today*, June 3. https://www.usatoday.com/story/opinion/2019/06/03/climate-change-requires-collective-action-more-than-single-acts-column/1275965001/.

Mann, Michael (@MichaelEMann). 2019. "'You Can't Save the Climate by Going Vegan. Corporate Polluters Must Be Held Accountable' | My Op-Ed with @Penn_State Colleague Jonathan Brockopp in @USAToday." Twitter (now X), June 3. https://twitter.com/MichaelEMann/status/1135523949922660352.

Mansbridge, Jane J., and Aldon Morris, eds. 2001. *Oppositional Consciousness: The Subjective Roots of Social Protest*. University of Chicago Press.

Marantz, Andrew. 2020. "How to Stop a Power Grab." *New Yorker*, November 16. https://www.newyorker.com/magazine/2020/11/23/how-to-stop-a-power-grab.

Marantz, Andrew. 2022. "The Youth Movement Trying to Revolutionize Climate Politics." *New Yorker*, February 28. https://www.newyorker.com/magazine/2022/03/07/the-youth-movement-trying-to-revolutionize-climate-politics.

Marchese, David. 2022. "An Evangelical Climate Scientist Wonders What Went Wrong." *New York Times*, January 3, sec. Magazine. https://www.nytimes.com/interactive/2022/01/03/magazine/katharine-hayhoe-interview.html.

Margolies, Jane. 2023. "Awash in Asphalt, Cities Rethink Their Parking Needs." *New York Times*, March 7, sec. Business. https://www.nytimes.com/2023/03/07/business/fewer-parking-spots.html.

Margolis, Jason. 2015. "Canadians Are Coming Out in Droves, Again, to Resettle Refugees—on Their Own Dime." *The World from PRX*, November 20. https://theworld.org/stories/2015-11-20/private-canadians-are-coming-out-droves-again-resettle-refugees.

Markus, Hazel Rose, and Shinobu Kitayama. 2010. "Cultures and Selves: A Cycle of Mutual Constitution." *Perspectives on Psychological Science* 5 (4): 420–430. https://doi.org/10.1177/1745691610375557.

Martela, Frank, Bent Greve, Bo Rothstein, and Juho Saari. 2020. "The Nordic Exceptionalism: What Explains Why the Nordic Countries Are Constantly Among the Happiest in the World." *World Happiness Report*. https://worldhappiness.report/ed/2020/the-nordic-exceptionalism-what-explains-why-the-nordic-countries-are-constantly-among-the-happiest-in-the-world/.

Martín, Annette. 2020. "Social Structure, Ignorance, and Oppression." PhD diss., New York University. http://search.proquest.com/docview/2461428857/abstract/CF0ED72D02ED41FFPQ/1.

Matthews, Dylan. 2015. "America's Biggest Housing Program Is Run by the IRS. It's a Huge Giveaway to Rich People." *Vox*, December 11. https://www.vox.com/policy-and-politics/2015/12/11/9901144/mortgage-interest-deduction.

Matthews, Dylan. 2019. "America Has a Housing Segregation Problem. Seattle May Just Have the Solution." *Vox*, August 4. https://www.vox.com/future-perfect/2019/8/4 /20726427/raj-chetty-segregation-moving-opportunity-seattle-experiment.

Matthews, Dylan. 2022. "Humanity Was Stagnant for Millennia—Then Something Big Changed 150 Years Ago." *Vox*, September 7. https://www.vox.com/future-perfect /2022/9/7/23332699/economic-growth-brad-delong-slouching-utopia.

Matthews, Dylan. 2023. "Seattle May Have Figured Out How to Get More Poor People into Better Housing." *Vox*, April 3. https://www.vox.com/future-perfect/2023/4/3/23 647615/raj-chetty-housing-vouchers-cmto-seattle.

May, Joshua, and Victor Kumar. 2023. "Harnessing Moral Psychology to Reduce Meat Consumption." *Journal of the American Philosophical Association* 9 (2): 367–387. https://doi.org/10.1017/apa.2022.2.

Mazar, Asaf, Geoff Tomaino, Ziv Carmon, and Wendy Wood. 2022. "Americans Discount the Effect of Friction on Voter Turnout." *Proceedings of the National Academy of Sciences* 119 (34): e2206072119. https://doi.org/10.1073/pnas.2206072119.

McAdam, Doug. 1986. "Recruitment to High-Risk Activism: The Case of Freedom Summer." *American Journal of Sociology* 92 (1): 64–90.

McDonough, Siobhan. 2022. "The Problem of Global Energy Inequity, Explained by American Refrigerators." *Vox*, May 21. https://www.vox.com/future-perfect/231060 61/energy-inequity-world-electricity-american-refrigerators.

McIntire, Mike. 2023. "The Secret History of Gun Rights: How Lawmakers Armed the NRA." *New York Times*, July 30, sec. US. https://www.nytimes.com/2023/07/30 /us/politics/nra-congress-firearms.html.

McKibben, Bill. 2022a. "Dimming the Sun to Cool the Planet Is a Desperate Idea, Yet We're Inching Toward It." *New Yorker*, November 22. https://www.newyorker .com/news/annals-of-a-warming-planet/dimming-the-sun-to-cool-the-planet-is-a -desperate-idea-yet-were-inching-toward-it.

McKibben, Bill. 2022b. "Wrong Turn: America's Car Culture and the Road Not Taken." *Yale Environment 360*, June 9. https://e360.yale.edu/features/wrong-turn -americas-car-culture-and-the-road-not-taken.

McManus, I. C., Matthew Freegard, James Moore, and Richard Rawles. 2010. "Science in the Making: Right Hand, Left Hand. II: The Duck-Rabbit Figure." *Laterality* 15 (1–2): 166–185. https://doi.org/10.1080/13576500802564266.

McRaney, David. 2022. *How Minds Change: The Surprising Science of Belief, Opinion, and Persuasion*. Portfolio.

Medina, José. 2013. *The Epistemology of Resistance: Gender and Racial Oppression, Epistemic Injustice, and Resistant Imaginations*. Oxford University Press. https://doi.org /10.1093/acprof:oso/9780199929023.001.0001.

Mehic, Adrian. 2019. "Immigration and Right-Wing Populism: Evidence from a Natural Experiment." Working Paper No. 2019:5. Lund University. https://www .econstor.eu/handle/10419/260275.

Mehta, Stephanie. 2019. "Despite Spending Billions, Companies Can't Buy Diversity." *Washington Post*, November 22. https://www.washingtonpost.com/outlook /despite-spending-billions-companies-cant-buy-diversity/2019/11/21/d8907b92-fb 1a-11e9-ac8c-8eced29ca6ef_story.html.

Me Too. 2024. "Healing in Action." https://metoomvmt.org/take-action/.

Melfi, Theodore, dir. 2006. *Hidden Figures*. Fox 2000 Pictures, Chernin Entertainment, Levantine Films.

Mendelson, Anne. 2023. *Spoiled: The Myth of Milk as Superfood*. Columbia University Press.

Menendian, Stephen, Samir Gambhir, and Arthur Gailes. 2021. "The Roots of Structural Racism Project." Othering & Belonging Institute, June 30. https://belonging .berkeley.edu/roots-structural-racism.

Merton, Robert K. 1968. "The Matthew Effect in Science." *Science* 159 (3810): 56–63. https://doi.org/10.1126/science.159.3810.56.

Mesoudi, Alex, Kesson Magid, and Delwar Hussain. 2016. "How Do People Become W.E.I.R.D.? Migration Reveals the Cultural Transmission Mechanisms Underlying Variation in Psychological Processes." *PLoS ONE* 11 (1): e0147162. https://doi.org /10.1371/journal.pone.0147162.

Metrix, Ace. 2014. "Even 40 Years Later, 'The Crying Indian' Still Rings True." *Ace Metrix* (blog), November 6. https://www.acemetrix.com/insights/blog/even-40-years -later-the-crying-indian-psa-still-rings-true/.

Mettler, Suzanne. 2005. *Soldiers to Citizens: The GI Bill and the Making of the Greatest Generation*. Oxford University Press.

Mettler, Suzanne. 2011a. "Our Hidden Government Benefits." *New York Times*, September 20, 2011, sec. Opinion. https://www.nytimes.com/2011/09/20/opinion /our-hidden-government-benefits.html.

Mettler, Suzanne. 2011b. *The Submerged State: How Invisible Government Policies Undermine American Democracy*. University of Chicago Press.

Meyer, David S., and Nancy Whittier. 1994. "Social Movement Spillover." *Social Problems* 41 (2): 277–298. https://doi.org/10.2307/3096934.

Meyer, Robinson. 2020. "The Secret Political Power of Fossil Fuels." *Atlantic*, October 27. https://www.theatlantic.com/newsletters/archive/2020/10/the-secret-political -power-of-fossil-fuels/616869/.

Meyer, Robinson. 2021. "What 2020's Bizarre Economy Taught Us About Climate Change." *Atlantic*, January 12. https://www.theatlantic.com/science/archive/2021/01/the-lowest-carbon-pollution-in-three-decades/617652/.

Meyer, Robinson. 2022. "'Greenwashing' Isn't About Consumers." *Atlantic*, June 29. https://www.theatlantic.com/science/archive/2022/06/corporate-climate-action-employee-work/661425/.

Meyers, Chanel, Amanda Williams, Kristin Pauker, and Evan P. Apfelbaum. 2022. "The Impact of Social Norms on Navigating Race in a Racially Diverse Context." *Group Processes & Intergroup Relations* 25 (4): 853–870. https://doi.org/10.1177/1368430220984228.

Mildenberger, Matto. 2019. "The Tragedy of 'The Tragedy of the Commons.'" *Scientific American Blog* (blog), April 23. https://blogs.scientificamerican.com/voices/the-tragedy-of-the-tragedy-of-the-commons/.

Mildenberger, Matto. 2020. *Carbon Captured: How Business and Labor Control Climate Politics*. MIT Press.

Milkoreit, Manjana, Jennifer Hodbod, Jacopo Baggio, et al. 2018. "Defining Tipping Points for Social-Ecological Systems Scholarship—an Interdisciplinary Literature Review." *Environmental Research Letters* 13 (3): 033005. https://doi.org/10.1088/1748-9326/aaaa75.

Millar, Mark. 2014. *Superman: Red Son*. New ed. DC Comics.

Miller, Dale T. 2023. "A Century of Pluralistic Ignorance: What We Have Learned about Its Origins, Forms, and Consequences." *Frontiers in Social Psychology* 1. https://www.frontiersin.org/articles/10.3389/frsps.2023.1260896.

Miller, Grant. 2008. "Women's Suffrage, Political Responsiveness, and Child Survival in American History." *Quarterly Journal of Economics* 123 (3): 1287–1327. https://doi.org/10.1162/qjec.2008.123.3.1287.

Miller, Gregory E., Tianyi Yu, Edith Chen, and Gene H. Brody. 2015. "Self-Control Forecasts Better Psychosocial Outcomes but Faster Epigenetic Aging in Low-SES Youth." *Proceedings of the National Academy of Sciences* 112 (33): 10325–10330. https://doi.org/10.1073/pnas.1505063112.

Millgram, Elijah. 2019. *John Stuart Mill and the Meaning of Life*. Oxford University Press.

Mistry, Rashmita S., Lindsey Nenadal, Katherine M. Griffin, Frederick J. Zimmerman, Hasmik Avetisian Cochran, Carla-Anne Thomas, and Christopher Wilson. 2016. "Children's Reasoning about Poverty, Economic Mobility, and Helping Behavior: Results of a Curriculum Intervention in the Early School Years." *Journal of Social Issues* 72 (4): 760–788. https://doi.org/10.1111/josi.12193.

MIT Election Data & Science Lab. 2021. "Voter ID Laws as of 2020." June 10, 2021. https://public.tableau.com/views/VoterIdentificationGraphics_cartogram/VoterID?: embed=y&:showVizHome=no&:host_url=https%3A%2F%2Fpublic.tableau.com %2F&:embed_code_version=3&:tabs=no&:toolbar=yes&:animate_transition=yes& :display_static_image=no&:display_spinner=no&:display_overlay=yes&:display _count=yes&:language=en-US&:loadOrderID=0.

Mitchell, Gregory, and Philip E. Tetlock. 2023. "Are Progressives in Denial About Progress? Yes, but So Is Almost Everyone Else." *Clinical Psychological Science* 11 (4): 683–704. https://doi.org/10.1177/21677026221114315.

Mohamed, Omayma. 2019. "How Intersectionalism Betrays the World's Muslim Women." *Quillette*, April 28. https://quillette.com/2019/04/28/how-intersectionalism -betrays-the-worlds-muslim-women/.

Molho, Catherine, Joshua M. Tybur, Paul A. M. Van Lange, and Daniel Balliet. 2020. "Direct and Indirect Punishment of Norm Violations in Daily Life." *Nature Communications* 11 (1): 3432. https://doi.org/10.1038/s41467-020-17286-2.

Molla, Rani. 2022. "Unions Are on the Rise in 2022. Four Charts Show Just How Much." *Vox*, August 30. https://www.vox.com/recode/2022/8/30/23326654/2022 -union-charts-elections-wins-strikes.

Montague, Zach. 2023. "Affirmative Action: Rejection of Affirmative Action Draws Strong Reactions From Right and Left." *New York Times*, June 29, sec. US. https:// www.nytimes.com/live/2023/06/29/us/affirmative-action-supreme-court.

Montanaro, Domenico. 2020. "Poll: Despite Record Turnout, 80 Million Americans Didn't Vote. Here's Why." *NPR*, December 15, sec. Politics. https://www.npr.org /2020/12/15/945031391/poll-despite-record-turnout-80-million-americans-didnt -vote-heres-why.

Moody-Adams, Michele. 2022. *Making Space for Justice: Social Movements, Collective Imagination, and Political Hope.* Columbia University Press.

Moore, Elena. 2024. "Biden Won Big with Young Voters. This Year, They Swung toward Trump in a Big Way." NPR, November 8, sec. 2024 Election. https://www .npr.org/2024/11/07/g-s1-33331/unpacking-the-2024-youth-vote-heres-what-we -know-so-far.

Moosapeta, Asheesh. 2023. "How Immigration and Multiculturalism Helped Shape Trudeau's New Cabinet." CIC News, August 6. https://www.cicnews.com/2023/08 /how-immigration-and-multiculturalism-helped-shape-trudeaus-new-cabinet-0836 590.html.

Morning Edition. 2022. "Purdue's Reputation for Affordability Results in Substantial Growth for the School." NPR, September 6. https://www.npr.org/2022/09/06

/1121201296/purdues-reputation-for-affordability-results-in-substantial-growth-for
-the-schoo.

Morton, Jennifer M. 2014. "Cultural Code-Switching: Straddling the Achievement
Gap." *Journal of Political Philosophy* 22 (3): 259–2581. https://doi.org/10.1111/jopp
.12019.

Morton, Jennifer. 2019. *Moving Up without Losing Your Way: The Ethical Costs of
Upward Mobility*. Princeton University Press.

Mujcic, Redzo, and Paul Frijters. 2021. "The Colour of a Free Ride." *The Economic
Journal* 131 (634): 970–999. https://doi.org/10.1093/ej/ueaa090.

Mulligan, Casey B., and Charles G. Hunter. 2003. "The Empirical Frequency of a Pivotal Vote." *Public Choice* 116 (1): 31–54. https://doi.org/10.1023/A:1024244329828.

Mummendey, Amélie, Thomas Kessler, Andreas Klink, and Rosemarie Mielke. 1999.
"Strategies to Cope with Negative Social Identity: Predictions by Social Identity
Theory and Relative Deprivation Theory." *Journal of Personality and Social Psychology*
76 (2): 229–245. https://doi.org/10.1037/0022-3514.76.2.229.

Munch-Jurisic, Ditte Marie. 2022. *Perpetrator Disgust: The Moral Limits of Gut Feelings*.
Oxford University Press.

Mutz, Diana C. 2018. "Status Threat, Not Economic Hardship, Explains the 2016
Presidential Vote." *Proceedings of the National Academy of Sciences* 115 (19). https://
doi.org/10.1073/pnas.1718155115.

Myers-Briggs Company. n.d. "Personality Assessment Inventory and Professional
Development." Accessed October 30, 2023. https://www.themyersbriggs.com/.

Nagel, Jennifer. 2015. "Effective Altruism and the Syrian Refugee Crisis: A Canadian Response." Daily Nous, November 25. https://dailynous.com/2015/11/25/phil
osophers-on-the-syrian-refugees/#nagel.

Nakate, Vanessa. 2021. *A Bigger Picture: My Fight to Bring a New African Voice to the
Climate Crisis*. Mariner Books.

National Association for the Advancement of Colored People. 2023. "Environment
& Climate Justice." https://naacp.org/know-issues/environmental-climate-justice.

National Association of Realtors. 2022. "US Homeownership Rate Experiences Largest Annual Increase on Record, Though Black Homeownership Remains Lower Than
a Decade Ago, NAR Analysis Finds." Posted February 22. https://www.nar.realtor
/newsroom/u-s-homeownership-rate-experiences-largest-annual-increase-on-record
-though-black-homeownership-remains-lower-than-decade-ago.

National Equity Atlas. n.d. "Car Access." Accessed January 4, 2024. https://nation
alequityatlas.org/indicators/Car_access#/.

National Geographic. n.d. "Permafrost." Accessed January 11, 2024. https://educa
tion.nationalgeographic.org/resource/permafrost.

National Geographic. 2023. "Humans Induce and Reduce Environmental Disasters,"
October 19. https://education.nationalgeographic.org/resource/humans-induce-and
-reduce-environmental-disasters.

Nefsky, Julia. 2017. "How You Can Help, Without Making a Difference." *Philosophical Studies* 174 (11): 2743–2767. https://doi.org/10.1007/s11098-016-0808-y.

Nelsen, Matthew D., and Christopher D. Petsko. 2021. "Race and White Rural
Consciousness." *Perspectives on Politics* 19 (4): 1205–1218. https://doi.org/10.1017
/S1537592721001948.

Nelson, Maggie. 2021. *On Freedom: Four Songs of Care and Constraint.* Graywolf Press.

Nelson, Robert K., LaDale Winling, Reagan Tobias, Cassandra Cogan, and Jared
Kimball. 2023. "Mapping Inequality: Redlining in New Deal America." University of
Richmond. https://dsl.richmond.edu/panorama/redlining/.

Nelson, William E. 2019. "The Shutdown: Drowning Government in the Bathtub."
The Conversation, February 12. http://theconversation.com/the-shutdown-drowning
-government-in-the-bathtub-111333.

Neufeld, Eleonore. 2022. "Psychological Essentialism and the Structure of Concepts." *Philosophy Compass* 17 (5): e12823. https://doi.org/10.1111/phc3.12823.

Newall, Mallory, and Sara Machi. 2020. "Why Don't People Vote?" Ipsos, December
15. https://www.ipsos.com/en-us/news-polls/medill-npr-nonvoters-2020.

Newkirk, Pamela. 2019. *Diversity, Inc.: The Failed Promise of a Billion-Dollar Business.*
Bold Type Books.

New York Preservation Archive Project. n.d. "Jane Jacobs." Accessed October 25,
2023. https://www.nypap.org/preservation-history/jane-jacobs/.

New York Times. 1858. "How We Poison Our Children." May 13, sec. Archives.
https://www.nytimes.com/1858/05/13/archives/how-we-poison-our-children.html.

New York Times. 1894. "Weeding Out Bad Sculpture." March 13. https://timesma
chine.nytimes.com/timesmachine/1894/03/13/106096693.pdf.

New York Times. 1931. "Nathan Straus Dies; Nation Mourns Loss of Philanthro-
pist," January 12. https://timesmachine.nytimes.com/timesmachine/1931/01/12
/102206984.pdf?pdf_redirect=true&ip=0.

Nielsen, Kristian S., Kimberly A. Nicholas, Felix Creutzig, Thomas Dietz, and Paul
C. Stern. 2021. "The Role of High-Socioeconomic-Status People in Locking in or
Rapidly Reducing Energy-Driven Greenhouse Gas Emissions." *Nature Energy* 6 (11):
1011–1116. https://doi.org/10.1038/s41560-021-00900-y.

Nielsen, Mark, and Keyan Tomaselli. 2010. "Overimitation in Kalahari Bushman Children and the Origins of Human Cultural Cognition." *Psychological Science* 21 (5): 729–736. https://doi.org/10.1177/0956797610368808.

Niu, Yanzhuo, and B. Bradford Brown. 2023. "Satisfaction and Closeness in Same- and Cross-National College Roommate Relationships: What Similarity Matters?" *International Journal of Intercultural Relations* 95 (July): 101813. https://doi.org/10.1016/j.ijintrel.2023.101813.

Noah, Timothy. 2009. "The Medicare-Isn't-Government Meme." *Slate*, August 5. https://slate.com/news-and-politics/2009/08/help-slate-track-the-medicare-isn-t-government-meme.html.

Nolan, Jessica M. 2010. "'An Inconvenient Truth' Increases Knowledge, Concern, and Willingness to Reduce Greenhouse Gases." *Environment and Behavior* 42 (5): 643–658. https://doi.org/10.1177/0013916509357696.

Nolen, Stephanie, and Natalija Gormalova. 2023. "The Gamble: Can Genetically Modified Mosquitoes End Disease?" *New York Times*, September 29, sec. Health. https://www.nytimes.com/2023/09/29/health/mosquitoes-genetic-engineering.html.

Nordell, Jessica. 2017. "Is This How Discrimination Ends? A New Approach to Implicit Bias." *Atlantic*, May 7. https://www.theatlantic.com/science/archive/2017/05/unconscious-bias-training/525405/.

Norlock, Kathryn J. 2010. "Forgivingness, Pessimism, and Environmental Citizenship." *Journal of Agricultural and Environmental Ethics* 23 (1): 29–42. https://doi.org/10.1007/s10806-009-9182-5.

North, Anna. 2019. "Me Too Movement Increased Reporting of Sex Crimes, Study Finds." *Vox*, December 11. https://www.vox.com/2019/12/11/21003592/me-too-movement-sexual-assault-crimes-reporting.

North, Douglass C. 1990. *Institutions, Institutional Change and Economic Performance*. Cambridge University Press.

North, Douglass C., and Robert P. Thomas. 1973. *The Rise of the Western World: A New Economic History*. Cambridge University Press.

Norton, Peter D. 2007. "Street Rivals: Jaywalking and the Invention of the Motor Age Street." *Technology and Culture* 48 (2): 331–359.

Norton, Peter D. 2008. *Fighting Traffic: The Dawn of the Motor Age in the American City*. MIT Press.

Norwood, Candice. 2021. "Racial Bias Trainings Surged After George Floyd's Death. A Year Later, Experts Are Still Waiting for 'Bold' Change." PBS NewsHour, May 25. https://www.pbs.org/newshour/nation/racial-bias-trainings-surged-after-george-floyds-death-a-year-later-experts-are-still-waiting-for-bold-change.

Nowicki, Jacqueline M. 2022. "K-12 Education: Student Population Has Significantly Diversified, but Many Schools Remain Divided along Racial, Ethnic, and Economic Lines. Report to the Chairman, Committee on Education and Labor, House of Representatives." GAO-22–104737. US Government Accountability Office. https://eric.ed.gov/?id=ED624690.

Noyes, Alexander, Frank C. Keil, Yarrow Dunham, and Katherine Ritchie. 2023. "Same People, Different Group: Social Structures Are a Central Component of Group Concepts." *Cognition* 240 (November): 105567. https://doi.org/10.1016/j.cognition.2023.105567.

Numbeo. n.d.a. "Pollution Comparison Between Stockholm, Sweden and Los Angeles, CA, United States." Accessed October 25, 2023. https://www.numbeo.com/pollution/compare_cities.jsp?country1=Sweden&city1=Stockholm&country2=United+States&city2=Los+Angeles%2C+CA.

Numbeo. n.d.b. "Traffic Comparison Between Stockholm, Sweden And Copenhagen, Denmark." Accessed October 25, 2023. https://www.numbeo.com/traffic/compare_cities.jsp?country1=Sweden&city1=Stockholm&country2=Denmark&city2=Copenhagen.

Nuño, Lidia E., Shawn L. Hill, Edward R. Maguire, and Howard Giles. 2023. "Experiencing VOICES: Police and Public Reactions to an Intergroup Communication Intervention." *Police Practice and Research* 24 (6): 631–645. https://doi.org/10.1080/15614263.2022.2147069.

Nyborg, Karine, John M. Anderies, Astrid Dannenberg, et al. 2016. "Social Norms as Solutions." *Science* 354 (6308): 42–43. https://doi.org/10.1126/science.aaf8317.

Obama, Barack. 2020. *A Promised Land.* Crown.

O'Brien, Ed. 2022. "Losing Sight of Piecemeal Progress: People Lump and Dismiss Improvement Efforts That Fall Short of Categorical Change—Despite Improving." *Psychological Science* 33 (8): 1278–1299. https://doi.org/10.1177/09567976221075302.

O'Connor, Anahad. 2015. "Coca-Cola Funds Scientists Who Shift Blame for Obesity Away from Bad Diets." *New York Times*, August 9, sec. Health. https://archive.nytimes.com/well.blogs.nytimes.com/2015/08/09/coca-cola-funds-scientists-who-shift-blame-for-obesity-away-from-bad-diets/.

Odstel, Dica. 2013. "Jimi Hendrix Guitar Feedback." March 5, 2013. YouTube, 1:42. https://www.youtube.com/watch?v=53JpbrxM7O0.

Office of Energy Efficiency and Renewable Energy. n.d. "Clean Energy Job Creation and Growth." Accessed December 31, 2023. https://www.energy.gov/eere/clean-energy-job-creation-and-growth.

Okrent, Daniel. 2011. *Last Call: The Rise and Fall of Prohibition.* Scribner.

Olasov, Ian. 2016. "Offensive Political Dog Whistles: You Know Them When You Hear Them. Or Do You?" *Vox*, November 7. https://www.vox.com/the-big-idea/2016/11/7/13549154/dog-whistles-campaign-racism.

Olson, Mancur. 1971. *The Logic of Collective Action: Public Goods and the Theory of Groups, With a New Preface and Appendix*. Revised ed. Harvard University Press.

O'Neill, Aaron. 2022. "United States: Child Mortality Rate 1800–2020." Statista, June 21. https://www.statista.com/statistics/1041693/united-states-all-time-child-mortality-rate/.

Our World in Data. 2024. "CO_2 and Greenhouse Gas Emissions Data Explorer." https://ourworldindata.org/explorers/co2.

Ortiz, L. M. 2021. "Could France's Approach to Combating NIMBYism Work in the United States?" Plantizen, November 19. https://www.planetizen.com/news/2021/11/115325-could-frances-approach-combating-nimbyism-work-united-states.

Ortiz-Ospina, Esteban, and Max Roser. 2016. "Trust." Our World in Data. https://ourworldindata.org/trust.

Osborn, Catherine. 2022. "How Latin American Feminists Won Abortion Rights." *Foreign Policy*, May 6. https://foreignpolicy.com/2022/05/06/mexico-argentina-brazil-abortion-united-states-roe-wade-green-tide/.

Ostrower, Gary B. 1979. *Collective Insecurity: The United States and the League of Nations During the Early Thirties*. Associated University Pr.

Otto, Ilona M., Jonathan F. Donges, Roger Cremades, et al. 2020. "Social Tipping Dynamics for Stabilizing Earth's Climate by 2050." *Proceedings of the National Academy of Sciences* 117 (5): 2354–2365. https://doi.org/10.1073/pnas.1900577117.

Overly, Steven. 2021. "This Government Loan Program Helped Tesla at a Critical Time. Trump Wants to Cut It." *Washington Post*, December 5. https://www.washingtonpost.com/news/innovations/wp/2017/03/16/this-government-loan-program-helped-tesla-at-a-critical-time-trump-wants-to-cut-it/.

Pager, Devah. 2003. "The Mark of a Criminal Record." *American Journal of Sociology* 108 (5): 937–975. https://doi.org/10.1086/374403.

Pager, Devah, Bruce Western, and Bart Bonikowski. 2009. "Discrimination in a Low-Wage Labor Market: A Field Experiment." *American Sociological Review* 74 (5): 777–799. https://doi.org/10.1177/000312240907400505.

Pager, Devah, Bruce Western, and Naomi Sugie. 2009. "Sequencing Disadvantage: Barriers to Employment Facing Young Black and White Men with Criminal Records." *Annals of the American Academy of Political and Social Science* 623 (1): 195–213. https://doi.org/10.1177/0002716208330793.

Paikeday, Tina Shah. 2019. "A Leader's Guide: Finding and Keeping Your Next Chief Diversity Officer." Russell Reynolds Associates, March 1. https://www.russellreyn olds.com/en/insights/reports-surveys/a-leaders-guide-finding-and-keeping-your -next-chief-diversity-officer.

Palm, Risa, Toby Bolsen, and Justin T. Kingsland. 2020. "'Don't Tell Me What to Do': Resistance to Climate Change Messages Suggesting Behavior Changes." *Weather, Climate, and Society* 12 (4): 827–835. https://doi.org/10.1175/WCAS-D-19-0141.1.

Paluck, Elizabeth Levy, Roni Porat, Chelsey S. Clark, and Donald P. Green. 2021. "Prejudice Reduction: Progress and Challenges." *Annual Review of Psychology* 72 (1): 533–560. https://doi.org/10.1146/annurev-psych-071620-030619.

Paluck, Elizabeth Levy, Hana Shepherd, and Peter M. Aronow. 2016. "Changing Climates of Conflict: A Social Network Experiment in 56 Schools." *Proceedings of the National Academy of Sciences of the United States of America* 113 (3): 566–571. https:// doi.org/10.1073/pnas.1514483113.

Pan, J. C. 2020. "Workplace 'Anti-Racism Trainings' Aren't Helping." Jacobin, September 9. https://jacobin.com/2020/09/workplace-anti-racism-trainings-trump -corporate-america.

Panagopoulos, Costas. 2010. "Affect, Social Pressure and Prosocial Motivation: Field Experimental Evidence of the Mobilizing Effects of Pride, Shame and Publi-cizing Voting Behavior." *Political Behavior* 32 (3): 369–886. https://doi.org/10.1007 /s11109-010-9114-0.

Pangambam, S. 2018. "The Great Migration and the Power of a Single Decision: Isabel Wilkerson (Full Transcript)." *Singju Post*, April 12. https://singjupost.com/the -great-migration-and-the-power-of-a-single-decision-isabel-wilkerson-full-transcript /?singlepage=1.

Parfit, Derek. 1984. *Reasons and Persons*. Oxford University Press.

Parker, Kim, Juliana Menasce Horowitz, Ruth Igielnik, J. Baxter Oliphant, and Anna Brown. 2017. "America's Complex Relationship with Guns." Pew Research Center, June 22. https://www.pewresearch.org/social-trends/2017/06/22/americas-complex -relationship-with-guns/.

Parkinson, Justin. 2016. "The Significance of Sarah Baartman." *BBC News*, January 7, sec. Magazine. https://www.bbc.com/news/magazine-35240987.

Paulson, Steve. "'I Am Because We Are': The African Philosophy of Ubuntu." To the Best of Our Knowledge. September 30. https://www.ttbook.org/interview/i-am -because-we-are-african-philosophy-ubuntu.

Payne, B. Keith, and Jason W. Hannay. 2021. "Implicit Bias Reflects Systemic Racism." *Trends in Cognitive Sciences* 25 (11): 927–936. https://doi.org/10.1016/j.tics .2021.08.001.

Payne, B. Keith, Jon A. Krosnick, Josh Pasek, Yphtach Lelkes, Omair Akhtar, and Trevor Tompson. 2010. "Implicit and Explicit Prejudice in the 2008 American Presidential Election." *Journal of Experimental Social Psychology* 46 (2): 367–374. https://doi.org/10.1016/j.jesp.2009.11.001.

Payne, B. Keith, and Heidi A. Vuletich. 2018. "Policy Insights From Advances in Implicit Bias Research." *Policy Insights from the Behavioral and Brain Sciences* 5 (1): 49–56. https://doi.org/10.1177/2372732217746190.

Payne, B. Keith, Heidi A. Vuletich, and Jazmin L. Brown-Iannuzzi. 2019. "Historical Roots of Implicit Bias in Slavery." *Proceedings of the National Academy of Sciences* 116 (24): 11693–11698. https://doi.org/10.1073/pnas.1818816116.

Pearson, Adam R., Jonathon P. Schuldt, Rainer Romero-Canyas, Matthew T. Ballew, and Dylan Larson-Konar. 2018. "Diverse Segments of the US Public Underestimate the Environmental Concerns of Minority and Low-Income Americans." *Proceedings of the National Academy of Sciences* 115 (49): 12429–12434. https://doi.org/10.1073/pnas.1804698115.

Peck, Raoul, dir. 2021. *Exterminate All the Brutes*. HBO Documentary Films, Velvet Film. https://www.hbo.com/exterminate-all-the-brutes.

Pennycook, Gordon. 2023. "A Framework for Understanding Reasoning Errors: From Fake News to Climate Change and Beyond." *Advances in Experimental Social Psychology* 67: 131–208. https://doi.org/10.1016/bs.aesp.2022.11.003.

Pennycook, Gordon, James Allan Cheyne, Nathaniel Barr, Derek J. Koehler, and Jonathan A. Fugelsang. 2015. "On the Reception and Detection of Pseudo-Profound Bullshit." *Judgment and Decision Making* 10 (6): 549–563. https://doi.org/10.1017/S1930297500006999.

Pennycook, Gordon, and David G. Rand. 2019. "Lazy, Not Biased: Susceptibility to Partisan Fake News Is Better Explained by Lack of Reasoning than by Motivated Reasoning." *Cognition* 188 (July): 39–50. https://doi.org/10.1016/j.cognition.2018.06.011.

Pepin, Joanna, and David Cotter. 2017. "Trending Towards Traditionalism? Changes in Youths' Gender Ideology." Council on Contemporary Families, March 31.

Perry, Andre, Jonathan Rothwell, and David Harshbarger. 2018. "The Devaluation of Assets in Black Neighborhoods." Brookings, November 27. https://www.brookings.edu/articles/devaluation-of-assets-in-black-neighborhoods/.

Peters, Adele. 2020. "These Are the Companies Leading the Trillion Trees Effort in the US." Fast Company, August 31. https://www.fastcompany.com/90544563/these-are-the-companies-leading-the-trillion-trees-effort-in-the-u-s.

Peterson, B. Bailie. 2021. "Supporting First-Generation Philosophers at Every Level." *APA Newsletter on Feminism and Philosophy* 20 (3): 38–43.

Pettigrew, Thomas F. 1998. "Intergroup Contact Theory." *Annual Review of Psychology* 49 (1): 65–85. https://doi.org/10.1146/annurev.psych.49.1.65.

Pettigrew, Thomas F. 2018. "The Emergence of Contextual Social Psychology." *Personality and Social Psychology Bulletin* 44 (7): 963–971. https://doi.org/10.1177/014 6167218756033.

Pfrimmer, David. 2019. "The Story behind the World's First Private Refugee Sponsorship Program." *The Conversation*, December 8. http://theconversation.com/the -story-behind-the-worlds-first-private-refugee-sponsorship-program-126257.

Phelan, Matthew. 2019. "Who Said 'History Is Written by the Victors'? The Origins of the Quote." *Slate*, November 26. https://slate.com/culture/2019/11/history-is-written -by-the-victors-quote-origin.html.

Philippe, Sébastien, Susan Alzner, Gilbert P. Compo, Mason Grimshaw, and Megan Smith. 2023. "Fallout from US Atmospheric Nuclear Tests in New Mexico and Nevada (1945–1962)." Working paper. https://doi.org/10.48550/arXiv.2307.11040.

Pichardo, Eduardo J., John T. Jost, and Verónica Benet-Martínez. 2022. "Internalization of Inferiority and Colonial System Justification: The Case of Puerto Rico." *Journal of Social Issues* 78 (1): 79–106. https://doi.org/10.1111/josi.12437.

Pierson, Emma, Camelia Simoiu, Jan Overgoor, et al. 2020. "A Large-Scale Analysis of Racial Disparities in Police Stops across the United States." *Nature Human Behaviour* 4 (7): 736–745. https://doi.org/10.1038/s41562-020-0858-1.

Piper, Kelsey. 2022a. "Stop Telling Kids That Climate Change Will Destroy Their World." *Vox*, June 8. https://www.vox.com/23158406/climate-change-tell-kids-wont -destroy-world.

Piper, Kelsey. 2022b. "Why Popularism Is Good—to a Point." *Vox*, April 27. https:// www.vox.com/future-perfect/23041412/popularism-election-voters.

Piscopo, Jennifer M. 2020. "When Do Quotas in Politics Work? Latin America Offers Lessons." *Americas Quarterly*, October 22. https://americasquarterly.org/article/when -do-quotas-in-politics-work-latin-america-offers-lessons/.

Pittenger, David J. 1993. "The Utility of the Myers-Briggs Type Indicator." *Review of Educational Research* 63 (4): 467–488. https://doi.org/10.3102/00346543063004467.

Plaut, Victoria C. 2010. "Diversity Science: Why and How Difference Makes a Difference." *Psychological Inquiry* 21 (2): 77–99. https://doi.org/10.1080/1047840 1003676501.

Post, Charles. 2016. "The New Deal and the Popular Front." *International Socialist Review* (108). https://isreview.org/issue/108/new-deal-and-popular-front/index.html.

Powell, Rachell. 2023. "Social Norms and Superorganisms." *Biology & Philosophy* 38 (3): 21. https://doi.org/10.1007/s10539-023-09909-x.

Pratto, Felicia, Jim Sidanius, Lisa M. Stallworth, and Bertram F. Malle. 1994. "Social Dominance Orientation: A Personality Variable Predicting Social and Political Attitudes." *Journal of Personality and Social Psychology* 67 (4): 741–763. https://doi.org /10.1037/0022-3514.67.4.741.

Proios, John. 2021. "Ethical Narratives and Oppositional Consciousness." Edited by Arianna Falbo and Heather Stewart. *APA Newsletter on Feminism and Philosophy* 20 (3): 11–15.

ProPublica. 2017. "Lost Mothers." https://www.propublica.org/series/lost-mothers.

Puddifoot, Katherine. 2021. *How Stereotypes Deceive Us*. Oxford University Press.

Purdue University Global Academic Success Center. 2024. "Hasty Generalizations and Other Logical Fallacies." https://purdueglobalwriting.center/hasty-generalizations -and-other-logical-fallacies/.

Purnell, Christopher. 2013. *Overimitation and Conformity—Lyons et al. (2007)*. November 14, 2013. YouTube, 0:49. https://www.youtube.com/watch?v=20Smx_nD9cw.

Putnam, Robert D. 2000. *Bowling Alone: The Collapse and Revival of American Community*. Simon & Schuster.

Quote Investigator. 2017. "Never Doubt That a Small Group of Thoughtful, Committed Citizens Can Change the World; Indeed, It's the Only Thing That Ever Has." Posted November 12. https://quoteinvestigator.com/2017/11/12/change-world/.

Rabin, Roni C. 2022. "Medical Care Alone Won't Halt the Spread of Diabetes, Scientists Say." *New York Times*, October 5, sec. Health. https://www.nytimes.com/2022 /10/05/health/diabetes-prevention-diet.html.

Race-Class Academy. 2022. "Race-Class Academy." https://race-class-academy.com.

Rahmanan, Anna. 2023. "We Don't All Wear Black At Funerals. Here's What Mourners Wear Across Cultures." *HuffPost*, April 11. https://www.huffpost.com/entry /wearing-black-at-funerals_l_640a12fee4b0653e296a4d35.

Ramos, Miguel R., Sandy Schumann, and Miles Hewstone. 2022. "The Role of Short-Term and Longer Term Immigration Trends on Voting for Populist Radical Right Parties in Europe." *Social Psychological and Personality Science* 13 (4): 816–826. https:// doi.org/10.1177/19485506211043681.

Ramzy, Austin. 2017. "McCain's Vote Provides Dramatic Moment in 7-Year Battle Over Obamacare." *New York Times*, July 28, sec. US. https://www.nytimes.com/2017 /07/28/us/politics/john-mccain-vote-trump-obamacare.html.

Ray, Michael. 2023. "Sandy Hook Elementary School Shooting." *Britannica*. https:// www.britannica.com/event/Sandy-Hook-Elementary-School-shooting.

Ray, Rashawn. 2020. "How Can We Enhance Police Accountability in the United States?" Brookings, August 5. https://www.brookings.edu/articles/how-can-we-enhance-police-accountability-in-the-united-states/.

Reaves, Brian. 2015. "Local Police Departments, 2013: Personnel, Policies, and Practices." Bureau of Justice Statistics, May. https://bjs.ojp.gov/library/publications/local-police-departments-2013-personnel-policies-and-practices.

Reed, Julian A., and D. Allen Phillips. 2005. "Relationships Between Physical Activity and the Proximity of Exercise Facilities and Home Exercise Equipment Used by Undergraduate University Students." *Journal of American College Health* 53 (6): 285–290. https://doi.org/10.3200/JACH.53.6.285-290.

Reed-Sandoval, Amy. 2020. *Socially Undocumented: Identity and Immigration Justice.* Oxford University Press.

Rees, Williams E., and Mathis Wackernagel. 1996. *Our Ecological Footprint: Reducing Human Impact on the Earth.* New Catalyst Books.

Reeves, Richard. 2022. *Of Boys and Men: Why the Modern Male Is Struggling, Why It Matters, and What to Do About It.* Brookings Institution Press. https://www.barnesandnoble.com/w/of-boys-and-men-richard-v-reeves/1141579690.

Reiland, Indrek. 2023. "Regulative Rules: A Distinctive Normative Kind." *Philosophy and Phenomenological Research* 8 (3): 772–791. https://doi.org/10.1111/phpr.13008.

Reisenwitz, Cathy. 2023. "The ACAB Case Against Proactive Policing." Medium, June 28. https://medium.com/@cathyreisenwitz/the-acab-case-against-proactive-policing-ad44717da2de.

Renger, Daniela, Silke Eschert, Mimke L. Teichgräber, and Sophus Renger. 2020. "Internalized Equality and Protest Against Injustice: The Role of Disadvantaged Group Members' Self-Respect in Collective Action Tendencies." *European Journal of Social Psychology* 50 (3): 547–560. https://doi.org/10.1002/ejsp.2637.

Research and Markets LTD. 2021. "Diversity and Inclusion (D&I)—Global Strategic Business Report." https://www.researchandmarkets.com/reports/5519706/diversity-and-inclusion-dandi-global-strategic.

Responsibility.org. 2022. "Drunk Driving Fatality Statistics." https://www.responsibility.org/alcohol-statistics/drunk-driving-statistics/drunk-driving-fatality-statistics/.

Reuters. 2022. "Human Activity Is Leading to More Disasters-UN Report," April 25, sec. Environment. https://www.reuters.com/business/environment/human-activity-is-leading-more-disasters-un-report-2022-04-25/.

Richard, Lawrence. 2023. "Biden Appoints Ed Siskel, Who Shielded Obama from GOP's Benghazi Investigation, as New White House Counsel." Fox News, August 22.

https://www.foxnews.com/politics/biden-appoints-ed-siskel-shielded-obama-gops
-benghazi-investigation-new-white-house-counsel.

Richerson, Peter J., and Robert Boyd. 2005. *Not by Genes Alone: How Culture Transformed Human Evolution*. University of Chicago Press.

richmond33. 2018. "Copenhagen, Strøget. 1960 and 2016: From Ruled by Cars to a City for People." Reddit post in r/Europe, September 1. www.reddit.com/r/europe/comments/9c2v3i/copenhagen_strøget_1960_and_2016_from_ruled_by/.

Riofrancos, Thea. 2020. *Resource Radicals: From Petro-Nationalism to Post-Extractivism in Ecuador*. Duke University Press Books.

Ritchie, Hannah. 2019. "Who Has Contributed Most to Global CO2 Emissions?" Our World in Data, October 1. https://ourworldindata.org/contributed-most-global-co2.

Rittel, Horst W. J., and Melvin M. Webber. 1973. "Dilemmas in a General Theory of Planning." *Policy Sciences* 4 (2): 155–169.

Robbins, Christopher. 2018. "Robert Caro Wonders What New York Is Going To Become." Gothamist, May 2. https://gothamist.com/news/robert-caro-wonders-what-new-york-is-going-to-become.

Roberts, David. 2013. "What Theda Skocpol Gets Right About the Cap-and-Trade Fight." Grist, January 15. https://grist.org/climate-energy/what-theda-skocpol-gets-right-about-the-cap-and-trade-fight/.

Roberts, David. 2015. "Are Trump Supporters Driven by Economic Anxiety or Racial Resentment? Yes." *Vox*, December 30. https://www.vox.com/2015/12/30/10690360/racism-economic-anxiety-trump.

Roberts, David. 2020. "Social Tipping Points Are the Only Hope for the Climate." *Vox*, January 29. https://www.vox.com/energy-and-environment/2020/1/29/21083250/climate-change-social-tipping-points.

Roberts, Steven O., Susan A. Gelman, and Arnold K. Ho. 2017. "So It Is, So It Shall Be: Group Regularities License Children's Prescriptive Judgments." *Cognitive Science* 41 (S3): 576–600. https://doi.org/10.1111/cogs.12443.

Robinson, Cedric J. 2005. *Black Marxism: The Making of the Black Radical Tradition*. University of North Carolina Press.

Rodia, Tina. 2022. "The Constitution Is the Crisis: Jamelle Bouie on the State of the US." SNF Paideia Program, September 2. http://snfpaideia.upenn.edu/news/the-constitution-is-the-crisis-jamelle-bouie-on-the-state-of-the-u-s/.

Romero, Simon, and Emiliano Rodríguez Mega. 2023. "Mexico's Supreme Court Decriminalizes Abortion Nationwide." *New York Times*, September 6, sec. World.

https://www.nytimes.com/2023/09/06/world/americas/mexico-abortion-decrimi
nalize-supreme-court.html.

Ronald Reagan Presidential Foundation and Institute. n.d. "News Conference—I'm
Here to Help." Accessed November 15, 2023. https://www.reaganfoundation.org
/ronald-reagan/reagan-quotes-speeches/news-conference-1/.

Rosenberg, Zach. 2009. "NIMBY Won't Stop California High-Speed Rail." *Wired*,
October. https://www.wired.com/2009/10/nimby-chsr/.

Roser, Max. 2023. "Mortality in the Past: Every Second Child Died." Our World in
Data, April 11. https://ourworldindata.org/child-mortality-in-the-past.

Roser, Max. 2024. "The Short History of Global Living Conditions and Why It Matters That We Know It." Our World in Data. https://ourworldindata.org/a-history-of
-global-living-conditions.

Ross, Lauren N. 2023. "What Is Social Structural Explanation? A Causal Account."
Noûs 58 (1): 163–179. https://doi.org/10.1111/nous.12446.

Rothstein, Richard. 2017. *The Color of Law: A Forgotten History of How Our Government
Segregated America*. Liveright Publishing.

Rouse, Cecilia, Lise Barrow, Kevin Rinz, and Kevin Soltas. 2021. "The Economic Benefits of Extending Permanent Legal Status to Unauthorized Immigrants." The White
House, September 17. https://www.whitehouse.gov/cea/written-materials/2021/09
/17/the-economic-benefits-of-extending-permanent-legal-status-to-unauthorized
-immigrants/.

Rullo, Marika, Emilio Paolo Visintin, Stella Milani, Alessandra Romano, and Loretta
Fabbri. 2022. "Stay Humble and Enjoy Diversity: The Interplay Between Intergroup
Contact and Cultural Humility on Prejudice." *International Journal of Intercultural
Relations* 87 (March): 169–182. https://doi.org/10.1016/j.ijintrel.2022.02.003.

Runciman, Walter G. 1966. *Relative Deprivation and Social Justice: A Study of Attitudes
to Social Inequality in Twentieth-Century England*. Routledge.

Rüsch, Nicolas, and Markus Kösters. 2021. "Honest, Open, Proud to Support Dis-
closure Decisions and to Decrease Stigma's Impact Among People with Mental Ill-
ness: Conceptual Review and Meta-Analysis of Program Efficacy." *Social Psychiatry
and Psychiatric Epidemiology* 56 (9): 1513–1526. https://doi.org/10.1007/s00127-021
-02076-y.

Russo, Anthony, and Joe Russo, dirs. 2016. *Captain America: Civil War*. Marvel Stu-
dios, Vita-Ray Dutch Productions (III), Studio Babelsberg.

Saletan, William. 2007. "Same Sex." *Slate*, August 30. https://slate.com/technology
/2007/08/larry-craig-s-anti-gay-hypocrisy.html.

Salvi, Carola, Paola Iannello, Alice Cancer, Samuel E. Cooper, Mason McClay, Joseph E. Dunsmoor, and Alessandro Antonietti. 2023. "Does Social Rigidity Predict Cognitive Rigidity? Profiles of Socio-Cognitive Polarization." *Psychological Research* 87 (8): 2533–2547. https://doi.org/10.1007/s00426-023-01832-w.

Samet, Jerry, and Deborah Zaitchik. 2022. "Innateness and Contemporary Theories of Cognition." *Stanford Encyclopedia of Philosophy.* https://plato.stanford.edu/archives/sum2022/entries/innateness-cognition/.

Samuels, Brett. 2020. "Trump Announces the US Will Join 1 Trillion Tree Initiative." *The Hill*, January 21. https://thehill.com/homenews/administration/479087-trump-announces-the-us-will-join-1-trillion-tree-initiative/.

Sandberg, Sheryl. 2013. *Lean In: Women, Work, and the Will to Lead.* Knopf.

Sanders, Bernie. n.d. "Racial Justice." Bernie Sanders official website. Accessed January 23, 2024. https://berniesanders.com/issues/racial-justice/.

Santhanagopalan, Radhika, Jasmine M. DeJesus, Ramya S. Moorthy, and Katherine D. Kinzler. 2021. "Nationality Cognition in India: Social Category Information Impacts Children's Judgments of People and Their National Identity." *Cognitive Development* 57 (January): 100990. https://doi.org/10.1016/j.cogdev.2020.100990.

Santos, Laurie, host. 2004. *The Happiness Lab with Dr. Laurie Santos.* "Why Our Brains Don't Fear Climate Change Enough." Podcast, January 2. https://www.pushkin.fm/podcasts/the-happiness-lab-with-dr-laurie-santos/why-our-brains-dont-fear-climate-change-enough.

Sarkissian, Hagop. 2010. "Minor Tweaks, Major Payoffs: The Problems and Promise of Situationism in Moral Philosophy." *Philosopher's Imprint* 10 (9): 1–15.

Sarkissian, Hagop. 2018. "Confucius and the Superorganism." In *The Oneness Hypothesis*, edited by Philip Ivanhoe, Owen Flanagan, Victoria Harrison, Eric Schwitzgebel, and Hagop Sarkissian. Columbia University Press. https://doi.org/10.7312/ivan18298-017.

Saul, Jennifer M. 2017. "Racial Figleaves, the Shifting Boundaries of the Permissible, and the Rise of Donald Trump." *Philosophical Topics* 45 (2): 97–116.

Saul, Jennifer M. 2018. "(How) Should We Tell Implicit Bias Stories?" *Disputatio* 10 (50): 217–244. https://doi.org/10.2478/disp-2018-0014.

Saul, Jennifer M. 2024. *Dogwhistles and Figleaves: How Manipulative Language Spreads Racism and Falsehood.* Oxford University Press.

Savranskaya, Svetlana V. 2005. "New Sources on the Role of Soviet Submarines in the Cuban Missile Crisis." *Journal of Strategic Studies* 28 (2): 233–259. https://doi.org/10.1080/01402390500088312.

Scalzi, John. 2012. "Straight White Male: The Lowest Difficulty Setting There Is." *Whatever*, May 15. https://whatever.scalzi.com/2012/05/15/straight-white-male-the-lowest-difficulty-setting-there-is/.

Schaeffer, Katherine. 2019. "Share of Americans Who Favor Stricter Gun Laws Has Increased since 2017." Pew Research Center, October 16. https://www.pewresearch.org/short-reads/2019/10/16/share-of-americans-who-favor-stricter-gun-laws-has-increased-since-2017/.

Scharrer, Erica, and Srividya Ramasubramanian. 2015. "Intervening in the Media's Influence on Stereotypes of Race and Ethnicity: The Role of Media Literacy Education." *Journal of Social Issues* 71 (1): 171–185. https://doi.org/10.1111/josi.12103.

Scharrer, Erica, Srividya Ramasubramanian, and Omotayo Banjo. 2022. "Media, Diversity, and Representation in the US: A Review of the Quantitative Research Literature on Media Content and Effects." *Journal of Broadcasting & Electronic Media* 66 (4): 723–749. https://doi.org/10.1080/08838151.2022.2138890.

Scheiber, Noam, Farah Stockman, and J. David Goodman. 2020. "How Police Unions Became Such Powerful Opponents to Reform Efforts." *New York Times*, June 6, sec. US. https://www.nytimes.com/2020/06/06/us/police-unions-minneapolis-kroll.html.

Schelling, Tucmas C. 1969. "Models of Segregation." *American Economic Review* 59 (2): 488–493.

Schiappa, Edward, Peter B. Gregg, and Dean E. Hewes. 2006. "Can One TV Show Make a Difference? Will & Grace and the Parasocial Contact Hypothesis." *Journal of Homosexuality* 51 (4): 15–37. https://doi.org/10.1300/J082v51n04_02.

Schleifer, Theodore. 2020. "Marc Benioff Picks a New Fight with Silicon Valley—over Trees." *Vox*, January 21. https://www.vox.com/recode/2020/1/21/21075804/marc-benioff-trees-silicon-valley-donald-trump-davos.

Schmidt, Marco F. H., Lucas P. Butler, Julia Heinz, and Michael Tomasello. 2016. "Young Children See a Single Action and Infer a Social Norm: Promiscuous Normativity in 3-Year-Olds." *Psychological Science* 27 (10): 1360–1370. https://doi.org/10.1177/0956797616661182.

Schwarz, Norbert. 2023. "Humility in Inquiry." *Journal of Positive Psychology* 18 (2): 267–270. https://doi.org/10.1080/17439760.2022.2155225.

Schwitzgebel, Eric, Bradford Cokelet, and Peter Singer. 2020. "Do Ethics Classes Influence Student Behavior? Case Study: Teaching the Ethics of Eating Meat." *Cognition* 203 (October): 104397. https://doi.org/10.1016/j.cognition.2020.104397.

Schwitzgebel, Eric, Bradford Cokelet, and Peter Singer. 2023. "Students Eat Less Meat After Studying Meat Ethics." *Review of Philosophy and Psychology* 14 (1): 113–138. https://doi.org/10.1007/s13164-021-00583-0.

Scott, Dylan. 2024. "How the World Has Radically Cut Child Deaths, in One Chart." *Vox*, March 15. https://www.vox.com/future-perfect/24100883/child-mortality-rate-worldwide-united-nations.

Seaside Institute. 2022. "Seaside Institute to Honor 2023 Seaside Prize Winner Donald Shoup." https://seasidefl.com/news/seaside-institute-to-honor-2023-seaside-prize-winner-donald-shoup.

Seattle Civil Rights and Labor History Project. n.d. "Racial Restrictive Covenants." Accessed October 23, 2023. https://depts.washington.edu/civilr/covenants.htm.

Selig, Kate, and Emily Guskin. 2023. "You're Doing It Wrong: Recycling and Other Myths about Tackling Climate Change." *Washington Post*, August 30. https://www.washingtonpost.com/climate-solutions/2023/08/28/climate-action-poll/.

Selinger, Evan. 2012. "The Philosophy of the Technology of the Gun." *Atlantic*, July 23. https://www.theatlantic.com/technology/archive/2012/07/the-philosophy-of-the-technology-of-the-gun/260220/.

Semuels, Alana. 2021. "The US Is Increasingly Diverse, So Why Is Segregation Getting Worse?" *Time*, June 21. https://time.com/6074243/segregation-america-increasing/.

Senator Scott Wiener. 2023. "Governor Signs Senator Wiener's Landmark Housing Bills." https://sd11.senate.ca.gov/news/20231011-governor-signs-senator-wiener%E2%80%99s-landmark-housing-bills%C2%A0.

Sengupta, Nikhil K., Nils K. Reimer, Chris G. Sibley, and Fiona Kate Barlow. 2023. "Does Intergroup Contact Foster Solidarity with the Disadvantaged? A Longitudinal Analysis Across 7 Years." *American Psychologist* 78 (6): 750–760. https://doi.org/10.1037/amp0001079.

Serafini, Paula. 2020. "'A Rapist in Your Path': Transnational Feminist Protest and Why (and How) Performance Matters." *European Journal of Cultural Studies* 23 (2): 290–295. https://doi.org/10.1177/1367549420912748.

Setiya, Kieran. 2022. "The New Moral Mathematics." *Boston Review*, August 15. https://www.bostonreview.net/articles/the-new-moral-mathematics/.

Setman, S. and Kelly, D. 2021. "Socializing Willpower: Resolve from the Outside In." *Behavioral and Brain Sciences* 44: E53. https://doi.org/10.1017/S0140525X20001065.

Shamir, Ronen. 2008. "The Age of Responsibilization: On Market-Embedded Morality." *Economy and Society* 37 (1): 1–19. https://doi.org/10.1080/03085140701760833.

Shehaj, Albana, Adrian J. Shin, and Ronald Inglehart. 2021. "Immigration and Right-Wing Populism: An Origin Story." *Party Politics* 27 (2): 282–293. https://doi.org/10.1177/1354068819849888.

Shelby, Tommie. 2008. "Comment on Glenn Loury." In *Race, Incarceration, and American Values*. MIT Press.

Shelby, Tommie. 2016. *Dark Ghettos: Injustice, Dissent, and Reform*. The Belknap Press of Harvard University Press.

Shepherd, Andrew, Erik Ivins, Eric Rignot, et al. 2020. "Mass Balance of the Greenland Ice Sheet from 1992 to 2018." *Nature* 579 (7798): 233–239. https://doi.org/10.1038/s41586-019-1855-2.

Shepley, Mardelle, Naomi Sachs, Hessam Sadatsafavi, Christine Fournier, and Kati Peditto. 2019. "The Impact of Green Space on Violent Crime in Urban Environments: An Evidence Synthesis." *International Journal of Environmental Research and Public Health* 16 (24): 5119. https://doi.org/10.3390/ijerph16245119.

Shoda, Yuichi. 2004. "Individual Differences in Social Psychology: Understanding Situations to Understanding People, Understanding People to Understand Situations." In *The Sage Handbook of Methods in Social Psychology*, edited by Carol Sansone, Carolyn C. Morf, and A. T. Panter. SAGE.

Shook, Natalie J., and Russell H. Fazio. 2008. "Interracial Roommate Relationships: An Experimental Field Test of the Contact Hypothesis." *Psychological Science* 19 (7): 717–723. https://doi.org/10.1111/j.1467-9280.2008.02147.x.

Shuman, Eric, Martijn van Zomeren, Tamar Saguy, and Eric Knowles. 2022. "Defend, Deny, Distance, and Dismantle: A Measure of How Advantaged Group Members Manage Their Identity." Working paper. Hebrew University. https://doi.org/10.31234/osf.io/6d4qc.

Sidanius, Jim, and Felicia Pratto. *Social Dominance: An Intergroup Theory of Social Hierarchy and Oppression*. Cambridge University Press, 1999. https://doi.org/10.1017/CBO9781139175043.

Siebert, Horst. 2002. *Der Kobra-Effekt. Wie man Irrwege der Wirtschaftspolitik vermeidet*. Dva.

Silverman, Alexandra L., Karl Cheng-Heng Fua, and Bethany A. Teachman. 2023. "More Than One Way to Say I Love You: An Internet-Based Intervention for Training Flexible Thinking in Romantic Relationships." *Journal of Clinical Psychology* 79 (4): 909–936. https://doi.org/10.1002/jclp.23443.

Simon, David, dir. 2002. *The Wire*. Blown Deadline Productions, HBO.

Sinnott-Armstrong, Walter. 2005. "It's Not My Fault: Global Warming and Individual Moral Obligations." In *Perspectives on Climate Change: Science, Economics, Politics, Ethics*, edited by Walter Sinnott-Armstrong and Richard B. Howarth. Emerald Group Publishing Limited. https://doi.org/10.1016/S1569-3740(05)05013-3.

Sintov, Nicole, Sally Geislar, and Lee V. White. 2019. "Cognitive Accessibility as a New Factor in Proenvironmental Spillover: Results from a Field Study of Household Food Waste Management." *Environment and Behavior* 51 (1): 50–80. https://doi.org/10.1177/0013916517735638.

Skinner-Dorkenoo, Allison L., Meghan George, James E. Wages, Sirenia Sánchez, and Sylvia P. Perry. 2023. "A Systemic Approach to the Psychology of Racial Bias Within Individuals and Society." *Nature Reviews Psychology* 2 (7): 392–406. https://doi.org/10.1038/s44159-023-00190-z.

Skocpol, Theda. 2013. "Naming the Problem: What It Will Take to Counter Extremism and Engage Americans in the Fight against Global Warming." Columbia School of Journalism and the Scholars Strategy Network.

Skogan, Wesley G. 2003. *Community Policing: Can It Work?* Cengage Learning.

Small, Mario L., Armin Akhavan, Mo Torres, and Qi Wang. 2021. "Banks, Alternative Institutions and the Spatial–Temporal Ecology of Racial Inequality in US Cities." *Nature Human Behaviour* 5 (12): 1622–1628. https://doi.org/10.1038/s41562-021-01153-1.

Smith, Heather J., Thomas F. Pettigrew, Gina M. Pippin, and Silvana Bialosiewicz. 2012. "Relative Deprivation: A Theoretical and Meta-Analytic Review." *Personality and Social Psychology Review* 16 (3): 203–232. https://doi.org/10.1177/1088868311430825.

Smith, Katherine Clegg, Samantha Cukier, and David H. Jernigan. 2014. "Defining Strategies for Promoting Product through 'Drink Responsibly' Messages in Magazine Ads for Beer, Spirits and Alcopops." *Drug and Alcohol Dependence* 142 (September): 168–173. https://doi.org/10.1016/j.drugalcdep.2014.06.007.

Snowden, Lonnie, and Genevieve Graaf. 2019. "The 'Undeserving Poor,' Racial Bias, and Medicaid Coverage of African Americans." *Journal of Black Psychology* 45 (3): 130–142. https://doi.org/10.1177/0095798419844129.

Sobel, Adam. 2021. "Making the Transition to a Green Economy: What Is Our Responsibility as Citizens?" *Bulletin of the Atomic Scientists* 77 (2): 67–69. https://doi.org/10.1080/00963402.2021.1885821.

Soon, Valerie. 2020. "Implicit Bias and Social Schema: A Transactive Memory Approach." *Philosophical Studies* 177 (7): 1857–1877. https://doi.org/10.1007/s11098-019-01288-y.

Soon, Valerie. 2021a. "An Intrapersonal, Intertemporal Solution to an Interpersonal Dilemma." *Philosophical Studies* 178 (February). https://doi.org/10.1007/s11098-021-01604-5.

Soon, Valerie. 2021b. "Social Structural Explanation." *Philosophy Compass* 16 (10): e12782. https://doi.org/10.1111/phc3.12782.

Sparkman, Gregg, Shahzeen Z. Attari, and Elke U. Weber. 2021. "Moderating Spillover: Focusing on Personal Sustainable Behavior Rarely Hinders and Can Boost Climate Policy Support." *Energy Research & Social Science* 78 (August): 102150. https://doi.org/10.1016/j.erss.2021.102150.

Sparkman, Gregg, Nathan Geiger, and Elke U. Weber. 2022. "Americans Experience a False Social Reality by Underestimating Popular Climate Policy Support by Nearly Half." *Nature Communications* 13 (1): 4779. https://doi.org/10.1038/s41467-022-32412-y.

Sparkman, Gregg, and Gregory M. Walton. 2017. "Dynamic Norms Promote Sustainable Behavior, Even If It Is Counternormative." *Psychological Science* 28 (11): 1663–1674. https://doi.org/10.1177/0956797617719950.

Srinivasan, Amia. 2015. "Stop the Robot Apocalypse." *London Review of Books*, September 23. https://www.lrb.co.uk/the-paper/v37/n18/amia-srinivasan/stop-the-robot-apocalypse.

Stanford, Mark. 2020. "The Cultural Evolution of Human Nature." *Acta Biotheoretica* 68 (2): 275–285. https://doi.org/10.1007/s10441-019-09367-7.

Stanselll, Amanda, and Daniel Zhao. 2020. "Diversity Now: How Companies and Workers Are Bringing Nationwide Social Justice Protests to the Workplace." Glassdoor, July 15. https://www.glassdoor.com/research/diversity-jobs-reviews.

Statista. 2023. "USA—Reported Forcible Rape Rate 1990–2022." https://www.statista.com/statistics/191226/reported-forcible-rape-rate-in-the-us-since-1990/.

Steffen, Will, Johan Rockström, Katherine Richardson, et al. 2018. "Trajectories of the Earth System in the Anthropocene." *Proceedings of the National Academy of Sciences* 115 (33): 8252–8259. https://doi.org/10.1073/pnas.1810141115.

Steinmetz, Katy. 2020. "She Coined the Term 'Intersectionality' Over 30 Years Ago. Here's What It Means to Her Today." *Time*, February 20. https://time.com/5786710/kimberle-crenshaw-intersectionality/.

Steuteville, Robert. 2023. "Parking Is a National Policy Issue, Thanks to Donald Shoup." Congress for the New Urbanism, March 8. https://www.cnu.org/publicsquare/2023/03/08/parking-national-policy-issue-thanks-donald-shoup.

Stewart, Abigail J., and Virginia Valian. 2018. *An Inclusive Academy: Achieving Diversity and Excellence*. MIT Press.

Stewart, Briar. 2016. "Nearly 40 Years Later, Life Comes Full Circle for Former Vietnamese Refugee." CBC, March 8. https://www.cbc.ca/news/canada/edmonton/vietnamese-refugee-pay-it-forward-syrian-family-1.3464777.

Stewart, Tracie L., Ioana M. Latu, Nyla R. Branscombe, and H. Ted Denney. 2010. "Yes We Can!: Prejudice Reduction Through Seeing (Inequality) and Believing (in Social Change)." *Psychological Science* 21 (11): 1557–1562. https://doi.org/10.1177/0956797610385354.

Stewart, Tracie L., Ioana M. Latu, Tim Martin, Seamus P. Walsh, Allyson Schmidt, and Kerry Kawakami. 2022. "Implicit Bias Reduction That Lasts: Putting Situational

Attribution Training to the Test." *Journal of Applied Social Psychology* 52 (11): 1062–1069. https://doi.org/10.1111/jasp.12912.

Stokes, Leah C. 2020. *Short Circuiting Policy: Interest Groups and the Battle Over Clean Energy and Climate Policy in the American States*. Oxford University Press.

Storer, Adam, Daniel Schneider, and Kristen Harknett. 2020. "What Explains Racial/Ethnic Inequality in Job Quality in the Service Sector?" *American Sociological Review* 85 (4): 537–572. https://doi.org/10.1177/0003122420930018.

Storr, Will. 2018. *Selfie: How We Became So Self-Obsessed and What It's Doing to Us*. Harry N. Abrams.

Strand, Ginger. 2008. "The Crying Indian." *Orion Magazine*, November 20. https://orionmagazine.org/article/the-crying-indian/.

Streitfeld, David. 2021. "How Amazon Crushes Unions." *New York Times*, March 16, sec. Technology. https://www.nytimes.com/2021/03/16/technology/amazon-unions-virginia.html.

Stromberg, Joseph, and Estelle Caswell. 2014. "Why the Myers-Briggs Test Is Totally Meaningless." *Vox*, July 15. https://www.vox.com/2014/7/15/5881947/myers-briggs-personality-test-meaningless.

Studdert, David M., Yifan Zhang, Erin E. Holsinger, et al. 2022. "Homicide Deaths Among Adult Cohabitants of Handgun Owners in California, 2004 to 2016." *Annals of Internal Medicine* 175 (6): 804–811. https://doi.org/10.7326/M21-3762.

Studdert, David M., Yifan Zhang, Sonja A. Swanson, et al. 2020. "Handgun Ownership and Suicide in California." *New England Journal of Medicine* 382 (23): 2220–2229. https://doi.org/10.1056/NEJMsa1916744.

Students for Fair Admissions Inc. v. President & Fellows of Harvard College. 2023.

Stürmer, Stefan, Bernd Simon, Michael Loewy, and Heike Jörger. 2003. "The Dual-Pathway Model of Social Movement Participation: The Case of the Fat Acceptance Movement." *Social Psychology Quarterly* 66 (1): 71–82. https://doi.org/10.2307/3090142.

Sugrue, Thomas J. 2014. *The Origins of the Urban Crisis: Race and Inequality in Postwar Detroit*. Princeton University Press.

Sunkara, Bhaskar. 2020. "Stop Trying to Fight Racism with Corporate Diversity Consultants." *The Guardian*, July 8, sec. Opinion. https://www.theguardian.com/commentisfree/2020/jul/08/diversity-consultants-racism-seminars-corporate-america.

Sunrise Movement. n.d.a. "About the Sunrise Movement." Accessed June 24, 2023. https://www.sunrisemovement.org/about/.

Sunrise Movement. n.d.b. "Sunrise's Principles." Accessed June 24, 2023. https://www.sunrisemovement.org/principles/.

Suozzo, Andrea. 2015. "Pasteurization and Its Discontents: Raw Milk, Risk, and the Reshaping of the Dairy Industry." University of Vermont. https://scholarworks.uvm.edu/graddis/320.

Supran, Geoffrey, and Naomi Oreskes. 2021. "Rhetoric and Frame Analysis of ExxonMobil's Climate Change Communications." *One Earth* 4 (5): 696–719. https://doi.org/10.1016/j.oneear.2021.04.014.

Supran, Geoffrey, Stefan Rahmstorf, and N. Oreskes. 2023. "Assessing ExxonMobil's Global Warming Projections." *Science* 379 (6628): eabk0063. https://doi.org/10.1126/science.abk0063.

Surico, John. 2023. "Make Way for the Bike Bus." *New York Times*, June 6, sec. New York. https://www.nytimes.com/2023/06/06/nyregion/bike-bus-cycling.html.

Tagar, Michal, Chelsea Hetherington, Deborah Shulman, and Melissa Koenig. 2017. "On the Path to Social Dominance? Individual Differences in Sensitivity to Intergroup Fairness Violations in Early Childhood." *Personality and Individual Differences* 113 (July): 246–250. https://doi.org/10.1016/j.paid.2017.03.020.

Táíwò, Olúfẹ́mi O. 2022. *Elite Capture: How the Powerful Took Over Identity Politics*. Haymarket Books.

Tajfel, Henri, and John Turner. 2000. "An Integrative Theory of Intergroup Conflict." In *Organizational Identity*, edited by Mary Jo Hatch and Majken Schultz. Oxford University Press. https://doi.org/10.1093/oso/9780199269464.003.0005.

Tankard, Margaret E., and Elizabeth Levy Paluck. 2017. "The Effect of a Supreme Court Decision Regarding Gay Marriage on Social Norms and Personal Attitudes." *Psychological Science* 28 (9): 1334–1344. https://doi.org/10.1177/0956797617709594.

Taylor, Helen, and Martin D. Vestergaard. 2022. "Developmental Dyslexia: Disorder or Specialization in Exploration?" *Frontiers in Psychology* 13. https://www.frontiersin.org/articles/10.3389/fpsyg.2022.889245.

Taylor, Jessica. 2015. "Trump Calls for 'total And Complete Shutdown of Muslims Entering' US." NPR, December 7, sec. Politics. https://www.npr.org/2015/12/07/458836388/trump-calls-for-total-and-complete-shutdown-of-muslims-entering-u-s.

Taylor, Paul. 2022. "Dutch Disruption: Drones, Digital Twins and Design." *Bromford LAB* (blog). June 23. https://www.bromfordlab.com/labblogcontent/2022/6/22/dutch-disruption-day-2-drones-digital-twins-and-design.

Telis, Gisela. 2010. "Kids Overimitate Adults, Regardless of Culture." *Science*, May 7. https://www.science.org/content/article/kids-overimitate-adults-regardless-culture.

Terriquez, Veronica. 2015. "Intersectional Mobilization, Social Movement Spillover, and Queer Youth Leadership in the Immigrant Rights Movement." *Social Problems* 62 (3): 343–362.

Tesler, Michael. 2012. "The Spillover of Racialization into Health Care: How President Obama Polarized Public Opinion by Racial Attitudes and Race." *American Journal of Political Science* 56 (3): 690–704. https://doi.org/10.1111/j.1540-5907.2011.00577.x.

Tetlock, Philip E., and Dan Gardner. 2016. *Superforecasting: The Art and Science of Prediction.* Crown.

Thoem, James. n.d. "What Makes Copenhagen the World's Most Bicycle Friendly Capital?" Visit Copenhagen. Accessed October 25, 2023. https://www.visitcopen hagen.com/copenhagen/activities/what-makes-copenhagen-worlds-most-bicycle -friendly-capital.

Thøgersen, John, and Caroline Noblet. 2012. "Does Green Consumerism Increase the Acceptance of Wind Power?" *Energy Policy* 51 (December): 854–862. https://doi .org/10.1016/j.enpol.2012.09.044.

Thomas, Angie. 2017. *The Hate U Give.* Balzer + Bray.

Thompson, Andrew. 2020. "Understanding the Meaning of Ubuntu: A Proudly South African Philosophy." Culture Trip, June 11. https://theculturetrip.com/africa /south-africa/articles/understanding-the-meaning-of-ubuntu-a-proudly-south-afri can-philosophy.

Thompson, Corinne N. 2020. "COVID-19 Outbreak—New York City, February 29– June 1, 2020." *Morbidity and Mortality Weekly Report* 69 (46): 1725–1729. https://doi .org/10.15585/mmwr.mm6946a2.

Thompson, Derek. 2019. "Workism Is Making Americans Miserable." *Atlantic*, February 24. https://www.theatlantic.com/ideas/archive/2019/02/religion-workism-mak ing-americans-miserable/583441/.

Thurber, Jon. 2020. "The Evangelist of Parking." UCLA Blueprint. https://blueprint .ucla.edu/feature/the-evangelist-of-parking/.

Timms, Ryan, and David Spurrett. 2023. "Hostile Scaffolding." *Philosophical Papers* 52 (1): 53–82. https://doi.org/10.1080/05568641.2023.2231652.

Tinggaard, Gert. 2020. "Researcher: Denmark's World-Record Level of Trust Is Helping Us in the Fight against Corona." ScienceNordic, April 1. https://sciencenordic .com/denmark-politics-society-and-culture/researcher-denmarks-world-record-level -of-trust-is-helping-us-in-the-fight-against-corona/1662939.

Tollefson, Jeff. 2021. "COVID Curbed Carbon Emissions in 2020—But Not by Much." *Nature* 589 (7842): 343. https://doi.org/10.1038/d41586-021-00090-3.

Toole, Briana. 2022. "Objectivity in Feminist Epistemology." *Philosophy Compass* 17 (11): 1–13. https://doi.org/10.1111/phc3.12885.

Tracy, Sarah W., and Caroline J. Acker, eds. 2004. *Altering American Consciousness: The History of Alcohol and Drug Use in the United States, 1800–2000.* University of Massachusetts Press.

Truelove, Heather Barnes, Amanda R. Carrico, Elke U. Weber, Kaitlin Toner Raimi, and Michael P. Vandenbergh. 2014. "Positive and Negative Spillover of Pro-Environmental Behavior: An Integrative Review and Theoretical Framework." *Global Environmental Change* 29 (November):127–138. https://doi.org/10.1016/j.gloenvcha.2014.09.004.

Tulshyan, Ruchika, and Jodi-Ann Burey. 2021. "Stop Telling Women They Have Imposter Syndrome." *Harvard Business Review*, February 11. https://hbr.org/2021/02/stop-telling-women-they-have-imposter-syndrome.

Ture, Kwame, and Charles V. Hamilton. 1992. *Black Power: The Politics of Liberation.* Vintage.

Turner, Jared. 2022. "Chesterton's Fence." *Thoughtbot* (blog), February 14. https://thoughtbot.com/blog/chestertons-fence.

Turner, Rhiannon N., Gordon Hodson, and Kristof Dhont. 2020. "The Role of Individual Differences in Understanding and Enhancing Intergroup Contact." *Social and Personality Psychology Compass* 14 (6): e12533. https://doi.org/10.1111/spc3.12533.

Turvey, Nigel. 2013. *Cane Toads: A Tale of Sugar, Politics and Flawed Science.* Sydney University Press.

Uenal, Fatih, Jim Sidanius, and Sander van der Linden. 2021. "Social and Ecological Dominance Orientations: Two Sides of the Same Coin? Social and Ecological Dominance Orientations Predict Decreased Support for Climate Change Mitigation Policies." *Group Processes & Intergroup Relations* 25 (6). https://doi.org/10.1177/13684302211010923.

Uluǧ, Özden Melis, and Linda R. Tropp. 2021. "Witnessing Racial Discrimination Shapes Collective Action for Racial Justice: Enhancing Awareness of Privilege Among Advantaged Groups." *Journal of Applied Social Psychology* 51 (3): 248–261. https://doi.org/10.1111/jasp.12731.

US Bureau of Labor Statistics. 2023. "Labor Force Characteristics by Race and Ethnicity, 2021." https://www.bls.gov/opub/reports/race-and-ethnicity/2021/home.htm.

US Census Bureau. 2022. "Census Bureau Releases 2020 Presidential Election Voting Report." Press Release No. CB22-TPS.14. https://www.census.gov/newsroom/press-releases/2022/2020-presidential-election-voting-report.html.

US Census Bureau. 2023. "National Poverty in America Awareness Month: January 2023." https://www.census.gov/newsroom/stories/poverty-awareness-month.html.

US Environmental Protection Agency. 2015. "Greenhouse Gas (GHG) Emissions and Removals." https://www.epa.gov/ghgemissions.

US Environmental Protection Agency. 2016. "Climate Change Indicators: US Greenhouse Gas Emissions." https://www.epa.gov/climate-indicators/climate-change-indicators-us-greenhouse-gas-emissions.

Valentino, Nicholas A., Carly Wayne, and Marzia Oceno. 2018. "Mobilizing Sexism: The Interaction of Emotion and Gender Attitudes in the 2016 US Presidential Election." *Public Opinion Quarterly* 82 (S1): 799–821. https://doi.org/10.1093/poq/nfy003.

Valian, Virginia. 1999. *Why So Slow? The Advancement of Women.* MIT Press.

Van Assche, Jasper, Kristof Dhont, and Thomas F. Pettigrew. 2019. "The Social-Psychological Bases of Far-Right Support in Europe and the United States." *Journal of Community & Applied Social Psychology* 29 (5): 385–401. https://doi.org/10.1002/casp.2407.

Van Assche, Jasper, Hermann Swart, Katharina Schmid, et al. 2023. "Intergroup Contact Is Reliably Associated with Reduced Prejudice, Even in the Face of Group Threat and Discrimination." *American Psychologist* 78 (6): 761–774. https://doi.org/10.1037/amp0001144.

Vartanian, Alex. n.d. "Retro Graphics—Vintage Charm for Your Projects." Pinterest. Accessed October 30, 2023. https://www.pinterest.com/pin/81698180710716151/.

Vasil, Ny, Mahesh Srinivasan, Monica E. Ellwood-Lowe, Sierra Delaney, Alison Gopnik, and Tania Lombrozo. 2024. "Structural Explanations Lead Young Children and Adults to Rectify Resource Inequalities." *Journal of Experimental Child Psychology* 242 (June): 105896. https://doi.org/10.1016/j.jecp.2024.105896.

Vasilyeva, Nadya, and Saray Ayala-López. 2019. "Structural Thinking and Epistemic Injustice." In *Overcoming Epistemic Injustice: Social and Psychological Perspectives,* edited by Benjamin R. Sherman and Goguen Stacey. Rowman & Littlefield International.

Vasilyeva, Nadya, Alison Gopnik, and Tania Lombrozo. 2018. "The Development of Structural Thinking About Social Categories." *Developmental Psychology* 54 (9): 1735–1744. https://doi.org/10.1037/dev0000555.

Vedantam, Shankar, host. 2016. *Hidden Brain.* "How to Build a Better Job." Podcast, March 29. https://www.npr.org/2016/03/28/471859161/how-to-build-a-better-job.

Vedantam, Shankar, host. 2018. *Hidden Brain.* "Zipcode Destiny: The Persistent Power of Place and Education" Podcast, November 12. https://www.npr.org/2018/11/12/666993130/zipcode-destiny-the-persistent-power-of-place-and-education.

Vedantam, Shankar, host. 2020. *Hidden Brain*. "Between Two Worlds." Podcast. https://hiddenbrain.org/podcast/between-two-worlds/.

Venter, Zander S., Charlie Shackleton, Andrew Faull, Lizette Lancaster, Gregory Breetzke, and Ian Edelstein. 2022. "Is Green Space Associated with Reduced Crime? A National-Scale Study from the Global South." *Science of The Total Environment* 825 (June): 154005. https://doi.org/10.1016/j.scitotenv.2022.154005.

Verme, Paolo. 2023. "Theory and Evidence on the Impact of Refugees on Host Communities." *World Bank Blogs* (blog), March 28. https://blogs.worldbank.org/dev4peace/theory-and-evidence-impact-refugees-host-communities.

Verme, Paolo, and Kirsten Schuettler. 2021. "The Impact of Forced Displacement on Host Communities: A Review of the Empirical Literature in Economics." *Journal of Development Economics* 150 (May): 102606. https://doi.org/10.1016/j.jdeveco.2020.102606.

Vernon, Jamie. 2017. "Understanding the Butterfly Effect." *American Scientist*, April 12. https://www.americanscientist.org/article/understanding-the-butterfly-effect.

Vezzali, Loris, Simon Lolliot, Elena Trifiletti, et al. 2023. "Effects of Intergroup Contact on Explicit and Implicit Outgroup Attitudes: A Longitudinal Field Study with Majority and Minority Group Members." *British Journal of Social Psychology* 62 (1): 215–240. https://doi.org/10.1111/bjso.12558.

Vial, Andrea C., Janine Bosak, Patrick C. Flood, and John F. Dovidio. 2021. "Individual Variation in Role Construal Predicts Responses to Third-Party Biases in Hiring Contexts." *PLOS ONE* 16 (2): e0244393. https://doi.org/10.1371/journal.pone.0244393.

Vidal, Xavier Medina, Rocío A. Páez, and Todd G. Shields. 2021. "Identity and the Racialized Politics of Violence in Gun Regulation Policy Preferences." *Social Science Quarterly* 103 (6): 1342–1358. https://doi.org/10.1111/ssqu.13023.

Vinyeta, Kirsten, Kyle P. Whyte, and Kathy Lynn. 2015. "Climate Change Through an Intersectional Lens: Gendered Vulnerability and Resilience in Indigenous Communities in the United States." US Department of Agriculture. https://doi.org/10.2737/PNW-GTR-923.

Visé, Daniel de. 2022. "Vegetarianism Is on the Rise—Especially the Part-Time Kind." *The Hill*, November 23. https://thehill.com/changing-america/sustainability/3747206-vegetarianism-is-on-the-rise-especially-the-part-time-kind/.

Voith, Richard, Jing Liu, Sean Zielenbach, Andrew Jakabovics, Brian An, Seva Rodnyansky, Anthony W. Orlando, and Raphael W. Bostic. 2022. "Effects of Concentrated LIHTC Development on Surrounding House Prices." *Journal of Housing Economics* 56 (June): 101838. https://doi.org/10.1016/j.jhe.2022.101838.

Vuletich, Heidi A., Nicolas Sommet, and B. Keith Payne. 2023. "The Great Migration and Implicit Bias in the Northern United States." *Social Psychological and Personality Science* 15 (5): 498–508. https://doi.org/10.1177/19485506231181718.

Waldman, Paul. 2020. "Republicans Are Serious About Voter Suppression. Here's How to Stop Them." *Washington Post*, May 18. https://www.washingtonpost.com /opinions/2020/05/18/republicans-are-serious-about-voter-suppression-heres-how -stop-them/.

Walker, Iain, and Heather J. Smith, eds. 2002. *Relative Deprivation: Specification, Development, and Integration.* Cambridge University Press.

Walker, Tim. 2022. "Later School Start Times More Popular, But What Are the Drawbacks?" National Education Association News, December 1. https://www.nea .org/nea-today/all-news-articles/later-school-start-times-more-popular-what-are -drawbacks.

Warren, Elizabeth. 2019. "Big, Structural Change: We've Done It Before, and We Can Do It Again." Medium, May 23. https://medium.com/@teamwarren/big-structural -change-weve-done-it-before-and-we-can-do-it-again-c9a042ed8b59.

Waters, Anne, ed. 2003. *American Indian Thought: Philosophical Essays.* Wiley-Blackwell.

Watts, Jonathan. 2019. "Greta Thunberg, Schoolgirl Climate Change Warrior: 'Some People Can Let Things Go. I Can't.'" *The Guardian*, March 11, sec. Environment. https://www.theguardian.com/world/2019/mar/11/greta-thunberg-schoolgirl -climate-change-warrior-some-people-can-let-things-go-i-cant.

Wax-Thibodeaux, Emily. 2013. "The 10 Best PSAs of All Time." *Washington Post*, September 13. https://www.washingtonpost.com/national/the-10-best-psas-of-all-time /2013/09/13/10cb0ebe-1bf2-11e3-8685-5021e0c41964_gallery.html.

Wayne, Carly, Nicholas Valentino, and Marzia Oceno. 2016. "How Sexism Drives Support for Donald Trump." *Washington Post*, October 23. https://www.washing tonpost.com/news/monkey-cage/wp/2016/10/23/how-sexism-drives-support-for -donald-trump/.

Wegner, Daniel M., David J. Schneider, Samuel R. Carter, and Teri L. White. 1987. "Paradoxical Effects of Thought Suppression." *Journal of Personality and Social Psychology* 53 (1): 5–13. https://doi.org/10.1037/0022-3514.53.1.5.

Weisbuch, Max, Kristin Pauker, and Nalini Ambady. 2009. "The Subtle Transmission of Race Bias via Televised Nonverbal Behavior." *Science* 326 (5960): 1711–1714.

Westra, Evan, and Daniel Kelly. 2025. "Natural Born Jerks? Virtue Signaling and the Social Scaffolding of Human Agency." In *The Routledge Handbook of Mindshaping*, edited by Tad Zawidzki and Rémi Tison. Routledge.

Whalen, J. R., host. 2023. "Mixed Feelings Over 'Round Up for Charity' Requests." *Your Money Briefing.* Podcast, August 31. https://www.wsj.com/podcasts/your-money -matters/mixed-feelings-over-round-up-for-charity-requests/fdb8f670-30f0-4e37 -9349-35a1ca59d6e4.

White, Gillian B. 2015. "Black Workers Really Do Need to Be Twice as Good." *Atlantic*, October 7, 2015. https://www.theatlantic.com/business/archive/2015/10/why -black-workers-really-do-need-to-be-twice-as-good/409276/.

White, Judith. 1999. "Ethical Comportment in Organizations: A Synthesis of the Feminist Ethic of Care and the Buddhist Ethic of Compassion." *International Journal of Value-Based Management* 12 (2): 109–128. https://doi.org/10.1023/A:1007779604630.

Whyte, Kyle, and Chris Cuomo. 2017. "Ethics of Caring in Environmental Ethics: Indigenous and Feminist Philosophies." In *The Oxford Handbook of Environmental Ethics*, edited by Stephen M. Gardiner and Allen Thompson. Oxford University Press. https://doi.org/10.1093/oxfordhb/9780199941339.013.22.

Wikipedia. 2023a. "Chris Smalls." Last updated October 16, 2023. https://en.wiki pedia.org/w/index.php?title=Chris_Smalls&oldid=1180335575.

Wikipedia. 2023b. "For Want of a Nail." Last updated October 30, 2023. https://en .wikipedia.org/w/index.php?title=For_Want_of_a_Nail&oldid=1182568317.

Wikipedia. 2023c. "Lenin Peace Prize." Last updated September 7, 2023. https://en .wikipedia.org/w/index.php?title=Lenin_Peace_Prize&oldid=1174228836.

Wikipedia. 2023d. "List of Close Election Results." Last updated November 6, 2023. https://en.wikipedia.org/wiki/List_of_close_election_results.

Wikipedia. 2023e. "Nathan Straus." Last updated October 22, 2023. https://en .wikipedia.org/w/index.php?title=Nathan_Straus&oldid=1181338104.

Wikipedia. 2023f. "Paradox of Voting." Last updated February 16, 2023. https://en .wikipedia.org/w/index.php?title=Paradox_of_voting&oldid=1139743246.

Wikipedia. 2023g. "The Old Man Lost His Horse." Last updated October 13, 2023. https://en.wikipedia.org/w/index.php?title=The_old_man_lost_his_horse&oldid =1179934200.

Wikipedia. 2024. "Funmilayo Ransome-Kuti." Last updated January 11, 2024. https:// en.wikipedia.org/w/index.php?title=Funmilayo_Ransome-Kuti&oldid=1195003777.

Wikisource. 2013. "The Encyclopedia Americana (1920)/Straus, Nathan." https://en .wikisource.org/wiki/The_Encyclopedia_Americana_(1920)/Straus,_Nathan.

Wildcat, Matt, and Daniel Voth. 2023. "Indigenous Relationality: Definitions and Methods." *AlterNative: An International Journal of Indigenous Peoples* 19 (2): 475–483. https://doi.org/10.1177/11771801231168380.

Wilkerson, Isabel. 2017. "Isabel Wilkerson: The Great Migration and the Power of a Single Decision." TED. https://www.ted.com/talks/isabel_wilkerson_the_great _migration_and_the_power_of_a_single_decision.

Wilkerson, Isabel. 2020. *Caste: The Origins of Our Discontents*. Random House.

Williams, David R., Yan Yu, James S. Jackson, and Norman B. Anderson. 1997. "Racial Differences in Physical and Mental Health: Socio-Economic Status, Stress and Discrimination." *Journal of Health Psychology* 2 (3): 335–451. https://doi.org /10.1177/135910539700200305.

Willis, Margaret M., and Juliet B. Schor. 2012. "Does Changing a Light Bulb Lead to Changing the World? Political Action and the Conscious Consumer." *Annals of the American Academy of Political and Social Science* 644 (1): 160–190. https://doi.org /10.1177/0002716212454831.

Wills, Vanessa C. 2018. "What Could It Mean to Say, 'Capitalism Causes Sexism and Racism?'" *Philosophical Topics* 46 (2): 229–246.

Wills, Vanessa C. 2021. "'And He Ate Jim Crow': Racist Ideology as False Consciousness." In *The Movement for Black Lives: Philosophical Perspectives*, edited by Brandon Hogan, Michael Cholbi, Alex Madva, and Benjamin S. Yost. Oxford University Press. https://doi.org/10.1093/oso/9780197507773.003.0003.

Willis, Vanessa C. 2024. *Marx's Ethical Vision*. Oxford University Press.

Wilson, William J. 2012. *The Truly Disadvantaged: The Inner City, the Underclass, and Public Policy*. University of Chicago Press.

Winkler, Adam. 2011. "The Secret History of Guns." *Atlantic*, July 25. https://www .theatlantic.com/magazine/archive/2011/09/the-secret-history-of-guns/308608/.

Wire Services. 1985. "Catalyst for MADD Arrested Again: Drunk Driver Served 9 Months in Fatal 1980 Accident." *Los Angeles Times*, April 19, sec. California. https:// www.latimes.com/archives/la-xpm-1985-04-19-mn-14951-story.html.

Witt, Charlotte. 2011. *The Metaphysics of Gender*. Oxford University Press.

Wolfers, Justin. 2017. "Pinpointing Racial Discrimination by Government Officials." *New York Times*, October 6, sec. Business. https://www.nytimes.com/2017/10/06 /business/economy/racial-discrimination-government-officials.html.

Wong, Julia C. 2020. "Amazon Execs Labeled Fired Worker 'Not Smart or Articulate' in Leaked PR Notes." *The Guardian*, April 2, sec. Technology. https://www.theguardian .com/technology/2020/apr/02/amazon-chris-smalls-smart-articulate-leaked-memo.

Wright, Stephen C., and Gamze Baray. 2012. "Models of Social Change in Social Psychology: Collective Action or Prejudice Reduction? Conflict or Harmony?"

In *Beyond Prejudice: Extending the Social Psychology of Conflict, Inequality and Social Change*, edited by John Dixon and M. Mark Levine. Cambridge University Press.

Wynes, Seth, and Kimberly A Nicholas. 2017. "The Climate Mitigation Gap: Education and Government Recommendations Miss the Most Effective Individual Actions." *Environmental Research Letters* 12 (7): 074024. https://doi.org/10.1088/1748-9326 /aa7541.

Xie, J., S. Sreenivasan, G. Korniss, W. Zhang, C. Lim, and B. K. Szymanski. 2011. "Social Consensus Through the Influence of Committed Minorities." *Physical Review E* 84 (1): 011130. https://doi.org/10.1103/PhysRevE.84.011130.

Yamada, Katherine. 2014. "Verdugo Views: The True Story of Iron Eyes Cody." *Glendale News-Press*, August 28. https://www.latimes.com/socal/glendale-news-press /opinion/columnists/katherine-yamada/tn-gnp-verdugo-views-the-true-story-of -iron-eyes-cody-20140828-story.html.

Yazdi, Haleh, David Barner, and Gail D. Heyman. 2020. "Children's Intergroup Attitudes: Insights from Iran." *Child Development* 91 (5): 1733–1744. https://doi.org /10.1111/cdev.13363.

Yeager, David S., Jamie M. Carroll, Jenny Buontempo, et al. 2022. "Teacher Mindsets Help Explain Where a Growth-Mindset Intervention Does and Doesn't Work." *Psychological Science* 33 (1): 18–32. https://doi.org/10.1177/09567976211028984.

Yglesias, Matt. 2015. "All Politics Is Identity Politics." *Vox*, June 5. https://www.vox .com/2015/1/29/7945119/all-politics-is-identity-politics.

Yglesias, Matthew. 2018. "The Best Thing You Can Do to Stop Climate Change Is to Vote against Republicans." *Vox*, November 27. https://www.vox.com/2018/11/27 /18112540/what-can-we-do-to-stop-climate-change.

Yglesias, Matthew. 2023. "YIMBYs Keep Winning." Slow Boring, August 9. https:// www.slowboring.com/p/yimbys-keep-winning.

York, Richard, and Julius Alexander McGee. 2016. "Understanding the Jevons Paradox." *Environmental Sociology* 2 (1): 77–87. https://doi.org/10.1080/23251042.2015 .1106060.

Young, Iris M. 2011. *Responsibility for Justice*. Oxford University Press.

Yousafzai, Sami. 2011. "10 Years of Afghan War: How the Taliban Go On." Newsweek, October 2. https://www.newsweek.com/10-years-afghan-war-how-taliban-go-68223.

Yune, Howard. 2023. "Passenger Dies in Napa County Crash; Driver Arrested on Felony DUI Allegation." *Napa Valley Register*, August 28. https://napavalleyregister .com/news/local/crime-courts/fatal-crash-napa-county-dui-arrest/article_80e40360 -45bb-11ee-85f6-dbf148320066.html.

Zhang, Xingyu, Maria Carabello, Tyler Hill, Kevin He, Christopher R. Friese, and Prashant Mahajan. 2019. "Racial and Ethnic Disparities in Emergency Department Care and Health Outcomes Among Children in the United States." *Frontiers in Pediatrics* 7. https://www.frontiersin.org/articles/10.3389/fped.2019.00525.

Zheng, Robin. 2018a. "Bias, Structure, and Injustice: A Reply to Haslanger." *Feminist Philosophy Quarterly* 4 (1): 1–30. https://doi.org/10.5206/fpq/2018.1.4.

Zheng, Robin. 2018b. "What Is My Role in Changing the System? A New Model of Responsibility for Structural Injustice." *Ethical Theory and Moral Practice* 21 (4): 869–885. https://doi.org/10.1007/s10677-018-9892-8.

Zheng, Robin. 2023. "Reconceptualizing Solidarity as Power from Below." *Philosophical Studies* 180 (3): 893–917. https://doi.org/10.1007/s11098-022-01845-y.

Zillow MediaRoom. 2022. "Renters of Color Pay Higher Security Deposits, More Application Fees." https://zillow.mediaroom.com/2022-04-06-Renters-of-color-pay-higher-security-deposits,-more-application-fees.

Zmigrod, Leor, Ian W. Eisenberg, Patrick G. Bissett, Trevor W. Robbins, and Russell A. Poldrack. 2021. "The Cognitive and Perceptual Correlates of Ideological Attitudes: A Data-Driven Approach." *Philosophical Transactions of the Royal Society B: Biological Sciences* 376 (1822): 20200424. https://doi.org/10.1098/rstb.2020.0424.

Zmigrod, Leor, Peter Jason Rentfrow, and Trevor W. Robbins. 2020. "The Partisan Mind: Is Extreme Political Partisanship Related to Cognitive Inflexibility?" *Journal of Experimental Psychology: General* 149 (3): 407–418. https://doi.org/10.1037/xge0000661.

Zmigrod, Leor, Sharon Zmigrod, Peter Jason Rentfrow, and Trevor W. Robbins. 2019. "The Psychological Roots of Intellectual Humility: The Role of Intelligence and Cognitive Flexibility." *Personality and Individual Differences* 141 (April): 200–208. https://doi.org/10.1016/j.paid.2019.01.016.

Zomeren, Martijn van, Maja Kutlaca, and Felicity Turner-Zwinkels. 2018. "Integrating Who 'We' Are with What 'We' (Will Not) Stand For: A Further Extension of the Social Identity Model of Collective Action." *European Review of Social Psychology* 29 (1): 122–160. https://doi.org/10.1080/10463283.2018.1479347.

Zurcher, Anthony. 2021. "COP26: Obama Tells Young People to Stay Angry on Climate Fight." *BBC*, November 8. https://www.bbc.com/news/science-environment-59210395.

Index